BLOODLINE

By the same author:

SOLDIER OF THE RAJ

ADMIRAL OF THE BLUE

BLOODLINE

THE ORIGINS AND DEVELOPMENT OF THE REGULAR FORMATIONS OF THE BRITISH ARMY

by

IAIN GORDON

Pen & Sword
MILITARY

First published in Great Britain in 2010 by
Pen & Sword Military
An imprint of
Pen & Sword Books Ltd
47 Church Street
Barnsley
South Yorkshire
S70 2AS

ISBN 978 1 84884 205 2

Printed and bound in England
By the MPG Books Group

Pen & Sword Books Ltd incorporates the Imprints of Pen & Sword Aviation,
Pen & Sword Family History, Pen & Sword Maritime, Pen & Sword Military,
Wharncliffe Local History, Pen & Sword Select, Pen & Sword Military Classics,
Leo Cooper, Remember When, Seaforth Publishing and Frontline Publishing

For a complete list of Pen & Sword titles please contact
PEN & SWORD BOOKS LIMITED
47 Church Street, Barnsley, South Yorkshire, S70 2AS, England
E-mail: enquiries@pen-and-sword.co.uk
Website: www.pen-and-sword.co.uk

ACKNOWLEDGEMENTS

The Author is deeply grateful to the following for their assistance in the preparation of this book:

Colonel S. C. H. Ashworth,
RHQ The Mercian Regiment.
Major M. L. Badham-Thornhill,
Royal Artillery.
John Baker, Curator "Airborne Assault",
Museum of The Parachute Regiment.
Colonel M. J. Ball, RHQ The Princess of Wales's Royal Regiment.
Lieutenant-Colonel R. J. Binks,
HHQ The Royal Scots Dragoon Guards.
David Blake,
Museum of Army Chaplaincy.
Carolyn Bleach,
HQ Intelligence Corps.
Colonel T. C. S. Bonas,
RHQ Welsh Guards.
Lieutenant-Colonel W. R. Brace MBE,
HHQ 1st The Queen's Dragoon Guards.
C. A. Campbell, Regimental Secretary,
Royal Regiment of Scotland.
Major D. N. Chappell,
HHQ 9th/12th Royal Lancers.
Lieutenant-Colonel C. P. Conlon,
RHQ Royal Corps of Signals.
Captain J. C. Cornish,
HHQ The King's Royal Hussars.
Corps Archivist, The Corps of Royal Electrical and Mechanical Engineers.
Corps Secretary,
HQ Army Physical Training Corps.
Major E. M. Crofton,
RHQ Coldstream Guards.
G. Edgerley-Harris,
The Gurkha Museum.
Major J. M. Evans, HQ Queen Alexandra's Royal Army Nursing Corps.
Major M. Everett,
Curator, Royal Welsh Museum.
Major R. C. Gould,
RHQ The Royal Anglian Regiment.
Colin Gray,
RHQ The Royal Irish Regiment.
Captain W. A. Henshall,
HHQ The Royal Dragoon Guards.
Lieutenant-Colonel C. N. Holman MBA,
HQ Corps of Royal Engineers.
Captain J. M. Holtby,
HHQ The Queen's Royal Lancers.
Lieutenant-Colonel C. J. Ions,
HQ Army Air Corps.
J. E. Lloyd, Household Cavalry Regiment Museum and Archive.
Captain G. E. Locker,
HHQ The Light Dragoons.
Lieutenant-Colonel D. J. Owen,
HQ The Royal Logistic Corps.
RHQ Scots Guards.
RHQ The Yorkshire Regiment.
Regimental Secretary, The Queen's Royal Hussars (Queen's Own and Royal Irish).
Regimental Secretary, City of London HQ,
Royal Regiment of Fusiliers.
Regimental Secretary, Royal Tank Regiment.
Captain J. J. J. L. Roberts,
RHQ Irish Guards.
Lieutenant-Colonel C. J. E. Seymour LVO,
RHQ Grenadier Guards.
Major J. Sharp,
HQ Royal Army Dental Corps.
Major W. J. Spiers,
RHQ The Rifles.
Captain P. Starling,
Army Medical Services Museum.
Colonel K. M. Tutt OBE,
HQ Adjutant General's Corps.

and the Directors and Staff of
The Templar Study Centre,
National Army Museum, Chelsea.

RESEARCHERS

Readers who are researching the service careers of relatives or others are advised, in the first instance, to contact the relevant Regimental Museum, as shown in the following pages, who will advise them on their best course of action. A small charge is usually made where specific research into an individual or event is requested.

Enquiries should not be directed to Regimental or Home Headquarters who do not hold archive material and cannot assist in such matters.

CONTENTS

Acknowledgements	5
Author's Note	8
The Origins and Principal Reforms of the British Regular Army	9
Tables of Precedence and Evolution	18

ROYAL HORSE ARTILLERY

The Royal Horse Artillery	52

HOUSEHOLD CAVALRY

The Household Cavalry Regiment	31

ROYAL ARMOURED CORPS — HEAVY CAVALRY

1st The Queen's Dragoon Guards	35
The Royal Scots Dragoon Guards (Carabiniers and Greys)	36
The Royal Dragoon Guards	38

ROYAL ARMOURED CORPS — LIGHT CAVALRY

The Queen's Royal Hussars (Queen's Own and Royal Irish)	40
The Queen's Royal Lancers	48
9th/12th Royal Lancers (Prince of Wales's)	43
The King's Royal Hussars	44
The Light Dragoons	46

ROYAL ARMOURED CORPS — ROYAL TANK REGIMENT

Royal Tank Regiment	50

ARTILLERY

Royal Regiment of Artillery	52

ENGINEERS

Corps of Royal Engineers	56

SIGNALS

Royal Corps of Signals	60

FOOT GUARDS — THE GUARDS DIVISION

Grenadier Guards	65
Coldstream Guards	66
Scots Guards	67
Irish Guards	68
Welsh Guards	69

INFANTRY OF THE LINE — THE SCOTTISH DIVISION

The Royal Regiment of Scotland	70

INFANTRY OF THE LINE — THE QUEEN'S DIVISION

The Princess of Wales's Royal Regiment (Queen's and Royal Hampshires)	82
The Royal Regiment of Fusiliers	86
The Royal Anglian Regiment	88

INFANTRY OF THE LINE — THE KING'S DIVISION

The Duke of Lancaster's Regiment (King's, Lancashire and Border)	94
The Yorkshire Regiment	98

INFANTRY OF THE LINE — THE PRINCE OF WALES'S DIVISION

The Mercian Regiment   102

The Royal Welsh   106

INFANTRY OF THE LINE

The Royal Irish Regiment   108

The Parachute Regiment   126

The Rifles   112

GURKHAS

The Brigade of Gurkhas   130

The Queen's Gurkha Engineers, Signals and Logistic Regiments   131

The Royal Gurkha Rifles   132

Indian Army Gurkha Regiments previously in British Service   134

AVIATION AND SPECIAL FORCES

Glider Pilot Regiment   127

Special Air Service Regiment   127

Army Air Corps   128

LOGISTICS

Royal Logistic Corps   136

ARMY MEDICAL SERVICES

Royal Army Medical Corps   142

Queen Alexandra's Royal Army Nursing Corps   142

Royal Army Dental Corps   143

Royal Army Veterinary Corps   143

ELECTRICAL AND MECHANICAL ENGINEERING

Corps of Royal Electrical and Mechanical Engineers   144

PERSONNEL AND ADMINISTRATION

Adjutant General's Corps   146

INTELLIGENCE

Intelligence Corps   150

SMALL ARMS TRAINING AND EVALUATION

Small Arms School Corps   153

COMPASSIONATE AND SPIRITUAL SUPPORT

Royal Army Chaplains' Department   152

PHYSICAL TRAINING

Army Physical Training Corps   153

MUSIC

Corps of Army Music   154

THE DISBANDED REGIMENTS

The Cameronians (Scottish Rifles)   159

The York and Lancaster Regiment   159

The Connaught Rangers (89th and 94th)   160

The Prince of Wales's Leinster Regiment (Royal Canadians) (100th and 109th) 160

The Royal Munster Fusiliers   161

The Royal Dublin Fusiliers   161

Battle Honours awarded to Regular Regiments of the British Army 1662-2008 162

Notes   168

AUTHOR'S NOTE

A volume of this size can only scratch the surface of a subject so vast as the formations of the British Army. It therefore confines itself to the Regular Army and makes no attempt to include the legions of Yeomanry, Volunteers and Militia, and the splendid formations of the modern Territorial Army, part-time soldiers who spring to the support of their Regular colleagues in troubled times and without whom Britain would, today, be wholly unable to fulfil her worldwide commitments.

It also confines itself to the more significant changes in each Regiment's development and does not attempt to record every one of the frequent changes in regimental titles due simply to a change in colonels in the days when regiments were known by the names of their colonels.

Readers who are interested in pursuing this fascinating subject in greater detail must turn to the eight volumes of Anthony Baker's definitive work: *The Genealogy of the Regiments of the British Army* which includes the Territorial Army formations and the hundreds of ephemeral regiments raised in times of crisis, often for local defence, and disbanded and forgotten as soon as the crisis had passed. But they should be aware that in formations as long-established and with histories as proudly-preserved as the Regiments of the British Army, some disagreement on dates and titles is inevitable and no two books on the subject are exactly the same. I have tried, by comparison with several published sources and consultation with each individual Regiment and Corps, to get it as right as possible but I realise there are those who will dispute some detail and I apologise if I have outraged anyone's strongly-held opinion.

IAIN GORDON
Barnstaple, Devon
September 2009

The Origins and Principal Reforms of the British Regular Army

The formation and development of a standing army in Britain was driven by the two separate, yet conjoined, forces which have shaped our constitution — the struggle for power between monarchy and parliament and the inter-denominational Christian conflict which resulted from the determination of King Henry VIII to change his wife.

It was also from these two forces that the traditional British mistrust and hostility for any form of regular army evolved. Whilst the need for a powerful navy, to keep us free from invasion and to spearhead and protect our commercial interests overseas has, until fairly recently, been accepted by politicians and populace alike, the existence of a standing army in peacetime has always been viewed with suspicion and unease. Similarly, while the Navy has enjoyed generous financial support from government and popularity with the people, (apart from in coastal communities when impressment was rife), the brutal and licentious soldiery has seldom won the affection of the public nor the approbation and financial indulgence of parliament.

In the early 17th century, inter-denominational bigotry had sunk to such depths that the morbid fear of being ruled or governed by anyone with differing Christian rituals to one's own led the country to a bloody civil war, the execution of one monarch and the deposition of another. During these troubled times, the presence of armed men indicated the power and purpose of one of the opposing factions, which simply fanned the hatred and prejudice of the other.

THE KING'S GUARD

In 1649 Charles I was executed and in 1651 Charles II, having been defeated by Cromwell at Worcester, fled into exile. He gathered around him a body of loyal guards who were raised in the Low Countries from royalists who had fought for his father in the Civil War. In 1660, the Parliamentary Army in Britain was disbanded and Charles II was restored to the throne. He brought with him his bodyguard of trusted horse and foot soldiers which became the first element of the Regular British Army and would eventually be known as The Life Guards and The Grenadier Guards. The following year these were joined by the mounted troops of what would become the Royal Horse Guards and the foot soldiers known as The Coldstreamers, an established parliamentary regiment under General Monck which was disbanded in 1661 and immediately reformed as part of the new King's Guard. The Coldstream Guards, as they became, were soon joined by the Scots Regiment of Foot Guards, later the Scots Guards, raised from the remnants of a Royalist regiment which had fought for Charles I in the Civil War.

These units were the elite bodyguard of the Sovereign as they remain, with some more recent additions, to this day, but they were clearly inadequate to deal with any serious civil unrest, not to mention any requirement for overseas service in the event of war.

> *While it's 'Tommy this', an' 'Tommy that', an' 'Tommy fall be'ind',*
> *But it's 'Please to walk in front Sir', when there's trouble in the wind.*
> *Rudyard Kipling*

THE FIRST LINE REGIMENTS

The King therefore exercised his right to recall a regiment of Scottish mercenaries which had been raised by Sir John Hepburn for the French service in 1633 under a Royal Warrant from Charles I. This unit became the 1st Regiment of Foot — The Royal Scots — the oldest and most senior infantry regiment of the line in the British Army, and it was upon the practices of this regiment that the organization, drills and procedures of the emerging army were largely to be based.

From this beginning, regiments of horse and of foot were gradually added with stealth and persistence on the part of the King and never without obstruction from a hostile and suspicious parliament.

On his marriage to Catherine of Braganza, the Portuguese Infanta, Charles inherited, as part of her dowry, the trading ports of Bombay and Tangier. Bombay was conveniently leased to the East India Company and Tangier provided a legitimate excuse for the King to raise another regiment of horse and one of foot for its defence. These were

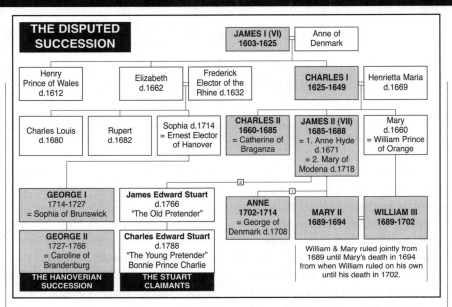

The Tangier Horse, which became The 1st Royal Dragoons, and The Tangier Regiment, 2nd of the Line, which later became The Queen's (Royal West Surrey) Regiment. The 2nd Tangier Regiment, raised in 1680, 4th of the Line, became The King's Own Royal Regiment (Lancaster).

In 1665 the King recalled the one remaining British regiment in Dutch service, consequently called The Holland Regiment, 3rd of the Line, which eventually became the famous Buffs

(Royal East Kent Regiment). Most of these original units have now been subsumed beneath the banners of today's "big" regiments and their progress can be followed in the tables on the following pages.

In 1672 in his *Declaration of Indulgence*, Charles II attempted to introduce what today would be hailed as a model of religious tolerance and civil enlightenment but parliament, in a furor of anti-catholic hysteria, refused to accept it and introduced instead the first

Test Act which effectively barred catholics and non-conformists from holding public office, both civil and military.

MONMOUTH'S REBELLION

Charles II died in 1685 and was succeeded by his brother James II (VII). In the first year of his reign, a rebellion by the protestant Duke of Monmouth, an illegitimate son of Charles II, gave James the excuse he needed for an immediate expansion of the Army. Nine regiments of horse and eight of foot were raised, Monmouth was defeated at Sedgemoor, convicted of treason and executed. The country had been shocked by how quickly and how easily the monarchy could be challenged and the case for retaining the additional regiments had been made. James had annulled the bar on catholics holding commissions in the Army but his attempt, two years later, to extend religious tolerance to all military and civil fields with a revised *Declaration of Indulgence* resulted in revolution and his deposition in favour of the protestant King William III, son of his sister Mary and the Dutch Prince of Orange.

JACOBITE RISINGS

In turn, the son of King James II (VII) was denied the Crown which passed instead through the female line first to Queen Anne and, on her death in 1714, to George, Elector of Hanover, whose remote claim to it was through his mother, Sophia, who was a granddaughter, again via the female line, of King James I (VI). But he was a protestant, and that was all that really mattered! Once again, catholics were barred from holding commissions in the Army and would remain so for most of the next century.

The years of internal strife and bloodshed that followed gave rise to a further augmentation of the standing army, this time largely unopposed by a parliament transfixed with fear that the throne should be regained by a catholic. William had experienced difficulties in imposing his authority, particularly in Scotland and Ireland, and several regiments had been raised for his support. But with the accession of George I, the bitter enmity between the tory Jacobites, supporters of the usurped, male-line, catholic Stewarts, and the whig Hanoverians, who gave their allegiance to the usurping, female-line, protestant Georges, came to a head and raged throughout the first half of the 18th century. Major Jacobite risings in 1715 and 1745 shook the confidence of the Hanoverian regime and called for further strengthening of the Army. After the failure of the second rising, the Jacobites were brutally suppressed, particularly in the Scottish Highlands from where the major part of the Jacobite forces had been drawn. But the Highlanders, with a long tradition of European mercenary service and a legendary reputation as fearless infantrymen, were yet to play a major role in the Army of Great Britain.

THE 1751 WARRANT

With the steady expansion of Empire and the changing nature of land warfare during the first half of the 18th century, a need for reform became apparent. Among many measures introduced in the Royal Warrant of 1751, line regiments ceased to be known by the name of their colonel, which had been the usual practice, and were given a number in accordance to their seniority.

The second half of the century saw the British Army engaged in the Seven Years War (1755-63), the War of American Independence (1775-83) and the start of hostilities with Revolutionary France (1793). Consequently, there was an expansion of some 50 new regiments between 1750 and 1780.

Then, during the last 20 years of the century, thousands of dispossessed Highlanders accepted the King's Shilling and the great Highland Regiments were born — Seaforths (1778), Gordons (1787), Argylls and Camerons (1794) and Sutherlands (the original Thin Red Line) in 1799.

THE DUKE OF YORK'S REFORMS

With the threat of French supremacy in Europe and the involved patronage of the Duke of York, second son of King George III and Commander-in-Chief from 1795 until his death in 1827, the Army enjoyed a period of modest progress and gentle reform. Its greatest professional test yet, the Napoleonic Wars, culminated in the defeat of Bonaparte at Waterloo in 1815. Once the threat had been removed, the soldiers who had fought tirelessly for a dozen years to keep Europe free received the usual shabby treatment from Government, being paid off, often far from their homes, without any form of support or finance to assist them with the transition back to civilian life. This had always been, and would continue to be, Britain's way of showing gratitude to the defenders of its freedom.

Wellington's army had done a good job which resulted in the longest period of peace and stability Europe had ever enjoyed. Needless to say, the Army was neglected and in 1854, by which time most of the veterans of Waterloo had died in poverty, another generation of young men was required for sacrifice in the Crimea. This time the dispute was not which nation should dominate Europe but which nation should be the Sovereign Christian Authority in the Holy Land — a cause which, in its stunningly bizarre frivolity, could never, ever justify the hardship and loss of life which followed. The years of parliamentary indifference and military intransigence resulted in the most scandalously mismanaged campaign in the history of the British Army. The public, alerted largely by the reports of William H Russell in *The Times*, demanded radical reforms.

POST-CRIMEAN REFORMS

The two most important weaknesses exposed in the Crimea were, on the combatant side, the poor quality of officers who were extremely brave but completely untrained and professionally incompetent. As a result, the sale of commissions came under scrutiny and the problems of patronage were addressed, if not wholly overcome.

The other fundamental flaw brought to light was the complete inadequacy of logistic and medical support for the field army. Transport and supply had previously come under the control of the Board of Ordnance, a civilian body set up by Henry VIII to control armaments, and had since become the governing body for artillery, engineering and the commissariat. In 1855 the Board was abolished, the Royal Artillery and Royal Engineers came under command of the War Office as did embryo organizations for supply, transport and, most noteworthy, army medicine and nursing.

The Post-Crimean Reforms were hardly in place when the nation was hit by another great trauma — the Indian Mutiny. After the transfer of power from the East India Company to the Crown, the British Army was further augmented by the inheritance of three cavalry and nine infantry regiments from the HEIC armies, the so-called "European" regiments, plus a major part of the Company artillery and sappers and miners. The balance formed the start of the great British-Indian Army.

The years which followed could be regarded as the high noon of empire and the time, perhaps, of the British Army's greatest prestige throughout the world even if its status had not improved with its own people. A prosperous and unthreatened public had little regard for the instrument of their own wealth and security and the traditional animosity and mistrust of government had not been assuaged by the pragmatic heroism of the soldiery in the Crimea and the Mutiny. The hostility between parliament and monarchy was perpetuated through the offices of the Duke of Cambridge, a grandson of George III, who was Commander-in-Chief from 1856-1895. The Duke, though deeply concerned with certain aspects of reform within the Army, was opposed to the fundamental changes in the structure and administration which were by now absolutely necessary. The lot therefore fell to Edward Cardwell, Secretary of State for War in Gladstone's first ministry (1868-74), whose name would be linked forever with the most radical restructuring of the Army which had taken place to date.

THE CARDWELL REFORMS 1870

Cardwell finally abolished the purchase of commissions — a system which had been condemned (apart from among a small group of diehards including the Duke of Wellington) since the mismanagement in the Crimea. Secondly, he introduced *The Army Enlistment Act* which allowed soldiers to join up for a twelve-year term, six with the Colours and six on the reserve, instead of the previous lifetime's commitment. This greatly increased the pool of potential recruits while, at the same time, creating, for the first time, a reserve army of experienced soldiers who were still young enough to form a viable expeditionary force.

Next, he removed the militia, for long regarded as parliament's safeguard against a rebellious regular army, from the control of the County Lord Lieutenants and placed it under proper command of the War Office.

Lastly, and perhaps the reform for which Cardwell is best remembered, was his *Localization Scheme* which involved a complete restructuring of the regimental system to capitalize on the new recruits created by the *Enlistment Act* and to consolidate the creation of a proper reserve force.

Put simply, this involved the division of the country into 66 Regimental Districts each with its own 2-battalion regular regiment and a third reserve battalion of former militia. At any given me, one regular battalion would be erving overseas and the other at home a Depot town within the regiment's eographical area. The home battalion ould maintain a regimental eadquarters and training facility, would rovide replacements for casualties and ther shortages in the overseas battalion nd had the ability, in theory, to provide a attalion of trained soldiers at short otice to any expeditionary force. The enior line infantry regiments already had wo battalions and the others were now aired to form 2-battalion regiments — he first of what was to be a continuous uccession of amalgamations. The avalry regiments remained unchanged; heir turn was to come later.

Under Cardwell's scheme, the infantry egiments of the line now acquired a true erritorial" character, each being allied to specific geographical area, the name of hich was incorporated in its title, with ecruits, for the first time, being able to pecify the regiment of their choice. This erritorial" element, with men from the ame town or county serving together, ould prove to be one of the greatest

strengths of the British regimental system during the next century.

THE CHILDERS REFORMS 1881

In 1874 Gladstone's government fell and Cardwell was out of office. Then in 1880 a Liberal government was again elected and Cardwell's successor as Secretary of State for War was Hugh Childers who developed the Cardwell Reforms still further.

In 1881 regimental numbers were dropped completely with regiments, from then on, being known by their territorial or other special designation. However, regimental numbers had become so much a part of the culture and tradition of the regiments that their unofficial use continued, and still continues in the sub-titles of some regiments to this day.

Just as the Crimea had exposed the weaknesses of logistic and medical support for the field army, so the Second Boer War (1899-1902) brought to public attention the inadequacy of the high command structure in London. In the course of this strategic shambles it took nearly 400,000 British and Dominion

troops, of which 22,000 lost their lives, nearly three years to muzzle a few deeply-committed, fast-moving guerillas.

THE ESHER COMMITTEE 1903

A committee set up in 1903 under Lord Esher came up with proposals for certain fundamental changes to the command structure, notably the creation of a Committee of Imperial Defence, to be chaired by the Prime Minister, and an Army Council comprising a mix of military and political members. The office of Commander-in-Chief was to be abolished and replaced by a Chief of the General Staff who would serve as the first military member of the Army Council.

THE HALDANE REFORMS 1905-1912

In December 1905 the Conservative government fell and was replaced by the Liberal Ministry of Campbell-Bannerman.

Preparations for the protection of Britain's national and imperial interests against the rising power and militancy of Germany were thus entrusted to a government whose roots were strongly anti-military and whose dislike of the

Army had not diminished since the days before Waterloo.

The Navy, which had been operating on the "Two Power Standard" (whereby the British Fleet should be kept more powerful than the next two most powerful navies in Europe combined), entered the War in a position of strength which kept the German High Seas Fleet blockaded in port for most of the War thereby minimising British naval casualties. The Army was a different matter.

Richard Haldane, the new Secretary of State for War, despite the continual paring and hindrance of his own party, did his best to prepare Britain for the coming conflict with the implementation and development of the Esher General Staff structure, the formation of an Expeditionary Force which could mobilize instantly when required and the organization of the Volunteers and Yeomanry into a Territorial Force for home defence.

Despite Haldane's best efforts, Britain entered the First World War scandalously under-manned for the job it was expected to do, the British Expeditionary

ARMY STRENGTHS AT START OF FIRST WORLD WAR		
	Infantry Divisions	Cavalry Divisions
Germany	82	11
Russia	110	36
France	63	10
Great Britain (BEF)	6	1 brigade

In 2008 British taxpayers were supporting 101,300 drug addicts and alcoholics living on benefits; about the same as the number of soldiers in the British Army.

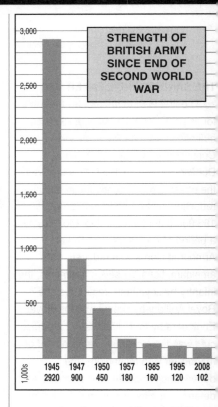

Force famously being described by the German Kaiser as: "Britain's Contemptible Little Army" (see table above). The initial blood sacrifice, upon which the British government and people had always insisted, was consequently made and the war unnecessarily protracted for four brutal years of unprecedented suffering and casualties.

INTER-WAR REFORMS

The First World War had seen the introduction of the two greatest military innovations since gunpowder — airpower and armour — both of which were the first priority for reform at the end of the War. The Royal Air Force had been formed in 1918 to take over aviation and the Tank Corps was founded in 1917 and had responsibility for the vital task of developing Britain's armoured vehicles and tactics between the Wars. In 1922 it acquired "Royal" status and by 1939 had

eight regular battalions and became the Royal Tank Regiment as the nucleus of the newly-formed Royal Armoured Corps. In order to preserve Britain's famous cavalry regiments, it was decided that they should be gradually mechanized and retrained as armoured regiments having been reduced in number by pairings which are detailed in the pages which follow.

The First World War, with its massive mobilization and casualties, had involved almost every family in the land and in its aftermath created for a time a better understanding between the populace and the soldiery. There were no longer signs outside public houses reading: "No Dogs. No Beggars. No Soldiers." and veterans enjoyed greater sympathy and esteem in the civilian world than had their fathers and grandfathers. It was not long, however, before civil demands upon the public purse once again engulfed the need to reform and re-equip the Army. Despite the continual and impassioned warnings of Winston Churchill of the need to prepare against the re-emergence of a militant Germany, the

Army was again neglected and entered the War in 1939 as absurdly outnumbered by its foe as in 1914. As a consequence, the ritual blood sacrifice was yet again made by the professional soldiers of Britain's pathetic little Expeditionary Force to be followed by the humiliation of watching its ill-prepared, ill-equipped army being swept out of France, leaving all its equipment behind, at Dunkirk. Once again, the conflict was unnecessarily protracted, and the costs and casualties unnecessarily escalated as Britain struggled to put together a citizen army and to activate its industrial base to arm and equip it.

POST WORLD WAR 2 REFORMS

Demobilization at the end of the War rapidly reduced the Army from nearly 3 million to around 900,000. With responsibility for policing an already-crumbling Empire, supporting and restructuring a devastated Europe, restoring democratic government and public services in Germany while, at the same time, manning Britain's section of the buttress against the spread of

communism throughout the world, the Army clearly had a massive post-war commitment. Conscription was introduced for the first time in peacetime and a part-regular, part-conscript army of around 400,000 kept the peace and protected British interests throughout the world during the turbulent and fragmentary decade following the War.

In 1984 Britain's Defence Budget as a percentage of Gross Domestic Product was 5.3%. Today it is 2.2%. Russia, on the other hand, has quadrupled its military expenditure over the past five years.

THE SANDYS WHITE PAPER 1957

The first plan to restructure the Army for its post-war, post-imperial role was outlined in a White Paper by the Conservative Minister of Defence, Duncan Sandys, in 1957. This involved the phasing out of conscription and a reduction in strength from 373,000 to 165,000 (later increased to 180,000) over a period of five years. The Royal Armoured Corps was reduced, with amalgamations, by seven regiments, the infantry by seventeen regiments, the Royal Artillery by twenty and the Royal Engineers by four. Justification for these cuts was the increasing replacement of manpower with technology, the dependence upon nuclear weapons as a deterrent against major conflict and the use of airmobility to aid rapid reaction in international flashpoints.

Despite this and the fact that Britain was withdrawing from its colonial involvements worldwide, the new, smaller army found itself seriously overstretched during the 1950s and 60s in dealing with a number of international situations in the Far and Middle East and in Northern Ireland where the IRA had embarked upon a new campaign of terrorism in 1956.

"OPTIONS FOR CHANGE" 1990

The collapse of the Soviet monolith in the late 1980s, and Britain's consequently reduced commitment in Europe, offered a further opportunity to slash defence expenditure. Once again the Army bore the brunt of the cuts with a reduction, by further amalgamations, of eight armoured regiments and fifteen infantry battalions with commensurate cuts in artillery and engineers. At the same time constitutional changes were made to the support services with the formation of the Royal Logistic Corps and the Adjutant General's Corps.

The so-called "peace dividend" included no intelligent appraisal of the ethnic upheavals which the demise of communism would bring about in the Balkans; nor did government foresee the Iraqi invasion of Kuwait — both situations which, it was decided, required the intervention of Britain's fundamentally-weakened and reduced Army.

"FUTURE ARMY STRUCTURE" 2007

In December 2004 the Labour Government, with ever-escalating welfare demands and a burgeoning immigrant community, looked again to cuts in the Armed Services to balance its books despite the country's involvement in the Balkans, Iraq and Afghanistan. Another restructuring of the Army was announced in which the infantry would be reduced by four battalions and many others amalgamated into the new multi-battalion regiments which the government, within which there was not a single member who had served in the Armed Forces, considered to be the best way forward for an Army which was already dangerously overstretched, underfunded and facing a consequent crisis in recruitment. The final phase of this restructuring was completed in September 2007 with the formation of The Mercian Regiment descended from nine famous regiments of the line.

A TRADITION OF ILL-USE

In the three hundred years since the British Army was formed, it has never let us down. Today, with the Nation reeling from recent disclosures of incompetence and venality endemic in so many of our previously-most-trusted institutions, the Army remains ever constant as an example of complete integrity and professionalism. Together with the other armed services, it must be regarded as the nation's most dependable and trustworthy institution.

We turn to it in times of international conflict when our liberty is threatened; and in civil turmoil when industrial action has crippled essential services; and in pestilence or catastrophe where the civil authorities are overwhelmed and the Army is the only consortium in which the skills, experience, cool judgement and administrative expertise needed to manage the situation can be found.

Yet the institution which is most worthy of our affection and trust is the one we have treated the worst.

During the first decade of the 21st century Britain expected its Army to fight two "hot" wars, in Iraq and Afghanistan, on top of its normal peacekeeping and humanitarian duties, with a strength

It was reported in *The Daily Telegraph* **on 5th July 2008 that, at a time when the Army was short of men and of supplies and equipment at the front lines in two major battle theatres, civil servants at the Ministry of Defence had awarded themselves bonuses for the year totalling £41 million.**

which defence experts considered inadequate for half this commitment. Part-time, Territorial soldiers have had to augment Regular troops for extended periods of front-line duty in a way which was never intended for the TA to be deployed in peacetime and which, in turn, has created a grave crisis in recruitment for the Territorial Army.

THE PRESENT

Today, an exchequer plundered by profligate and indiscriminate welfare spending and fraud is evidently unable to support the country's perilously-overstretched soldiers with adequate and suitable weapons and equipment. When they are wounded they must rely, for all but primary battlefield treatment, upon the already overburdened civilian National Health Service, the superb Army Medical Services having been reduced to skeletal proportions and the Military Hospitals, with their reputation for excellence, all closed down.

If, in today's culture of reduced personal responsibility, a soldier may become eligible for compensation for grievous wounds incurred in the service of his country, his award may well be less than that received by a civilian claimant for some trivial injury incurred in a warm, comfortable office. Some of the married quarters in which service families are expected to live are so sub-standard that they would not be accepted by an out-of-work council house tenant and the amount Britain pays its soldiers is wholly inadequate for the skilled and dangerous work they undertake and morally insupportable when compared to the absurd pay scales in the civil service and parts of the commercial sector.

Only after a massive public protest, led by a popular actress, did the government recognise the gross injustice of giving Gurkha soldiers, our best and most loyal friends, inferior residency rights to immigrants with no allegiance to, or regard for, Britain other than as a comfortable and secure place in which to live: comfortable and secure thanks, in no small part, to the loyalty and gallantry of generations of Gurkhas to whose descendants we were then, to our eternal shame, denying the same privilege.

Today there are are signs that similar feelings of public outrage may be growing over the government's neglect of British troops in Afghanistan. For reasons that are difficult for us, as supposedly equal members of the European Community, to understand, the British contingent outnumbers those of France, Germany and the Netherlands combined and British casualties are around three times greater.

It is also difficult to understand how, though the number of civilian civil servants in the Ministry of Defence is approximately equal to the number of soldiers in the British Army, they seem incapable even of instituting and controlling defence industry contracts

which do not bolt grossly over budget, are not scandalously overdue on their contracted delivery dates and which, when they do eventually arrive, are found to be unfit for purpose.

At last, our national conscience is becoming uncomfortable with the way we are treating our soldiers who are the cream of our youth and deserving of the best we have to offer in all things. But it was ever thus! There is nothing new about the shabby way Britain treats her Army and can one realistically hope that, if and when the present world crisis is resolved, the heroes of Helmand Province will not soon be forgotten and a more pressing social use found for the funds which should be spent on preparing and equipping the next generation of British soldiers to protect us from the next international cataclysm?

So, the pages which follow chronicle the development and progressive dissipation of what many believe to be the finest Army in the world. Its achievements are recorded with pride lest they should ever be forgotten by those who have used it so ill. ❑

> *"The British Infantry are the best in the world –*
> *fortunately there are very few of them."*
>
> Marquis de la Piconnerie (1784-1849)

CONTENTS

The section which follows shows the names of regiments and corps in six columns as they were known in:

1751	1861	1881 post-Cardwell *(General Order 41)*	1881 post-Childers *(General Order 70)*	1922	2008

They appear in their Order of Precedence.

Where a title appears in BLACK it indicates that the regiment was current in the year to which the column refers.

Where a title goes from BLACK to GREY it indicates that it is now part of an amalgamated regiment which has been included previously. Simply follow the column back until the name of the extant regiment is shown in BLACK.

The page number on which it appears is shown on the extreme right.

1751	1861		1881 post CARDWELL (General Order No 41)	
		ROYAL HORSE ARTILLERY		ROYAL HORSE ARTILLERY
LIFE GUARDS	1st	LIFE GUARDS	1st	LIFE GUARDS
	2nd	LIFE GUARDS	2nd	LIFE GUARDS
ROYAL HORSE GUARDS (The Blues)		ROYAL HORSE GUARDS		ROYAL HORSE GUARDS
1st KING'S REGIMENT OF DRAGOON GUARDS	1st	THE KING'S DRAGOON GUARDS	1st	THE KING'S DRAGOON GUARDS
2nd QUEEN'S REGIMENT OF DRAGOON GUARDS	2nd	THE QUEEN'S DRAGOON GUARDS	2nd	THE QUEEN'S DRAGOON GUARDS
3rd REGIMENT OF DRAGOON GUARDS	3rd	(Prince of Wales's) DRAGOON GUARDS	3rd	(Prince of Wales's) DRAGOON GUARDS
1st REGIMENT OF HORSE	4th	(Royal Irish) DRAGOON GUARDS	4th	(Royal Irish) DRAGOON GUARDS
2nd REGIMENT OF HORSE	5th	(Princess Charlotte of Wales's) DRAGOON GUARDS	5th	(Princess Charlotte of Wales's) DRAGOON GUARDS
3rd REGIMENT OF HORSE (or The Carbineers)	6th	DRAGOON GUARDS (Carabiniers)	6th	DRAGOON GUARDS (Carabiniers)
4th REGIMENT OF HORSE	7th	(The Princess Royal's) DRAGOON GUARDS	7th	(The Princess Royal's) DRAGOON GUARDS
1st ROYAL DRAGOONS	1st	(Royal) DRAGOONS	1st	(Royal) DRAGOONS
2nd ROYAL NORTH BRITISH DRAGOONS	2nd	ROYAL NORTH BRITISH DRAGOONS (Scots Greys)	2nd	ROYAL NORTH BRITISH DRAGOONS (Scots Greys)
3rd KING'S OWN REGIMENT OF DRAGOONS	3rd	(King's Own) HUSSARS	3rd	(King's Own) HUSSARS
4th REGIMENT OF DRAGOONS	4th	(The Queen's Own) HUSSARS	4th	(The Queen's Own) HUSSARS
5th ROYAL IRISH DRAGOONS	5th	(Royal Irish) LANCERS	5th	(Royal Irish) LANCERS
6th THE INNISKILLING DRAGOONS	6th	(Inniskilling) DRAGOONS	6th	(Inniskilling) DRAGOONS
7th THE QUEEN'S REGIMENT OF DRAGOONS	7th	(Queen's Own) HUSSARS	7th	(Queen's Own) HUSSARS
8th REGIMENT OF DRAGOONS	8th	(The King's Royal Irish) HUSSARS	8th	(The King's Royal Irish) HUSSARS
9th REGIMENT OF DRAGOONS	9th	(Queen's Royal) LANCERS	9th	(Queen's Royal) LANCERS
10th REGIMENT OF DRAGOONS	10th	THE PRINCE OF WALES'S OWN ROYAL HUSSARS	10th	THE PRINCE OF WALES'S OWN ROYAL HUSSARS
11th REGIMENT OF DRAGOONS	11th	PRINCE ALBERT'S OWN HUSSARS	11th	PRINCE ALBERT'S OWN HUSSARS
12th REGIMENT OF DRAGOONS	12th	(Prince of Wales's Royal) LANCERS	12th	(Prince of Wales's Royal) LANCERS
13th REGIMENT OF DRAGOONS	13th	HUSSARS	13th	HUSSARS
14th REGIMENT OF DRAGOONS	14th	(King's) HUSSARS	14th	(King's) HUSSARS
	15th	(King's) HUSSARS	15th	(King's) HUSSARS
	16th	(The Queen's) LANCERS	16th	(The Queen's) LANCERS
	17th	LANCERS	17th	LANCERS
	18th	HUSSARS	18th	HUSSARS
	18th	HUSSARS	19th	HUSSARS
	20th	HUSSARS	20th	HUSSARS
	21st	HUSSARS	21st	HUSSARS

NOTE
When on parade with its guns, the Royal Horse Artillery has overall precedence parading on the "Right of the Line" and marching ahead of the Household Cavalry.

1881 post CHILDERS (General Order No 70)	1922	2008	PAGE NO.
		ROYAL HORSE ARTILLERY	
ROYAL HORSE ARTILLERY	ROYAL HORSE ARTILLERY	THE ROYAL HORSE ARTILLERY (see note on page 18)	52
		HOUSEHOLD CAVALRY	
1st LIFEGUARDS	THE LIFEGUARDS	THE HOUSEHOLD CAVALRY REGIMENT	31
2nd LIFEGUARDS	THE LIFEGUARDS	THE HOUSEHOLD CAVALRY REGIMENT	
ROYAL HORSE GUARDS	ROYAL REGIMENT OF HORSE GUARDS (The Blues)	THE HOUSEHOLD CAVALRY REGIMENT	
		HEAVY CAVALRY	
1st THE KING'S DRAGOON GUARDS	1st KING'S DRAGOON GUARDS	1st THE QUEEN'S DRAGOON GUARDS	35
2nd THE QUEEN'S DRAGOON GUARDS	THE QUEEN'S BAYS (2nd Dragoon Guards)	1st THE QUEEN'S DRAGOON GUARDS	
3rd (Prince of Wales's) DRAGOON GUARDS	3rd / 6th DRAGOON GUARDS	THE ROYAL SCOTS DRAGOON GUARDS (Carabiniers and Greys)	36
4th (Royal Irish) DRAGOON GUARDS	4th / 7th ROYAL DRAGOON GUARDS	THE ROYAL DRAGOON GUARDS	38
5th (Princess Charlotte of Wales's) DRAGOON GUARDS	5th / 6th DRAGOONS	THE ROYAL DRAGOON GUARDS	
6th DRAGOON GUARDS (Carabiniers)	3rd / 6th DRAGOON GUARDS	THE ROYAL SCOTS DRAGOON GUARDS (Carabiniers and Greys)	
7th (The Princess Royal's) DRAGOON GUARDS	4th / 7th DRAGOON GUARDS	THE ROYAL DRAGOON GUARDS	
		LIGHT CAVALRY	
1st (Royal) DRAGOONS	1st THE ROYAL DRAGOONS	THE HOUSEHOLD CAVALRY REGIMENT	
2nd ROYAL NORTH BRITISH DRAGOONS (Scots Greys)	THE ROYAL SCOTS GREYS (2nd Dragoons)	THE ROYAL SCOTS DRAGOON GUARDS (Carabiniers and Greys)	
3rd (King's Own) HUSSARS	3rd THE KING'S OWN HUSSARS	THE QUEEN'S ROYAL HUSSARS (Queen's Own and Royal Irish)	40
4th (The Queen's Own) HUSSARS	4th QUEEN'S OWN HUSSARS	THE QUEEN'S ROYAL HUSSARS (Queen's Own and Royal Irish)	
5th (Royal Irish) LANCERS	16th / 5th LANCERS	THE QUEEN'S ROYAL LANCERS	48
6th (Inniskilling) DRAGOONS	3rd / 6th DRAGOON GUARDS	THE ROYAL SCOTS DRAGOON GUARDS (Carabiniers and Greys)	
7th (Queen's Own) HUSSARS	7th QUEEN'S OWN HUSSARS	THE QUEEN'S ROYAL HUSSARS (Queen's Own and Royal Irish)	
8th (The King's Royal Irish) HUSSARS	8th KING'S ROYAL IRISH HUSSARS	THE QUEEN'S ROYAL HUSSARS (Queen's Own and Royal Irish)	
9th (Queen's Royal) LANCERS	9th QUEEN'S ROYAL LANCERS	9th / 12th ROYAL LANCERS (Prince of Wales's)	43
10th (The Prince of Wales's Own Royal) HUSSARS	10th ROYAL HUSSARS (Prince of Wales's Own)	THE KING'S ROYAL HUSSARS	44
11th (Prince Albert's Own) HUSSARS	11th HUSSARS (Prince Albert's Own)	THE KING'S ROYAL HUSSARS	
12th (Prince of Wales's Royal) LANCERS	12th ROYAL LANCERS (Prince of Wales's)	9th / 12th ROYAL LANCERS (Prince of Wales's)	
13th HUSSARS	13th / 18th ROYAL HUSSARS	THE LIGHT DRAGOONS	46
14th (King's) HUSSARS	14th / 20th HUSSARS	THE KING'S ROYAL HUSSARS	
15th (The King's) HUSSARS	15th / 19th HUSSARS	THE LIGHT DRAGOONS	
16th (The Queen's) LANCERS	16th / 5th LANCERS	THE QUEEN'S ROYAL LANCERS	
17th LANCERS	17th / 21st LANCERS	THE QUEEN'S ROYAL LANCERS	
18th HUSSARS	13th / 18th ROYAL HUSSARS	THE LIGHT DRAGOONS	
19th HUSSARS	15th / 19th HUSSARS	THE LIGHT DRAGOONS	
20th HUSSARS	14th / 20th HUSSARS	THE KING'S ROYAL HUSSARS	
21st HUSSARS	17th / 21st LANCERS	THE QUEEN'S ROYAL LANCERS	
		ROYAL TANK REGIMENT	
	TANK CORPS	ROYAL TANK REGIMENT	50

1751	1861	1881 post CARDWELL (General Order No 41)
	ROYAL REGIMENT OF ARTILLERY	ROYAL REGIMENT OF ARTILLERY
	CORPS OF ROYAL ENGINEERS	CORPS OF ROYAL ENGINEERS
1st FOOT GUARDS	GRENADIER GUARDS	GRENADIER GUARDS
2nd FOOT GUARDS	COLDSTREAM GUARDS	COLDSTREAM GUARDS
3rd FOOT GUARDS	SCOTS FUSILIER GUARDS	SCOTS FUSILIER GUARDS
1st (or Royal) REGIMENT OF FOOT	1st or THE ROYAL REGIMENT	1st Foot THE LOTHIAN REGIMENT (Royal Scots)
2nd (or The Queen's Royal) REGIMENT OF FOOT	2nd (The Queen's Royal) REGIMENT	2nd Foot THE ROYAL WEST SURREY REGIMENT (The Queen's)
3rd (or The Buffs) REGIMENT OF FOOT	3rd (East Kent) REGIMENT OF FOOT (The Buffs)	3rd Foot THE KENTISH REGIMENT (The Buffs)
4th (or The King's Own) REGIMENT OF FOOT	4th THE KING'S OWN REGIMENT	4th Foot THE ROYAL LANCASTER REGIMENT (The King's Own)
5th (Northumberland) REGIMENT OF FOOT	5th REGIMENT OF FOOT (Northumberland Fusiliers)	5th Foot THE NORTHUMBERLAND FUSILIERS
6th REGIMENT OF FOOT	6th (Royal 1st Warwickshire) REGIMENT OF FOOT	6th Foot THE ROYAL WARWICKSHIRE REGIMENT
7th REGIMENT OF FOOT (The Royal Fuziliers)	7th THE ROYAL FUSILIERS	7th Foot THE CITY OF LONDON REGIMENT (Royal Fusiliers)
8th (or The King's) REGIMENT OF FOOT	8th (The King's) REGIMENT OF FOOT	8th Foot THE LIVERPOOL REGIMENT (The King's)
9th REGIMENT OF FOOT	9th (East Norfolk) REGIMENT	9th Foot THE NORFOLK REGIMENT
10th REGIMENT OF FOOT	10th (North Lincolnshire) REGIMENT	10th Foot THE LINCOLNSHIRE REGIMENT
11th REGIMENT OF FOOT	11th (North Devonshire) REGIMENT	11th Foot THE DEVONSHIRE REGIMENT
12th REGIMENT OF FOOT	12th (East Suffolk) REGIMENT	12th Foot THE SUFFOLK REGIMENT
13th REGIMENT OF FOOT	13th (1st Somersetshire) (Prince Albert's Light Infantry) REGIMENT	13th Foot THE SOMERSETSHIRE REGIMENT (Prince Albert's Light Infantry)
14th REGIMENT OF FOOT	14th (Buckinghamshire) REGIMENT	14th Foot THE WEST YORKSHIRE REGIMENT (Prince of Wales's Own)
15th REGIMENT OF FOOT	15th (Yorkshire East Riding) REGIMENT	15th Foot THE EAST YORKSHIRE REGIMENT
16th REGIMENT OF FOOT	16th (Bedfordshire) REGIMENT	16th Foot THE BEDFORDSHIRE REGIMENT
17th REGIMENT OF FOOT	17th (Leicestershire) REGIMENT	17th Foot THE LEICESTERSHIRE REGIMENT
18th REGIMENT OF FOOT (or The Royal Irish)	18th (The Royal Irish) REGIMENT	18th Foot THE ROYAL IRISH REGIMENT
19th REGIMENT OF FOOT	19th (1st Yorkshire North Riding) REGIMENT	19th Foot THE NORTH YORKSHIRE REGIMENT (Prince of Wales's Own)
20th REGIMENT OF FOOT	20th (East Devonshire) REGIMENT	20th Foot THE LANCASHIRE FUSILIERS
21st REGIMENT OF FOOT	21st (Royal North British) FUSILIERS	21st Foot THE ROYAL SCOTS FUSILIERS
22nd REGIMENT OF FOOT	22nd (Cheshire) REGIMENT	22nd Foot THE CHESHIRE REGIMENT
23rd REGIMENT OF FOOT (or The Royal Welch Fusiliers)	23rd (Royal Welsh) FUSILIERS	23rd Foot THE ROYAL WELSH FUSILIERS
24th REGIMENT OF FOOT	24th (2nd Warwickshire) REGIMENT	24th Foot THE SOUTH WALES BORDERERS
25th REGIMENT OF FOOT	25th (King's Own Borderers) REGIMENT	25th Foot THE YORK REGIMENT (King's Own Borderers)

1881 post CHILDERS (General Order No 70)	1922	2008	PAGE NO.
		ROYAL ARTILLERY	
ROYAL REGIMENT OF ARTILLERY	ROYAL REGIMENT OF ARTILLERY	ROYAL REGIMENT OF ARTILLERY	52
		ROYAL ENGINEERS	
CORPS OF ROYAL ENGINEERS	CORPS OF ROYAL ENGINEERS	CORPS OF ROYAL ENGINEERS	56
		ROYAL SIGNALS	
	ROYAL CORPS OF SIGNALS	ROYAL CORPS OF SIGNALS	60
		FOOT GUARDS	
GRENADIER GUARDS	GRENADIER GUARDS	GRENADIER GUARDS	65
COLDSTREAM GUARDS	COLDSTREAM GUARDS	COLDSTREAM GUARDS	66
SCOTS FUSILIER GUARDS	SCOTS GUARDS	SCOTS GUARDS	67
	IRISH GUARDS	IRISH GUARDS	68
	WELSH GUARDS	WELSH GUARDS	69
		INFANTRY OF THE LINE	
THE ROYAL SCOTS (Lothian Regiment)	THE ROYAL SCOTS (The Royal Regiment)	THE ROYAL REGIMENT OF SCOTLAND	70
THE QUEEN'S (Royal West Surrey Regiment)	THE QUEEN'S ROYAL REGIMENT (West Surrey)	THE PRINCESS OF WALES'S ROYAL REGT (Queen's and Royal Hants)	82
THE BUFFS (East Kent Regiment)	THE BUFFS (East Kent Regiment)	THE PRINCESS OF WALES'S ROYAL REGT (Queen's and Royal Hants)	
THE KING'S OWN (Royal Lancaster Regiment)	THE KING'S OWN ROYAL REGIMENT (Lancaster)	THE DUKE OF LANCASTER'S REGIMENT (King's Lancashire and Border)	94
THE NORTHUMBERLAND FUSILIERS	THE NORTHUMBERLAND FUSILIERS	THE ROYAL REGIMENT OF FUSILIERS	86
THE ROYAL WARWICKSHIRE REGIMENT	THE ROYAL WARWICKSHIRE REGIMENT	THE ROYAL REGIMENT OF FUSILIERS	
THE ROYAL FUSILIERS (City of London Regiment)	THE ROYAL FUSILIERS (City of London Regiment)	THE ROYAL REGIMENT OF FUSILIERS	
THE KING'S (Liverpool Regiment)	THE KING'S REGIMENT (Liverpool)	THE DUKE OF LANCASTER'S REGIMENT (King's Lancashire and Border)	
THE NORFOLK REGIMENT	THE NORFOLK REGIMENT	THE ROYAL ANGLIAN REGIMENT	88
THE LINCOLNSHIRE REGIMENT	THE LINCOLNSHIRE REGIMENT	THE ROYAL ANGLIAN REGIMENT	
THE DEVONSHIRE REGIMENT	THE DEVONSHIRE REGIMENT	THE RIFLES	112
THE SUFFOLK REGIMENT	THE SUFFOLK REGIMENT	THE ROYAL ANGLIAN REGIMENT	
PRINCE ALBERT'S LIGHT INFANTRY (Somersetshire Regiment)	THE SOMERSET LIGHT INFANTRY (Prince Albert's)	THE RIFLES	
THE PRINCE OF WALES'S OWN (West Yorkshire Regiment)	THE WEST YORKSHIRE REGIMENT (The Prince of Wales's Own)	THE YORKSHIRE REGIMENT	98
THE EAST YORKSHIRE REGIMENT	THE EAST YORKSHIRE REGIMENT	THE YORKSHIRE REGIMENT	
THE BEDFORDSHIRE REGIMENT	THE BEDFORDSHIRE and HERTFORDSHIRE REGIMENT	THE ROYAL ANGLIAN REGIMENT	
THE LEICESTERSHIRE REGIMENT	THE LEICESTERSHIRE REGIMENT	THE ROYAL ANGLIAN REGIMENT	
THE ROYAL IRISH REGIMENT	*DISBANDED*	*DISBANDED*	110
THE PRINCESS OF WALES'S OWN (Yorkshire Regiment)	THE GREEN HOWARDS (Alexandra Princess of Wales's Own Yorkshire Regt)	THE YORKSHIRE REGIMENT	
THE LANCASHIRE FUSILIERS	THE LANCASHIRE FUSILIERS	THE ROYAL REGIMENT OF FUSILIERS	
THE ROYAL SCOTS FUSILIERS	THE ROYAL SCOTS FUSILIERS	THE ROYAL REGIMENT OF SCOTLAND	
THE CHESHIRE REGIMENT	THE CHESHIRE REGIMENT	THE MERCIAN REGIMENT	102
THE ROYAL WELSH FUSILIERS	THE ROYAL WELCH FUSILIERS	THE ROYAL WELSH	106
THE SOUTH WALES BORDERERS	THE SOUTH WALES BORDERERS	THE ROYAL WELSH	
THE KING'S OWN BORDERERS	THE KING'S OWN SCOTTISH BORDERERS	THE ROYAL REGIMENT OF SCOTLAND	

1751	1861	1881 post CARDWELL (General Order No 41)
26th REGIMENT OF FOOT	26th CAMERONIAN REGIMENT	26th / 90th Foot THE SCOTCH RIFLES (Cameronians)
27th (or The Iniskilling) REGIMENT OF FOOT	27th (Iniskilling) REGIMENT	27th / 108th Foot THE ROYAL INISKILLING FUSILIERS
28th REGIMENT OF FOOT	28th (North Gloucestershire) REGIMENT	28th / 61st Foot THE GLOUCESTERSHIRE REGIMENT
29th REGIMENT OF FOOT	29th (Worcestershire) REGIMENT	29th / 36th Foot THE WORCESTERSHIRE REGIMENT
30th REGIMENT OF FOOT	30th (Cambridgeshire) REGIMENT	30th / 59th Foot THE WEST LANCASHIRE REGIMENT
31st REGIMENT OF FOOT	31st (Huntingdonshire) REGIMENT	31st / 70th Foot THE EAST SURREY REGIMENT
32nd REGIMENT OF FOOT	32nd (Cornwall) LIGHT INFANTRY	32nd / 46th Foot THE DUKE OF CORNWALL'S LIGHT INFANTRY
33rd REGIMENT OF FOOT	33rd (Duke of Wellington's) REGIMENT	33rd / 76th Foot THE HALIFAX REGIMENT (Duke of Wellington's)
34th REGIMENT OF FOOT	34th (Cumberland) REGIMENT	34th / 55th Foot THE CUMBERLAND REGIMENT
35th REGIMENT OF FOOT	35th (Royal Sussex) REGIMENT	35th / 107th Foot THE ROYAL SUSSEX REGIMENT
36th REGIMENT OF FOOT	36th (Herefordshire) REGIMENT	29th / 36th Foot THE WORCESTERSHIRE REGIMENT
37th REGIMENT OF FOOT	37th (North Hampshire) REGIMENT	37th / 67th Foot THE HAMPSHIRE REGIMENT
38th REGIMENT OF FOOT	38th (1st Staffordshire) REGIMENT	38th / 80th Foot THE NORTH STAFFORDSHIRE REGIMENT
39th REGIMENT OF FOOT	39th (Dorsetshire) REGIMENT	39th / 54th Foot THE DORSETSHIRE REGIMENT
40th REGIMENT OF FOOT	40th (2nd Somersetshire) REGIMENT	40th / 82nd Foot THE SOUTH LANCASHIRE REGIMENT (Prince of Wales's Volunteers
41st ROYAL INVALIDS REGIMENT OF FOOT	41st (The Welsh) REGIMENT	41st / 69th Foot THE WELSH REGIMENT
42nd REGIMENT OF FOOT	42nd (Royal Highland) REGIMENT (Black Watch)	42nd / 73rd Foot THE ROYAL HIGHLANDERS (Black Watch)
43rd REGIMENT OF FOOT	43rd (Monmouthshire Light Infantry) REGIMENT	43rd / 52nd Foot THE OXFORDSHIRE LIGHT INFANTRY
44th REGIMENT OF FOOT	44th (East Essex) REGIMENT	44th / 56th Foot THE ESSEX REGIMENT
45th REGIMENT OF FOOT	45th (1st Nottinghamshire) REGIMENT	45th / 95th Foot THE DERBYSHIRE REGIMENT (Sherwood Foresters)
46th REGIMENT OF FOOT	46th (South Devonshire) REGIMENT	32nd / 46th Foot THE DUKE OF CORNWALL'S LIGHT INFANTRY
47th REGIMENT OF FOOT	47th (Lancashire) REGIMENT	47th / 81st Foot THE NORTH LANCASHIRE REGIMENT
48th REGIMENT OF FOOT	48th (Northamptonshire) REGIMENT	48th / 58th Foot THE NORTHAMPTONSHIRE REGIMENT
49th REGIMENT OF FOOT	49th (Princess Charlotte of Wales's Hertfordshire) REGIMENT	49th / 66th Foot THE BERKSHIRE REGIMENT (Princess Charlotte of Wales's)
	50th (The Queen's Own) REGIMENT	50th / 97th Foot THE ROYAL WEST KENT REGIMENT (Queen's Own)
	51st (2nd Yorkshire West Riding) (King's Own Light Infantry) REGIMENT	51st / 105th Foot THE SOUTH YORKSHIRE REGIMENT (King's Own Light Infantry)
	52nd (Oxfordshire Light Infantry) REGIMENT	43rd / 52nd Foot THE OXFORDSHIRE LIGHT INFANTRY
	53rd (Shropshire) REGIMENT	53rd / 85th Foot THE SHROPSHIRE REGIMENT (King's Light Infantry)
	54th (West Norfolk) REGIMENT	39th / 54th Foot THE DORSETSHIRE REGIMENT
	55th (Westmoreland) REGIMENT	34th / 55th Foot THE CUMBERLAND REGIMENT
	56th (West Essex) REGIMENT	44th / 56th Foot THE ESSEX REGIMENT
	57th (West Middlesex) REGIMENT	57th / 77th Foot THE MIDDLESEX REGIMENT (Duke of Cambridge's Own)
	58th (Rutlandshire) REGIMENT	48th / 58th Foot THE NORTHAMPTONSHIRE REGIMENT
	59th (2nd Nottinghamshire) REGIMENT	30th / 59th Foot THE WEST LANCASHIRE REGIMENT
	60th THE KING'S ROYAL RIFLE CORPS	60th Foot THE KING'S ROYAL RIFLE CORPS
	61st (South Gloucestershire) REGIMENT	28th / 61st Foot THE GLOUCESTERSHIRE REGIMENT
	62nd (Wiltshire) REGIMENT	62nd / 99th Foot THE WILTSHIRE REGIMENT (Duke of Edinburgh's)

1881 post CHILDERS (General Order No 70)	1922	2008	PAGE NO.
		INFANTRY OF THE LINE (continued)	
THE CAMERONIANS (Scottish Rifles)	THE CAMERONIANS (Scottish Rifles)	DISBANDED 1968	159
THE ROYAL INISKILLING FUSILIERS	THE ROYAL INISKILLING FUSILIERS	THE ROYAL IRISH REGIMENT	108
THE GLOUCESTERSHIRE REGIMENT	THE GLOUCESTERSHIRE REGIMENT	THE RIFLES	
THE WORCESTERSHIRE REGIMENT	THE WORCESTERSHIRE REGIMENT	THE MERCIAN REGIMENT	
THE EAST LANCASHIRE REGIMENT	THE EAST LANCASHIRE REGIMENT	THE DUKE OF LANCASTER'S REGIMENT (King's Lancs and Border)	
THE EAST SURREY REGIMENT	THE EAST SURREY REGIMENT	THE PRINCESS OF WALES'S ROYAL REGT (Queen's and Royal Hants)	
THE DUKE OF CORNWALL'S LIGHT INFANTRY	THE DUKE OF CORNWALL'S LIGHT INFANTRY	THE RIFLES	
THE DUKE OF WELLINGTON'S (West Riding Regiment)	THE DUKE OF WELLINGTON'S REGIMENT (West Riding)	THE YORKSHIRE REGIMENT	
THE BORDER REGIMENT	THE BORDER REGIMENT	THE DUKE OF LANCASTER'S REGIMENT (King's Lancs and Border)	
THE ROYAL SUSSEX REGIMENT	THE ROYAL SUSSEX REGIMENT	THE PRINCESS OF WALES'S ROYAL REGT (Queen's and Royal Hants)	
THE WORCESTERSHIRE REGIMENT	THE WORCESTERSHIRE REGIMENT	THE MERCIAN REGIMENT	
THE HAMPSHIRE REGIMENT	THE HAMPSHIRE REGIMENT	THE PRINCESS OF WALES'S ROYAL REGT (Queen's and Royal Hants)	
THE SOUTH STAFFORDSHIRE REGIMENT	THE SOUTH STAFFORDSHIRE REGIMENT	THE MERCIAN REGIMENT	
THE DORSETSHIRE REGIMENT	THE DORSETSHIRE REGIMENT	THE RIFLES	
THE PRINCE OF WALES'S VOLUNTEERS (South Lancashire Regt)	THE PRINCE OF WALES'S VOLUNTEERS (South Lancashire Regt)	THE DUKE OF LANCASTER'S REGIMENT (King's Lancs and Border)	
THE WELSH REGIMENT	THE WELCH REGIMENT	THE ROYAL WELSH	
THE BLACK WATCH (Royal Highlanders)	THE BLACK WATCH (Royal Highlanders)	THE ROYAL REGIMENT OF SCOTLAND	
THE OXFORDSHIRE LIGHT INFANTRY	THE OXFORDSHIRE and BUCKINGHAMSHIRE LIGHT INFANTRY	THE RIFLES	
THE ESSEX REGIMENT	THE ESSEX REGIMENT	THE ROYAL ANGLIAN REGIMENT	
THE SHERWOOD FORESTERS (Derbyshire Regiment)	THE SHERWOOD FORESTERS (Nottinghamshire and Derbyshire Regt)	THE MERCIAN REGIMENT	
THE DUKE OF CORNWALL'S LIGHT INFANTRY	THE DUKE OF CORNWALL'S LIGHT INFANTRY	THE RIFLES	
THE LOYAL NORTH LANCASHIRE REGIMENT	THE LOYAL REGIMENT (North Lancashire)	THE DUKE OF LANCASTER'S REGIMENT (King's Lancs and Border)	
THE NORTHAMPTONSHIRE REGIMENT	THE NORTHAMPTONSHIRE REGIMENT	THE ROYAL ANGLIAN REGIMENT	
PRINCESS CHARLOTTE OF WALES'S (Berkshire Regiment)	THE ROYAL BERKSHIRE REGIMENT (Princess Charlotte of Wales's)	THE RIFLES	
THE QUEEN'S OWN (Royal West Kent Regiment)	THE QUEEN'S OWN (Royal West Kent Regiment)	THE PRINCESS OF WALES'S ROYAL REGT (Queen's and Royal Hants)	
THE KING'S OWN YORKSHIRE LIGHT INFANTRY	THE KING'S OWN YORKSHIRE LIGHT INFANTRY	THE RIFLES	
THE OXFORDSHIRE LIGHT INFANTRY	THE OXFORDSHIRE and BUCKINGHAMSHIRE LIGHT INFANTRY	THE RIFLES	
THE KING'S SHROPSHIRE LIGHT INFANTRY	THE KING'S SHROPSHIRE LIGHT INFANTRY	THE RIFLES	
THE DORSETSHIRE REGIMENT	THE DORSETSHIRE REGIMENT	THE RIFLES	
THE BORDER REGIMENT	THE BORDER REGIMENT	THE DUKE OF LANCASTER'S REGIMENT (King's Lancs and Border)	
THE ESSEX REGIMENT	THE ESSEX REGIMENT	THE ROYAL ANGLIAN REGIMENT	
THE MIDDLESEX REGIMENT (Duke of Cambridge's Own)	THE MIDDLESEX REGIMENT (Duke of Cambridge's Own)	THE PRINCESS OF WALES'S ROYAL REGT (Queen's and Royal Hants)	
THE NORTHAMPTONSHIRE REGIMENT	THE NORTHAMPTONSHIRE REGIMENT	THE ROYAL ANGLIAN REGIMENT	
THE EAST LANCASHIRE REGIMENT	THE EAST LANCASHIRE REGIMENT	THE DUKE OF LANCASTER'S REGIMENT (King's Lancs and Border)	
THE KING'S ROYAL RIFLE CORPS	THE KING'S ROYAL RIFLE CORPS	THE RIFLES	
THE GLOUCESTERSHIRE REGIMENT	THE GLOUCESTERSHIRE REGIMENT	THE RIFLES	
THE WILTSHIRE REGIMENT (Duke of Edinburgh's)	THE WILTSHIRE REGIMENT (Duke of Edinburgh's)	THE RIFLES	

1751	1861		1881 post CARDWELL (General Order No 41)	
	63rd	(West Suffolk) REGIMENT	63rd / 96th Foot	THE MANCHESTER REGIMENT
	64th	(2nd Staffordshire) REGIMENT	64th / 98th Foot	THE NORTH STAFFORDSHIRE REGT (Prince of Wales's)
	65th	(2nd Yorkshire West Riding) REGIMENT	65th / 84th Foot	THE YORK and LANCASTER REGIMENT
	66th	(Berkshire) REGIMENT	49th / 66th Foot	PRINCESS CHARLOTTE OF WALES'S (Berkshire Regiment)
	67th	(South Hampshire) REGIMENT	37th / 67th Foot	THE HAMPSHIRE REGIMENT
	68th	(Durham Light Infantry) REGIMENT	68th / 106th Foot	THE DURHAM LIGHT INFANTRY
	69th	(South Lincolnshire) REGIMENT	41st / 69th Foot	THE WELSH REGIMENT
	70th	(Surrey) REGIMENT	31st / 70th Foot	THE EAST SURREY REGIMENT
	71st	(Highland) LIGHT INFANTRY	71st / 74th Foot	THE HIGHLAND LIGHT INFANTRY (City of Glasgow Regiment)
	72nd	(Duke of Albany's Own Highlanders) REGIMENT	72nd / 78th Foot	THE SEAFORTH HIGHLANDERS
	73rd	(Perthshire) REGIMENT	42nd / 73rd Foot	THE ROYAL HIGHLANDERS (Black Watch)
	74th	(Highlanders) REGIMENT	71st / 74th Foot	THE HIGHLAND LIGHT INFANTRY
	75th	(Stirlingshire) REGIMENT	75th / 92nd Foot	THE GORDON HIGHLANDERS
	76th	REGIMENT	33rd / 76th Foot	THE HALIFAX REGIMENT (Duke of Wellington's)
	77th	(East Middlesex) REGIMENT	57th / 77th Foot	THE MIDDLESEX REGIMENT (Duke of Cambridge's Own)
	78th	(Highland) REGIMENT (The Ross-shire Buffs)	72nd / 78th Foot	THE SEAFORTH HIGHLANDERS
	79th	REGIMENT (Cameron Highlanders)	79th Foot	THE QUEEN'S OWN CAMERON HIGHLANDERS
	80th	(Staffordshire Volunteers) REGIMENT	38th / 80th Foot	THE NORTH STAFFORDSHIRE REGIMENT
	81st	(Royal Lincoln Volunteers) REGIMENT	47th / 81st Foot	THE NORTH LANCASHIRE REGIMENT
	82nd	(The Prince of Wales's Volunteers) REGIMENT	40th / 82nd Foot	THE SOUTH LANCASHIRE REGIMENT (Prince of Wales's Volunteers)
	83rd	(County of Dublin) REGIMENT	83rd / 86th Foot	THE ROYAL IRISH RIFLES
	84th	(York and Lancaster) REGIMENT	65th / 84th Foot	THE YORK and LANCASTER REGIMENT
	85th	(Bucks Volunteers) REGIMENT (King's Light Infantry)	53rd / 85th Foot	THE SHROPSHIRE REGIMENT (King's Light Infantry)
	86th	(Royal County Down) REGIMENT	83rd / 86th Foot	THE ROYAL IRISH RIFLES
	87th	(The Royal Irish Fusiliers) REGIMENT	87th / 89th Foot	THE ROYAL IRISH FUSILIERS (Princess Victoria's)
	88th	(Connaught Rangers) REGIMENT	88th / 94th Foot	THE CONNAUGHT RANGERS
	89th	REGIMENT	87th / 89th Foot	THE ROYAL IRISH FUSILIERS (Princess Victoria's)
	90th	PERTHSHIRE LIGHT INFANTRY	26th / 90th Foot	THE SCOTCH RIFLES (Cameronians)
	91st	(Argyllshire) REGIMENT	91st / 93rd Foot	THE PRINCESS LOUISE'S (Sutherland and Argyll) HIGHLANDERS
	92nd	(Gordon Highlanders) REGIMENT	75th / 92nd Foot	THE GORDON HIGHLANDERS
	93rd	(Sutherland Highlanders) REGIMENT	91st / 93rd Foot	THE PRINCESS LOUISE'S (Sutherland and Argyll) HIGHLANDERS
	94th	REGIMENT	88th / 94th Foot	THE CONNAUGHT RANGERS
	95th	(Derbyshire) REGIMENT	45th / 95th Foot	THE DERBYSHIRE REGIMENT (Sherwood Foresters)
	96th	REGIMENT	63rd / 96th Foot	THE MANCHESTER REGIMENT
	97th	(The Earl of Ulster's) REGIMENT	50th / 97th Foot	THE ROYAL WEST KENT REGIMENT (Queen's Own)
	98th	REGIMENT	64th / 98th Foot	THE NORTH STAFFORDSHIRE REGT (Prince of Wales's)
	99th	(Lanarkshire) REGIMENT	62nd / 99th Foot	THE WILTSHIRE REGIMENT (Duke of Edinburgh's)

1881 post CHILDERS (General Order No 70)	1922	2008	PAGE NO.
		INFANTRY OF THE LINE (continued)	
THE MANCHESTER REGIMENT	THE MANCHESTER REGIMENT	THE DUKE OF LANCASTER'S REGIMENT (King's Lancs and Border)	
THE NORTH STAFFORDSHIRE REGT (Prince of Wales's)	THE NORTH STAFFORDSHIRE REGT (Prince of Wales's)	THE MERCIAN REGIMENT	
THE YORK and LANCASTER REGIMENT	THE YORK and LANCASTER REGIMENT	DISBANDED 1968	159
PRINCESS CHARLOTTE OF WALES'S (Berkshire Regiment)	THE ROYAL BERKSHIRE REGIMENT (Princess Caroline of Wales's)	THE RIFLES	
THE HAMPSHIRE REGIMENT	THE HAMPSHIRE REGIMENT	THE PRINCESS OF WALES'S ROYAL REGT (Queen's and Royal Hants)	
THE DURHAM LIGHT INFANTRY	THE DURHAM LIGHT INFANTRY	THE RIFLES	
THE WELSH REGIMENT	THE WELCH REGIMENT	THE ROYAL WELSH	
THE EAST SURREY REGIMENT	THE EAST SURREY REGIMENT	THE PRINCESS OF WALES'S ROYAL REGT (Queen's and Royal Hants)	
THE HIGHLAND LIGHT INFANTRY (City of Glasgow Regiment)	THE HIGHLAND LIGHT INFANTRY (City of Glasgow Regiment)	THE ROYAL REGIMENT OF SCOTLAND	
THE SEAFORTH HIGHLANDERS	THE SEAFORTH HIGHLANDERS	THE ROYAL REGIMENT OF SCOTLAND	
THE BLACK WATCH (Royal Highlanders)	THE BLACK WATCH (Royal Highlanders)	THE ROYAL REGIMENT OF SCOTLAND	
THE HIGHLAND LIGHT INFANTRY (City of Glasgow Regiment)	THE HIGHLAND LIGHT INFANTRY (City of Glasgow Regiment)	THE ROYAL REGIMENT OF SCOTLAND	
THE GORDON HIGHLANDERS	THE GORDON HIGHLANDERS	THE ROYAL REGIMENT OF SCOTLAND	
THE DUKE OF WELLINGTON'S (West Riding Regiment)	THE DUKE OF WELLINGTON'S REGIMENT (West Riding)	THE YORKSHIRE REGIMENT	
THE MIDDLESEX REGIMENT (Duke of Cambridge's Own)	THE MIDDLESEX REGIMENT (Duke of Cambridge's Own)	THE PRINCESS OF WALES'S ROYAL REGT (Queen's and Royal Hants)	
THE SEAFORTH HIGHLANDERS	THE SEAFORTH HIGHLANDERS	THE ROYAL REGIMENT OF SCOTLAND	
THE QUEEN'S OWN CAMERON HIGHLANDERS	THE QUEEN'S OWN CAMERON HIGHLANDERS	THE ROYAL REGIMENT OF SCOTLAND	
THE SOUTH STAFFORDSHIRE REGIMENT	THE SOUTH STAFFORDSHIRE REGIMENT	THE MERCIAN REGIMENT	
THE LOYAL NORTH LANCASHIRE REGIMENT	THE LOYAL REGIMENT (North Lancashire)	THE DUKE OF LANCASTER'S REGIMENT (King's Lancs and Border)	
THE PRINCE OF WALES'S VOLUNTEERS (South Lancashire Regt)	THE PRINCE OF WALES'S VOLUNTEERS (South Lancashire Regt)	THE DUKE OF LANCASTER'S REGIMENT (King's Lancs and Border)	
THE ROYAL IRISH RIFLES	THE ROYAL ULSTER RIFLES	THE ROYAL IRISH REGIMENT	
THE YORK and LANCASTER REGIMENT	THE YORK and LANCASTER REGIMENT	DISBANDED 1968	
THE KING'S SHROPSHIRE LIGHT INFANTRY	THE KING'S SHROPSHIRE LIGHT INFANTRY	THE RIFLES	
THE ROYAL IRISH RIFLES	THE ROYAL ULSTER RIFLES	THE ROYAL IRISH REGIMENT	
THE ROYAL IRISH FUSILIERS (Princess Victoria's)	THE ROYAL IRISH FUSILIERS (Princess Victoria's)	THE ROYAL IRISH REGIMENT	
THE CONNAUGHT RANGERS	DISBANDED 1922	DISBANDED 1922	160
THE ROYAL IRISH FUSILIERS (Princess Victoria's)	THE ROYAL IRISH FUSILIERS (Princess Victoria's)	THE ROYAL IRISH REGIMENT	
THE CAMERONIANS (Scottish Rifles)	THE CAMERONIANS (Scottish Rifles)	DISBANDED 1968	
THE PRINCESS LOUISE'S (Argyll and Sutherland) HIGHLANDERS	THE ARGYLL and SUTHERLAND HIGHLANDERS (Princess Louise's)	THE ROYAL REGIMENT OF SCOTLAND	
THE GORDON HIGHLANDERS	THE GORDON HIGHLANDERS	THE ROYAL REGIMENT OF SCOTLAND	
THE PRINCESS LOUISE'S (Argyll and Sutherland) HIGHLANDERS	THE ARGYLL and SUTHERLAND HIGHLANDERS (Princess Louise's)	THE ROYAL REGIMENT OF SCOTLAND	
THE CONNAUGHT RANGERS	DISBANDED 1922	DISBANDED 1922	
THE SHERWOOD FORESTERS (Derbyshire Regiment)	THE SHERWOOD FORESTERS (Notts and Derbyshire Regt)	THE MERCIAN REGIMENT	
THE MANCHESTER REGIMENT	THE MANCHESTER REGIMENT	THE DUKE OF LANCASTER'S REGIMENT (King's Lancs and Border)	
THE QUEEN'S OWN (Royal West Kent Regiment)	THE QUEEN'S OWN (Royal West Kent Regiment)	THE PRINCESS OF WALES'S ROYAL REGT (Queen's and Royal Hants)	
THE NORTH STAFFORDSHIRE REGT (Prince of Wales's)	THE NORTH STAFFORDSHIRE REGT (Prince of Wales's)	THE MERCIAN REGIMENT	
THE WILTSHIRE REGIMENT (Duke of Edinburgh's)	THE WILTSHIRE REGIMENT (Duke of Edinburgh's)	THE RIFLES	

1751	1861		1881 post CARDWELL (General Order No 41)	
	100th	(Prince of Wales's Royal Canadian) REGIMENT	100th / 109th Foot	THE PRINCE OF WALES'S ROYAL CANADIAN REGIMENT
	101st	ROYAL BENGAL FUSILIERS	101st / 104th Foot	THE ROYAL MUNSTER FUSILIERS
	102nd	ROYAL MADRAS FUSILIERS	102nd / 103rd Foot	THE ROYAL DUBLIN FUSILIERS
	103rd	ROYAL BOMBAY FUSILIERS	102nd / 103rd Foot	THE ROYAL DUBLIN FUSILIERS
	104th	BENGAL FUSILIERS	101st / 104th Foot	THE ROYAL MUNSTER FUSILIERS
	105th	MADRAS LIGHT INFANTRY	51st / 105th Foot	THE SOUTH YORKSHIRE REGIMENT (King's Own Light Infantry)
	106th	BOMBAY LIGHT INFANTRY	68th / 106th Foot	THE DURHAM LIGHT INFANTRY
	107th	BENGAL INFANTRY REGIMENT	35th / 107th Foot	THE ROYAL SUSSEX REGIMENT
	108th	MADRAS INFANTRY REGIMENT	27th / 108th Foot	THE ROYAL INISKILLING FUSILIERS
	109th	BOMBAY INFANTRY REGIMENT	100th / 109th Foot	THE PRINCE OF WALES'S ROYAL CANADIAN REGT
		THE RIFLE BRIGADE (4 battalions)		THE PRINCE CONSORT'S OWN RIFLE BRIGADE
	1st	GURKHA REGIMENT (Light Infantry)	1st	GURKHA RIFLE REGIMENT (Light Infantry)
	17th	BENGAL NATIVE INFANTRY	2nd	(Prince of Wales's Own) GURKHA REGIMENT (The Sirmoor Regiment
	18th	BENGAL NATIVE INFANTRY	3rd	(The Kumaon) GURKHA REGIMENT
	19th	BENGAL NATIVE INFANTRY	4th	GURKHA REGIMENT
	7th	REGIMENT OF INFANTRY (The Hazara Gurkha Battalion)	5th	GURKHA REGIMENT (The Hazara Gurkha Battalion) (1886)
	46th	(1st Assam) BENGAL NATIVE INFANTRY	42nd	GURKHA (Light) INFANTRY (1886)
47th / 48th		BENGAL NATIVE INFANTRY	43rd / 44th	BENGAL NATIVE INFANTRY
	9th	BENGAL NATIVE INFANTRY	32nd	BENGAL NATIVE INFANTRY (1823)
	10th	MADRAS NATIVE INFANTRY	10th	MADRAS INFANTRY (1885)

1881 post CHILDERS (General Order No 70)	1922	2008	PAGE NO.
		INFANTRY OF THE LINE (continued)	
THE PRINCE OF WALES'S LEINSTER REGT (Royal Canadians)	DISBANDED 1922	DISBANDED 1922	160
THE ROYAL MUNSTER FUSILIERS	DISBANDED 1922	DISBANDED 1922	161
THE ROYAL DUBLIN FUSILIERS	DISBANDED 1922	DISBANDED 1922	161
THE ROYAL DUBLIN FUSILIERS	DISBANDED 1922	DISBANDED 1922	
THE ROYAL MUNSTER FUSILIERS	DISBANDED 1922	DISBANDED 1922	
THE KING'S OWN YORKSHIRE LIGHT INFANTRY	THE KING'S OWN YORKSHIRE LIGHT INFANTRY	THE RIFLES	
THE DURHAM LIGHT INFANTRY	THE DURHAM LIGHT INFANTRY	THE RIFLES	
THE ROYAL SUSSEX REGIMENT	THE ROYAL SUSSEX REGIMENT	THE PRINCESS OF WALES'S ROYAL REGT (Queen's and Royal Hants)	
THE ROYAL INISKILLING FUSILIERS	THE ROYAL INISKILLING FUSILIERS	THE ROYAL IRISH REGIMENT	
THE PRINCE OF WALES'S LEINSTER REGT (Royal Canadians)	DISBANDED 1922	DISBANDED 1922	
THE PRINCE CONSORT'S OWN RIFLE BRIGADE	THE RIFLE BRIGADE (Prince Consort's Own)	THE RIFLES	
		THE PARACHUTE REGIMENT (1942)	126
		GURKHA INFANTRY	
1st GURKHA RIFLE REGIMENT (Light Infantry)	1st KING GEORGE'S OWN GURKHA RIFLES (The Malaun Regt)	TRANSFERRED TO INDIAN ARMY 1947	134
2nd (POWO) GURKHA REGIMENT (The Sirmoor Rifles)	2nd (King Edward's Own) GURKHA RIFLES (The Sirmoor Rifles)	THE ROYAL GURKHA RIFLES	132
3rd (The Kumaon) GURKHA REGIMENT	3rd (Queen Alexandra's Own) GURKHA RIFLES	TRANSFERRED TO INDIAN ARMY 1947	134
4th GURKHA REGIMENT	4th GURKHA RIFLES	TRANSFERRED TO INDIAN ARMY 1947	134
5th GURKHA REGIMENT (The Hazara Gurkha Battalion) (1886)	5th ROYAL GURKHA RIFLES (Frontier Force)	TRANSFERRED TO INDIAN ARMY 1947	134
2nd GURKHA (Light) INFANTRY (1886)	6th GURKHA RIFLES	THE ROYAL GURKHA RIFLES	132
	7th GURKHA RIFLES	THE ROYAL GURKHA RIFLES	133
3rd / 44th BENGAL NATIVE INFANTRY	8th GURKHA RIFLES	TRANSFERRED TO INDIAN ARMY 1947	135
2nd BENGAL NATIVE INFANTRY (1823)	9th GURKHA RIFLES	TRANSFERRED TO INDIAN ARMY 1947	135
4th MADRAS INFANTRY (1885)	10th GURKHA RIFLES	THE ROYAL GURKHA RIFLES	133
	11th GURKHA RIFLES	(RAISED 1918, DISBANDED 1922)	135
		GURKHA ENGINEERS	
		THE QUEEN'S GURKHA ENGINEERS (1951)	131
		GURKHA SIGNALS	
		QUEEN'S GURKHA SIGNALS (1948)	131
		GURKHA LOGISTICS	
		THE QUEEN'S OWN GURKHA LOGISTIC REGT (1958)	131
		GLIDER PILOT REGIMENT	
		GLIDER PILOT REGIMENT (1942 - 1947)	127
		SAS	
		SPECIAL AIR SERVICE REGIMENT (1944)	127
		ARMY AIR CORPS	
		ARMY AIR CORPS (1942)	128

1751	1861	1881 post CARDWELL (General Order No 41)
	ARMY CHAPLAINS' DEPARTMENT	ARMY CHAPLAINS' DEPARTMENT
	COMMISSARIAT STAFF CORPS	COMMISSARIAT and TRANSPORT CORPS
	CORPS OF ARMOURER-SERGEANTS	ORDNANCE STORE CORPS
ROYAL PIONEERS *(1762)*	ARMY WORKS CORPS *(1855)*	
	ARMY HOSPITAL CORPS	ARMY MEDICAL STAFF CORPS *(1884)*
	VETERINARY MEDICAL DEPARTMENT	VETERINARY MEDICAL DEPARTMENT
		ARMY NURSING SERVICE
	ARMY PAY DEPARTMENT *(1877)*	ARMY PAY CORPS *(1893)*
	MOUNTED MILITARY POLICE	CORPS OF MILITARY MOUNTED POLICE
		CORPS OF ARMY SCHOOLMASTERS *(1846)*
	THE SCHOOL OF MUSKETRY	THE SCHOOL OF MUSKETRY
		ARMY GYMNASTIC STAFF

1881 post CHILDERS (General Order No 70)	1922	2008	PAGE NO.
		ROYAL ARMY CHAPLAINS' DEPARTMENT	
ARMY CHAPLAINS' DEPARTMENT	ROYAL ARMY CHAPLAINS' DEPARTMENT	ROYAL ARMY CHAPLAINS' DEPARTMENT	152
		ROYAL LOGISTIC CORPS	
ARMY SERVICE CORPS (1889)	ROYAL ARMY SERVICE CORPS	ROYAL LOGISTIC CORPS	136
ARMY ORDNANCECORPS (1896)	ROYAL ARMY ORDNANCE CORPS	ROYAL LOGISTIC CORPS	
	ROYAL PIONEER CORPS (1946)	ROYAL LOGISTIC CORPS	
	ARMY CATERING CORPS (1965)	ROYAL LOGISTIC CORPS	
		ARMY MEDICAL SERVICES	
ARMY MEDICAL STAFF CORPS (1884)	ROYAL ARMY MEDICAL CORPS	ROYAL ARMY MEDICAL CORPS	142
ARMY VETERINARY CORPS (1903)	ROYAL ARMY VETERINARY CORPS	ROYAL ARMY VETERINARY CORPS	143
	ARMY DENTAL CORPS	ROYAL ARMY DENTAL CORPS	143
ARMY NURSING SERVICE	QUEEN ALEXANDRA'S IMPERIAL MILITARY NURSING SERVICE	QUEEN ALEXANDRA'S ROYAL ARMY NURSING CORPS	142
		ROYAL ELECTRICAL & MECHANICAL ENGINEERS	
		CORPS OF ROYAL ELECTRICAL and MECHANICAL ENGINEERS	144
		ADJUTANT GENERAL'S CORPS	
ARMY PAY CORPS (1893)	ROYAL ARMY PAY CORPS	ADJUTANT GENERAL'S CORPS (SPS)	146
CORPS OF MILITARY MOUNTED POLICE	CORPS OF MILITARY POLICE (1926)	ADJUTANT GENERAL'S CORPS (PRO)	
	MILITARY PROVOST STAFF CORPS (1906)	ADJUTANT GENERAL'S CORPS (PRO)	
CORPS OF ARMY SCHOOLMASTERS (1846)	ARMY EDUCATIONAL CORPS	ADJUTANT GENERAL'S CORPS (ETS)	
	AUXILIARY TERRITORIAL SERVICE (1938)	ADJUTANT GENERAL'S CORPS (SPS)	
	ARMY LEGAL CORPS (1978)	ADJUTANT GENERAL'S CORPS (ALS)	
		SMALL ARMS SCHOOL CORPS	
THE SCHOOL OF MUSKETRY	SMALL ARMS SCHOOL	SMALL ARMS SCHOOL CORPS	153
		INTELLIGENCE CORPS	
	INTELLIGENCE CORPS	INTELLIGENCE CORPS	150
		ARMY PHYSICAL TRAINING CORPS	
ARMY GYMNASTIC STAFF	ARMY PHYSICAL TRAINING STAFF	ARMY PHYSICAL TRAINING CORPS	153
		CORPS OF ARMY MUSIC	
		CORPS OF ARMY MUSIC	154

The Household Cavalry

The regiments comprising today's Household Cavalry Regiment are the oldest and most senior regular formations in the Army dating, as they do, from the birth of Britain's first standing army after the Restoration of King Charles II in 1660.

After the defeat of the Royal army at the Battle of Worcester in 1652, King Charles II returned to exile in France where he remained until1660 when he was invited to return to the throne. To ensure his personal safety, a body of horse guards was raised in Holland by Lord Gerard of Brandon from soldiers who had gone into exile with the King and upon whose loyalty he could depend. Originally formed into independent troops, the 1st (King's) Troop was commanded by Lord Gerard himself; the 2nd (Duke of York's) Troop by Sir Charles Berkeley and the 3rd (Duke of Albermarle's) Troop by Sir Philip Howard.

In 1661 a 4th (Scots) Troop was raised in Edinburgh by the Earl of Newburgh which was joined by a further two troops over the next few years. In 1666 the troops were ranked as regiments and given precedence over all other regiments in the army. In 1670 the King travelled in State to Parliament escorted, for the first time, by a troop of his own Life Guards and two years later a precedent was set for a tradition which prevails to this day: the troops of Life Guards were consolidated into one regiment which went to fight in Holland where they showed that the Household Cavalry were superb fighting troops in addition to their ceremonial excellence.

Over the next century there were many troop disbandments, amalgamations and restorations until 1788 when the 1st and 2nd Life Guards were established.

The origins of the Royal Horse Guards also dates back to the Restoration when the Earl of Oxford raised The King's Royal Regiment of Horse and dressed them in blue uniforms to match his personal livery. Their consequent nickname "The Blues" has endured as part of their official title for over three centuries to the present day.

In 1812 two squadrons of the Regiment together with two squadrons from the Life Guards formed the Household Cavalry Brigade which distinguished itself in the Peninsula and at Waterloo to such an extent that in 1820 "The Blues" were made an integral part of the Household Cavalry. Since this time a composite Household Cavalry Regiment of Life Guards and Horse Guards has served with distinction in many theatres, including both World Wars, and is the form in which both operate today though preserving their individual identities.

The third constituent of the Household Cavalry, "The Royals", was raised in 1661 by the Earl of Peterborough from veterans of Cromwell's army. It was raised as The Tangier Horse for service in Tangier which had become British as part of the dowry of Catherine of Braganza on her marriage to King Charles II. In 1674 it was ranked as the 1st Regiment of Dragoons and ten years later returned to England and was placed on the English establishment as The King's Own Royal Regiment of Dragoons.

At Waterloo an officer of the Regiment captured the Eagle of the French 105th Infantry Regiment which later became the Regiment's badge. In 1969, after three centuries of distinguished service in all theatres, "The Royals" were granted the ultimate honour of amalgamation with "The Blues" as part of the Monarch's Household Cavalry.

Today, soldiers of the Household Cavalry Regiment man a fully-operational armoured reconnaissance unit as well as providing the mounted troops for state ceremonial occasions for which the Regiment is rightly renowned.

NOTES

(1) Formed in Holland from Royalists who went into exile with King Charles II after the Battle of Worcester in 1652 and returned with him on his Restoration in 1660.

(2) On the death of the Duke of Albermarle.

(3) Lorry-borne without horses. In 1919, after very heavy casualties, both regiments were remounted as cavalry.

From 1882 until World War II there were several temporary amalgamations of Life Guards and Horse Guards into Household Cavalry Composite Regiments. From 1941 to 1945 they were consolidated into the 1st and 2nd Household Cavalry Regiments.

1658
1st (King's) Troop of Life Guards (1)

1788
1st Regiment of Life Guards

1918
1st Life Guards Battalion Guards Machine Gun Regiment (3)

1659
2nd (Duke of York's) and 3rd (Duke of Albermarle's) Troops of Life Guards (1)

1670
2nd became Queen's Troop and 3rd became Duke of York's (2)

1788
2nd Regiment of Life Guards

1918
2nd Life Guards Battalion Guards Machine Gun Regiment (3)

1661
1st King's Royal Regiment of Horse (4)

1714
Royal Regiment of Horse Guards

1750
Royal Horse Guards Blue

1819
Royal Regiment of Horse Guards (The Blues) (5)

1877
Royal Horse Guards

1891
Royal Horse Guards (The Blues)

1918
3rd (Royal Horse Guards) Battalion Guards Machine Gun Regiment

NOTES

(4) Raised as the 1st Horse on creation of the Regular Army and known popularly as "The Oxford Blues".

(5) The regiment was honoured by King George III by the appointment of the Duke of Wellington as its Colonel in 1813 and its elevation to the status of Household Cavalry in 1820.

1661
The Tangier Horse (6)

1674
1st Regiment of Dragoons

1684
The King's Own Royal Regiment of Dragoons

1691
The Royal Regiment of Dragoons

1st DRAGOONS

1751
1st (Royal) Regiment of Dragoons

1877
1st (Royal) Dragoons

NOTES

(6) Raised by the Earl of Peterborough from veterans of Cromwell's army for service in Tangier which was part of the dow of Catherine of Braganza on her marriage to King Charles II.

1921
THE LIFE GUARDS

1921
ROYAL REGIMENT OF HORSE GUARDS (The Blues)

1921
1st THE ROYAL DRAGOONS
1961
THE ROYAL DRAGOONS (1st Dragoons)

1969
THE BLUES AND ROYALS (Royal Horse Guards and 1st Dragoons)

1993

THE HOUSEHOLD CAVALRY REGIMENT	THE HOUSEHOLD CAVALRY MOUNTED REGIMENT
A fully-operational armoured reconnaissance unit	A traditional mounted unit for State ceremonial duties

Headquarters Household Cavalry:
Horse Guards, Whitehall, London SW1A 2AX
Tel: 0207 4142392
email: headquarters@householdcavalry.co.uk
Website: www.householdcavalry.gvon.com

LIFE GUARDS

REGIMENTAL MARCHES

Quick Marches: Milanollo
Men of Harlech

Slow Marches: The Life Guards Slow March
Men of Harlech

COLONEL-IN-CHIEF

HM The Queen

COLONEL OF THE LIFE GUARDS AND GOLD STICK

General the Lord Guthrie of Craigiebank GCB, LVO, OBE

ALLIED REGIMENT

The President's Bodyguard of the Pakistan Army

BLUES AND ROYALS

REGIMENTAL MARCHES

Quick Marches: March of the Princess from Aida
The Blues (The Royals)

Slow March: Slow March of The Blues and Royals

COLONEL-IN-CHIEF

HM The Queen

COLONEL OF THE BLUES AND ROYALS AND GOLD STICK HRH The Princess Royal KG, KT, GCVO, QSO

ALLIANCES

Canadian Armed Forces:

The Royal Canadian Dragoons
The Governor General's Horse Guards

BATTLE HONOURS

HE LIFE GUARDS

Pre-1914:

tingen [1743]; **Peninsula** [1808-14];
terloo [1815]; **Egypt, 1882; Tel-el-Kebir** [1882];
uth Africa, 1899-1900; Relief of Kimberley [1900];
rdeberg [1900].

First World War:

ns; **Le Cateau;** Retreat from Mons; **Marne 1914;**
ne 1914; **Messines 1914;** Armentières 1914;
es 1914, 15, 17; Langemarck 1914; Gheluvelt;
nne Bosschen; St. Julien; Frezenberg;
mme 1916, 18; Albert 1916; **Arras 1917, 18;**
rpe 1917, 18; Broodseinde; Poelcapelle;
schendaele; Bapaume 1918; **Hindenburg Line;**
hy; St. Quentin Canal; Beaurevoir; Cambrai 1918;
e; **France and Flanders 1914-18.**

Second World War:

nt Pincon; **Souleuvre;** Noireau Crossing;
ens 1944; **Brussels;** Neerpelt; **Nederrijn;** Nijmegen;
en; Bentheim; **North-West Europe 1944-45;**
hdad 1941; **Iraq 1941; Palmyra; Syria 1941;**
lamein; North Africa 1942-43; Arezzo;
ance to Florence; Gothic Line; **Italy 1944.**

Post-1945:

f 1991; Wadi al Batin; **Iraq 2003;** Al Basrah.

THE ROYAL REGIMENT OF HORSE GUARDS (The Blues)

Pre-1914:

Dettingen [1743]; **Warburg** [1760]; **Beaumont** [1794];
Willems [1794]; **Peninsula** [1808-14]; **Waterloo** [1815];
Egypt, 1882; Tel-el-Kebir [1882];
South Africa, 1899-1900; Relief of Kimberley [1900];
Paardeberg [1900].

First World War:

Mons; **Le Cateau;** Retreat from Mons; **Marne 1914;**
Aisne 1914; **Messines 1914;** Armentières 1914;
Ypres 1914, 15, 17; Langemarck 1914; **Gheluvelt;**
Nonne Bosschen; St. Julien; **Frezenberg; Loos;**
Arras 1917; Scarpe 1917; Broodseinde; Poelcapelle;
Passchendaele; Hindenburg Line; Cambrai 1918;
Sambre; France and Flanders 1914-18.

Second World War:

Mont Pincon; **Souleuvre;** Noireau Crossing;
Amiens 1944; **Brussels;** Neerpelt; **Nederrijn;** Nijmegen;
Lingen; Bentheim; **North-West Europe 1944-45;**
Baghdad 1941; **Iraq 1941; Palmyra; Syria 1941;**
El Alamein; North Africa 1942-43; Arezzo;
Advance to Florence; Gothic Line; **Italy 1944.**

THE ROYAL DRAGOONS (1st Dragoons)

Pre-1914:

Tangier, 1662-1680; Warburg [1760]; **Willems** [1794];
Peninsula [1808-14]; **Fuentes d'Onor** [1811];
Waterloo [1815]; **Sevastapol** [1854-55];
Balaklava [1854]; **South Africa, 1899-1902;**
Relief of Ladysmith [1900].

First World War:

Ypres 1914, 15; Langemarck 1914; Gheluvelt;
Nonne Bosschen; **Frezenberg; Loos; Arras 1917;**
Scarpe 1917; **Somme 1918;** St. Quentin; Avre; **Amiens;**
Hindenburg Line; Beaurevoir; **Cambrai 1918;**
Pursuit to Mons; France and Flanders 1914-18.

Second World War;

Nederrijn; Veghel; **Rhine; North-West Europe 1944-45;**
Syria 1941; Msus; Gazala; **Knightsbridge;**
Defence of Alamein Line; **El Alamein;** El Agheila;
Advance on Tripoli; North Africa 1941-43; Sicily 1943;
Italy 1943.

THE BLUES AND ROYALS (Royal Horse Guards and 1st Dragoons)

Post-1945:

Falkland Islands 1982; Iraq 2003; Al Basrah.

REGIMENTAL MUSEUM

HOUSEHOLD CAVALRY MUSEUM
Horse Guards, Whitehall, London SW1A 2AX
Tel: 0207 414 2392   Fax: 0207 414 2212
email: museum@householdcavalry.co.uk
Website: householdcavalry.co.uk

The Royal Armoured Corps

The first regular regiments of horse in the British Army were raised during the short reign of King James II (VII). As the range and accuracy of infantry weapons improved through the 18th and 19th centuries, so the role of cavalry as a shock assault force declined; until the horse was replaced by the tank between the two World Wars.

The Royal Armoured Corps was created in 1939 as the collective formation for the recently-mechanised cavalry regiments of the line and the Royal Tank Corps the name of which was changed at that time to Royal Tank Regiment. There are presently ten regiments in the corps — the Household Cavalry, although an armoured regiment, is not part of the Royal Armoured Corps.

In the early days of the British Army, mounted regiments were simply designated Regiments of Horse but a distinction soon began to emerge between heavy and light cavalry. Heavy cavalry, sometimes wearing partial armour, with strong weapons and mounted on large horses, were the shock troops of the field army used to charge and pulverise infantry formations. Light cavalry, lightly armed and mounted, were faster moving, more mobile troops used for reconnaissance and skirmishing.

The early regiments of Dragoon Guards followed the style of the French cuirassiers with metal helmets and breastplates which are retained today in the ceremonial uniforms of the Household Cavalry. Dragoons were originally mounted infantry who travelled on horseback but dismounted and fought on foot. However, the term came to mean heavy cavalry and, apart from the helmets retained by the Dragoon Guards and their senior status, by the 19th century there was little difference between Dragoon Guards and Dragoons. During the 19th century the regiments of Light Dragoons, following the trends being set in

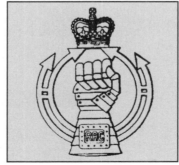

Hungary and Poland, began to be redesignated as Hussars and Lancers which names they retain to this day though the historical heavy/light role of each regiment does not necessarily reflect its modern equipment and role (see table on page 42).

Both Hussars and Lancers originated as heavy cavalry in Eastern Europe in the middle ages. During the 18th century they began converting to the light role, wearing the distinctive uniforms with which they became associated and which were adopted in the British Army as regiments of Light Dragoons were redesignated Hussars and Lancers. The Hussars were famous for their magnificent uniforms — the heavily-braided dolman jackets and the Hungarian fur kucsma headdress with a cloth bag hanging down the side. The Lancer regiments adopted the distinctive flat-topped Polish Uhlan helmet.

The lance was withdrawn from service after the Boer War but was reintroduced from 1908 to 1928 when it was finally dropped except for ceremonial purposes and for the sport of tent-pegging which still a measure of supreme equestrian skill in mounted formations.

Mounted cavalry was maintained throughout World War I and, although the static conditions of the Western Front gave few opportunities for its use in Europe, it was used successfully in the Middle Eastern theatre.

An interesting historical reversal took place in 1992 with the creation of The Light Dragoons from four regiments of Hussars which had, themselves, been created from Light Dragoon regiments more than a century earlier.

1685
2nd (The Queen Consort's) (1) Regiment of Horse (Lanier's)

1714
The King's (2) Own Regiment of Horse

1st
DRAGOON GUARDS

1746
1st King's (3) Dragoon Guards

NOTES

Descended from the 2nd and 3rd Regiments of Horse, the 1st Queen's Dragoon Guards is the oldest and most senior cavalry regiment of the line.

(1) Queen Anne, Consort of King James II (VII)

(2) King George I.

(3) King George II.

1685
3rd (Earl of Peterborough's) Regiment of Horse

1715
The Princess of Wales's (4) Own Royal Regiment of Horse

1727
The Queen's Own Royal Regiment of Horse

2nd
DRAGOON GUARDS

1746
2nd Queen's Dragoon Guards

1868
2nd Dragoon Guards (Queen's Bays) (5)

1921
The Queen's Bays (2nd Dragoon Guards)

(4) Princess Caroline of Brandenburg-Anspach, wife of the future King George II and Queen Consort from his accession in 1727.

(5) In 1767 the regiment was remounted on bay horses instead of black since when they were known as "The Bays".

(6) They were also known as "Rusty Buckles" — a name given to the regiment on its return from Ireland in the 18th century after a period of continuous rain had rusted their horse irons.

BATTLE HONOURS

1st KING'S DRAGOON GUARDS

Pre-1914:

Blenheim [1704]; **Ramillies** [1706]; **Oudenarde** [1708]; **Malplaquet** [1709]; **Dettingen** [1743]; **Warburg** [1760]; **Beaumont** [1794]; **Waterloo** [1815]; **Sevastopol** [1854-55]; **Pekin, 1860; Taku Forts** [1860]; **South Africa, 1879; South Africa, 1901-02.**

First World War:

Somme 1916; Morval; France and Flanders 1914-17.

Afghanistan 1919.

Second World War:

Beda Fomm; Defence of Tobruk; Tobruk 1941; Tobruk Sortie; Relief of Tobruk; Gazala; Bir Hacheim; **Defence of Alamein Line;** Alam el Halfa; El Agheila; **Advance on Tripoli; Tebaga Gap;** Point 201 (Roman Wall); El Hamma; Akarit; **Tunis; North Africa 1941-43;** Capture of Naples; Scafati Bridge; **Monte Camino;** Garigliano Crossing; Capture of Perugia; Arezzo; **Gothic Line; Italy 1943-44;** Athens; Greece 1944-45.

THE QUEEN'S BAYS (2nd DRAGOON GUARDS)

Pre-1914:

Warburg [1760]; **Willems** [1794]; **Lucknow** [1857-58]; **South Africa, 1901-02.**

First World War:

Mons; Le Cateau; Retreat from Mons; **Marne 1914;** Aisne 1914; **Messines 1914;** Armentières 1914; **Ypres 1914-15;** Frezenberg; Bellewaarde; **Somme 1916-18;** Flers-Courcelette; Arras 1917; **Scarpe 1917; Cambrai 1917, 18;** St. Quentin; Bapaume 1918; Rosières; **Amiens;** Albert 1918; Hindenburg Line; St. Quentin Canal; Beaurevoir; **Pursuit to Mons;** France and Flanders 1914-18.

Second World War:

Somme 1940; Withdrawal to Seine; North-West Europe 1940; Msus; **Gazala;** Bir el Aslagh; Cauldron; Knightsbridge; Via Balbia; Mersa Matruh; **El Alamein;** Tebaga Gap; **El Hamma;** El Kourzia; Djebel Kournine; **Tunis;** Creteville Pass; **North Africa 1941-43; Coriano;** Carpineta; **Lamone Crossing;** Lamone Bridgehead; **Rimini Line;** Ceriano Ridge; Cesena; **Argenta Gap;** Italy 1944-45.

1st KING'S DRAGOON GUARDS

THE QUEEN'S BAYS (2nd DRAGOON GUARDS)

1959
1st THE QUEEN'S DRAGOON GUARDS

1st THE QUEEN'S DRAGOON GUARDS

Post-1945:

Gulf 1991; Wadi Al Batin; **Iraq 2003;** Al Basrah.

HOME HEADQUARTERS

Maindy Barracks, Whitchurch Road, Cardiff CF14 3YE
Tel: Civ. 02920 781213 Mil. 8213/8227
Fax: 02920 781384
email: adminofficer@qdg.org.uk
Website: www.qdg.org.uk

REGIMENTAL MARCHES

Quick March: Regimental March of 1st The Queen's Dragoon Guards (Radetsky March and Rusty Buckles) (6)

Slow Marches: 1st Dragoon Guards Slow March and 2nd Dragoon Guards Slow March.

ALLIANCES

Canadian Armed Forces:
The Governor General's Horse Guards

Australian Military Forces:
1st/15th Royal New South Wales Lancers

Pakistan Army:
11th Cavalry (Frontier Force)

Sri Lanka Army:
1st Reconnaissance Regiment

South African Defence Forces:
1st Special Service Battalion

COLONEL-IN-CHIEF

Lieutenant-General HRH The Prince of Wales
KG, KT, OM, GCB, AK, QSO, ADC

REGIMENTAL MUSEUM

1st THE QUEEN'S DRAGOON GUARDS MUSEUM
Cardiff Castle, Castle Street, Cardiff CF10 2RB
Tel: 02920 781213 Fax: 02920 781384
email: curator@qdg.org.uk
Website: www.qdg.org.uk

1685
The Earl of Plymouth's Regiment of Horse (2)

1687
4th Regiment of Horse

3rd
DRAGOON GUARDS

1751
3rd Regiment of Dragoon Guards

(2) Formed from independent troops of Horse mainly in Bedfordshire and Surrey.

(3) The future King George IV.

1685
The Queen Dowager's (4) Regiment of Horse (5)

1690
8th Regiment of Horse

1691
The King's Carabineers

1756
3rd Irish Horse (Carabineers)

6th
DRAGOON GUARDS

1788
6th Regiment of Dragoon Guards

1826
6th Dragoon Guards (Carabiniers) (6)

(4) Queen Catherine of Braganza, widow of Charles II.

(5) 9th Horse formed from independent troops of Horse by Viscount Lumley, later 1st Earl of Scarborough.

(6) In 1840 "Carabineers" was changed to "Carabiniers".

1681
The Royal Regiment of Dragoons of Scotland (1)

2nd
DRAGOONS

1688
2nd Regiment of Dragoons

1692
The Royal Regiment of Scots Dragoons

1707
The Royal Regiment of North British Dragoons

1751
2nd Royal North British Dragoons

1866
2nd Royal North British Dragoons (Royal Scots Greys)

1877
2nd Dragoons (Royal Scots Greys)

NOTES

(1) Formed in Scotland by Colonel Thomas Dalziel (Dalyell) of the Binns by the addition of three troops of dragoons to three independent companies previously raised in 1678.

1765
3rd DRAGOON GUARDS
(Prince of Wales's) (3)

1921
THE CARABINIERS
(6th Dragoon Guards)

1922
3rd/6th DRAGOON GUARDS

1928
3rd CARABINIERS
(Prince of Wales's Dragoon Guards)

1921
THE ROYAL SCOTS GREYS
(2nd Dragoons)

1971
THE ROYAL SCOTS
DRAGOON GUARDS
(Carabiniers and Greys)

HOME HEADQUARTERS

The Castle, Edinburgh EH1 2YT
Tel: Civ. 0131 3105100 Fax: 0131 3105101
Website: www.scotsdg.mod.uk

REGIMENTAL MARCHES

Military Band

Quick March: 3rd Dragoon Guards

Slow March: The Garb of Old Gaul

Pipes and Drums

Quick March: Heilan' Laddie

Slow March: My Home

ALLIANCES

Canadian Armed Forces:
The Windsor Regiment (RCAC)

Australian Military Forces:
12th/16th Hunter River Lancers (RAAC)

New Zealand Army:
The New Zealand Scottish (RNZAC)

South African Defence Forces:
The Natal Carabineers

COLONEL-IN-CHIEF

HM The Queen

DEPUTY COLONEL-IN-CHIEF

HRH Field Marshal The Duke of Kent
KG, GCMG, GCVO, ADC

BATTLE HONOURS

3rd DRAGOON GUARDS (Prince of Wales's)

THE CARABINIERS (6th Dragoon Guards)

THE ROYAL SCOTS GREYS (2nd Dragoons)

3rd CARABINIERS (Prince of Wales's Dragoon Guards)

Pre-1914:

Blenheim [1704]; Ramillies [1706]; Oudenarde [1708]; Malplaquet [1709]; Warburg [1760]; Beaumont [1794]; Willems [1794]; Peninsula [1808-14]; Talavera [1809]; Albuhera [1811]; Vittoria [1813]; Abyssinia [1867-68]; South Africa, 1899-1902.

First World War:

Ypres 1914, 15; Nonne Bosschen; Frezenberg; Loos; Arras 1917; Scarpe 1917; Somme 1918; St. Quentin; Avre; Amiens; Hindenburg Line; Beaurevoir; Cambrai 1918; Pursuit to Mons; France and Flanders 1914-18.

Pre-1914:

Blenheim [1704]; Ramillies [1706]; Oudenarde [1708]; Malplaquet [1709]; Warburg [1760]; Willems [1794]; Sevastapol [1854-55]; Delhi, 1857; Afghanistan, 1879-80; South Africa, 1899-1902; Relief of Kimberley [1900]; Paardeberg [1900].

First World War:

Mons; Le Cateau; Retreat from Mons; Marne 1914; Aisne 1914; Messines 1914; Armentières 1914; Ypres 1915; St. Julien; Bellewaarde; Arras 1917; Scarpe 1917; Cambrai 1917, 18; Somme 1918; St. Quentin; Lys; Hazebrouck; Amiens; Bapaume 1918; Hindenburg Line; Canal du Nord; Selle; Sambre; France and Flanders 1914-18.

Pre-1914:

Blenheim [1704]; Ramillies [1706]; Oudenarde [1708]; Malplaquet [1709]; Dettingen [1743]; Warburg [1760]; Willems [1794]; Waterloo [1815]; Balaklava [1854]; Sevastapol [1854-55]; South Africa, 1899-1902; Relief of Kimberley [1900]; Paardeberg [1900].

First World War:

Mons; Retreat from Mons; Marne 1914; Aisne 1914; Messines 1914; Ypres 1914, 15; Gheluvelt; Neuve Chapelle; St. Julien; Bellewaarde; Arras 1917; Scarpe 1917; Cambrai 1917, 18; Lys; Hazebrouck; Amiens; Somme 1918; Albert 1918; Bapaume 1918; Hindenburg Line; St. Quentin Canal; Beaurevoir; Pursuit to Mons; France and Flanders 1914-18.

Second World War:

Caen; Hill 112; Falaise; Venlo Pocket; Hochwald; Aller; Bremen; North-West Europe 1944-45; Merjayun; Syria 1941; Alam El Halfa; El Alamein; Al Agheila; Nofilia; Advance on Tripoli; North Africa 1942, 43; Salerno; Battipaglia; Volturno Crossing; Italy 1943.

Second World War:

Imphal; Tamu Road; Nungshigum; Bishenpur; Kanglatongbi; Kennedy Peak; Shwebo; Sagaing; Mandalay; Ava; Irrawaddy; Yenangyaung 1945; Burma 1944-45.

THE ROYAL SCOTS DRAGOON GUARDS (Carabiniers and Greys)

Post-1945:

Wadi al Batin; Gulf 1991; Al Basrah; Iraq 2003.

1685
The Earl of Arran's
Cuirassiers (1)

1690
5th Regiment of Horse

1715
The Prince of Wales's (2)
Own Regiment of Horse

1746
1st Irish Horse
(The Blue Horse)

4th
DRAGOON GUARDS

1788
4th (Royal Irish)
Dragoon Guards

NOTES

(1) Raised for King James II (VII) from independent troops of horse to defend London from the expected invasion by William of Orange.

(2) The future King George II.

1688
10th Regiment of Horse
(Earl of Devonshire's) (3)

1690
8th Regiment of Horse
(Schomberg's Horse)

1720
Ligonier's Horse

1746
4th Irish Horse
(The Black Horse)

7th
DRAGOON GUARDS

1788
7th (The Princess Royal's) (4)
Dragoon Guards

(3) Raised by William Cavendish, Earl of Devonshire, from protestant members of five disbanded regiments of horse previously loyal to King James II (VII).

(4) The eldest daughter of King George III who later became Empress of Prussia.

1685
The Duke of Shrewsbury's Regiment of Horse (1)

1687
6th Regiment of Horse

1717
2nd Irish Horse
(The Green Horse)

5th
DRAGOONS

1784
5th Dragoon Guards

1804
5th (Princess Charlotte of Wales's) (5)
Dragoon Guards

(5) The only daughter of the future King George IV. She died in 1817.

1689
Cunningham's Regiment of Dragoons (6)
(The Black Dragoons)

6th
DRAGOONS

1751
6th (Inniskilling) Dragoons

(6) Raised from the protestant inhabitants of Enniskillen to defend the town from the expected invasion of King James II (VII).

1921
4th ROYAL IRISH DRAGOON GUARDS

1921
7th DRAGOON GUARDS
(Princess Royal's)

1921
5th DRAGOON GUARDS
(Princess Charlotte of Wales's)

1921
THE INNISKILLINGS
(6th Dragoons)

1922
4th / 7th ROYAL DRAGOON GUARDS

1922
5th/6th Dragoons

1927
5th Inniskilling Dragoon Guards

1935
5th ROYAL INNISKILLING DRAGOON GUARDS

1992
THE ROYAL DRAGOON GUARDS

Although the origins of all four of the original constituents of this great regiment lie in Ireland, the only visible reminder today of its Irish heritage is the representation of the Castle of Inniskilling in the regiment's cap badge.

HOME HEADQUARTERS

3 Tower Street, York YO1 9SB

Tel: Civ. 01904 642036 Mil. York 2310
Fax. 01904 642036

email: hhq@rdgmuseum.org.uk
Website: www.rdgmuseum.org.uk/

REGIMENTAL MARCHES

Quick March: Fare thee well Iniskilling

Slow March: A combination of the Slow Marches of 4th Dragoon Guards and 7th Dragoon Guards

COLONEL-IN-CHIEF

Lieutenant-General HRH The Prince of Wales
KG, KT, OM, GCB, AK, QSO, ADC

ALLIANCES

Canadian Armed Forces:
The Fort Garry Horse
The British Colombia Dragoons

Australian Military Forces:
4th/9th Prince of Wales's Light Horse
3rd/9th South Australian Mounted Rifles

New Zealand Army:
Queen Alexandra's Mounted Rifles

Pakistan Army:
15th Lancers

Indian Army:
The Deccan Horse

REGIMENTAL MUSEUM

ROYAL DRAGOON GUARDS MUSEUM
3 Tower Street, York YO1 9SB
Tel: 01904 642036 Fax: 01904 642036
email: hhq@rdgmuseum.org.uk
Website: www.rdgmuseum.org.uk

BATTLE HONOURS

4th ROYAL IRISH DRAGOON GUARDS

Pre-1914:

...ninsula [1808-14]; **Balaklava** [1854]; ...vastapol [1854-55]; **Tel-el-Kebir** [1882]; ...ypt, 1882-84.

First World War:

...ns; Le Cateau; **Retreat from Mons; Marne 1914;** ...sne 1914; La Bassée 1914; **Messines 1914;** ...nentières 1914; **Ypres 1914, 15;** St. Julien; ...zenberg; Bellewaarde; **Somme 1916, 18;** ...rs-Courcelette; Arras 1917; Scarpe 1917; ...mbrai 1917, 18; St. Quentin; Rosières; Amiens; ...ert 1918; Hindenburg Line; **Pursuit to Mons;** ...nce and Flanders 1914-18.

7th DRAGOON GUARDS (Princess Royal's)

Pre-1914:

Blenheim [1704]; **Ramillies** [1706]; **Oudenarde** [1708]; Malplaquet [1709]; **Dettingen** [1743]; **Warburg** [1760]; South Africa, 1846-47; **Tel-el-Kebir** [1882]; **Egypt, 1882-84;** South Africa, 1899-1902.

First World War:

La Bassée 1914; **Givenchy 1914; Somme 1916-18; Bazentin;** Flers-Courcelette; **Cambrai 1917-18; St. Quentin; Avre;** Lys; Hazebrouck; **Amiens; Hindenburg Line;** St. Quentin Canal; Beaurevoir; **Pursuit to Mons;** France and Flanders 1914-18.

4th / 7th ROYAL DRAGOON GUARDS

Second World War:

Dyle; **Dunkirk 1940; Normandy Landing; Odon; Mont Pincon;** Seine 1944; **Nederrijn; Geilenkirchen;** Roer; **Rhineland;** Cleve; **Rhine;** Bremen; North-West Europe 1940, 44-45.

5th DRAGOON GUARDS (Princess Charlotte of Wales's)

Pre-1914:

Blenheim [1704]; **Ramillies** [1706]; **Oudenarde** [1708]; Malplaquet [1709]; **Beaumont** [1794]; Peninsula [1808-14]; **Salamanca** [1812]; Vittoria [1813]; **Toulouse** [1814]; **Balaklava** [1854]; Sevastopol [1854-55]; **Defence of Ladysmith** [1899-1900]; South Africa, 1899-1902.

First World War:

Mons; Le Cateau; Retreat from Mons; **Marne 1914;** Aisne 1914; La Bassée 1914; **Messines 1914;** Armentières 1914; **Ypres 1914, 15;** Frezenberg; **Bellewaarde; Somme 1916, 18;** Flers-Courcelette; Arras 1917; Scarpe 1917; **Cambrai 1917, 18;** St. Quentin; Rosières; **Amiens;** Albert 1918; Hindenburg Line; St. Quentin Canal; Beaurevoir; **Pursuit to Mons;** France and Flanders 1914-18.

THE INNISKILLINGS (6th Dragoons)

Pre-1914:

Dettingen [1743]; **Warburg** [1760]; **Willems** [1794]; Waterloo [1815]; **Balaklava** [1854]; Sevastapol [1854-55]; South Africa, 1899-1902.

First World War:

Somme 1916, 18; Morval; **Cambrai 1917, 18; St. Quentin; Avre;** Lys; Hazebrouck; **Amiens; Hindenburg Line; St. Quentin Canal;** Beaurevoir; **Pursuit to Mons; France and Flanders 1914-18.**

5th ROYAL INNISKILLING DRAGOON GUARDS

Second World War:

Withdrawal to Escaut; **St. Omer-La Bassée; Dunkirk 1940; Mont Pincon;** St. Pierre la Vielle; Lisieux; Risle Crossing; **Lower Maas;** Roer; Ibbenburen; North-West Europe 1940, 44-45.

Post-1945:

The Hook 1952; Korea 1951-52.

1685
The Queen Consort's (1)
Own Regiment of
Dragoons (2)

1714
The King's Own
Regiment of Dragoons

3rd DRAGOONS

1751
3rd (King's Own)
Dragoons

1818
3rd (King's Own)
Light Dragoons

1861
3rd (King's Own)
Hussars

NOTES

(1) Queen Mary of Modena, 2nd wife of King James II (VII).

(2) Raised by King James II (VII) for defence of the Realm against William of Orange. Changed its allegiance in 1688.

1690
8th Dragoons (3)

1715
The Princess of Wales's
Own Royal Dragoons

1727
The Queen's (4) Own
Dragoons

7th DRAGOONS

1751
7th Dragoons
(Queen's Own)

1783
7th Light Dragoons
(Queen's Own) (5)

1805
7th (Queen's Own)
Hussars

(3) Raised in Scotland from independent troops of horse for service with William of Orange against King James II (VII).

(4) Queen Caroline of Brandenburg-Anspach, wife of King George II.

(5) Queen Charlotte of Mecklenburg-Strelitz, wife of King George III.

1685
Princess Anne of
Denmark's Dragoons (6)

4th DRAGOONS

1751
4th Dragoons

1788
4th Dragoons
(Queen's (5) Own)

1818
4th Light Dragoons
(Queen's Own)

1861
4th (The Queen's
Own (7)) Hussars

(6) The younger daughter of King James II (VII) who married King George of Denmark. She later became Queen Anne of Great Britain.

The regiment was raised in Wessex by Col Hon John Berkeley who in 1688 defected to William of Orange though the regiment remained loyal to James II (VII).

(7) Queen Victoria.

1693
Henry Conyngham's
Regiment of Dragoons (8)

8th DRAGOONS

1751
8th Dragoons

1775
8th Light Dragoons

1777
8th (The King's Royal
Irish) Light Dragoons

1822
8th (The King's Royal
Irish) Hussars

(8) Raised by Henry Cunningham (Conyngham), Colon of the Inniskillings, from Irish protestants who had fought at the Battle of the Boyne

1921
3rd THE KING'S OWN
HUSSARS

1921
7th QUEEN'S OWN
HUSSARS

1921
4th QUEEN'S OWN
HUSSARS

1921
8th KING'S ROYAL IRISH
HUSSARS

1958
THE QUEEN'S OWN
HUSSARS

1958
THE QUEEN'S ROYAL IRISH
HUSSARS

1993
**THE QUEEN'S ROYAL
HUSSARS**
(The Queen's Own and
Royal Irish)

HOME HEADQUARTERS

Regent's Park Barracks, Albany St., London NW1 4AL
Tel: 0207 7562275 Fax: 0207 7562276

email: regsec@qrhussars.co.uk
Website: www.qrh.org.uk/

REGIMENTAL MARCHES

Quick March: Regimental Quick March of
      The Queen's Royal Hussars

Slow Marches: The 3rd Hussars Slow March
      Litany of Loretto (4th Hussars)
      The Garb of Old Gaul (7th Hussars)
      The Scottish Archers (8th Hussars)

ALLIANCES

Canadian Armed Forces:
   The Sherbrooke Hussars
   The Royal Canadian Hussars (Montreal)
   8th Canadian Hussars (Princess Louise's)

Australian Military Forces:
   3rd/9th South Australian Mounted Rifles
   2nd/14th Light Horse (Queensland Mounted Infantry)
   3rd Battalion The Royal Australian Regiment
   Victorian Mounted Rifles Squadron,
     4th/9th Prince of Wales's Light Horse

New Zealand Army:
   Queen Alexandra's Mounted Rifles

South African Defence Force:
   Natal Mounted Rifles
   Umvoti Mounted Rifles
   Light Horse Regiment

COLONEL-IN-CHIEF

Field Marshal HRH The Prince Philip, Duke of Edinburgh
   KG, KT, OM, GBE, AC, QSO

With origins dating back to 168[
The Queen's Royal Hussars is
the senior Light Cavalry
Regiment of the British Army.

BATTLE HONOURS

3rd THE KING'S OWN HUSSARS

Pre-1914:

ttingen [1743]; **Peninsula** [1808-14]; lamanca [1812], Vittoria [1813]; **Toulouse** [1814]; ndahar [1842]; **Ferozeshah** [1845]; **Moodkee** [1845]; braon [1846]; **Chillianwallah** [1849]; njaub [1848-49]; Goojerat [1849]; **South Africa, 1902.**

First World War:

ns; Le Cateau; **Retreat from Mons; Marne 1914;** sne 1914; **Messines 1914;** Armentières 1914; res 1914, 15; Gheluvelt; St. Julien; Bellewaarde; ras 1917; Scarpe 1917; Cambrai 1917, 18; mme 1918; St. Quentin; Lys; Hazebrouck; niens 1918; Bapaume 1918; Hindenburg Line; nal du Nord; Selle; Sambre; ance and Flanders 1914-18.

Second World War:

di Barrani; Buq Buq; **Beda Fomm; Sidi Suleiman;** Alamein; **North Africa 1940-42; Citta del Pieve;** tta di Castello; Italy 1944; **Crete.**

REGIMENTAL MUSEUMS

THE QUEEN'S ROYAL HUSSARS MUSEUM

The Queen's Own Hussars
Lord Leycester Hospital,
60 High Street, Warwick CV34 4BH
Tel: 01926 492035 Fax: 01926 492035
email: qohmuseum@qrh.org.uk
Website: www.qohmuseum.org.uk

The Queen's Royal Irish Hussars
Redoubt Fortress,
Eastbourne, East Sussex BN22 7AQ
Tel: 01323 410300 Fax: 01323 439882
redoubtmuseum@ eastbourne.gov.uk
Website: www.eastbournemuseums.co.uk

Curator's Office *(HHQ London):* Tel: 020 7756 2274

7th QUEEN'S OWN HUSSARS

Pre-1914:

Warburg [1760]; Beaumont [1794]; Willems [1794]; **Peninsula** [1808-14]; **Orthes** [1814]; **Waterloo** [1815]; Lucknow [1857-58]; **South Africa, 1901-02.**

First World War:

Khan Baghdadi; Sharqat; Mesopotamia 1917-18.

Second World War:

Egyptian Frontier 1940; Beda Fomm; **Sidi Rezegh 1941; North Africa 1940-41; Ancona;** **Rimini Line; Italy 1944-45; Pegu; Paungde;** **Burma 1942.**

4th QUEEN'S OWN HUSSARS

Pre-1914:

Dettingen [1743]; **Peninsula** [1808-14]; Talavera [1809]; **Albuhera** [1811]; **Salamanca** [1812]; Vittoria [1813]; **Toulouse** [1814]; **Afghanistan, 1839;** Ghuznee, 1839; Alma [1854]; **Balaklava** [1854]; Inkerman [1854]; **Sevastapol** [1854-55].

First World War:

Mons; Le Cateau; Retreat from Mons; **Marne 1914;** **Aisne 1914;** Messines 1914; Armentières 1914; **Ypres 1914, 15;** Langemarck 1914; Gheluvelt; **St. Julien;** Bellewaarde; **Arras 1917;** Scarpe 1917; **Cambrai 1917; Somme 1918; Amiens;** Hindenburg Line; Canal du Nord; Pursuit to Mons; France and Flanders 1914-18.

Second World War:

Gazala; Defence of Alamein Line; **Ruweisat;** **Alam el Halfa; El Alamein;** North Africa 1942; **Coriano;** San Clemente; **Senio Pocket; Rimini Line;** Conventello-Comacchio; Santerno Crossing; **Argenta Gap;** Italy 1944-45; **Proasteion; Corinth Xanal; Greece 1941.**

8th KING'S ROYAL IRISH HUSSARS

Pre-1914:

Hindoostan [1790-1823]; **Leswarree** [1803]; Alma [1854]; **Balaklava** [1854]; Inkerman [1854]; **Sevastopol** [1854-55]; **Central India** [1857-58]; Afghanistan, 1879-1880; **South Africa, 1900-02.**

First World War:

Givenchy 1914; Somme 1916, 18; Bazentin; Flers-Courcelette; **Cambrai 1917, 18;** St. Quentin; **Bapaume 1918; Rosières; Amiens; Albert 1918;** Hindenburg Line; St. Quentin Canal; **Beaurevoir; Pursuit to Mons; France and Flanders 1914-18.**

Second World War:

Villers Bocage; Mont Pincon; Dives Crossing; Nederrijn; Best; **Lower Maas; Roer; Rhine;** **North-West Europe 1944-45;** Egyptian Frontier 1940; Sidi Barrani; **Buq Buq; Sidi Rezegh 1941;** Relief of Tobruk; **Gazala;** Bir el Igela; Mersa Matruh; Alam el Halfa; **El Alamein; North Africa 1940-42.**

Post-1945:

Seoul; Hill 327; **Imjin;** Kowang-San; **Korea 1950-51.**

THE QUEEN'S ROYAL IRISH HUSSARS

Wadi al Batin; **Gulf 1991.**

PRESENT ROLE & DEPLOYMENT OF REGIMENTS

THE HOUSEHOLD CAVALRY REGIMENT

Windsor

FORMATION RECONNAISSANCE REGIMENT

SCIMITAR

1st THE QUEEN'S DRAGOON GUARDS

Osnabrück, Germany

FORMATION RECONNAISSANCE REGIMENT

SCIMITAR

THE ROYAL SCOTS DRAGOON GUARDS

Fallingbostel, Germany

ARMOURED REGIMENT

CHALLENGER 2

THE ROYAL DRAGOON GUARDS

Catterick

ARMOURED REGIMENT

CHALLENGER 2

THE QUEEN'S ROYAL HUSSARS

Sennelager, Germany

ARMOURED REGIMENT

CHALLENGER 2

9th/12th ROYAL LANCERS

Hohne, Germany

FORMATION RECONNAISSANCE REGIMENT

SCIMITAR

THE KING'S ROYAL HUSSARS

Tidworth

ARMOURED REGIMENT

CHALLENGER 2

THE LIGHT DRAGOONS

Swanton Morley, Norfolk

FORMATION RECONNAISSANCE REGIMENT

SCIMITAR

THE QUEEN'S ROYAL LANCERS

Catterick

FORMATION RECONNAISSANCE REGIMENT

SCIMITAR

1st ROYAL TANK REGIMENT

One squadron based at Warminster as part of the Combined Arms Training Centre and equipped with CHALLENGER 2.

Two squadrons based at RAF Honington as the Army element of the Joint NBC Regiment equipped with the FUCHS CBRN RECONNAISSANCE VEHICLE.

2nd ROYAL TANK REGIMENT

Based at Tidworth as an element of the Allied Joint Rapid deployment Force (JRDF)

Three squadrons equipped with CHALLENGER 2

One squadron equipped with SCIMITAR

THE ARMOURED REGIMENT
(Type 58)

The Armoured Regiment would typically be equipped with 58 CHALLENGER 2 Main Battle Tanks divided equally between each of its 4 Armoured Squadrons. Each Armoured Squadron would comprise 4 Troops of 3 or 4 tanks. There would also be a Headquarters Squadron containing a Reconnaissance Troop equipped with 8 SCIMITARS, the Quartermaster's and Motor Transport Sections and all the supporting services such as: Light Aid Detachment (REME); Administration Office (AGC[SPS]); Medical Centre (RAMC); Catering Troop (RLC); Gymnasium (APTC);

THE FORMATION RECONNAISSANCE REGIMENT

The Formation Reconnaissance Regiment (formerly Armoured Reconnaissance Regiment) would typically have 3 SABRE Squadrons each comprising 2/3 SCIMITAR Troops and 2/3 Fire Support Troops equipped with JAVELIN ATGW which are carried in CVR but fired dismounted. As with the Armoured Regiment, a Headquarters Squadron would contain the Quartermaster's and Motor Transport Sections as well as the supporting services provided by elements from the other Corps.

In addition to the vehicles which constitute their main armament, both types of regiment are also equipped with a variety of specialist vehicles such as SPARTAN (Armoured Personnel Carrier), SULTAN (Command Vehicle) and the SAMARITAN (Ambulance).

9th DRAGOONS lineage

1715
Wynne's Regiment of Dragoons (1)

9th DRAGOONS

1751
9th Dragoons

1783
9th Light Dragoons

1816
9th Light Dragoons (Lancers)

1830
9th (Queen's Royal) (2) Lancers

1921
9th QUEEN'S ROYAL LANCERS

NOTES

(1) Raised in the southern counties of England by Major General Owen Wynne.

(2) Queen Adelaide of Saxe-Meiningen, wife of King William IV.

During the Indian Mutiny, in which the 9th Lancers were awarded 13 Victoria Crosses, the Regiment was referred to by the mutineers as "The Delhi Spearman" — a nickname which has endured to this day.

12th DRAGOONS lineage

1715
Bowles's Regiment of Dragoons (3)

12th DRAGOONS

1751
12th Dragoons

1768
The 12th (or The Prince of Wales's) (4) Regiment of (Light) Dragoons

1816
The 12th (or The Prince of Wales's) Regiment of Light Dragoons (Lancers)

1817
The 12th (or The Prince of Wales's) Royal Regiment of Lancers

The 12th Prince of Wales's Royal Lancers

1921
12th ROYAL LANCERS
(Prince of Wales's)

(3) Raised in Hampshire and Berkshire by Colonel Phineas Bowles.

(4) The future King George IV.

1960
9th / 12th ROYAL LANCERS
(Prince of Wales's)

BATTLE HONOURS

9th QUEEN'S ROYAL LANCERS

Pre-1914:

Peninsula [1808-14]; **Punniar** [1843]; **Sobraon** [1846]; **Chillianwallah** [1849]; **Goojerat** [1849]; **Punjaub** [1848-49]; **Delhi, 1857; Lucknow** [1857-58]; **Afghanistan, 1878-1880; Charasiah** [1879]; **Kabul, 1879; Kandahar, 1880; Modder River** [1899]; **South Africa, 1899-1902; Relief of Kimberley** [1900]; **Paardeberg** [1900].

First World War:

Mons; Le Cateau; **Retreat from Mons; Marne 1914; Aisne 1914;** La Basée 1914; **Messines 1914;** Armentières 1914; **Ypres 1914, 15;** Gravenstafel; St. Julien; Frezenburg; Bellewaarde; **Somme 1916, 18;** Pozières; Flers-Courcelette; **Arras 1917;** Scarpe 1917; **Cambrai 1917,18;** St. Quentin; **Rosières;** Avre; Amiens; Albert 1918; Hindenburg Line; **Pursuit to Mons;** France and Flanders 1914-18.

Second World War:

Somme 1940; Withdrawal to Seine; **North-West Europe 1940;** Saunnu; **Gazala;** Bir el Aslagh; Sidi Rezegh 1942; Defence of Alamein Line; **Ruweisat;** Ruweisat Ridge; **El Alamein;** Tebaga Gap; **El Hamma;** El Kourzia; Tunis; Creteville Pass; **North Africa 1942-43;** Coriano; Capture of Forli; Lamone Crossing; Pideura; **Lamone Bridgehead; Argenta Gap; Italy 1944-45.**

12th ROYAL LANCERS (Prince of Wales's)

Pre-1914:

Egypt (with the Sphinx) [1801]; **Peninsula** [1808-14]; **Salamanca** [1812]; **Waterloo** [1815]; **South Africa, 1851-53; Central India** [1857-58]; **South Africa, 1899-1902; Relief of Kimberley** [1900]; **Paardeberg** [1900].

First World War:

Mons; Retreat from Mons; Marne 1914; Aisne 1914; Messines 1914; Ypres 1914, 15; Neuve Chapelle; St. Julien; Bellewaarde; **Arras 1917;** Scarpe 1917; **Cambrai 1917, 18; Somme 1918;** St. Quentin; Lys; Hazebrouck; Amiens; Albert 1918; Hindenburg Line; St. Quentin Canal; Beaurevoir; **Sambre;** France and Flanders 1914-18.

Second World War:

Dyle; Defence of Arras; Arras Counter Attack; **Dunkirk 1940; North-West Europe 1940; Chor es Sufan; Gazala;** Alam el Halfa; **El Alamein;** Advance on Tripoli; Tebaga Gap; El Hamma; Akarit; El Kourzia; Djebel Kournine; **Tunis;** Creteville Pass; **North Africa 1941-43;** Citerna; Gothic Line; Capture of Forli; Conventello-Comacchio; **Bologna;** Sillaro Crossing; Idice Bridgehead; **Italy 1944-45.**

HOME HEADQUARTERS

TA Centre, Saffron Rd., Wigston, Leicester LE18 4UX
Tel: 0116 2759572/9573/9577 Fax: 0116 2759571
Website: www.delhispearman.org.uk

REGIMENTAL MARCHES

Quick March: God Bless the Prince of Wales
Slow Marches: Men of Harlech (9th Lancers)
Coburg (12th Lancers)

ALLIANCES

Canadian Armed Forces:
The Prince Edward Island Regiment

Pakistan Army:
12th Cavalry

COLONEL-IN-CHIEF

HRH The Duke of York KCVO ADC

REGIMENTAL MUSEUM

9th / 12th ROYAL LANCERS MUSEUM
Derby Museum and Art Gallery.
The Strand, Derby DE1 1BS
Tel: 01332 716659 Fax: 01332 716670
email: Mike.Galer@ derby.gov.uk
Website: www.derby.gov.uk

1715
Gore's Regiment of Dragoons (1)

10th DRAGOONS

1751
10th Dragoons

1783
10th (The Prince of Wales's Own) Light Dragoons

1806
10th (The Prince of Wales's Own) Hussars (3)

1811
10th (The Prince of Wales's Own Royal) Hussars

NOTES

(1) Raised in Hertfordshire by Brigadier General Humphrey Gore.

(2) The future King George IV.

(3) The first regiment to be designated "Hussars".

The 10th Royal Hussars, renowned for their magnificent uniforms, were originally known as "The Chainy Tenth" because of their elaborate cross belts. This gradually changed to "The Shiny Tenth"

1715
Honeywood's Regiment of Dragoons (4)

11th DRAGOONS

1751
11th Dragoons

1783
11th Light Dragoons

1840
11th (Prince Albert's Own) (5) Hussars

(4) Raised in Essex by Brigadier General Philip Honeywood.

(5) In 1840 the Regiment escorted Prince Albert of Saxe-Coburg-Gotha from Dover to Canterbury before his marriage to Queen Victoria. He requested that they should henceforth bear his name.

Known as "The Cherrypickers" from an action in the Peninsula fought in a cherry orchard, the regiment was also known as "Lord Cardigan's Cherrybums" from their crimson overalls.

1715
Dormer's Regiment of Dragoons (6)

14th DRAGOONS

1751
14th Dragoons

1776
14th Light Dragoons

1798
14th (Duchess of York's Own) (7) Light Dragoons

1830
14th (The King's) (8) Light Dragoons

1861
14th (King's) Hussars

(6) Raised in the south of England by Brigadier General James Dormer.

(7) Wife of Frederick, Duke of York, second son of King George III.

(8) King William IV.

Known as "The Chambermaids" from their capture at Vittoria of a silver chamber pot belonging to Joseph Bonaparte, created King of Spain by his brother Napoleon.

20th LIGHT DRAGOONS

1792
20th (Jamaica) Light Dragoons (9)

1805
20th Light Dragoons

1818
DISBANDED

1861
20th Light Dragoons (10)

(9) Raised from existing regiments in England and Ireland by Colonel Henry Gardner for service in the Maroon War in Jamaica.

(10) Regiment reformed including 250 volunteers from the 2nd Bengal European Light Cavalry. The new Regiment inherited the honours of the previous 20th Light Dragoons in spite of the period of disbandment.

The Regiment was know, waggishly, during the 19th century as "Nobody's Own".

1921
10th ROYAL HUSSARS
(Prince of Wales's Own)

1921
11th HUSSARS
(Prince Albert's Own)

1921
14th KING'S HUSSARS

1862
20th HUSSARS

1969
THE ROYAL HUSSARS
(Prince of Wales's Own)

1922
14th / 20th HUSSARS

1936
14th / 20th KING'S HUSSARS

1992
THE KING'S ROYAL HUSSARS

HOME HEADQUARTERS

North: Fulwood Barracks, Preston, Lancs. PR2 8AA
Tel: 01772 260310 / 260480

South: Peninsula Barracks, Winchester, Hants
SO23 8TS Tel: 01962 828539

email: regimental-secretary@krh.army.mod.uk

REGIMENTAL MARCHES

Quick March: The King's Royal Hussars
Slow March: Coburg

AFFILIATED REGIMENT
The Royal Gurkha Rifles

ALLIANCES

Canadian Armed Forces:
1st Hussars

Australian Military Forces:
10th Light Horse
2nd/14th Light Horse
(Queensland Mounted Infantry)

New Zealand Army:
Queen Alexandra's Mounted Rifles

Pakistan Army:
The Guides Cavalry (Frontier Regiment)

Zambia Army:
Zambia Armoured Car Regiment

COLONEL-IN-CHIEF

HRH The Princess Royal KG KT GCVO QSO

BATTLE HONOURS

10th ROYAL HUSSARS (Prince of Wales's Own)

Pre-1914:

arburg [1760]; Peninsula [1808-14]; **Vittoria** [1813]; aterloo [1815]; **Sevastapol** [1854-55]; ghanistan, 1878-1879; **Ali Masjid** [1878]; ypt, **1884**; South Africa, 1899-1902; lief of Kimberley [1900]; **Paardeberg** [1900].

First World War:

res 1914, 15; Langemarck 1914; Gheluvelt; nne Bosschen; **Rezenberg; Loos; Arras 1917-18;** arpe 1917; **Somme 1918;** St. Quentin; **Avre; Amiens;** ocourt-Quéant; Hindenburg Line; Beaurevoir; mbrai 1918; **Pursuit to Mons;** ance and Flanders 1914-18.

Second World War:

mme 1940; North-West Europe 1940; **Saunnu;** zala; Bir el Aslagh; Alam el Halfa; **El Alamein;** Hamma; El Kourzia; Djebel Kournine; **Tunis;** rth Africa 1942-43; **Coriano; Santarcangelo;** sina Canal Crossing; Senio Pocket; Cesena; lli di Comacchio; **Argenta Gap;** Italy 1944-45.

REGIMENTAL MUSEUMS

"HORSEPOWER" — THE MUSEUM OF THE KING'S ROYAL HUSSARS
Peninsula Barracks, Romsey Road, Winchester, Hants. SO23 8TS
Tel: 01962 828541 Fax; 01862 828538
email: curator@horsepowermuseum.co.uk
Website: www.horsepowermuseum.co.uk

14th / 20th KING'S HUSSARS COLLECTION
Museum of Lancashire, Stanley street, Preston, Lancs. PR1 4YP
Tel: 01772 264075 Fax: 01772 264079
Website: www.lancashire.gov.uk

11th HUSSARS (Prince Albert's Own)

Pre-1914:

Warburg [1760]; **Beaumont** [1794]; **Willems** [1794]; Peninsula [1808-14]; **Salamanca** [1812]; **Waterloo [1815]; Bhurtpore** [1826]; **Alma** [1854]; **Balaklava** [1854]; **Inkerman** [1854]; **Sevastapol** [1854-55].

First World War:

Mons; **Le Cateau; Retreat from Mons; Marne 1914; Aisne 1914; Messines 1914;** Armentières 1914; **Ypres 1914-15;** Frezenberg; Bellewaarde; **Somme 1916-18;** Flers-Courcelette; Arras 1917; Scarpe 1917; **Cambrai 1917-18;** St. Quentin; Rosières; **Amiens;** Albert 1918; Hindenburg Line; St. Quentin Canal; Beaurevoir; Selle; **France and Flanders 1914-18.**

Second World War:

Villers Bocage; Bourguebus Ridge; Mont Pincon; Jurques; Dives Crossing; La Vie Crossing; Lisieux; Le Touques Crossing; Risle Crossing; **Roer; Rhine;** Ibbenburen; Aller; North-West Europe 1944-45; **Egyptian Frontier 1940;** Withdrawal to Matruh; Bir Enba; **Sidi Barrani;** Buq Buq; Bardia 1941; Capture of Tobruk; **Beda Fomm;** Halfaya 1941; Sidi Suleiman; Tobruk 1941; Gubi I, II; Gabr Saleh; **Sidi Rezegh 1941;** Taieb el Essom; Relief of Tobruk; Saunnu; Msus; Defence of Alamein Line; Alam el Halfa; **El Alamein;** Advance on Tripoli; Enfidaville; **Tunis;** North Africa 1940-43; Capture of Naples; Volturno Crossing; **Italy 1943.**

14th KING'S HUSSARS

Pre-1914:

Peninsula [1808-14]; **Douro** [1809]; **Talavera** [1809]; **Fuentes d'Onor** [1811]; **Salamanca** [1812]; **Pyrenees** [1813]; **Vittoria** [1813]; **Orthes** [1814]; Punjaub [1848-49]; **Chillianwallah** [1849]; **Goojerat** [1849]; **Persia** [1856-57]; **Central India** [1857-58]; **Relief of Ladysmith** [1900]; South Africa, 1900-02.

First World War:

Tigris 1916; Kut al Amara 1917; Baghdad; Mesopotamia 1915-18; Persia 1918.

20th HUSSARS

Pre-1914:

Peninsula [1808-14]; **Vimiera** [1808]; **Suakin** [1885]; South Africa, 1900-02.

First World War:

Mons; Retreat from Mons; Marne 1914; Aisne 1914; Messines 1914; Ypres 1914-15; Neuve Chapelle; St. Julien; Bellewaarde; Arras 1917; Scarpe 1917; **Cambrai 1917, 18; Somme 1918;** St. Quentin; Lys; Hazebrouck; **Amiens;** Albert 1918; Bapaume 1918; Hindenburg Line; St. Quentin Canal; Beaurevoir; **Sambre;** France and Flanders 1914-18.

14th / 20th KING'S HUSSARS

Second World War:

Bologna; Medicina; Italy 1945.

Post-1945:

Gulf 1991; Wadi al Batin.

1715
Munden's Regiment of Dragoons (1)

13th
DRAGOONS

1751
13th Dragoons

1782
13th Light Dragoons

NOTES

(1) Raised in the Midlands by Brigadier Richard Munden.

1759
19th Light Dragoons (2)

18th
LIGHT DRAGOONS

1763
18th Light Dragoons

1807
18th King's Irish Hussars

1821
DISBANDED

1858
18th Hussars (3)

1903
18th (Princess of Wales's) (4) Hussars

1910
18th (Queen Mary's Own) (4) Hussars

(2) Raised in Ireland by Charles Moor, Earl (later Marquis) of Drogheda and known popularly as Drogheda's Light Horse.

(3) Raised in Leeds and granted the right to succeed to certain of the honours of the previous regiment.

(4) Princess, and subsequently Queen, Victoria Mary of Teck, wife of King George V. Awarded in recognition of the Regiment's outstanding service in South Africa 1901-03.

15th
LIGHT DRAGOONS

1759
15th Light Dragoons (5)

1765
1st (The King's Royal) Light Dragoons

1769
15th (The King's) Light Dragoons

1807
15th (The King's) Light Dragoons (Hussars)

1861
15th (King's) Hussars

1901
15th (The King's) Hussars

(5) Raised by Major General George Eliott (later Lord Heathfield) and known as Eliott's Light Horse. This was the first regiment to be raised as Light Dragoons.

1781
23rd Light Dragoons (6)

19th
LIGHT DRAGOONS

1783
19th Light Dragoons (7)

1821
DISBANDED

1858
1st Bengal European Light Cavalry (HEIC)

1860
19th Hussars (8)

1886
19th (Princess of Wales's Own) (9) Hussars

1908
19th (Queen Alexandra's Own Royal) Hussars

(6) Raised by General Burgoyne for service in India.

(7) In 1817 the regiment was dressed and equipped in the style of Polish Lancers.

(8) Taken on to the British Establishment and granted the right to inherit the honours of the previous regiment.

(9) Princess Alexandra of Denmark, wife of the future King Edward VII.

1861
13th HUSSARS

1919
18th ROYAL HUSSARS
(Queen Mary's Own)

1921
15th THE KING'S HUSSARS

1921
19th ROYAL HUSSARS
(Queen Alexandra's Own)

1922
13th / 18th ROYAL HUSSARS

1935
13th / 18th ROYAL HUSSARS
(Queen Mary's Own)

1922
15th / 19th HUSSARS

1933
15th / 19th THE KING'S ROYAL HUSSARS

1992
THE LIGHT DRAGOONS

HOME HEADQUARTERS
Fenham Barracks, Newcastle-upon-Tyne NE2 4NP
Tel: 0191 239 3138 / 3140 / 3141 Fax: 0191 2393139
Website: www.lightdragoons.org.uk/

REGIMENTAL MARCHES
Quick March: Balaklava
Slow March: Denmark — 19th Hussars Slow March

ALLIANCES
Canadian Armed Forces:
The Royal Canadian Hussars (Montreal)
The South Alberta Light Horse
Australian Military Forces:
1st/15th Royal New South Wales Lancers
Indian Army:
Skinner's Horse
(1st Duke of York's Own Cavalry)

Pakistan Army:
6th Lancers
19th Lancers
Malaysian Armed Forces:
2nd Royal Armoured Regiment

COLONEL-IN-CHIEF
HM King Abdullah II
of the Hashemite Kingdom of Jordan

BATTLE HONOURS

13th HUSSARS

Pre-1914:

Peninsula [1808-14]; Albuhera [1811]; Vittoria [1813]; Orthes [1814]; Toulouse [1814]; Waterloo [1815]; Alma [1854]; Balaklava [1854]; Inkerman [1854]; Sevastapol [1854-55]; South Africa, 1899-1902; Relief of Ladysmith [1900].

First World War:

France and Flanders 1914-16; Kut al Amara 1917; Baghdad; Sharqat; Mesopotamia 1916-18.

18th ROYAL HUSSARS (Queen Mary's Own)

Pre-1914:

Peninsula [1808-14]; Waterloo [1815]; Defence of Ladysmith [1899-1900]; South Africa, 1899-1902.

First World War:

Mons; Le Cateau; Retreat from Mons; Marne 1914; Aisne 1914; La Bassée 1914; Messines 1914; Armentières 1914; Ypres 1914,15; Gravenstafel; St. Julien; Frezenberg; Bellewaarde; Somme 1916-18; Flers-Courcelette; Arras 1917; Scarpe 1917; Cambrai 1917-18; St. Quentin; Rosières; Amiens; Albert 1918; Hindenburg Line; Pursuit to Mons; France and Flanders 1914-18.

15th THE KING'S HUSSARS

Pre-1914:

Emsdorff [1760]; Villers-en-Cauchies [1794]; Willems [1794]; Egmont-op-Zee [1799]; Peninsula [1808-14]; Sahagun [1808]; Vittoria [1813]; Waterloo [1815]; Afghanistan, 1878-1880;

First World War:

Mons; Retreat from Mons; Marne 1914; Aisne 1914; Ypres 1914, 15; Langemarck1914; Gheluvelt; Nonne Bosschen; Frezenberg; Bellewaarde; Somme 1916, 18; Flers-Courcelette; Cambrai 1917, 18; St. Quentin; Rosières; Amiens; Albert 1918; Bapaume 1918; Hindenburg Line; St. Quentin Canal; Beaurevoir; Pursuit to Mons; France and Flanders 1914-18.

19th ROYAL HUSSARS (Queen Alexandra's Own)

Pre-1914:

Mysore [1789-91]; Seringapatam [1799]; Assaye [1803]; Niagara [1813]; Egypt, 1882-84; Tel-el-Kebir [1882]; Nile, 1884-85; Abu Klea [1885]; Defence of Ladysmith [1899-1900]; South Africa, 1899-1902.

First World War:

Le Cateau; Retreat from Mons; Marne 1914; Aisne 1914; Armentières 1914; Ypres 1915; Frezenberg; Bellewaarde; Somme 1916, 18; Flers-Courcelette; Cambrai 1917, 18; St. Quentin; Rosières; Amiens; Albert 1918; Bapaume 1918; Hindenburg Line; St. Quentin Canal; Beaurevoir; Pursuit to Mons; France and Flanders 1914-18.

REGIMENTAL MUSEUMS

THE LIGHT DRAGOONS MUSEUM
13th / 18th Royal Hussars (Queen Mary's Own)
Cannon Hall, Cawthorne, Barnsley,
South Yorkshire S75 4AT
Tel: 01226 790270 Fax: 01226 792117
email: lightdragoons.org.uk
Website: www.lightdragoons.org.uk

THE LIGHT DRAGOONS MUSEUM
15th / 19th King's Royal Hussars
"A SOLDIER'S LIFE"
Discovery Museum, Blandford Square,
Newcastle-upon-Tyne NE1 4JA
Tel: 0191 2326789 Fax: 0191 230264
email: roberta.twinn@twmuseums.org.uk
Website: twmuseums.org.uk

13th / 18th ROYAL HUSSARS (Queen Mary's Own)

Second World War:

Dyle; Withdrawal to Escaut; Ypres-Comines Canal; Normandy Landing; Bretteville; Caen; Bourguebus Ridge; Mont Pincon; St. Pierre la Vielle; Geilenkirchen; Roer; Rhineland; Waal Flats; Goch; Rhine; Bremen; North-West Europe 1940, 44-45.

15th / 19th THE KING'S ROYAL HUSSARS

Second World War:

Withdrawal to Escaut; Seine 1944; Hechtel; Nederrijn; Venraij; Rhineland; Hochwald; Rhine; Ibbenburen; Aller; North-West Europe 1940, 44-45.

1759
Burgoyne's Light Horse (1)

1766
2nd (Queen's) (2) Light Dragoons

16th
LIGHT DRAGOONS

1769
16th (Queen's Own) Light Dragoons

1815
16th (Queen's Own) Light Dragoons (Lancers)

1861
16th (The Queen's) Lancers

NOTES

(1) An unofficial regiment raised in the London area and Northampton by Colonel John Burgoyne.

(2) Taken on to the regular establishment and granted the right to bear the cypher of Queen Charlotte of Mecklenberg-Strelitz, wife of King George III.

Known as "The Scarlet Lancers", the 16th were the first British regiment to use the lance in action at Bhurtpore in 1825.

1689
The Royal Irish Dragoons (3)

1704
The Royal Dragoons of Ireland

5th
DRAGOONS

1751
5th (Royal Irish) Dragoons

1799
DISBANDED (4)

1858
5th (Royal Irish) Lancers (5)

---

(3) Raised in Ireland by Colonel Owen Wynne from independent troops of protestant horse.

(4) Disbanded in disgrace due to infiltration of Irish rebels.

(5) Reinstated but with loss of its original seniority

1759
18th Light Dragoons (6)

17th
LIGHT DRAGOONS

1763
17th Light Dragoons

1822
17th Light Dragoons (Lancers)

1861
17th Lancers

---

(6) Raised by Colonel John Hale in the London and Hertford areas and known as Hale's Light Horse.

(7) George, Duke of Cambridge, cousin of Queen Victoria and Commander-in-Chief of the Army 1856-95.

21st
LIGHT DRAGOONS

1760
21st Light Dragoons (8)

1763
DISBANDED (9)

1861 (May)
21st Light Dragoons (10)

1861 (July)
21st Hussars

1897
21st Lancers (11)

1899
21st (Empress of India's) (12) Lancers

---

(8) Raised by the Marquis of Granby for the Seven Years War.

(9) The Regiment was twice more raised and disbanded before reconstitution in its final form in 1861.

(10) Formed from the 3rd Bengal European Light Cavalry HEIC.

(11) The last regiment to be converted to lancers.

(12) Queen Victoria.

1921
16th THE QUEEN'S LANCERS

1921
5th ROYAL IRISH LANCERS

1876
17th LANCERS
(Duke of Cambridge's Own) (7)

1921
21st LANCERS
(Empress of India's)

1922
16th / 5th LANCERS

1954
16th / 5th THE QUEEN'S ROYAL LANCERS

1922
17th / 21st LANCERS

1993
THE QUEEN'S ROYAL LANCERS

HOME HEADQUARTERS
Lancer House, Prince William of Gloucester Barracks, Grantham, Lincs. NG31 7TJ
Tel: 0115 9573195 Fax: 0115 9573195
Website: www.qrl.uk.com

REGIMENTAL MARCHES
Quick March: Stable Jacket
Slow March: Omdurman

ALLIANCES
Canadian Armed Forces:
Lord Strathcona's Horse (Royal Canadians)

Australian Military Forces:
12th / 16th Hunter River Lancers

COLONEL-IN-CHIEF
HM The Queen

BATTLE HONOURS

16th THE QUEEN'S LANCERS

Pre-1914:

Beaumont [1794]; Willems [1794]; Peninsula [1808-14]; Talavera [1809]; Fuentes d'Onor [1811]; Salamanca [1812]; Nive [1813]; Vittoria [1813]; Waterloo [1815]; Bhurtpore [1826]; Afghanistan, 1839; Ghuznee, 1839; Maharajpore [1843]; Aliwal [1846]; Sobraon [1846]; Relief of Kimberley [1900]; Paardeberg [1900]; South Africa, 1900-02.

First World War:

Mons; Le Cateau; Retreat from Mons; Marne 1914; Aisne 1914; Messines 1914; Armentières 1914; Ypres 1914, 15; Gheluvelt; St. Julien; Bellewaarde; Arras 1817; Scarpe 1917; Cambrai 1917; Somme 1918; Amiens; Hindenburg Line; Canal du Nord; Pursuit to Mons; France and Flanders 1914-18.

5th ROYAL IRISH LANCERS

Pre-1914:

Blenheim [1704]; Ramillies [1706]; Oudenarde [1708]; Malplaquet [1709]; Suakin [1885]; South Africa, 1899-1902; Defence of Ladysmith [1899-1900].

First World War:

Mons; Le Cateau; Retreat from Mons; Marne 1914; Aisne 1914; Messines 1914; Ypres 1914, 15; Gheluvelt; St. Julien; Bellewaarde; Arras 1917; Scarpe 1917; Cambrai 1917; Somme 1918; St. Quentin; Amiens; Hindenburg Line; Canal du Nord; Pursuit to Mons; France and Flanders 1914-18.

17th LANCERS (Duke of Cambridge's Own)

Pre-1914:

Alma [1854]; Balaklava [1854]; Inkerman [1854]; Sevastapol [1854-55]; Central India [1857-58]; South Africa, 1879; South Africa, 1900-02.

First World War:

Festubert 1914; Somme 1916, 18; Morval; Cambrai 1917, 18; St. Quentin; Avre; Lys; Hazebrouck; Amiens; Hindenburg Line; St. Quentin Canal; Beaurevoir; Pursuit to Mons; France and Flanders 1914-18.

21st LANCERS (Empress of India's)

Pre-1914:

Khartoum, 1898.

First World War:

N. W. Frontier India 1915, 16.

16th / 5th THE QUEEN'S ROYAL LANCERS

Second World War:

Kasserine; Fondouk; Kairouan; Bordj; Djebel Kournine; Tunis; Gromballa; Bou Ficha; North Africa 1942-43; Cassino II; Liri Valley; Monte Piccolo; Capture of Perugia; Arezzo; Advance to Florence; Argenta Gap; Traghetto; Italy 1944-45.

Post-1945:

Wadi al Batin; Gulf 1991.

17th / 21st LANCERS

Second World War:

Tebourba Gap; Bou Arada; Kasserine; Thala; Fondouk; El Kourzia; Tunis; Hammam Lif; North Africa 1942-43; Cassino II; Monte Piccolo; Capture of Perugia; Advance to Florence; Argenta Gap; Fossa Cembalina; Italy 1944-45.

THE QUEEN'S ROYAL LANCERS

Post-1945:

Iraq 2003; Al Basrah.

REGIMENTAL MUSEUM

THE QUEEN'S ROYAL LANCERS MUSEUM
Lancer House,
Prince William of Gloucester Barracks,
Grantham, Lincs. NG31 7TJ
Tel: 0115 9573 295 Fax: 0115 9573 195
email: qrlmuseum@btinternet.com
Website: www.qrl.uk.com

1916 (February)
Six companies of tanks formed as
The Armoured Car Section
of the Motor Machine Gun Service

1916 (May)
Heavy Section Machine Gun Corps

1916 (November)
Heavy Branch Machine Gun Corps

1917
Tank Corps (1)

1923
Royal Tank Corps

1939
ROYAL TANK REGIMENT (2)

NOTES

(1) By the Armistice in 1918, 25 battalions of the Tank Corps had been formed.

(2) In 1939 there were 8 regular battalions of the Royal Tank Regiment with 4 more added in 1940. By 1945 there were 24 RTR regiments which were reduced to 8 at the end of the war.

Today there are two regiments — the 1st and 2nd Royal Tank Regiments, the 1st recruiting in Scotland and the north of England and the 2nd in the south.

REGIMENTAL HEADQUARTERS

Stanley Barracks, Bovington Camp, Dorset BH20 5JA

Tel: 01929 403331 Fax: 01929 403488

email: regsec@rtr.org.uk
Website: www.royaltankregiment.com

REGIMENTAL MARCHES

Quick March: Regimental March of the Royal Tank Regiment "My Boy Willie".

Slow March: Royal Tank Regiment Slow March

ALLIANCES

Canadian Armed Forces:
12e Régiment Blindé du Canada RCAC

Australian Military Forces:
1st Armoured Regiment RAAC

New Zealand Army:
Royal New Zealand Armoured Corps

Indian Army:
2nd Lancers (Gardner's Horse)
Indian Armoured Corps

Pakistan Army:
13th Lancers Pakistan Armoured Corps

COLONEL-IN-CHIEF

HM The Queen

BATTLE HONOURS

TANK
CORPS

First World War:

Somme 1916, 18; Arras 1917, 18; Messines 1917; Ypres 1917; Cambrai 1917; St. Quentin 1918; **Villers Bretonneux; Amiens; Bapaume 1918; Hindenburg Line;** Epéhy; Selle; **France and Flanders 1916-18;** Gaza.

ROYAL
TANK
REGIMENT

Second World War:

Arras Counter Attack; Calais 1940; St. Omer-La Bassée; Pincon; Falaise; Nederrijn; Scheldt; Venlo Pocket; Rhineland; **Rhine;** Bremen; **North-West Europe 1940, 44-45; Abyssinia 1940;** Sidi Barrani; **Tobruk 1941;** Sidi Rezegh 1941; Belhamed; Gazala; Cauldron; Knightsbridge; Defence of Alamein Line; Alam el Halfa; **El Alamein;** Mareth; Akarit; Fondouk; El Kourzia; Medjez Plain; Tunis; **North Africa 1940-43;** Primosole Bridge; Gerbini; Adrano; **Sicily 1943;** Sangro; Salerno; Volturno Crossing; Garigliano Crossing; Anzio; Advance to Florence; Gothic Line; Coriano; Lamone Crossing; Rimini Line; Argenta Gap; **Italy 1943-45; Greece 1941; Burma 1942.**

Post-1945:

Korea 1951-53; Iraq 2003; Al Basrah.

REGIMENTAL MUSEUM

THE TANK MUSEUM
Bovington Camp, Dorset BH20 6JG

Tel: 01929 405096 Fax: 01929 405360

Website: www.tankmuseum.org

FIRST WORLD WAR

In November 1916 the six original companies of tanks were expanded to battalion size. By the end of the War The Tank Corps comprised 25 tank battalions 18 of which were in action in France.

BETWEEN THE WARS

In 1919 all the tank battalions were disbanded except the 1st to the 5th plus 12 armoured car companies. In 1933 the 6th Battalion was reformed and the following year an experimental Light Battalion was formed but the concept was dropped in 1938. In the inter-war years the extended family of The Royal Tank Corps, and latterly The Royal Tank Regiment, was augmented firstly by mechanising yeomanry units and secondly by TA infantry battalions converting to tank units. In 1939 The Royal Tank Regiment became part of the newly-formed Royal Armoured Corps at which time there were 8 regular RTR battalions.

SECOND WORLD WAR

In 1941 an additional 4 regular RTR battalions were formed giving the regiment a strength of 12 regular and 12 TA battalions. During the course of the War, many infantry units converted to armour becoming temporary tank or reconnaissance regiments Royal Armoured Corps. At the famous Battle of El Alamein in 1942 the 1st, 2nd, 3rd, 4th, 5th, 6th, 7th, 8th, 40th, 41st, 44th, 45th, 46th, 47th and 50th battalions Royal Tank Regiment were present.

POST-1945

At the end of the Second World War, the Royal Tank Regiment was again reduced to eight regular regiments which were further reduced to the present two as shown below:

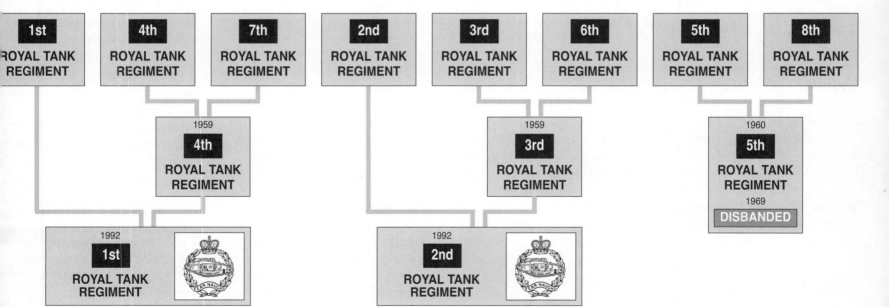

The Royal Regiment of Artillery

Since the invention of gunpowder and the subsequent development of cannons, artillery has formed a vital element in every battle force. Though used extensively in ships of war for many years previously, it was not until 1716 that a permanent artillery establishment was formed within the British Army.

Prior to this, artillery trains were raised by Royal Warrant for specific campaigns and disbanded as soon as the fighting was concluded. In 1716, after the weakness of this system had been exposed by delays in raising artillery to suppress the first Jacobite Rising, two permanent companies of 100 men each were formed at Woolwich which was to become the home of British artillery and remain so for nearly 300 years.

By the end of the century there were some 40 companies (batteries in today's terms) of artillery and a new formation "The Corps of Captains Commissaries and Drivers" had been introduced to bring the provision of horses and drivers within the service. This developed as a separate entity for nearly 30 years until its functions were absorbed by the Regiment in 1822.

For nearly three centuries the Royal Regiment of Artillery has provided battlefield fire support to the British Army in its campaigns in every corner of the world. From a corps of 200 men, employing civilian drivers and horses to pull its guns, it has developed into one of the largest and most technically-advanced formations in today's Army.

Today, with a strength of around 7,500 officers and men, the Royal Regiment of Artillery is the largest formation in the British army to be called "Regiment" though it is, itself, then subdivided into, currently, a further 15 regiments as shown on the following pages. Each of these regiments has its own role and equipments within the very wide spectrum of modern artillery — from conventional field guns to the latest guided weapons systems and including regiments of commando and parachute gunners.

The Royal Artillery bear no Colours as they are present at almost every engagement; nor do they receive individual Battle Honours. Instead, by order of King William IV in 1833, they bear the overall Honour of the motto "UBIQUE" (Everywhere) reflecting their omnipresent role. At the same time the King decreed that the Guns of the Royal Artillery should serve as their Colours and be accorded the same degree of protection and respect. Most batteries within the individual Gunner regiments also bear an Honour sub-title which commemorates a notable action or individual in the battery's history.

The Royal Horse Artillery is an integral part of the Royal Regiment yet retains its separate identity and customs. Personnel are freely interchangeable between the two formations. When on parade with its guns, the RHA has overall precedence parading on the "Right of the Line" and marching ahead of the Household Cavalry. Although the last mounted battery was mechanised in 1939, King George VI expressed the wish that, after the war, a mounted troop should be reformed, dressed and equipped in traditional style, for ceremonial duties. After inspecting this "Riding Troop" in 1947 he granted it the honour of bearing his name and it has since been designated "The King's Troop". Based in London, the Troop parades on State Occasions and serves as the Queen's Life Guard at Whitehall for one month of each year.

On Saturday 26th May 2007 The Royal Regiment of Artillery held a Parade and Sunset Ceremony at the Royal Artillery Barracks, Woolwich to mark its departure from Woolwich, its regimental home for the past 291 years.

GIBRALTAR INDEPENDENT ARTILLERY COMPANY

MINORCA INDEPENDENT ARTILLERY COMPANY

1716
Two regular companies (batteries) of Field Artillery (1) raised at Woolwich by Royal Warrant of George I

1722
Independent Artillery Companies (batteries) of Gibraltar and Minorca absorbed to form
THE ROYAL REGIMENT OF ARTILLERY (2)

ROYAL HORSE ARTILLERY
four troops raised

1793
Four troops of the newly-formed Royal Horse Artillery absorbed

ROYAL IRISH ARTILLERY

1801
Royal Irish Artillery Absorbed

1794
CORPS OF CAPTAINS COMMISSARIES AND DRIVERS
formed to bring the provision of horses and drivers within the Service (3)

1801
renamed
CORPS OF GUNNER DRIVERS

1822
Absorbed functions of Royal Artillery Drivers (4)

1806
renamed
ROYAL ARTILLERY DRIVERS

1855
Board of Ordnance abolished. Regiment came under control of the War Office

1822
Disbanded as separate entity with its functions absorbed into the Regiment

HONOURABLE EAST INDIA COMPANY ARTILLERY
21 Horse Batteries
48 Field Batteries

1861
Absorbed the Artillery of the Honourable East India Company giving a total strength of:
29 Horse Batteries
73 Field Batteries
88 Heavy Batteries

1899
ROYAL HORSE ARTILLERY (5)
Horse Artillery

ROYAL FIELD ARTILLERY
Field Artillery

1899
ROYAL GARRISON ARTILLERY
Heavy Batteries, Coastal Defence, Mountain and Siege Artillery

1924
THE ROYAL REGIMENT OF ARTILLERY

ROYAL HORSE ARTILLERY

ROYAL ARTILLERY

NOTES

Prior to 1716 Artillery Trains were raised for specific campaigns at the end of which they were disbanded.

The first Commanding Officer was Colonel Albert Borgard.

Prior to this, horses and drivers to haul the guns were provided by civilian contractors.

From 1822 until 1918 private soldiers of the Royal Artillery were ranked as Gunner Drivers. Since 1918 they have simply been Gunners.

Though included in the same group as the Field Artillery, it was decided that the Royal Horse Artillery would retain its separate identity which it does to this day although personnel are freely interchangeable between the two formations.

NOMENCLATURE OF ARTILLERY FORMATIONS		
1716 -1859	BATTALIONS	COMPANIES
1859 -1938	BRIGADES	BATTERIES
1938 -PRESENT	REGIMENTS	BATTERIES

REGIMENTAL HEADQUARTERS

The Artillery Centre, Stirling Barracks, Larkhill, Salisbury SP4 8QT

Website: www.army.mod.uk/artillery

REGIMENTAL MARCHES

Quick March: The Royal Artillery Quick March

Slow March: The Royal Artillery Slow March

ALLIANCES

Canadian Armed Forces:
The Royal Regiment of Canadian Artillery

Australian Military Forces:
The Royal Regiment of Australian Artillery

New Zealand Army:
The Royal Regiment of New Zealand Artillery

Fiji:
The Fiji Artillery

Indian Army:
Regiment of Artillery

Pakistan Army:
Artillery of Pakistan

Sri Lanka Army:
The Sri Lanka Artillery

Malaysian Armed Forces:
Malaysian Artillery

Singapore Armed Forces:
The Singapore Volunteer Artillery

Malta:
Armed Forces of Malta

Colonial Forces:
The Royal Gibraltar Regiment

South African Defence Force:
South African Artillery Corps

CAPTAIN-GENERAL

HM The Queen

REGIMENTAL MUSEUM

"FIREPOWER"
THE ROYAL ARTILLERY MUSEUM
Royal Arsenal, Woolwich, London SE18 6ST
Tel: 020 8855 7755 Fax: 020 8855 7100
email: info@firepower.org.uk
Website: www.firepower.org.uk

ACTIVE REGULAR ROYAL HORSE ARTILLERY AND ROYAL ARTILLERY REGIMENTS AND BATTERIES

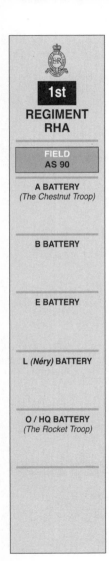

1st
REGIMENT RHA

FIELD
AS 90

A BATTERY
(The Chestnut Troop)

B BATTERY

E BATTERY

L *(Néry)* BATTERY

O / HQ BATTERY
(The Rocket Troop)

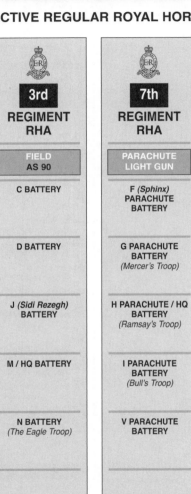

3rd
REGIMENT RHA

FIELD
AS 90

C BATTERY

D BATTERY

J *(Sidi Rezegh)* BATTERY

M / HQ BATTERY

N BATTERY
(The Eagle Troop)

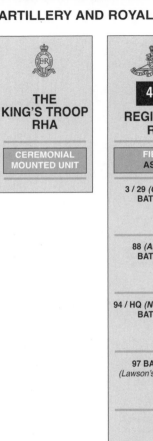

7th
REGIMENT RHA

PARACHUTE
LIGHT GUN

F *(Sphinx)*
PARACHUTE BATTERY

G PARACHUTE BATTERY
(Mercer's Troop)

H PARACHUTE / HQ BATTERY
(Ramsay's Troop)

I PARACHUTE BATTERY
(Bull's Troop)

V PARACHUTE BATTERY

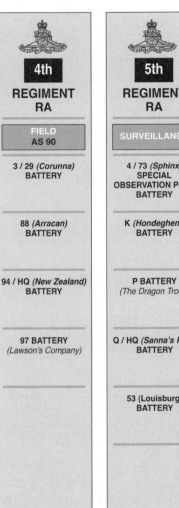

THE KING'S TROOP RHA

CEREMONIAL
MOUNTED UNIT

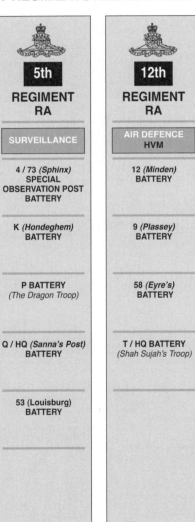

4th
REGIMENT RA

FIELD
AS 90

3 / 29 *(Corunna)*
BATTERY

88 *(Arracan)*
BATTERY

94 / HQ *(New Zealand)*
BATTERY

97 BATTERY
(Lawson's Company)

5th
REGIMENT RA

SURVEILLANCE

4 / 73 *(Sphinx)*
SPECIAL
OBSERVATION POST
BATTERY

K *(Hondeghem)*
BATTERY

P BATTERY
(The Dragon Troop)

Q / HQ *(Sanna's Post)*
BATTERY

53 *(Louisburg)*
BATTERY

12th
REGIMENT RA

AIR DEFENCE
HVM

12 *(Minden)*
BATTERY

9 *(Plassey)*
BATTERY

58 *(Eyre's)*
BATTERY

T / HQ BATTERY
(Shah Sujah's Troop)

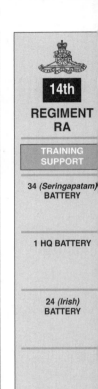

14th
REGIMENT RA

TRAINING
SUPPORT

34 *(Seringapatam)*
BATTERY

1 HQ BATTERY

24 *(Irish)*
BATTERY

ACTIVE REGULAR ROYAL HORSE ARTILLERY AND ROYAL ARTILLERY REGIMENTS AND BATTERIES

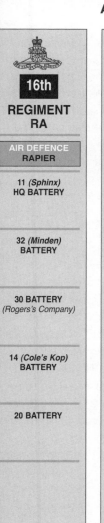

16th REGIMENT RA

AIR DEFENCE RAPIER

11 *(Sphinx)* HQ BATTERY

32 *(Minden)* BATTERY

30 BATTERY *(Rogers's Company)*

14 *(Cole's Kop)* BATTERY

20 BATTERY

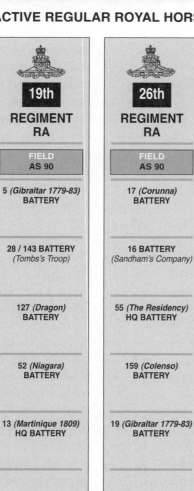

19th REGIMENT RA

FIELD AS 90

5 *(Gibraltar 1779-83)* BATTERY

28 / 143 BATTERY *(Tombs's Troop)*

127 *(Dragon)* BATTERY

52 *(Niagara)* BATTERY

13 *(Martinique 1809)* HQ BATTERY

26th REGIMENT RA

FIELD AS 90

17 *(Corunna)* BATTERY

16 BATTERY *(Sandham's Company)*

55 *(The Residency)* HQ BATTERY

159 *(Colenso)* BATTERY

19 *(Gibraltar 1779-83)* BATTERY

29th REGIMENT RA

COMMANDO LIGHT GUN

7 *(Sphinx)* COMMANDO BATTERY

8 *(Alma)* COMMANDO BATTERY

23 *(Gibraltar 1779-83)* HQ COMMANDO BATTERY

79 *(Kirkee)* COMMANDO BATTERY

148 *(Meiktila)* COMMANDO BATTERY

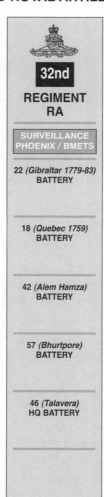

32nd REGIMENT RA

SURVEILLANCE PHOENIX / BMETS

22 *(Gibraltar 1779-83)* BATTERY

18 *(Quebec 1759)* BATTERY

42 *(Alem Hamza)* BATTERY

57 *(Bhurtpore)* BATTERY

46 *(Talavera)* HQ BATTERY

39th REGIMENT RA

MLRS / BMETS

56 *(Olphert's)* HQ BATTERY

74 BATTERY *(The Battle Axe Company)*

132 BATTERY *(The Bengal Rocket Troop)*

176 *(Abu Klea)* BATTERY

35 BATTERY

40th REGIMENT RA

FIELD LIGHT GUN

6 / 36 *(Arcot)* BATTERY

38 *(Seringapatam)* BATTERY

137 *(Java)* BATTERY

49 *(Inkerman)* HQ BATTERY

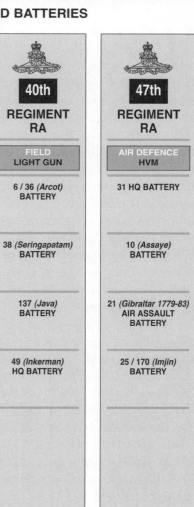

47th REGIMENT RA

AIR DEFENCE HVM

31 HQ BATTERY

10 *(Assaye)* BATTERY

21 *(Gibraltar 1779-83)* AIR ASSAULT BATTERY

25 / 170 *(Imjin)* BATTERY

---

59 *(Asten)* BATTERY and 76 **(Maude's)** BATTERY are currently attached to the Army Training Regiment.

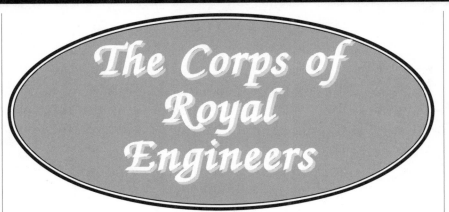

The Corps of Royal Engineers

Military engineering is as old as warfare itself though only formalised in Britain as a corps in 1716. Since this date, the Royal Engineers have performed all the traditional tasks such as fortification, demolition, bridge, road and camp construction, mine and explosive ordnance disposal, water supply and cartographic survey as well as pioneering almost every field of technical activity such as aviation, signalling and electrical and mechanical engineering.

With fortifications and earthworks a fundamental part of their remit, military engineers have played their part in warfare from earliest times. The first example of sophisticated military engineering in Britain is recorded on the Bayeux Tapestry where a prefabricated fort, transported in sections from France, is shown being erected in Britain during the Norman Conquest.

The monk Gundulph, Chief Engineer of William the Conqueror and later Bishop of Rochester, was responsible for several military structures which can be seen to this day including the White Tower, the earliest part of the Tower of London.

With the invention of gunpowder and the development of artillery, an Office of Ordnance was created in 1544 by King Henry VIII to control the issue of cannons and ammunition to the King's ships and armies in times of war. In 1597 this became the Board of Ordnance under the auspices of which gunners and military engineers were to operate for nearly three centuries until abolishment of the Board in 1855.

In 1716, by Royal Warrant of King George I, the Corps of Engineers was established and became "Royal" in 1787. Meanwhile, in Gibraltar, the wisdom of having the civilian engineering force under military rules and discipline was recognised with the formation of the first Artificer Company of soldiers, an example which was followed by the British establishment in 1787 with non-commissioned ranks formed into the Royal Military Artificers which in 1813 became the Royal Sappers and Miners.

This, in turn, was absorbed into the Corps of Royal Engineers in 1856 since which time engineer officers and soldiers have served together in the same organisation.

In 1806 the Royal Military Academy Woolwich ("The Shop") was built to provide professional education for officers of the Royal Artillery and Royal Engineers (and ultimately the Royal Corps of Signals) until its closure in 1947. Commissions in the RA and RE were always gained by competitive examination and not by purchase as was the practice in the cavalry and infantry.

Just as in mediaeval times when military engineers pioneered artillery with the development of siege engines, catapults and trebuchets so, over the ensuing years, did the Royal Engineers become involved in the experimental and development stages of almost every technical field in the Army though, as shown opposite, they have relinquished many functions to specialist units as the technologies have advanced. Though their range of skills is enormous, Royal Engineers are also trained as fully-combatant soldiers: there have been 55 awards of the Victoria Cross to Sappers and many Sapper officers have reached positions of high command — Field Marshals Burgoyne, Nicholson and Napier of Magdala, General Gordon of Khartoum, Field Marshal Lord Kitchener and General Glubb Pasha of the Arab Legion to name but a few.

As with the Gunners, they are awarded no individual Battle Honours but bear the Honour of the motto "UBIQUE" reflecting their vital role and presence in every theatre and campaign.

1716
CORPS OF ENGINEERS
(officers) (1)

1787
ROYAL MILITARY ARTIFICERS
(officers)

1856
Absorbed Royal Sappers and Miners (2)

1862
Absorbed the Sappers and Miners from
the three Presidency Armies
of the Honourable East India Company —
Bengal, Bombay and Madras

1902
Transferred Mechanical Transport Section to
Army Service Corps

1905
Transferred Submarine Mining Section to
Royal Navy

1912
Aviation activity transferred to Royal Flying Corps

1914
Absorbed responsibility for Inland Water Transport
from Army Service Corps

1920
Signal Service transferred to Royal Corps of Signals

1965
Transportation and Movement Control transferred to
Royal Corps of Transport

Absorbed responsibility for Airfield Construction
from Royal Air Force

1993
Transferred Postal and Courier Service
and responsibility for home and terrorist EOD
to Royal Logistic Corps (3)

1772
ARTIFICER COMPANY
(soldiers) formed at
Gibraltar

1787
ROYAL MILITARY ARTIFICERS
(soldiers) formed

1797
Absorbed Gibraltar
Artificer Company

1816
ROYAL SAPPERS and MINERS

HONOURABLE EAST INDIA COMPANY CORPS OF SAPPERS and MINERS

ARMY SERVICE CORPS
Inland Water Transport

ROYAL AIR FORCE
Airfield Construction
Branch

ARMY SERVICE CORPS

ROYAL NAVY

ROYAL FLYING CORPS
(formed for purpose)

ROYAL CORPS OF SIGNALS
(formed for purpose)

ROYAL CORPS OF TRANSPORT

ROYAL LOGISTIC CORPS

NOTES

(1) Although this was the first established formation of military engineers in the British Army, the Corps can claim descent from Gundulph who commanded the engineers in William the Conqueror's army and some of whose fortifications stand to this day.

(2) An important part of early military engineering was the construction of saps and mines in order to lay explosive charges beneath enemy fortifications. Hence the universal byname for the Royal Engineers — the Sappers.

(3) The responsibility for EOD (Explosive Ordnance Disposal), or Bomb Disposal as it is popularly known, is shared between the Royal Navy, the Royal Engineers, the Royal Logistic Corps and the Royal Air Force. Traditionally, the Royal Engineers were responsible for mines and enemy ordnance laid in wartime but the roles of the four agencies are today rather more involved.

CORPS HEADQUARTERS

Brompton Barracks, Chatham, Kent ME4 4UG

Tel: Civ. 01634 822121 Chatham Mil. 94661 2121

email: corps.secretary@rhqre.co.uk

Website: www.army.mod.uk/royalengineers/

REGIMENTAL MARCHES

Wings
The British Grenadiers

ALLIANCES

Canadian Armed Forces:
Military Engineering Branch

Australian Military Forces:
The Corps of Royal Australian Engineers

New Zealand Army:
The Corps of Royal New Zealand Engineers

Indian Army:
Indian Engineers

Pakistan Army:
Pakistan Engineers

Sri Lanka Army:
The Sri Lanka Engineers

Malaysian Armed Forces:
Malaysian Engineer Corps

Zambian Army:
Zambia Corps of Engineers

South African Defence Force:
South African Engineer Corps

Gibraltar:
The Royal Gibraltar Regiment

AFFILIATED REGIMENT

The Queen's Gurkha Engineers

COLONEL-IN-CHIEF

HM The Queen

REGULAR ROYAL ENGINEER REGIMENTS AND SQUADRONS

21 **ENGINEER REGIMENT RE**	**22** **ENGINEER REGIMENT RE**	**23** **ENGINEER REGIMENT RE** (AIR ASSAULT)	**24** **ENGINEER REGIMENT RE** (COMMANDO)	**25** **ENGINEER REGIMENT RE**	**26** **ENGINEER REGIMENT RE**	**28** **ENGINEER REGIMENT RE**	**32** **ENGINEER REGIMENT RE**
Ripon	Perham Down	Waterbeach	Chivenor	Waterbeach	Ludgershall	Hameln	Hohne
XX1	XX11	XX111	XX1V	XXV	XXV1	XXV111	XXX11
4 ARMOURED BRIGADE	1 MECHANISED BRIGADE	16 AIR ASSAULT BRIGADE	3 COMMANDO BRIGADE	12 (AIR SUPPORT) ENGINEER GROUP	12 MECHANISED BRIGADE	1 (UK) ARMD DIVISION	7th ARMOURED BRIGADE
7 HQ and SUPPORT SQUADRON	6 HQ SQUADRON	12 (*Nova Scotia*) HQ SQUADRON (AIR ASSAULT)	54 COMMANDO HQ and SUPPORT SQUADRON	43 HQ and SUPPORT SQUADRON (Air Support)	38 HQ and SUPPORT SQUADRON	64 HQ SQUADRON	2 HQ SQUADRON
1 ARMOURED ENGINEER SQUADRON	3 ARMOURED ENGINEER SQUADRON	9 PARACHUTE SQUADRON	59 COMMANDO SQUADRON	34 FIELD SQUADRON (Air Support)	30 FIELD SQUADRON	23 AMPHIBIOUS SQUADRON	26 ARMOURED ENGINEER SQUADRON
4 ARMOURED ENGINEER SQUADRON	5 FIELD SQUADRON	51 PARACHUTE SQUADRON (AIR ASSAULT)		53 FIELD SQUADRON (Air Support)	8 ARMOURED ENGINEER SQUADRON	42 FIELD SUPPORT SQUADRON	31 ARMOURED ENGINEER SQUADRON
73 ARMOURED ENGINEER SQUADRON	52 ARMOURED ENGINEER SQUADRON	61 FIELD SUPPORT SQUADRON (AIR ASSAULT)			33 ARMOURED ENGINEER SQUADRON	45 FIELD SUPPORT SQUADRON	39 ARMOURED ENGINEER SQUADRON
15 FIELD SUPPORT SQUADRON						65 FIELD SUPPORT SQUADRON	

REGULAR ROYAL ENGINEER REGIMENTS AND SQUADRONS

33 ENGINEER REGIMENT RE (EOD)

Wimbish

XXXIII

DEFENCE FORCES

HQ and SUPPORT SQUADRON (EOD)

21 FIELD SQUADRON (EOD)

49 FIELD SQUADRON (EOD)

58 FIELD SQUADRON (EOD)

17 FIELD SQUADRON (EOD)

35 ENGINEER REGIMENT RE

Paderborn

XXXV

20 ARMOURED BRIGADE

44 HQ SQUADRON

29 ARMOURED ENGINEER SQUADRON

37 ARMOURED ENGINEER SQUADRON

77 ARMOURED ENGINEER SQUADRON

36 ENGINEER REGIMENT RE

Maidstone

XXXVI

3 (UK) DIVISION

50 HQ SQUADRON

20 FIELD SQUADRON

69 GURKHA FIELD SQUADRON QGE

70 GURKHA FIELD SUPPORT SQUADRON QGE

38 ENGINEER REGIMENT RE

Antrim

XXXVIII

19 LIGHT BRIGADE

32 HQ and SUPPORT SQUADRON

11 FIELD SQUADRON

25 FIELD SQUADRON

39 ENGINEER REGIMENT RE (AIR SUPPORT)

Waterbeach

XXXIX

ROYAL AIR FORCE

60 HQ and SUPPORT SQUADRON

10 FIELD SQUADRON (AIR SUPPORT)

48 FIELD SQUADRON (AIR SUPPORT)

42 ENGINEER REGIMENT RE (GEOGRAPHIC)

Hermitage

XLII

FIELD DEPLOYABLE

HQ 42 ENGINEER REGIMENT (GEOGRAPHIC)

13 GEOGRAPHIC SQUADRON

14 GEOGRAPHIC SQUADRON

16 GEOGRAPHIC SUPPORT SQUADRON

ROYAL ENGINEERS SPECIALIST UNITS

62 Cyprus Support Squadron RE
(Provides engineer support to British Forces Cyprus) *Dhekelia.*

12 (Air Support) Engineer Group
Waterbeach.

29 (Land Support) Engineer Group
Aldershot.

170 (Infrastructure Support) Engineer Group
Chilwell. 62, 63, 64 and 66 Works Groups.

Band of the Corps of Royal Engineers
Chatham.

Works Group RE (Airfields)
Wallingford.

Engineer Resources
Bicester.

Engineer Training Advisory Team (ETAT)
Sennelager.

Export Support Team (RE EST)
Chatham.

Geographic Engineer Group
Hermitage.

Manning Career Management Division
Glasgow.

CORPS MUSEUM

ROYAL ENGINEERS MUSEUM

Brompton Barracks, Prince Arthur Road, Gillingham, Kent ME4 4UG

Tel: 01634 822839 Fax: 01634 822371

email: mail@re-museum.co.uk

Website: www.remuseum.org.uk

*T*he ability to pass orders and messages accurately and quickly has always been a vital constituent of success on the battlefield; in ancient times the Greeks used a torch telegraph and the Roman legions communicated with coloured smoke. During the Napoleonic Wars the Royal Navy communicated with a complex system of coloured flags — more suited to naval than land warfare — and it was not until the Crimean War in 1854 that more sophisticated communications systems began to be used by the Army with the introduction of the Morse Code and electric telegraph.

As with most technical activities, the early pioneering work on signalling in the Army was undertaken by the Royal Engineers who in 1867 formed a Signal Wing at Chatham which was the precursor of the Royal Corps of Signals. In 1884 this became the Telegraph Battalion RE which saw service in Egypt and the Sudan but really won its spurs during the Ashanti Campaign of 1895/6 when men of the Telegraph Battalion laid a telegraph cable from the Cape coast to Prahu, hacking their way through dense jungle for 72 miles and so surprising the

Signalling in the British Army prior to 1920 was the responsibility of specialist units of the Corps of Royal Engineers from which the Royal Corps of Signals emerged. Today, Royal Signals units provide command and control communications wherever the Army is deployed and are responsible for the operation and maintenance of some of the most technologically-advanced communications systems in the world.

Ashanti King Prempeh that he surrendered on the spot! His throne can be seen today in the Royal Signals Museum at Blandford.

The Telegraph Battalion continued to provide communications for the Army through the Zulu War and the Boer Wars and in 1912 the Royal Engineers Signal Service was formed. This expanded enormously during the First World War in the course of which it introduced the first wireless sets and the ubiquitous

despatch rider on his motorcycle who was to become such a familiar sight throughout both World Wars.

By the end of World War I, the growing importance and complexity of signalling demanded the formation of a separate corps and in June 1920 the Corps of Signals was formed by Royal Warrant and six weeks later became the Royal Corps of Signals by order of the King.

In the inter-war years the new Corps, with its horse-drawn cable wagons, saw

extensive service in India and throughout the Empire. Being a highly-technical body, its officers received their professional education at "The Shop" (The Royal Military Academy Woolwich) together with officers of the RA and RE until its closure in 1947.

In the Second World War, Royal Signals units served with every formation in every theatre. The Corps bears no Colours and is not awarded Battle Honours since, as with the Gunners and Sappers, its personnel are present at every action. In 1945 Royal Signals had a strength of over 150,000 officers and men compared with around 8,500 today.

With the rapid advance of communications and information technology over the past 25 years, the Corps has had to keep pace with its use in military systems and today operates and maintains some of the most advanced electronic equipment in the world. In the field army, battalions will normally be responsible for their own communications but at brigade and division level Royal Signals units are responsible. The size and content of each unit is structured to meet the specific command and control requirements of the formation it supports so no two units are exactly the same.

1867
ROYAL ENGINEERS SIGNAL WING
formed at Chatham (1)

1884
TELEGRAPH BATTALION
ROYAL ENGINEERS (2)

1912
ROYAL ENGINEERS
SIGNAL SERVICE

1920
CORPS OF SIGNALS
ROYAL CORPS OF SIGNALS

ROYAL SIGNALS MUSEUM
Blandford Camp, Blandford Forum, Dorset DT11 8RH
Tel: 01258 482248 Fax: 01258 482084
email: info@royalsignalsmuseum.com
Website: www.royalsignalsmuseum.com

NOTES

(1) In 1870 'C' Telegraph Troop Royal Engineers coprprised two officers and 130 sappers under Captain Montague Lambert and was the first dedicated signals formation to provide communications support to the Army. It first saw service in the Zulu War of 1879 using visual signalling and mounted messengers — the predecessors of the despatch rider.

(2) In 1884 the 22nd and 34th Companies Royal Engineers combined with 'C' Telegraph Troop to form the Telegraph Battalion Royal Engineers.

Though there are several motorcycle display teams in the Army, Royal Signals with their long and historic association with the motorcycle claim pride of place for their own team "The White Helmets".

CORPS HEADQUARTERS
Griffin House, Blandford Camp, Blandford Forum, Dorset DT11 8RH

Tel: Civ. 01258 482083 Mil. 94371 2083

email: rhq@royalsignals.mod.uk

Website: www.army.mod.uk/royalsignals/

REGIMENTAL MARCHES
Quick March: The Royal Signals March — "Begone Dull Care"

Slow March: HRH The Princess Royal

ALLIANCES
Canadian Armed Forces:
The Communications and Electronics Branch, Canadian Armed Forces

Australian Military Forces:
The Royal Australian Corps of Signals

New Zealand Army:
Royal New Zealand Corps of Signals

Indian Army:
Corps of Signals

Pakistan Army:
Signal Corps

Sri Lanka Army:
The Signal Corps

Malaysian Armed Forces:
Malaysian Signal Corps

Zambia Army:
Zambia Corps of Signals

AFFILIATED REGIMENT
Queen's Gurkha Signals

COLONEL-IN-CHIEF
HRH The Princess Royal, KG, KT, GCVO, QSO

ACTIVE REGULAR ROYAL SIGNALS REGIMENTS AND SQUADRONS — UK

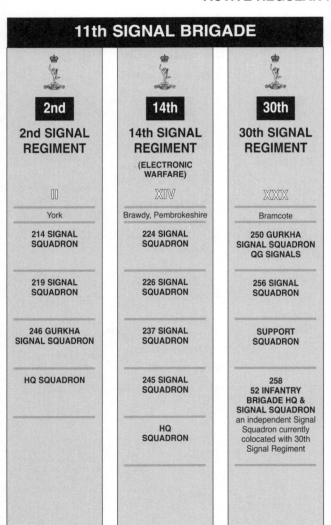

11th SIGNAL BRIGADE

2nd
2nd SIGNAL REGIMENT

II

York

214 SIGNAL SQUADRON

219 SIGNAL SQUADRON

246 GURKHA SIGNAL SQUADRON

HQ SQUADRON

14th
14th SIGNAL REGIMENT

(ELECTRONIC WARFARE)

XIV

Brawdy, Pembrokeshire

224 SIGNAL SQUADRON

226 SIGNAL SQUADRON

237 SIGNAL SQUADRON

245 SIGNAL SQUADRON

HQ SQUADRON

30th
30th SIGNAL REGIMENT

XXX

Bramcote

250 GURKHA SIGNAL SQUADRON QG SIGNALS

256 SIGNAL SQUADRON

SUPPORT SQUADRON

258
52 INFANTRY BRIGADE HQ & SIGNAL SQUADRON
an independent Signal Squadron currently colocated with 30th Signal Regiment

10th
10th SIGNAL REGIMENT

X

Northern Ireland

233 SIGNAL SQUADRON

ECM(FP) SIGNAL SQUADRON

Corsham

241 SIGNAL SQUADRON

Wilton

243 SIGNAL SQUADRON

Aldershot

251 SIGNAL SQUADRON

The only Regular Army Signal Regiment serving within 2 (National Communications) Signal Brigade.

3 (UK) DIVISION
HQ and SIGNAL REGIMENT

Bulford

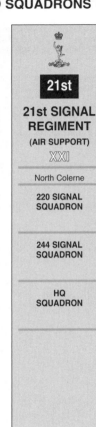

11th
11th SIGNAL REGIMENT

XI

Blandford

Within the
ROYAL SCHOOL OF SIGNALS

202 SIGNAL SQUADRON

206 SIGNAL SQUADRON

HQ SQUADRON

21st
21st SIGNAL REGIMENT

(AIR SUPPORT)

XXI

North Colerne

220 SIGNAL SQUADRON

244 SIGNAL SQUADRON

HQ SQUADRON

18 (UKSF)
SIGNAL REGIMENT

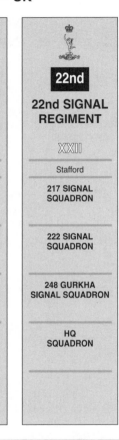

22nd
22nd SIGNAL REGIMENT

XXII

Stafford

217 SIGNAL SQUADRON

222 SIGNAL SQUADRON

248 GURKHA SIGNAL SQUADRON

HQ SQUADRON

Formed in 2005 to provide secure communications and support to Special Forces operations

(formerly 264 (SAS) Signal Squadron)

BRIGADE HEADQUARTERS and SIGNAL SQUADRONS UK

204
4 MECHANISED SIGNAL SQUADRON
Catterick

215
1 MECHANISED BRIGADE HQ and SIGNAL SQUADRON
Tidworth

228
12 MECHANISED BRIGADE HQ and SIGNAL SQUADRON
Aldershot

216
16 AIR ASSAULT BRIGADE HQ and SIGNAL SQUADRON
Colchester

209
19 LIGHT BRIGADE HQ and SIGNAL SQUADRON
Lisburn

261
101 LOGISTIC BRIGADE HQ and SIGNAL SQUADRON
Aldershot

ACTIVE REGULAR ROYAL SIGNALS REGIMENTS AND SQUADRONS — OVERSEAS

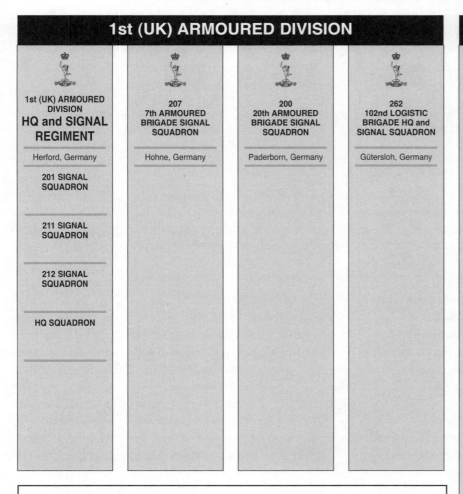

1st (UK) ARMOURED DIVISION

1st (UK) ARMOURED DIVISION HQ and SIGNAL REGIMENT

Herford, Germany

201 SIGNAL SQUADRON

211 SIGNAL SQUADRON

212 SIGNAL SQUADRON

HQ SQUADRON

207 7th ARMOURED BRIGADE SIGNAL SQUADRON

Hohne, Germany

200 20th ARMOURED BRIGADE SIGNAL SQUADRON

Paderborn, Germany

262 102nd LOGISTIC BRIGADE HQ and SIGNAL SQUADRON

Gütersloh, Germany

1st SIGNAL BRIGADE
SUPPORTING THE ALLIED RAPID REACTION CORPS (ARRC)

7th

7th (ARRC) SIGNAL REGIMENT

VII

Elmpt, Germany

229 SIGNAL SQUADRON

231 SIGNAL SQUADRON

232 SIGNAL SQUADRON

HQ SQUADRON

16th

16th SIGNAL REGIMENT

XVI

Elmpt, Germany

230 SIGNAL SQUADRON

255 SIGNAL SQUADRON

252 SIGNAL SQUADRON

HQ SQUADRON

HQ 1st SIGNAL BRIGADE

Rheindalen, Germany

Royal Signals Personnel also serve within the ARRC Support Battalion, Rheindalen

628 SIGNAL TROOP (FORMERLY 280 SIGNAL SQUADRON)

Elmpt, Germany

Provides communications support for the Allied Joint Force Command Headquarters Allied Force Northern Europe (AFNORTH)

Royal Signals personnel also serve within the Joint Service Communications Units in **CYPRUS** and the **FALKLAND ISLANDS.**

The Guards Division, known until 1968 as The Brigade of Guards, comprises the five regiments of Foot Guards which together with The Household Cavalry form The Household Division. As the Sovereign's personal troops, the Foot Guards take seniority and precedence ahead of all other infantry regiments of the Army regardless of formation dates.

The three oldest regiments, the Grenadiers, Coldstream and Scots Guards, had been raised by the time of the Restoration of King Charles II in 1660. The Irish Guards were formed in 1900 on the orders of Queen Victoria as a tribute to the bravery shown by the Irish Regiments in South Africa during the Second Boer War. Its original soldiers were Irishmen who volunteered for transfer from existing regiments of Foot Guards or infantry of the line.

The existence of a regiment of Foot Guards for each constituent country of the United Kingdom was completed in 1915 with the formation of The Welsh Guards. Two days after its formation on 26 February the Regiment mounted its first King's Guard at Buckingham Palace and within five months had been

With their scarlet tunics, black bearskins and impeccable turnout and drill, the regiments of The Guards Division are known throughout the world as ceremonial troops par excellence. However, their primary role is as highly-trained and competent infantry soldiers as a glance at their individual Battle Honours will immediately confirm.

awarded its first Victoria Cross on the Western Front at Pilckem.

During the First World War the five regiments produced 19 battalions of which 13 were service battalions, and 21 service battalions were formed in the Second. Though their individual identities and traditions are jealously guarded and carefully preserved, the common ethos and high standards of the five regiments have

Seven Joined in One: the badge of The Household Division.

always facilitated the interchange of personnel and working in composite formations. In World War II several of the Guards battalions were mechanised and 8 battalions formed the Guards Armoured Division which played a major role in the invasion of Europe in 1944. At the end of World War II all five regiments were reduced, the Grenadiers and Coldstreams to three battalions each, the

Scots to two battalions, and the Irish and Welsh to one battalion each. All have now been whittled down by successive defence cuts to a single battalion each.

The Foot Guards today are deployed the armoured infantry role, mechanised infantry role and light role and also make up the Guards Parachute Platoon in 3 PARA. Many guardsmen also volunteer for, and are selected to train and serve with, Special Forces.

The Foot Guards companies based in London perform the Public Duties and State Ceremonial for which they are renowned. Among these events are the Changing of the Guard ceremony at Buckingham Palace. The Guard also change at the Tower of London and at Windsor Castle, both of which are former or current residences of the Sovereign.

At the Tower of London guardsmen each night undertake the Ceremony of the Keys, a ritual locking up of the Tower which has been enacted for the past 7 years and every year on the Sovereign's official birthday in June the Foot Guard regiments take it in turn to Troop their Colour, an ancient and highly impressive ceremony derived from the practice of trooping each regiment's Colour in front of its soldiers so they would recognise as their rallying point on the battlefield.

1656
Royal Regiment of Guards (Wentworth's) (1)

1660
H M Foot Regiment of Guards (Russell's) (2)

1665
The King's Regiment of Guards (3)

c1685
1st Regiment of Foot Guards (4)

1815
1st or Grenadier (5) Regiment of Foot Guards

1815 GRENADIER GUARDS

GIMENTAL HEADQUARTERS

'ellington Barracks, Birdcage Walk,
ondon SW1E 6HQ

el: 0207414 3282/3284 Fax: 0207414 3443

'ebsite: www.army.mod.uk/grenadier

GIMENTAL MARCHES

uick Marches: The British Grenadiers
   The Grenadiers' March
ow Marches: March from Scipio
   The Duke of York's March

LIANCES

adian Armed Forces:
he Canadian Grenadier Guards

stralian Military Forces:
st Battalion The Royal Australian Regiment

idad and Tobago:
rinidad and Tobago Regiment

LONEL-IN-CHIEF

M The Queen

LONEL

RH The Prince Philip, Duke of Edinburgh
   KG, KT, OM, GBE, AC, QSO

NOTES

(1) Raised by Thomas, Lord Wentworth, in Bruges for the service of the exiled King Charles II. The Regiment was composed mainly of royalists in exile who had fought for the King in the Civil War and during Cromwell's invasion of the Netherlands. It became the senior regiment of Foot Guards upon the King's Restoration in 1660.

(2) Raised in England by Colonel John Russell, son of the Earl of Bedford.

(3) On its return to England, Wentworth's amalgamated with Russell's to form a 2-battalion regiment. In 1666 the Regiment was given precedence as the First Regiment of Guards which, at the time, ranked senior to the regiments of horse.

(4) In 1689 the senior right-flank company of the regiment was designated the Sovereign's personal Company and remains so to this day.

(5) A title awarded to the Regiment following the defeat by First Guards of the French Imperial Guard at the Battle of Waterloo in 1815.

> *Though today each reduced to a single battalion, the three senior Regiments of Foot Guards, Grenadiers, Coldstream and Scots Guards. also maintain a Public Duties Incremental Company, based in London, which retains the traditions, and the Colours, of the 2nd Battalion.*

BATTLE HONOURS

GRENADIER GUARDS

Pre-1914:

Tangier, 1680; Namur, 1695; Blenheim [1704]; **Gibraltar, 1704-05; Ramillies** [1706]; **Oudenarde** [1708]; **Malplaquet** [1709]; **Dettingen** [1743]; **Lincelles** [1793]; **Egmont-op-Zee** [1799]; **Peninsula** [1808-14]; **Corunna** [1809]; **Barrosa** [1811]; **Nive** [1813]; **Waterloo** [1815]; **Alma** [1854]; **Inkerman** [1854]; **Sevastopol** [1854-55]; **Egypt, 1882-84; Tel-el-Kebir** [1882]; **Suakin, 1885; Khartoum** [1898]; **Modder River** [1899]; **South Africa 1899-1902.**

First World War:

Mons; Retreat from Mons; **Marne 1914; Aisne 1914; Ypres 1914, 17;** Langemarck 1914; Gheluvelt; Nonne Bosschen; Neuve Chapelle; Aubers; Festubert 1915; **Loos; Somme 1916, 18;** Ginchy; Flers-Courcelette; Morval; Pilckem; Menin Road; Poelcapelle; Passchendaele; **Cambrai 1917, 18;** St. Quentin; Bapaume 1918; **Arras 1918;** Lys; **Hazebrouck;** Albert 1918; Scarpe 1918; **Hindenburg Line;** Havrincourt; Canal du Nord; Selle; Sambre; **France and Flanders 1914-18.**

Second World War:

Dyle; **Dunkirk 1940;** Cagny; **Mont Pincon; Nijmegen;** Reichswald; **Rhine;** North-West Europe 1940, 44-45; **Mareth; Medjez Plain;** North Africa 1942-43; **Salerno;** Volturno Crossing; **Monte Camino; Anzio; Gothic Line;** Battaglia; Italy 1943-45.

Post-1945:

Gulf 1991; Wadi al Batin.

REGIMENTAL MUSEUM

THE GUARDS MUSEUM
Wellington Barracks, Birdcage Walk,
London SW1E 6HQ
Tel: 02074 143428 Fax: 02074 143429
email: Guardsmuseum@aol.com
Website: www.theguardsmuseum.com

1660
The Lord General's Regiment of Foot Guards (1)

1670
The Coldstream Regiment of Foot Guards (2)

1817
COLDSTREAM GUARDS

NOTES

(1) Raised originally in 1650 from elements of the Parliamentary Army by General George Monck (later Duke of Albemarle). The regiment fought against the Scottish Royalist army at Dunbar but was later involved in the Restoration of the Monarchy in London in 1660. In February 1661 the regiment was disbanded and immediately reconstituted as part of the King's bodyguard.

(2) Long known popularly as "Coldstreamers" (from the town in Scotland where General Monck resided), the title became official on Monck's death in 1670.

The Coldstream did not enter Royal service until 1661 and therefore ranks second in seniority to the Grenadier Guards.

REGIMENTAL HEADQUARTERS

Wellington Barracks, Birdcage Walk,
London SW1E 6HQ

Tel: 02074 143246 Fax: 02074 143444

email: ara.rhqcoldmgds@milnet.uk.net

Website: www.ShinyCapstar.com

REGIMENTAL MARCHES;

Quick March: 'Milanollo'

Slow March: Excerpt from 'The Marriage of Figaro'

ALLIANCES

Canadian Armed Forces:

Governor General's Foot Guards

Australian Military Forces:

2nd Battalion The Royal Australian Regiment

COLONEL-IN-CHIEF

HM The Queen

COLONEL

General Sir Michael Rose
KCB, CBE, DSO, QGM, DL

Though today each reduced to a single battalion, the three senior Regiments of Foot Guards, Grenadiers, Coldstream and Scots Guards. also maintain a Public Duties Incremental Company, based in London, which retains the traditions, and the Colours, of the 2nd Battalion.

BATTLE HONOURS

COLDSTREAM GUARDS

Pre-1914:

Tangier 1680; Namur 1695; Gibraltar 1704-05; Oudenarde [1708]; **Malplaquet** [1709]; **Dettingen** [1743]; **Lincelles** [1793]; **The Sphinx** (superscribed 'Egypt') [1801]; **Peninsula** [1808-14]; **Talavera** [1809]; **Barrosa** [1811]; **Fuentes d'Onor** [1811]; **Salamanca** [1812]; **Nive** [1813]; **Waterloo** [1815]; **Alma** [1854]; **Inkerman** [1854]; **Sevastopol** [1854-55]; **Egypt, 1882; Tel-el-Kebir** [1882]; **Suakin, 1885; Modder River** [1899]; **South Africa 1899-1902.**

First World War:

Mons; **Retreat from Mons; Marne 1914; Aisne 1914; Ypres 1914, 17;** Langemarck 1914; Gheluvelt; Nonne Bosschen; Givenchy 1914; Neuve Chapelle; Aubers; Festubert 1915; **Loos;** Mount Sorrel; **Somme 1916, 18;** Flers-Courcelette; Morval; Pilckem; Menin Road; Poelcapelle; Passchendaele; **Cambrai 1917, 18;** St. Quentin; Bapaume 1918; **Arras 1918;** Lys; **Hazebrouck;** Albert 1918; Scarpe 1918; Drocourt-Quéant; **Hindenburg Line;** Havrincourt; Canal du Nord; Selle; Sambre; France and Flanders 1914-18.

Second World War:

Dyle; Defence of Escaut; **Dunkirk 1940;** Cagny; **Mont Pincon;** Quarry Hill; Estry; Heppen; Nederrijn; Venraij; Meijel; Roer; **Rhineland;** Reichswald; Cleve; Goch; Moyland; Hochwald; Rhine; Lingen; Uelzen; **North-West Europe 1940, 44-45;** Egyptian Frontier 1940; **Sidi Barrani;** Halfaya 1941; **Tobruk 1941, 1942;** Msus; Knightsbridge; Defence of Alamein Line; Medenine; Mareth; Longstop Hill 1942; Sbiba; Steamroller Farm; **Tunis;** Hammam Lif; North Africa 1940-43; **Salerno;** Battipaglia; Cappezano; Volturno Crossing; Monte Camino; Calabritto; Garigliano Crossing; **Monte Ornito;** Monte Piccolo; Capture of Perugia; Arezzo; Advance to Florence; Monte Domini; Catarelto Ridge; Argenta Gap; **Italy 1943-45.**

Post-1945:

Gulf 1991.

REGIMENTAL MUSEUM

THE GUARDS MUSEUM

Wellington Barracks, Birdcage Walk,
London SW1E 6HQ

Tel: 02074 143428 Fax: 02074 143429

email: Guardsmuseum@aol.com

Website: www.theguardsmuseum.com

1660
The Scottish Regiment of Foot Guards (1)

1712
The 3rd Regiment of Foot Guards

1831
The Scots Fusilier Guards

1877
SCOTS GUARDS

NOTES

(1) Two companies of footguards raised in Scotland by George, Earl of Linlithgow, from the remnants of a regiment which had fought for King Charles I in the Civil War and had remained loyal to Charles II in his attempt to regain the throne in 1650.

Prior to being taken on to the English Establishment in 1685, the Regiment was known variously as "His Majesty's Regiment of Guards", "The King's Regiment" and "The King's Footguards".

All the early records of the Regiment were destroyed in a serious fire at the Tower of London in 1841.

BATTLE HONOURS

SCOTS GUARDS

Pre-1914:

Namur, 1695; Dettingen [1743]; **Lincelles** [1793];
Peninsula [1808-14]; **Talavera** [1809]; **Barrosa** [1811];
Fuentes d'Onor [1811]; **Salamanca** [1812];
Nive [1813]; **Waterloo** [1815]; **Alma** [1854];
Inkerman [1854]; **Sevastopol** [1854-55];
Egypt, 1882-84; Tel-el-Kebir [1882]; **Suakin, 1885;**
Modder River [1899]; **South Africa 1899-1902.**

First World War:

Retreat from Mons; Marne 1914; Aisne 1914;
Ypres 1914, 17; Langemarck 1914; Gheluvelt;
Nonne Bosschen; Givenchy 1914; Neuve Chapelle;
Aubers; **Festubert 1915; Loos; Somme 1916, 18;**
Flers-Courcelette; Morval; Pilckem; Poelcapelle;
Passchendaele; **Cambrai 1917, 18;** St. Quentin;
Albert 1918; Bapaume 1918; Arras 1918;
Drocourt-Quéant; **Hindenburg Line;** Havrincourt;
Canal du Nord; Selle; Sambre;
France and Flanders 1914-18.

Second World War:

Stien; Norway 1940; Mont Pincon; **Quarry Hill;** Estry;
Venlo Pocket; **Rhineland;** Reichswald; Cleve; Moyland;
Hochwald; Rhine; Lingen; Uelzen;
North-West Europe 1940, 44-45; Halfaya 1941;
Sidi Suleiman; Tobruk 1941; **Gazala;** Knightsbridge;
Defence of Alamein Line; **Medenine;** Tadjera Khir;
Medjez Plain; Grich el Oued;
Djebel Bou Aoukaz 1943, 1; North Africa 1941-43;
Salerno; Battipaglia; Volturno Crossing;
Rochetta e Croce; **Monte Camino; Anzio;** Campoleone;
Carroceto; Trasimene Line; Advance to Florence; Monte
San Michele; Catarelto Ridge; Argenta Gap;
Italy 1943-45.

Post-1945:

Tumbledown Mountain; **Falkland Islands 1982;**
Gulf 1991.

REGIMENTAL HEADQUARTERS

Wellington Barracks, Birdcage Walk,
London SW1E 6HQ

Tel: 02074 143333/143321 Fax: 02074 143445

email: general@rhqscotsguards.co.uk

Website: www.army.mod.uk/scotsguards

REGIMENTAL MARCHES

Pipes and Drums
Quick March: Heilan Laddie
Slow March: The Garb of Old Gaul

Regimental Band
Quick March: Heilan Laddie
Slow March: The Garb of Old Gaul

ALLIANCES

Australian Military Forces:
3rd Battalion The Royal Australian Regiment

Royal Navy:
HMS Sceptre

COLONEL-IN-CHIEF

HM The Queen

COLONEL

HRH The Duke of Kent KG, CCMG, GCVO, ADC

Though today each reduced to a single battalion, the three senior Regiments of Foot Guards, Grenadiers, Coldstream and Scots Guards, also maintain a Public Duties Incremental Company, based in London, which retains the traditions, and the Colours, of the 2nd Battalion.

REGIMENTAL MUSEUM

THE GUARDS MUSEUM
Wellington Barracks, Birdcage Walk,
London SW1E 6HQ
Tel: 02074 143428 Fax: 02074 143429
email: Guardsmuseum@aol.com
Website: www.theguardsmuseum.com

**1900
IRISH GUARDS**

NOTES

The Irish Guards were raised in 1900 in recognition of the bravery shown by the Irish regiments in South Africa during the Second Boer War.

A free transfer was offered to any Irishman serving in one of the other regiments of Foot Guards or any infantry regiment of the line.

Originally nicknamed "Bob's Own" after its first Colonel, Field Marshal Lord Roberts, the Regiment is now universally, and affectionately, known as "The Micks".

Although the regiment cannot actively recruit in the Irish Republic, its members come from both North and South, Protestant and Catholic, maintaining Ireland's long and devoted tradition of service to the British Army and what it stands for.

BATTLE HONOURS

**IRISH
GUARDS**

First World War:

Mons; **Retreat from Mons; Marne 1914; Aisne 1914; Ypres 1914, 17;** Langemarck 1914; Gheluvelt; Nonne Bosschen; **Festubert 1915; Loos; Somme 1916, 18;** Flers-Courcelette; Morval; Pilckem; Poelcapelle; Passchendaele; **Cambrai 1917, 18;** St. Quentin; Lys; **Hazebrouck;** Albert 1918; Bapaume 1918; Arras 1918; Scarpe 1918; Drocourt-Quéant; **Hindenburg Line;** Canal du Nord; Selle; Sambre; France and Flanders 1914-18.

Second World War:

Pothus; **Norway 1940; Boulogne 1940;** Cagny; **Mont Pincon; Neerpelt; Nijmegen;** Aalst; **Rhineland;** Hochwald; Rhine; Bentheim; **North-West Europe 1944-45;** Medjez Plain; **Djebel Bou Aoukaz 1943; North Africa 1943; Anzio;** Aprilia; Carroceto; Italy 1943-44.

Post-1945:

Al Basrah; **Iraq 2003.**

REGIMENTAL HEADQUARTERS

Wellington Barracks, Birdcage Walk,
London SW1E 6HQ

Tel: 02074 14 3295/3254 Fax: 02074 14 3446

email: igwebmaster@btconnect.com

Website: www.army.mod.uk/irishguards

REGIMENTAL MARCHES

Quick March: St. Patrick's Day
Slow March: Let Erin Remember

ALLIANCES

Australian Military Forces:
4th Battalion The Royal Australian Regiment

Leeward Islands:
Montserrat Defence Force

COLONEL-IN-CHIEF

HM The Queen

COLONEL

Major-General Sir Sebastian Roberts KCVO, OBE

**1915
WELSH GUARDS**

NOTES

The Welsh Guards were raised on 26 February 1915 to complete the disposition of a regiment of foot guards for each constituent country of the United Kingdom.

Two days later the Regiment mounted its first King's Guard at Buckingham Palace and within five months had won its first Victoria Cross on the Western Front at Pilckem.

REGIMENTAL HEADQUARTERS

Wellington Barracks, Birdcage Walk, London SW1E 6HQ

Tel: 02074 14 3291 Fax: 02074 14 3447

email: rhq@welshguards.army.mod.uk

Website: www.army.mod.uk/welsh_guards

REGIMENTAL MARCHES

Quick March: Rising of the Lark

Slow March: Men of Harlech

ALLIANCES

Australian Military Forces:
5th/7th Battalion The Royal Australian Regiment

Royal Navy:
HMS Campbeltown

COLONEL-IN-CHIEF

HM The Queen

COLONEL

HRH The Prince of Wales
KG, KT, OM, GCB, AK, QSO, ADC

BATTLE HONOURS

WELSH GUARDS

First World War:

Loos; Somme 1916, 18; **Ginchy; Flers-Courcelette; Morval;** Ypres 1917; **Pilckem; Poelcapelle;** Passchendaele; **Cambrai 1917, 18; Bapaume 1918;** Arras 1918; Albert 1918; Drocourt-Quéant; Hindenburg Line; Havrincourt; **Canal du Nord;** Selle; **Sambre;** France and Flanders 1915-18.

Second World War:

Defence of Arras; Boulogne 1940; St. Omer-La Bassée; Bourguebus Ridge; Cagny; **Mont Pincon; Brussels; Hechtel;** Nederrijn; Rhineland; Lingen; North-West Europe 1940, 44-45; **Fondouk;** Djebel el Rhorab; Tunis; **Hammam Lif;** North Africa 1943; **Monte Ornito;** Liri Valley; **Monte Piccolo;** Capture of Perugia; Arezzo; Advance to Florence; Gothic Line; **Battaglia;** Italy 1944-45.

Post-1945:

Falkland Islands 1982.

REGIMENTAL MUSEUM

THE GUARDS MUSEUM
Wellington Barracks, Birdcage Walk, London SW1E 6HQ
Tel: 02074 143428 Fax: 02074 143429
email: Guardsmuseum@aol.com
Website: www.theguardsmuseum.com

*I*t has been said that Scotland's greatest export has always been her soldiers and, certainly, from earliest times, Scottish mercenaries were renowned throughout Europe for their bravery and competence.

From the mid-13th century, Irish resistance to Anglo-Norman invasion was bolstered by the *Gallóglaigh* (Gallowglass) the Gaelic-Norse mercenary elite from the Highlands and Islands of Scotland which continued in the service of the Irish lordships for the next 350 years. Throughout the 16th and 17th centuries, Scottish mercenaries proved their worth in Bohemian, Dutch, Swedish, Polish, Russian, Danish and French service. The famous Scots, or Green, Brigade was in Dutch service from 1572-1697 and became known as "The Bulwark of Holland". During the Thirty Years War (1618-1648) it is estimated that between 20,000 and 30,000 Highland Scots fought against Germany as mercenaries in the service of King Gustavus Adolphus of Sweden.

Prior to the Union of the Crowns of Scotland and England in 1603, Scottish armies and Scottish mercenaries in foreign service had regularly fought

The Scottish Division comprises one large regiment, The Royal Regiment of Scotland, with five regular and two TA battalions each retaining some elements of the individual regiments from which it is descended — some of the finest and most renowned infantry regiments of all time.

against English troops and it was a fitting gesture that in the new Union of Great Britain the first regular regiment of infantry of the line should be raised from Scots soldiers of the Green Brigade in foreign service. This was to become 1st

Royal Scots, the oldest and most senior line infantry regiment in the Army.

During the sad period of religious and political strife of the 17th/18th centuries, Scotsman often fought Scotsman and the old, Jacobite clan regiments were

defeated and disarmed. But from the debris of this crushed society emerged the new Highland Regiments which would acquire legendary reputations in the service of the Crown.

During Queen Victoria's reign, her love of the Highlands gave rise to an upsurge in popularity for all things Highland and the talismen of the Highlanders — principally the bagpipes and tartan dress — were adopted by all Scottish regiments. Since then, they have left their mark in the armies of every Commonwealth country where kilts and pipe bands are fiercely-preserved symbols of, sometimes very remote but no less jealously guarded, Scottish origins.

Each battalion in the new regiment carries forward elements of the identity of its predecessors. Although members of the Regiment wear the new Royal Regiment of Scotland cap badge, each battalion retains its own Pipes & Drums whose musicians continue to wear the tartan of the former regiment. For instant recognition, each battalion also wears a different coloured hackle in its bonnets:
1 SCOTS, black;   2 SCOTS, white;
3 SCOTS, red;   4 SCOTS, blue and
5 SCOTS, green.

PRESENT ROLES & ATTACHMENTS OF THE REGULAR BATTALIONS THE ROYAL REGIMENT OF SCOTLAND	
1 SCOTS (Royal Scots Borderers)	Light Role *(4th Mechanised Brigade)*
2 SCOTS (Royal Highland Fusiliers)	Light Role *(16th Air Assault Brigade)*
3 SCOTS (Black Watch)	Light Role *(19th Light Brigade)*
4 SCOTS (Highlanders)	Armoured Infantry *(7th Armoured Brigade)*
5 SCOTS (Argyll and Sutherland Highlanders)	Light Role Air Assault *(16th Air Assault Brigade)*

THE ROYAL SCOTS

THE KING'S OWN SCOTTISH BORDERERS

THE ROYAL SCOTS FUSILIERS

THE HIGHLAND LIGHT INFANTRY

THE BLACK WATCH

THE SEAFORTH HIGHLANDERS

THE QUEEN'S OWN CAMERON HIGHLANDERS

THE GORDON HIGHLANDERS

THE ARGYLL and SUTHERLAND HIGHLANDERS

THE ROYAL HIGHLAND FUSILIERS

THE QUEEN'S OWN HIGHLANDERS

THE HIGHLANDERS

1st BATTALION

(ROYAL SCOTS BORDERERS)

PAGE 72 / 73

2nd BATTALION

(ROYAL HIGHLAND FUSILIERS)

PAGE 74-75

3rd BATTALION

(BLACK WATCH)

PAGE 76

4th BATTALION

(HIGHLANDERS)

PAGE 78-79

5th BATTALION

(ARGYLL and SUTHERLAND HIGHLANDERS)

PAGE 77

THE ROYAL REGIMENT OF SCOTLAND

1633 Le Régiment d'Hébron (1) *(in French service)*	1633 Le Régiment Douglas *(in French service)*

1678 (2)
Earl of Dumbarton's Regiment of Foot

1684
The Royal Regiment of Foot

1st

1751
1st *or* Royal Regiment of Foot

1812
1st Regiment of Foot *or* Royal Scots

1821
1st *or* The Royal Regiment of Foot

1871
1st *or* The Royal Scots Regiment

1881 (May)
The Lothian Regiment (Royal Scots)

1881 (July)
The Royal Scots (The Lothian Regiment)

1920
THE ROYAL SCOTS
(The Royal Regiment)

2006
Amalgamated with
The King's Own Scottish Borderers
to form:

1st BATTALION
THE ROYAL REGIMENT
OF SCOTLAND
(Royal Scots Borderers)

NOTES

(1) In 1633 Sir John Hepburn, under a Royal Warrant from King Charles I, raised a body of 1,200 Scots for the French service. By 1635 the Regiment had increased to over 8,000 men many of whom had previously been serving in the 'Green Brigade' as mercenaries to the Swedish crown.

(2) In 1661 the Regiment was recalled to Britain to bridge the gap between the disbandment of Cromwell's New Model Army and the establishment of a Regular British Army which was organised on the lines of the British units then in foreign service. The Regiment was thus the First Regiment of the British Army and is the senior infantry regiment of the line.

Although elements of the Regiment returned to French service remaining on the continent until 1678, the precedence of the Regiment dates from 1661 when it was first recalled to Britain.

Derisively referred to as "Pontius Pilate's Bodyguard" by the French Picardie Regiment which disputed the claim of the Scots Brigade to be the oldest regiment in the French Army, the nickname was adopted with pride and is borne by the Regiment to this day.

REGIMENTAL MARCHES of
THE ROYAL REGIMENT OF SCOTLAND

Pipes & Drums

Quick March:	Scotland the Brave
Slow March:	The Slow March of the Royal Regiment of Scotland

Military Band

Quick March:	Scotland the Brave
Slow March:	The Slow March of the Royal Regiment of Scotland

The individual battalions have their own Marches carried forward from the antecedent regiments which are shown on the following pages.

REGIMENTAL MUSEUM

ROYAL SCOTS REGIMENTAL MUSEUM
The Castle, Edinburgh EH1 2YT
Tel: 0131 310 5016
email: rhqrs@btconnect.com
Website: www.theroyalscots.co.uk

THE
ROYAL SCOTS
(The Royal
Regiment)

Pre-1914:

Tangier, 1680; Namur, 1695; Blenheim [1704]; **Ramillies** [1706]; **Oudenarde** [1708]; **Malplaquet** [1709]; **Louisburg** [1758]; **Havannah** [1762]; **Egmont-op-Zee** [1799]; **Egypt** [1801]; **St. Lucia 1803; Corunna** [1809]; **Busaco** [1810]; **Salamanca** [1812]; **Vittoria** [1813]; **San Sebastian** [1813]; **Nive** [1813]; **Peninsula** [1808-14]; **Niagara** [1813]; **Waterloo** [1815]; **Nagpore** [1817]; **Maheidpoor** [1817]; **Ava** [1824-26]; **Alma** [1854]; **Inkerman** [1854]; **Sevastopol** [1854-55]; **Taku Forts** [1860]; **Pekin** 1860; **South Africa 1899-1902.**

First World War:

Mons; **Le Cateau;** Retreat from Mons; **Marne 1914, 18;** Aisne 1914; La Bassée 1914; Neuve Chapelle;

REGIMENTAL HEADQUARTERS
ROYAL REGIMENT OF SCOTLAND

The Castle, Edinburgh EH1 2YT
Tel: 0131 310 5060

HOME HEADQUARTERS
Royal Scots

The Castle, Edinburgh EH1 2YT
Tel: 0131 310 5016
email: rhqrs@btconnect.com
Website: www.theroyalscots.co.uk

REGIMENTAL MARCHES (Royal Scots)

Pipes & Drums

Quick March:	Dumbarton's Drums
Slow March:	The Garb of Old Gaul

Military Band

Quick March:	Dumbarton's Drums
Slow March:	The Garb of Old Gaul

BATTLE HONOURS

Ypres 1915, 17, 18; Gravenstafel; St. Julien; Frezenburg; Bellewaarde; Aubers; Festubert 1915; **Loos; Somme 1916, 18;** Albert 1916, 18; Bazentin; Pozières; Flers-Courcelette; Le Transloy; Ancre Heights; Ancre 1916, 18; **Arras 1917, 18;** Scarpe 1917, 18; Arleux; Pilckem; Langemarck 1917; Menin Road; Polygon Wood; Poelcappelle; Passchendaele; Cambrai 1917; St. Quentin; Rosieres; **Lys;** Estaires; Messines 1918; Hazebrouck; Bailleul; Kemmel; Béthune; Soissonnais-Ourcq; Tardenois; Amiens; Bapaume 1918; Drocourt-Queant; Hindenberg Line; Canal du Nord; St. Quentin Canal; Beaurevoir; Courtrai; Selle; Sambre; France and Flanders 1914-18; **Struma;** Macedonia 1915-18; Helles; Landing at Helles; Krithia; Suvla; Scimitar Hill; **Gallipoli 1915-16;** Rumani; Egypt 1915-16; Gaza; El Mughar; Nebi Samwil; Jaffa; **Palestine 1917-18;** Archangel 1918-19.

Second World War:

Dyle; **Defence of Escaut;** St. Omer-La Bassée; **Odon;** Cheux; Defence of Rauray; Caen; Esquay; Mont Pincon; **Aart;** Nederrijn; Best; Scheldt; **Flushing;** Meijel; Venlo Pocket; Roer; Rhineland; Reichswald; Cleve; Goch; **Rhine;** Uelzen; Bremen; Artlenberg; **North-West Europe 1940, 44-45; Gothic Line;** Marradi; Monte Gamberaldi; **Italy 1944-45;** South-East Asia 1941; Donbaik; **Kohima;** Relief of Kohima; Aradura; Shwebo; Mandalay; Burma 1943-45.

Post-1945:

Gulf 1991; Wadi al Batin.

ALLIANCES (Royal Scots)

Canadian Armed Force:

The Canadian Scottish Regiment (Princess Mary's)

The Royal Newfoundland Regiment

Royal Navy:

HMS Edinburgh

AFFILIATED REGIMENT (Royal Scots)

Royal Gurkha Rifles

COLONEL-IN-CHIEF

HM The Queen

ROYAL COLONEL

HRH The Princess Royal KG, KT, GCVO, QSO

1689
The Edinburgh Regiment of Foot (1)

25th

1751
25th (Edinburgh) Foot

1782
25th (Sussex) Foot

1805
25th (The King's Own Borderers) Foot

1881 (May)
The York Regiment (King's Own Borderers)

1881 (July)
The King's Own Borderers

1887
**THE KING'S OWN
SCOTTISH BORDERERS**

2006
Amalgamated with
The Royal Scots to form:

**1st BATTALION
THE ROYAL REGIMENT
OF SCOTLAND
(Royal Scots Borderers)**

NOTES

(1) The Regiment was raised as an emergency measure in 1689 to defend Edinburgh against the Jacobite threat. It was recruited "by beat of drum" along the Royal Mile in the record time of two hours with men flocking to join the Earl of Leven for the defence of their city.

REGIMENTAL MUSEUM

**KING'S OWN SCOTTISH BORDERERS
REGIMENTAL MUSEUM**
The Barracks, Berwick-upon-Tweed,
Northumberland TD15 1DG
Tel: 01289 307426 Fax: 01289 331928
email: kosbmus@milnet.uk.net
Website: www.kosb.co.uk/museum.htm

BATTLE HONOURS

**THE
KING'S OWN
SCOTTISH
BORDERERS**

Pre-1914:

Namur, 1695; **Minden** [1759]; **Egmont-op-Zee** [1799]; **Martinique**, 1809; **Afghanistan, 1878-80;** **Chitral** [1895]; **Tirah** [1897-98]; **Paardeberg** [1900]; **South Africa, 1900-02.**

First World War:

Mons; Le Cateau; Retreat from Mons; Marne 1914, 18; **Aisne 1914;** La Bassée 1914; Messines 1914; **Ypres 1914, 15, 17, 18;** Nonne Bosschen; Hill 60; Gravenstafel; St. Julien; Frezenberg; Bellewaarde; **Loos;** **Somme 1916, 18;** Albert 1916, 18; Bazentin; Delville Wood; Pozières; Guillemont; Flers-Courcelette; Morval; Le Transloy; Ancre Heights; **Arras 1917, 18;**

Vimy 1917; Scarpe 1917, 18; Arleux; Pilckem; Langemarck 1917; Menin Road; Polygon Wood; Broodseinde; Poelcappelle; Passchendaele; Cambrai 1917-18; St. Quentin; Lys; Estaires; Hazebrouck; Kemmel; **Soissonnais-Ourcq;** Bapaume 1918; Drocourt-Queant; **Hindenberg Line;** Epéhy; Canal du Nord; Courtrai; Selle; Sambre; France and Flanders 1914-18; Italy 1917-18; Helles; Landing at Helles; Krithia; Suvla; Scimitar Hill; **Gallipoli 1915-16;** Rumani; Egypt 1916; **Gaza;** **El Mughar; Nebi Samwil; Jaffa; Palestine 1917-18.**

Second World War:

Dunkirk 1940; Cambes; **Odon;** Cheux; Defence of Rauray; **Caen;** Esquay; Troarn; Mont Pincon; Estry; Aart; Nederrijn; **Arnhem 1944;** Best; Scheldt; **Flushing;** Venraij; Meijel; Venlo Pocket; Roer; Rhineland; Reichswald; Cleve; Goch; **Rhine;** Ibbenburen; Lingen; Dreirwalde; Uelzen; **Bremen;** Artlenberg; North-West Europe 1940, 44-45; North Arakan; Buthidaung; **Ngakyedauk Pass; Imphal;** Kanglatongbi; Ukhrul; Meiktila; **Irrawaddy; Kama;** **Burma 1943-45.**

Post-1945:

Kowang-San; Maryang-San; **Korea 1951-52;** **Gulf 1991.**

REGIMENTAL HEADQUARTERS
ROYAL REGIMENT OF SCOTLAND

The Castle, Edinburgh EH1 2YT

Tel: 0131 310 5060

HOME HEADQUARTERS
King's Own Scottish Borderers

The Barracks, Berwick-upon-Tweed,
Northumberland TD15 1DG

email: info@kosb.co.uk

Website: www.kosb.co.uk

REGIMENTAL MARCHES (KOSB)
Pipes & Drums

Quick March: Blue Bonnets are over the Border

Slow March: The Borderers

Military Band

Quick March: Blue Bonnets are over the Border

Slow March: The Garb of Old Gaul

ALLIANCES (KOSB)

Canadian Armed Forces:
1st Battalion The Royal New Brunswick
Regiment (Carleton and York)

Australian Military Forces:
25th/49th The Royal Queensland Regiment

Malaysian Armed Forces:
5th Battalion The Royal Malay Regiment

South African Defence Force:
The Witwatersrand Rifles

COLONEL-IN-CHIEF

HM The Queen

ROYAL COLONEL

HRH The Princess Royal KG, KT, GCVO, QSO

1678
Earl of Mar's
Regiment of Foot

1686
The Scots Fusiliers
Regiment of Foot (2)

1712
The Royal North British
Fusiliers

21st

1751
21st (Royal North British)
Fusiliers

1877
21st (Royal Scots
Fusiliers)

73rd

1777
1st Bn. 73rd (Highland)
Foot (1)

71st

1786
71st (Highland) Foot

1808
71st (Glasgow Highland)
Foot

1809
71st (Glasgow Highland
Light Infantry) Regt.

1810
71st (Highland) Light
Infantry

74th

1787
74th (Highland) Foot

1803
74th Highland Foot
(The Assaye Regiment)

1816
74th Foot

1845
74th (Highlanders) Foot

2nd BATTALION

1881
**THE ROYAL SCOTS
FUSILIERS**

1881
**THE HIGHLAND LIGHT
INFANTRY**
(City of Glasgow Regiment)

1959
**THE ROYAL HIGHLAND
FUSILIERS**
(Princess Margaret's (3) Own
Glasgow and Ayrshire Regiment)

2006
2nd BATTALION
**THE ROYAL REGIMENT
OF SCOTLAND**
(Royal Highland
Fusiliers)

NOTES

(1) The 73rd Foot was raised in 1777 by John MacKenzie, Lord Macleod, in response to the outbreak of the War of American Independence. In 1786 it was renumbered 71st and the number 73 allocated to the 2nd Bn. of the 42nd (The Royal Highland) Foot, later to become the Black Watch.

In tribute to these origins, the Royal Highland Fusiliers wore trews of the MacKenzie tartan.

(2) Having served under the Duke of Marlborough from 1702 to 1712, and been present at many of his major victories, the Royal Scots Fusiliers adopted the unofficial title of "Marlborough's Own".

(3) Younger daughter of King George VI.

**REGIMENTAL HEADQUARTERS
ROYAL REGIMENT OF SCOTLAND**
The Castle, Edinburgh EH1 2YT
Tel: 0131 310 5060

**HOME HEADQUARTERS
Royal Highland Fusiliers**
518 Sauchiehall Street, Glasgow G2 3LW
Tel: 0141 332 5639 Fax: 0141 353 1493
email: reg.sec@rhf.org.uk
Website: www.army.mod.uk/infantry/regts/sc

REGIMENTAL MARCHES (RHF)

Pipes & Drums

Quick Marches: Heilan Laddie
     Blue Bonnets are over the Bor

Slow March: My Home

Military Band

Quick Marches: British Grenadiers
     Whistle o'er the Lave o't

Slow Marches: The Garb of Old Gaul
     March of the 21st Regiment

ALLIANCES (RHF)

Canadian Armed Forces:
The Royal Highland Fusiliers of Canada

New Zealand Army:
1st Battalion The Royal New Zealand Infantry
 Regiment

Pakistan Army:
11th Battalion The Baloch Regiment

South African Defence Force:
Prince Alfred's Guard

COLONEL-IN-CHIEF
HM The Queen

ROYAL COLONEL
HRH The Duke of York KCVO, ADC

REGIMENTAL MUSEUM

ROYAL HIGHLAND FUSILIERS MUSEUM
518 Sauchiehall Street, Glasgow G2 3LW
Tel: 0141 332 5639 Fax: 0141 353 1493
email: assregsec@rhf.org.uk
Website: www.rhf.org.uk

BATTLE HONOURS

**THE
ROYAL SCOTS
FUSILIERS**

**THE HIGHLAND
LIGHT INFANTRY**

(City of Glasgow
Regiment)

**THE
ROYAL HIGHLAND
FUSILIERS**

(Princess Margaret's[3]
Own Glasgow and
Ayrshire Regiment)

THE ROYAL SCOTS FUSILIERS

Pre-1914:

Blenheim [1704]; **Ramillies** [1706]; **Oudenarde** [1708]; **Malplaquet** [1709]; **Dettingen** [1743]; **Belleisle** [1761]; **Martinique, 1794; Bladensburg** [1814]; **Alma** [1854]; **nkerman** [1854]; **Sevastopol** [1854-55]; **South Africa, 1879; Burmah, 1885-1887; Tirah** [1897-98]; **South Africa, 1899-1902; Relief of Ladysmith** [1900].

First World War:

Mons; Le Cateau; Retreat from Mons; **Marne 1914;** Aisne 1914; La Bassée 1914; **Ypres 1914, 17, 18;** Langemarck 1914; Gheluvelt; Nonne Bosschen; Neuve Chapelle; Aubers; Festubert 1915; Loos; **Somme 1916, 18;** Albert 1916, 18; Bazentin; Delville Wood; Pozières; Flers-Courcelette; Le Transloy; Ancre Heights; Ancre 1916; **Arras 1917, 18;** Scarpe 1917, 18; Arleux; Messines 1917; Pilckem; Menin Road; Polygon Wood; St. Quentin; Bapaume 1918; **Lys;** Estaires; Hazebrouck; Bailleul; Béthune; Scherpenberg; Drocourt-Quéant; **Hindenberg Line;** Canal du Nord; Courtrai; Selle; France and Flanders 1914-18; **Doiran 1917, 18;** Macedonia 1916-18; Helles; **Gallipoli 1915-18;** Rumani; Egypt 1916-17; Gaza; El Mughar; Nebi Samwil; Jerusalem; Jaffa; Tell Asur; **Palestine 1917-18.**

Second World War:

Defence of Arras; **Ypres-Comines Canal;** Somme 1940; Withdrawal to Seine; **Odon;** Fontenay le Pesnil; Cheux; Defence of Rauray; Mont Pincon; Estry; **Falaise;** La Vie Crossing; La Touques Crossing; Aart; Nederrijn; Best; Le Havre; Antwerp-Turnhout Canal; **Scheldt;** Soth Beveland; Lower Maas; Meijel; Venlo Pocket; Roer; Rhineland; Reichswald; Cleve; Goch; **Rhine;** Dreirwalde; Uelzen; **Bremen;** Artlenberg; North-West Europe 1940, 44-45; **Landing in Sicily;** Sicily 1943; Sangro; **Garigliano Crossing;** Minturno; Anzio; Advance to Tiber; Italy 1943-44; Madagascar; Middle East 1942; **North Arakan;** Razabil; **Pinwe;** Schweli; Mandalay; Burma 1944-45.

THE HIGHLAND LIGHT INFANTRY

Pre-1914:

Carnatic [1778-91]; **Gibraltar, 1780-83; Sholinghur** [1781]; **Mysore** [1789-91]; **Hindoostan** [1790]; **Seringapatam** [1799]; **Assaye** [1803]; **Cape of Good Hope, 1806; Rolica** [1808]; **Vimera** [1808]; **Peninsula** [1808-14]; **Corunna** [1809]; **Busaco** [1810]; **Almaraz** [1812]; **Badajos** [1812]; **Ciudad Rodrigo** [1812]; **Salamanca** [1812]; **Nive** [1813]; **Nivelle** [1813]; **Pyrenees** [1813]; **Vittoria** [1813]; **Orthes** [1814]; **Toulouse** [1814]; **Waterloo** [1815]; **South Africa. 1851-53; Sevastopol** [1854-55]; **Central India** [1856-58]; **Egypt, 1882-84; Tel-el-Kebir** [1882]; **Modder River** [1899]; **South Africa, 1899-1902.**

First World War:

Mons; Retreat from Mons; Marne 1914; Aisne 1914; **Ypres 1914, 15, 17, 18;** Langemarck 1914, 17; Gheluvelt; Nonne Bosschen; Givenchy 1914; Neuve Chapelle; St. Julien; Aubers; Festubert 1915; **Loos; Somme 1916, 18;** Albert 1916, 18; Bazentin; Delville Wood; Pozières; Flers-Courcelette; Le Transloy; Ancre Heights; Ancre 1916, 18; **Arras 1917, 18;** Vimy 1917; Scarpe 1917-18; Arleaux; Pilckem; Menin Road; Polygon Wood; Passchendaele; Cambrai 1917, 18; St. Quentin; Bapaume 1918; Lys; Estaires; Messines 1918; Hazebrouck; Bailleul; Kemmel; Amiens; Drocourt-Quéant; **Hindenberg Line;** Havrincourt; Canal du Nord; St. Quentin Canal; Beaurevoir; Courtrai; Selle; Sambre; France and Flanders 1914-18; **Gallipoli 1915-18;** Rumani; Egypt 1916; Gaza; El Mughar; Nebi Samwil; Jaffa; **Palestine 1917-18;** Tigris 1916; Kut al Amara 1917; Sharqat; **Mesopotamia 1916-18;** Murman 1919; **Archangel 1919.**

Second World War:

Withdrawal to Cherbourg; **Odon;** Cheux; Esquay; Mont Pincon; Quarry Hill; Estry; Falaise; Seine 1944; Alart; Nederrijn; Best; **Scheldt;** Lower Maas; South Beveland; **Walcheren Causeway;** Asten; Roer; Ourthe; Rhineland; **Reichswald;** Goch; Moyland Wood; Weeze; **Rhine;** Ibbenburen; Dreirwalde; Aller; Uelzen; Bremen; Artlenberg; **North-West Europe 1940, 44-45;** Jebel Shiba; Barentu; **Keren;** Massawa; Abyssinia 1941; Gazala; **Cauldron;** Mersa Matruh; Fuka; North Africa 1940-42; **Landing in Sicily;** Sicily 1943; Italy 1943, 45; Athens; **Greece 1944-45;** Adriatic; Middle East 1944.

THE ROYAL HIGHLAND FUSILIERS

Post-1945:

Gulf 1991.

1725
Independent Companies known as "The Black Watch" (1)

1739
The Highland Regiment of Foot (2)

42nd

1751
The 42nd Foot

1758
42nd (The Royal Highland) Foot

1861
42nd (The Royal Highland) Foot (The Black Watch)

42nd

1758-62
1779-86
2nd Bn. 42nd (The Royal Highland) Foot

73rd

1786
73rd Highland Regiment of Foot

1809
73rd Foot

1862
73rd (Perthshire) Foot

1881
The Black Watch (Royal Highlanders)

1934
THE BLACK WATCH
(Royal Highland Regiment)

2006
2nd BATTALION
THE ROYAL REGIMENT
OF SCOTLAND
(Black Watch)

NOTES

(1) Six independent companies, recruited from clans who were loyal to the Hanoverian monarchy, were raised from 1725 to be stationed in different parts of the Highlands. Their purpose was to enforce law and order among the Jacobite clans who were loyal to the Royal Stewarts. Due to the dark tartan they wore, these units became known as "The Black Watch".

(2) In 1739 King George II authorised the raising of an additional four companies the whole to be formed into a new Regiment of the Line to be known as "The Highland Regiment of Foot".

REGIMENTAL HEADQUARTERS
ROYAL REGIMENT OF SCOTLAND

The Castle, Edinburgh EH1 2YT

Tel: 0131 310 5060

HOME HEADQUARTERS
Black Watch

Balhousie Castle, Hay Street, Perth PH1 5HR

Tel: 01738 638152   Fax: 01738 643245

email: info@the blackwatch.co.uk

Website: www.theblackwatch.co.uk

REGIMENTAL MARCHES

Pipes & Drums

Quick March: Heilan Laddie

Slow March: My Home
               Highland Cradle Song

Military Band

Quick March: Blue Bonnets are over the Border

Slow March: The Garb of Old Gaul

**THE
BLACK WATCH**
(Royal Highland
Regiment)

Pre-1914:

Havannah [1762]; **Martinique** [1762]; **North America 1763-64; Mangalore** [1783]; **Mysore** [1789]; **Seringapatam** [1799]; **Peninsula** [1808]; **Corunna** [1809]; **Busaco** [1810]; **Fuentes d'Onor** [1811]; **Salamanca** [1812]; **Nive** [1813]; **Nivelle** [1813]; **Pyrenees** [1813]; **Toulouse** [1814]; **Orthes** [1814]; **Waterloo** [1815]; **South Africa, 1846-47; South Africa, 1851-53; Alma** [1854]; **Sevastopol** [1854-55]; **Lucknow** [1857]; **Ashantee, 1873-74; Tel-el-Kebir** [1882]; **Egypt, 1882-84; Nile, 1884-85; Kirbekan** [1885]; **South Africa, 1899-1902; Paardeberg** [1900].

First World War:

Retreat from Mons; **Marne 1914;** Aisne 1914; La Bassée 1914; **Ypres 1914, 17, 18;** Langemarck 1914; Gheluvelt; Nonne Bosschen; Givenchy 1914; Neuve Chapelle; Aubers; Festubert 1915; **Loos; Somme 1916, 18;** Albert 1916; Bazentin; Delville Wood; Pozières; Flers-Courcelette; Morval; Thiepval; Le Ancre Heights; Ancre 1916; **Arras 1917, 18;** Vimy 1917; Scarpe 1917, 18; Arleux; Pilckem;

BATTLE HONOURS

Menin Road; Polygon Wood; Poelcappelle; Passchendaele; Cambrai 1917, 18; St. Quentin; Bapaume 1918; Rosières; **Lys;** Estaires; Messines 1918; Hazebrouck; Kemmel; Béthune; Scherpenberg; Soissonnais-Ourcq; Tardenois; Drocourt-Queant; **Hindenberg Line;** Epéhy; St. Quentin Canal; Beaurevoir; Courtrai. Selle; Sambre; France and Flanders 1914-18; **Doiran 1917;** Macedonia 1915-18; Egypt 1916; Gaza; Jerusalem; Tell Asur; **Megiddo;** Sharon; Damascus; Palestine 1917-18; Tigris 1916; **Kut al Amara 1917;** Baghdad; Mesopotamia 1915-17.

Second World War:

Defence of Arras; Ypres-Comines Canal; Dunkirk 1940; Somme 19140; St. Valery-en-Caux; Saar; Breville; Odon; Fontenay le Pesnil; Defence of Rauray; Caen; Falaise; **Falaise Road;** La Vie Crossing; Le Havre; Lower Maas; Venlo Pocket; Ourthe; Rhineland; Reichswald; Goch; **Rhine;** North-West Europe 1940, 44-45; Barkasan; British Somaliland 1940; **Tobruk 1941;** Tobruk Sortie; **El Alamein;** Advance on Tripoli; Medenine; Zemlet el Lebene; Mareth; **Akarit;** Wadi Akarit East; Djebel Roumana; Medjez Plain; Si Mediene; Tunis; North Africa 1941-43; Landing in Sicily; Vizzini; Sferro; Gerbini; Adrano; Sferro Hills; **Sicily 1943; Cassino II;** Liri Valley; Advance to Florence; Monte Scalari; Casa Fortis; Rimini Line; Casa Fabbri Ridge; Savio Bridgehead; Italy 1944-45; Athens; Greece 1944-45; **Crete;** Haraklion; Middle East 1941; Chindits 1944; Burma 1944.

Post-1945;

The Hook 1952; Korea 1952-53; Al Basrah; **Iraq 2003.**

ALLIANCES

Canadian Armed Forces:
The Prince Edward Island Regiment
The Black Watch (Royal Highland Regiment) of Canada
The Lanark and Renfrew Scottish Regiment

Australian Military Forces:
The Royal Queensland Regiment
The Royal New South Wales Regiment

New Zealand Army:
1st and 2nd Squadron New Zealand Scottish, RNZAC

South African Defence Force:
Transvaal Scottish

Royal Navy:
HMS Montrose

COLONEL-IN-CHIEF

HM The Queen

ROYAL COLONEL

Lieutenant-General HRH Prince Charles, Duke of Rothesay, KG, KT, GCB, OM, AK

REGIMENTAL MUSEUM

BLACK WATCH REGIMENTAL MUSEUM
Balhousie Castle, Hay Street, Perth PH1 5HR
Tel: 01738 638152   Fax: 643245
email: info@theblackwatch.co.uk
Website: www.theblackwatch.co.uk

98th

1794
98th (Argyllshire Highlanders) Foot (1)

91st

1796
91st (Argyllshire Highlanders) Foot

1809
91st Foot

1821
1st (Argyllshire) Foot

1864
91st (Argyllshire) Highlanders

1872
t (Princess Louise's) (2) gyllshire Highlanders

93rd

1799
93rd Highlanders

1861
93rd (Sutherland Highlanders) Foot (3)

1881 (May)
The Princess Louise's (Sutherland and Argyll) Highlanders

1882 (July)
The Princess Louise's (Argyll and Sutherland) Highlanders

1920
THE ARGYLL AND SUTHERLAND HIGHLANDERS
(Princess Louise's)

2006
5th BATTALION
THE ROYAL REGIMENT OF SCOTLAND
(Argyll and Sutherland Highlanders)

NOTES

(1) In 1796 the 98th was renumbered 91st. The number 98 was allocated to the Regiment of Foot which eventually became the North Staffordshire Regiment.

(2) Princess Louise, Duchess of Argyll, fourth daughter of Queen Victoria.

(3) Of all the old Highland Regiments, the 93rd was the most territorial being recruited almost entirely from the disbanded Sutherland Fencibles and the tenantry of the Countess of Sutherland in the far north of Scotland. It was the 93rd which gave rise to the unofficial title "The Thin Red Line" when it withstood the charge of the Russian cavalry at Balaklava in a long, double-ranked line with bayonets fixed.

BATTLE HONOURS

THE ARGYLL AND SUTHERLAND HIGHLANDERS
(Princess Louise's)

Pre-1914:

Cape of Good Hope, 1806; Peninsula [1808]; **Rolica** [1808]; **Vimiera** [1808]; **Corunna** [1809]; **Pyrenees** [1813]; **Nive** [1813]; **Nivelle** [1813]; **Orthes** [1814]; **Toulouse** [1814]; **South Africa, 1846-47; South Africa, 1851-53; Alma** [1854]; **Balaklava** [1854]; **Sevastopol** [1854-55]; **Lucknow** [1857]; **South Africa, 1879; Modder River** [1899]; **South Africa, 1899-1902; Paardeberg** [1900].

First World War:

Mons; Le Cateau; Retreat from Mons; **Marne 1914, 18;** Aisne 1914; La Bassée 1914; Messines 1914, 18; Armentières 1914; **Ypres 1915, 17, 18;** Gravenstafel; St. Julien; Frezenberg; Bellewaarde; Festubert 1915; **Loos; Somme 1916, 18;** Albert 1916, 18; Bazentin; Delville Wood; Pozières; Flers-Courcelette; Morval; Le Transloy; Ancre Heights; Ancre 1916; **Arras 1917, 18;**
Scarpe 1917, 18; Arleux; Pilckem; Menin Road; Polygon Wood; Broodseinde; Poelcappelle; Passchendaele; **Cambrai 1917, 18;** St. Quentin; Bapaume 1918; Rosières; Lys; Estaires; Hazebrouck; Bailleul; Kemmel; Béthune; Soissonnais-Ourcq; Tardenois; Amiens; Hindenberg Line; Epéhy; Canal du Nord; St. Quentin Canal; Beaurevoir; Courtrai; Selle; Sambre; France and Flanders 1914-18; Italy 1917-18; Struma; **Doiran 1917, 18;** Macedonia 1915-18; Gallipoli 1915-16; Rumani; Egypt 1916; **Gaza;** El Mughar; Nebi Samwil; Jaffa; Palestine 1917-18.

Second World War:

Somme 1940; **Odon;** Tourmauville Bridge; Caen; Esquay; Mont Pincon; Quarry Hill; Estry; Falaise; Dives Crossing; Aart; Lower Maas; Meijel; Venlo Pocket; Ourthe; Rhineland; Reichswald; **Rhine;** Uelzen; Artlenberg; North-West Europe 1940, 44-45; Abyssinia 1941; **Sidi Barrani; El Alamein;** Medenine; **Akarit;** Djebel Azzag 1942; Kef Ouiba Pass; Mine de Sedjenane; Medjez Plain; **Longstop Hill 1943;** North Africa 1940-43; Landing in Sicily; Gerbini; Adrano; Centuripe; Sicily 1943; Termoli; Sangro; Cassino II; Liri Valley; Aquino; Monte Casalino; Monte Spaduro; Monte Grande; Senio; Santerno Crossing; Argenta Gap; **Italy 1943-45; Crete;** Heraklion; Middle East 1941; North Malaya; **Grik Road;** Central Malaya; Ipoh; Slim River; Singapore Island; **Malaya 1941-42.**

Post-1945:

Pakchon; Korea 1950-51.

REGIMENTAL HEADQUARTERS
ROYAL REGIMENT OF SCOTLAND

The Castle, Edinburgh EH1 2YT

Tel: 0131 310 5060

HOME HEADQUARTERS
Argyll and Sutherland Highlanders

The Castle, Stirling FK8 1EH

Tel: 01786 475165 Fax: 01786 446038

email: regsec@argylls.co.uk

Website: www.argylls.co.uk

REGIMENTAL MARCHES (A&SH)

Pipes & Drums

Quick Marches: The Campbells are Coming
Heilan' Laddie

Slow March: The Skye Boat Song

Military Band

Quick March: The Thin Red Line

Slow March: The Garb of Old Gaul

ALLIANCES (A&SH)

Canadian Armed Forces:
The Argyll and Sutherland Highlanders of Canada
(Princess Louise's)
The Calgary Highlanders

Australian Military Forces:
The Royal New South Wales Regiment

Pakistan Army:
1st Battalion (SCINDE) The Frontier Force
Regiment

Royal Navy:
HMS Argyll

COLONEL-IN-CHIEF and ROYAL COLONEL

HM The Queen

1778
78th (Seaforth Highland)
Regiment of Foot (1)

72nd

1786
72nd (Seaforth Highland)
Regiment of Foot

1823
72nd Duke of Albany's (2)
Own Highlanders

78th

1793
78th (Highland)
Regiment of Foot (3)

1794
2nd Battalion raised as
The Ross-shire Buffs

79th

1794
79th (Cameronian
Volunteers) (Highland)
Regiment of Foot (4)

1806
79th (Cameron
Highlanders) Regiment
of Foot

1873
79th (Queen's Own (5)
Cameron Highlanders)
Regiment of Foot

75th

1787
75th (Highland)
Regiment of Foot (6)

1809
75th Regiment of Foot

1862
75th (Stirlingshire)
Regiment of Foot

1794
100th (Gordon
Highlanders)
Regiment of Foot (7)

92nd

1798
92nd (Highland)
Regiment of Foot

1809
92nd Regiment of Foot

1861
92nd (Gordon
Highlanders)
Regiment of Foot

1881
SEAFORTH HIGHLANDERS
(Ross-shire Buffs,
The Duke of Albany's)

1881
THE QUEEN'S OWN CAMERON HIGHLANDERS

1961
QUEEN'S OWN HIGHLANDERS
(Seaforth and Cameron)

1881
THE GORDON HIGHLANDERS

1994
THE HIGHLANDERS
(Seaforth, Gordons and Camerons)

2006
4th BATTALION THE ROYAL REGIMENT OF SCOTLAND
(Highlanders)

NOTES:

(1) Raised in Ross-shire by the Earl of Seaforth and mainly comprising MacKenzies.

(2) Frederick, Duke of York and Albany, second son of King George III, Commander-in-Chief 1811-27.

(3) Raised at Fort George, Inverness, by Colonel Francis MacKenzie, last Earl of Seaforth.

(4) Raised the year before in 1793 by Sir Alan Cameron of Erracht from volunteers in Lochaber. This was a West Highland Cameron regiment, not to be confused with the Glasgow and Borders Cameronians.

(5) Queen Victoria.

(6) Raised by Colonel Robert Abercrombie for service in India. Also known as Abercrombie's Highlanders.

(7) Raised in Aberdeenshire by the Duke of Gordon. Legend has it that the beautiful Duchess Jean acquired recruits at county gatherings by holding the King's Shilling between her teeth and inviting recruits to claim it with a kiss!

REGIMENTAL HEADQUARTERS
The Castle, Edinburgh EH1 2YT
Tel: 0131 310 5060

HOME HEADQUARTERS
Queen's Own Highlanders
(Seaforth and Camerons)
Cameron Barracks, Inverness IV2 3XD
Tel: 01463 224380
email: rhqthehighlanders@btopenworld.com
Website: www.qohldrs.co.uk

HOME HEADQUARTERS
The Gordon Highlanders
St Luke's, Viewfield Road, Aberdeen AB15 7XH
Tel: 01224 318174 Fax: 01224 208652
email: highlanders.aberdeen@delta4u.co.uk
Website: www.gordonhighlanders.com

REGIMENTAL MARCHES (HLDRS)

Pipes & Drums:

Quick Marches:	Pibroch of Donuil Dubh Cock o' the North
Slow March:	The Highlanders Slow March

Military Band:

Quick March:	The Wee Highland Laddie
Slow March:	The Garb of Old Gaul

ALLIANCES (HLDRS)

Canadian Armed Forces:
The Cameron Highlanders of Ottawa
48th Highlanders of Canada
The Queen's Own Cameron Highlanders
of Canada
The Seaforth Highlanders of Canada
The Toronto Scottish Regiment (Queen
Elizabeth the Queen Mother's Own)

Australian Armed Forces:
5th/7th Battalion The Royal Australian
Regiment
10th/27th Battalion The Royal South Australia
Regiment
16th Battalion The Royal Western Australia
Regiment
5th/6th Battalion The Royal Victoria Regiment

New Zealand Army:
4th Battalion (Otago and Southland)
Royal New Zealand Infantry Regiment
7th Battalion (Wellington (City of Wellington's
Own) and Hawkes Bay) Royal New
Zealand Infantry Regiment

South African Defence Force:
The Cape Town Highlanders

Royal Navy:
HMS Sutherland
HMS Victorious

COLONEL-IN-CHIEF
HM The Queen

ROYAL COLONEL
Field Marshal HRH The Prince Philip, Duke of
Edinburgh KG, KT, OM, GBE, AC, QSO

BATTLE HONOURS

THE SEAFORTH HIGHLANDERS
(Ross-shire Buffs, The Duke of Albany's)

THE GORDON HIGHLANDERS

THE QUEEN'S OWN CAMERON HIGHLANDERS

QUEEN'S OWN HIGHLANDERS
(Seaforth and Camerons)

THE SEAFORTH HIGHLANDERS

Pre-1914:

Carnatic [1778-91]; **Mysore** [1789-91]; **Hindoostan** [1790-1823]; **Assaye** [1803]; **Cape of Good Hope, 1806**; **Maida** [1806]; **Java** [1811]; **South Africa, 1835**; **Sevastopol** [1854-55]; **Persia** [1856-57]; **Central India** [1857-58]; **Koosh-Ab** [1857]; **Lucknow** [1857-58]; **Afghanistan, 1878-1880**; **Peiwar Kotal** [1878]; **Charasiah** [1879]; **Kabul, 1879**; **Kandahar, 1880**; **Tel-el-Kebir** [1882]; **Egypt, 1882-84**; **Chitral** [1895]; **Atbara** [1898]; **Khartoum** [1898]; **South Africa, 1899-1902**; **Paardeberg** [1900].

First World War:

Le Cateau; Retreat from Mons; **Marne 1914, 18**; Aisne 1914; La Bassée 1914; Armentières 1914; Festubert 1914, 15; Givenchy, 1914; Neuve Chapelle; **Ypres, 1915, 17, 18**; St. Julien; Frezenberg, Bellewaarde; Aubers; **Loos; Somme, 1916, 18**; Albert, 1916; Bazentin; Delville Wood; Pozières; Flers Courcelette; Le Transloy; Ancre Heights; Ancre, 1916; **Arras, 1917,18; Vimy, 1917**; Scarpe, 1917, 18; Arleux; Pilckem; Menin Road; Polygon Wood; Broodseinde; Poelcapelle; Passchendaele; **Cambrai, 1917, 18**; St. Quentin; Bapaume, 1918; Lys; Estaires; Messines 1918; Hazebrouck; Bailleul; Kennel; Béthune; Soissonnais-Ourcq; Tardenois; Drocourt-Quéant; Hindenburg Line; Courtai; Selle; Valenciennes; France and Flanders 1914-18; Macedonia 1917-18; Megiddo; Sharon; **Palestine 1918; Tigris 1916**; Kut al Amara 1917; **Baghdad;** Mesopotamia 1915-18.

Second World War:

Ypres-Comines Canal; Somme 1940; Withdrawal to Seine; **St. Valéry-en-Caux**; Odon; Cheux; **Caen;** Troarn; Mont Pincon; Quarry Hill; Falaise; Falaise Road; Dives Crossing; La Vie Crossing; Lisieux; Nederrijn; Best; Le Havre; Lower Maas; Meijel; Venlo Pocket; Ourthe; **Rhineland;** Reichswald; Goch; Moyland; Rhine; Uelzen; Artlenberg; North-West Europe 1940, 44-45; **El Alamein;** Advance to Tripoli; Mareth; Wadi Zigzaou; **Akarit;** Djebel Roumana; North Africa 1942-43; Landing in Sicily; Augusta; Francofonte; Adrano; Sferro Hills; **Sicily 1943;** Garigliano Crossing; **Anzio;** Italy 1943-44; **Madagascar;** Middle East 1942; **Imphal;** Shenam Pass; Litan; Tengnoupal; **Burma 1942-44;**

THE GORDON HIGHLANDERS

Pre-1914:

Mysore [1789-91]; **Egmont-op-Zee** [1799]; **Seringapatam** [1799]; **Mandora** [1801]; **Peninsula** [1808-14]; **Corunna** [1809]; **Fuentes d'Onor** [1811]; **Almaraz** [1812]; **Nive** [1813]; **Pyrenees** [1813]; **Vittoria** [1813]; **Orthes** [1814]; **Waterloo** [1815]; **South Africa, 1835; Delhi, 1857; Lucknow** [1857-58]; **Afghanistan, 1878-1880; Charasiah** [1879]; **Kabul, 1879; Kandahar, 1880; Egypt, 1882-84; Tel-el-Kebir** [1882]; **Nile, 1884-85; Chitral** [1895]; **Tirah** [1897-98]; **Defence of Ladysmith** [1899-1900]; **South Africa, 1899-1902; Paardeberg** [1900].

First World War:

Mons; Le Cateau; Retreat from Mons; **Marne 1914, 18**; Aisne 1914; La Bassée 1914; Messines 1914; Armentières 1914; **Ypres 1914, 15, 17**; Langemarck 1914; Gheluvelt; Nonne Bosschen; Neuve Chapelle; Frezenberg; Bellewaarde; Aubers; Festubert 1915; Hooge 1915; **Loos; Somme 1916, 18**; Albert 1916, 18; Bazentin; Delville Wood; Pozières; Guillemont; Flers-Courcelette; Le Transloy; **Ancre 1916; Arras 1917, 18**; Vimy 1917; Scarpe 1917, 18; Arleux; Bullecourt; Pilckem; Menin Road; Polygon Wood; Broodseinde; Poelcapelle; Passchendaele; **Cambrai 1917, 18**; St. Quentin; Bapaume 1918; Rosières; Lys; Estaires; Hazebrouck; Béthune; Soissonnais-Ourcq; Tardenois; Hindenburg Line; Canal du Nord; Selle; Sambre; France and Flanders 1914-18; Piave; **Vittorio Veneto;** Italy 1917-18.

Second World War:

Withdrawal to Escaut; Ypres-Comines Canal; Dunkirk 1940; Somme 1940; St. Valéry-en-Caux; **Odon;** La Vie Crossing; Lower Maas; Venlo Pocket; Rhineland; **Reichswald;** Cleve; **Goch; Rhine; North-West Europe 1940, 44-45; El Alamein;** Advance on Tripoli; **Mareth;** Medjez Plain; North Africa 1942-43; Landing in Sicily; **Sferro;** Sicily 1943; **Anzio;** Rome; Italy 1944-45.

THE QUEEN'S OWN CAMERON HIGHLANDERS

Pre-1914:

Egmont-op-Zee [1799]; **Peninsula** [1808-14]; **Corunna** [1809]; **Busaco** [1810]; **Fuentes d'Onor** [1811]; **Salamanca** [1812]; **Nive** [1813]; **Nivelle** [1813]; **Pyrenees** [1813]; **Toulouse** [1814]; **Waterloo** [1815]; **Alma** [1854]; **Sevastopol** [1854-55]; **Lucknow** [1857-58]; **Tel-el-Kebir** [1882]; **Egypt, 1882-84; Nile, 1884-85; Atbara** [1898]; **Khartoum** [1898]; **South Africa, 1900-02.**

First World War:

Retreat from Mons; **Marne 1914, 18; Aisne 1914; Ypres 1914, 15, 17, 18;** Langemarck 1914; Gheluvelt; Nonne Bosschen; Givenchy 1914; **Neuve Chapelle;** Hill 60; Gravenstafel; St. Julien; Frezenberg; Bellewaarde; Aubers; Festubert 1915; **Loos; Somme 1916, 18;** Albert 1916; Bazentin; **Delville Wood;** Pozières; Flers-Courcelette; Morval; Le Transloy; Ancre Heights; **Arras 1917, 18;** Scarpe 1917; Arleux; Pilckem; Menin Road; Polygon Wood; Poelcapelle; Passchendaele; St. Quentin; Bapaume 1918; Lys; Estaires; Messines 1918; Kemmel; Béthune; Soissonnais-Ourcq; Drocourt-Quéant; Hindenberg Line; Epéhy; St. Quentin Canal; Courtrai; Selle; **Sambre;** France and Flanders 1914-18; Struma; **Macedonia 1915-18.**

Second World War:

Defence of Escaut; **St. Omer-La Bassée;** Somme 1940; St. Valéry-en-Caux; Falaise; Falaise Road; La Vie Crossing; Le Havre; Lower Maas; Venlo Pocket; Rhineland; **Reichswald;** Goch; **Rhine;** North-West Europe 1940, 44-45; Agordat; **Keren;** Abyssinia 1941; **Sidi Barrani;** Tobruk 1941, 42; Gubi II; Carmusa; Gazala; **El Alamein;** Mareth; Wadi Zigzaou; **Akarit;** Djebel Roumana; North Africa 1940-43; Francofonte; Adrano; Sferro Hills; Sicily 1943; Cassino I; Poggio del Grillo; **Gothic Line;** Tavoleto; Coriano; Pian di Castello; Monte Reggiano; Rimini Line; San Marino; Italy 1944; **Kohima;** Relief of Kohima; Naga Village; Aradura; Shwebo; **Mandalay;** Ava; Irrawaddy; Mt. Popa; Burma 1944-45.

QUEEN'S OWN HIGHLANDERS

Post-1945:

Gulf 1991.

REGIMENTAL MUSEUMS

THE HIGHLANDERS REGIMENTAL MUSEUM
Fort George, Ardersier, Inverness-shire IV2 7TD
Tel: 01463 224380
email: rhqthehighlanders@btopenworld.com

THE GORDON HIGHLANDERS MUSEUM
St. Luke's, Viewfield Road, Aberdeen AB15 7XY
Tel: 01224 311200 Fax: 01224 319323
email: museum@gordonhighlanders.com
Website: www.gordonhighlanders.com

The most senior constituent of the Queen's Division, The Princess of Wales's Royal Regiment, is itself descended from twelve old regiments of the line including the 2nd Foot ("The Queens") and the 3rd Foot ("The Buffs") which, next to The Royal Scots, are the two oldest line infantry regiments in the British Army.

Known as "The Tigers", a nickname bestowed upon the 67th Regiment after 21 years of unbroken service in India, The Princess of Wales's Royal Regiment has an essentially south-eastern heritage; its former regiments originated predominantly in Kent, Sussex, Surrey, Middlesex, Hampshire and the Channel Islands which areas remain the Regiment's principal recruiting ground today. The Royal Hampshires were more fortunate than most in maintaining their exclusive county identity, avoiding amalgamation until formation of The Princess of Wales's Royal Regiment in 1992 and the name of the old regiment lives on in the subtitle of the new.

The second element of The Queen's Division is the Royal Regiment of Fusiliers. The original role of fusiliers in the late 17th century was to guard the

The Queen's Division consists of three "large" regiments, each of two battalions which are descended from no less than 25 original regiments of the line as shown opposite and on the pages which follow.

artillery train where the light, flintlock rifles known as *fusils*, with which they were equipped, were safer to use than matchlock weapons around the open gunpowder barrels used by the gunners.

As flintlocks gradually became standard issue, fusilier regiments adopted more of a light infantry role while maintaining their customs and distinctive dress including a racoon skin headdress, similar to but

smaller than a guardsman's bearskin. Though today's fusiliers wear the ubiquitous beret, they are distinguished by the red and white hackle still worn behind the cap badge.

The third element of The Queen's Division is The Royal Anglian Regiment which was the first amalgam of nine original county infantry regiments to be formed into a "large" regiment in 1964. Its then four battalions have today been whittled down to two.

As its name implies, the Royal Anglian has a strong heritage in East Anglia and the East Midlands and embodies the former county regiments of Norfolk, Suffolk, Lincolnshire, Northamptonshire, Rutlandshire, Bedfordshire, Hertfordshire, Essex and Leicestershire which area, together with Cambridgeshire, remains its principal recruiting territory today. The 1st Battalion is known as "The Vikings" and the 2nd Battalion "The Poachers" — a reminder of the Regiment's ancient connection with Lincolnshire and the folksong *"The Lincolnshire Poacher"*.

The Queen's Division also includes, for administrative purposes, The Royal Gibraltar Regiment, a home defence unit of one infantry battalion formed in 1958 from the Gibraltar Defence Forces and granted their "Royal" title in 1991.

PRESENT ROLES & ATTACHMENTS OF THE REGULAR BATTALIONS THE QUEEN'S DIVISION	
1 PWRR	Armoured Infantry *(20th Armoured Brigade)*
2 PWRR	Light Role *(Cyprus)*
1 RRF	Armoured Infantry *(7th Armoured Brigade)*
2 RRF	Light Role *(London District)*
1 R ANGLIAN	Mechanised Infantry *(12th Mechanised Brigade)*
2 R ANGLIAN	Light Role *(7th Armoured Brigade)*

THE ORIGINAL FUSILIER REGIMENTS

Royal Northumberland Fusiliers Royal Warwickshire Fusiliers Royal Fusiliers (City of London Regiment) Lancashire Fusiliers	*Reformed into four battalions and subsequently reduced to 1st & 2nd Battalions* **Royal Regiment of Fusiliers** *a constituent of* ***The Queen's Division***
Royal Iniskilling Fusiliers Royal Irish Fusiliers (Princess Victoria's)	*Amalgamated into* *1st Battalion* **Royal Irish Regiment**
Royal Munster Fusiliers Royal Dublin Fusiliers	*Disbanded 1922*
Royal Highland Fusiliers (Princess Margaret's Own Glasgow and Ayrshire Regiment)	*2nd Battalion* **Royal Regiment of Scotland**
Royal Welch Fusiliers	*1st Battalion* **Royal Welsh**

2nd — 57th
3rd — 67th
31st — 70th
35th — 77th
37th — 97th
50th — 107th

9th — 44th
10th — 48th
12th — 56th
16th — 58th
17th

5th — 7th
6th — 20th

1st BATTALION	2nd BATTALION
THE PRINCESS OF WALES'S ROYAL REGIMENT (Queen's and Royal Hampshires)	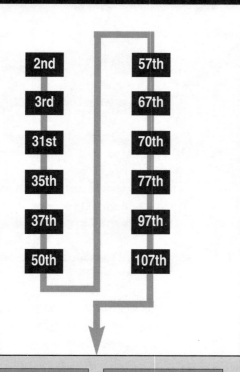

PAGE 82-85

1st BATTALION	2nd BATTALION
THE ROYAL REGIMENT OF FUSILIERS	

PAGE 86-87

1st BATTALION	2nd BATTALION
THE ROYAL ANGLIAN REGIMENT	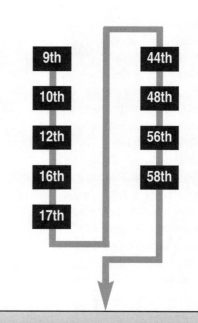

PAGE 88-91

THE QUEEN'S DIVISION

1661
The Tangier Regiment (1)

1684
The Queen's Regiment (2)

1686
The Queen Dowager's Regiment

1703
The Queen Dowager's Royal Regiment

1714
The Princess of Wales's Royal Regiment

1727
The Queen's Own Royal Regiment

2nd

1751
2nd (The Queen's Royal) Regiment

1881 (May)
The Royal West Surrey Regiment (The Queen's)

1881 (July)
The Queen's (Royal West Surrey Regiment)

1702
Villier's Regiment of Marines (3)

1711
Goring's Regiment of Foot

31st

1751
31st Regiment of Foot

1782
31st (Huntingdonshire) Regiment of Foot

1756
2nd Battalion 31st Foot

70th

1758
70th Regiment of Foot

1782
70th (Surrey (4)) Regiment of Foot

1812
70th (Glasgow Lowland) Regiment of Foot

1825
70th (The Surrey) Regiment of Foot

1665
The Holland Regiment (5)

1689
Prince George of Denmark's Regiment

3rd

1689
3rd Regiment of Foot

1711
The Buffs (6)

1751
3rd (or The Buffs) Regiment of Foot

1782
3rd (East Kent) Regiment of Foot (The Buffs)

1881 (May)
The Kentish Regiment (The Buffs)

1881 (July)
The Buffs (East Kent Regiment)

50th

1757
50th Regiment of Foot (7)

1782
50th (West Kent) Regiment of Foot

1827
50th (Duke of Clarence's) (8) Regiment of Foot

1831
50th (The Queen's Own) (9) Regiment of Foot

97th

1824
97th Regiment of Foot (10)

1826
97th (Earl of Ulster's) Regiment of Foot

1701
The Earl of Donegal's Regiment of Foot (11)

35th

1751
35th Regiment of Foot

1782
35th (Dorsetshire) Regiment of Foot

1804
35th (Sussex) Regiment of Foot

1832
35th (Royal Sussex) Regiment of Foot

1854
3rd (Bengal) European Light Infantry (12)

1858
3rd Bengal Light Infantry (13)

107th

1861
107th Bengal Infantry Regiment

1881
THE QUEEN'S OWN
(Royal West Kent Regiment)
50, 97

1881
THE ROYAL SUSSEX REGIMENT
35, 107

1881
THE EAST SURREY REGIMENT
31, 70

1921
THE QUEEN'S ROYAL REGIMENT
(West Surrey)

1935
THE BUFFS
(Royal East Kent Regiment)

1966
THE QUEEN'S REGIMENT
2, 3, 31, 35, 50, 57, 70, 77, 97, 107

1959
THE QUEEN'S ROYAL SURREY REGIMENT
2, 31, 70

1961
THE QUEEN'S OWN BUFFS
(The Royal Kent Regiment)
3, 50, 97

1992
THE PRINCESS OF WALES'S ROYAL REGIMENT
(Queen's and Royal Hampshires)
2, 3, 31, 35, 37, 50, 57, 67, 70, 77, 97, 107

Lineage (left chart)

1755
59th Regiment of Foot (14)

1756
Middlesex Militia (15)

57th

1757
57th Regiment of Foot

1782
th (West Middlesex) Regiment of Foot

77th

1787
77th (Hindoostan) Regiment of Foot

1807
77th (East Middlesex) Regiment of Foot

1876
77th (East Middlesex) Regiment of Foot (Duke of Cambridge's Own) (16)

1881
THE MIDDLESEX REGIMENT
(Duke of Cambridge's Own)
57, 77

1702
Meredith's Regiment of Foot (17)

37th

1751
37th Regiment of Foot

1782
37th (North Hampshire) Regiment of Foot

1756
2nd Battalion 20th Regiment of Foot

67th

1758
67th Regiment of Foot (18)

1782
67th (South Hampshire) Regiment of Foot

1881
The Hampshire Regiment
37, 67

1946
THE ROYAL HAMPSHIRE REGIMENT
37, 67

NOTES:

(1) Raised by Henry Mordaunt, Earl of Peterborough, for the Defence of Tangier which was acquired by King Charles II on his marriage to Catherine of Braganza.

(2) Queen Catherine of Braganza, wife of Charles II.

(3) Raised by Colonel George Villiers as the 2nd Regiment of Marines.

(4) Sic.

(5) Raised from the remnants of four English regiments which had previously been in Dutch service but had been disbanded in the previous year by the Netherlands States General for refusing to swear the Oath of Allegiance.

(6) Known as "The Buffs" from the colour of their uniform facings. The Tudor dragon in the regimental badge was awarded to the Regiment by Queen Anne c.1707 and is one of the oldest regimental badges.

(7) Formed from the 52nd Regiment of Foot which had been raised by Colonel James Abercrombie in the previous year.

(8) Prince William Henry, Duke of Clarence, third son of King George III and future King William IV.

(9) Queen Adelaide, wife of William IV.

(10) Raised in Winchester by Colonel C. Hamilton.

(11) Raised in Northern Ireland by the Earl of Donegal and also known as The Belfast Regiment.

(12) Honourable East India Company.

(13) British Indian Army.

(14) Raised in Gloucestershire and Somerset by Colonel John Arabin.

(15) Three regiments of militia raised by Sir William Beauchamp Proctor — the East and West Middlesex and the Westminster Militia.

(16) George, Duke of Cambridge, cousin of Queen Victoria.

(17) Raised in Ireland by Colonel Thomas Meredith.

(18) The Regiment's first Commanding Officer was Colonel James Wolfe.

Containing the elements of the old 2nd and 3rd Regiments of Foot, The Princess of Wales's Royal Regiment is the oldest English line infantry regiment in the Army. Its nickname "The Tigers" derives from an honour bestowed upon the 67th (South Hampshire) Foot in 1826 by King George IV. After 21 years of unbroken active service in India, the King authorised the adoption of a tiger sleeve badge which is worn by the Regiment to this day.

REGIMENTAL MUSEUMS

QUEEN'S ROYAL SURREY REGIMENT MUSEUM
Clandon Park, Guildford, Surrey GU4 7RQ
Tel: 01483 223419 Fax: 01483 223419
email: qrsregimentalmuseum@btconnect.com
Website: www.queensroyalsurreys.org.uk

THE BUFFS, ROYAL EAST KENT REGIMENT COLLECTION
Royal Museum and Art Gallery, 18 High Street, Canterbury, Kent CT1 2RA
Tel: 01227 452747 Fax: 01227 455047
email: martin.crowther@canterbury.gov.uk

QUEEN'S OWN ROYAL WEST KENT REGIMENT COLLECTION
Maidstone Museum and Art Gallery, St. Faith's Street, Maidstone, Kent ME4 1LH
Tel: 01622 602838
email: qorwkmuseum@maidstone.gov.uk

ROYAL SUSSEX REGIMENT COLLECTION
The Redoubt, Royal Parade, Eastbourne, East Sussex BN22 7AQ
Tel: 01323 410300 Fax: 01323 438827
email: redoubtmuseum@eastbourne.gov.uk
Website: eastbournemuseums.co.uk

ROYAL HAMPSHIRE REGIMENT MUSEUM
Serle's House, Southgate Street, Winchester, Hampshire SO23 9EG
Tel: 01962 863658 Fax: 01962 863658
email: serieshouse@aol.com
Website: www.royalhampshireregimentmuseum.co.uk

PRINCESS OF WALES'S ROYAL REGIMENT and QUEEN'S REGIMENT MUSEUM
5 Keep Yard, Dover Castle, Dover, Kent CT16 1HU
Tel: 01304 240121 Fax: 01304 240121
email: pwrrqueensmuseum@tinyworld.co.uk
Website: www.army.mod.uk/pwrr

REGIMENTAL HEADQUARTERS

Howe Barracks, Canterbury, Kent CT1 1JY

Tel: Civ: 01227 818056 Mil: Canterbury 4256

Fax: 01227 818057

Website: www.army.mod.uk/tigers/

REGIMENTAL MARCHES

Quick March: The Farmer's Boy leading into The Soldiers of the Queen

Slow March: The Minden Rose

ALLIANCES

Canadian Armed Forces:
The Queen's York Rangers
(1st American Regiment) RCAC
The South Alberta Light Horse (RCAC)
The Queen's Own Rifles of Canada
The Hastings and Prince Edward Regiment
1st Battalion The Royal New Brunswick Regiment (Carleton and York)
The Essex and Kent Scottish
49th (Sault Ste Marie) Field Artillery Regiment RCA

Australian Military Forces:
The Royal New South Wales Regiment
The Royal Western Australia Regiment
The University of New South Wales Regiment

New Zealand Army:
2nd Battalion (Canterbury, Nelson, Marlborough and West Coast) The Royal New Zealand Infantry Regiment
5th Battalion (Wellington, West Coast and Taranaki) The Royal New Zealand Infantry Regiment

Pakistan Army:
12th, 14th, 15th and 17th Battalions The Punjab Regiment

COLONEL-IN-CHIEF

HM Queen Margrethe II of Denmark

BATTLE HONOURS

THE QUEEN'S ROYAL REGIMENT (West Surrey)

THE EAST SURREY REGIMENT

THE BUFFS (Royal East Kent Regiment)

THE QUEEN'S OWN (Royal West Kent Regiment)

Pre-1914:

Tangier, 1662-1680; Namur, 1695;
Naval Crown, 1st June 1794; Egypt (Sphinx) [1801];
Vimiera [1808]; **Corunna** [1809]; **Salamanca** [1812];
Peninsula [1808-14]; **Nivelle** [1813]; **Pyrenees** [1813];
Vittoria [1813]; **Toulouse** [1814]; **Afghanistan, 1839;**
Ghuznee, 1839; Khelat [1839]; **South Africa, 1851-53;**
Pekin, 1860; Taku Forts [1860]; **Burmah, 1885-1887;**
Tirah [1897-98]; **South Africa, 1899-1902;**
Relief of Ladysmith [1900].

First World War:

Mons; **Retreat from Mons;** Marne 1914, 18; Aisne 1914;
Ypres 1914, 17, 18; Langemarck 1914; Gheluvelt;
Aubers; Festubert 1915; Loos; **Somme 1916, 18;**
Albert 1916, 18; Bazentin; Delville Wood; Pozières;
Guillemont; Flers-Courcelette; Morval; Thiepval;
Le Transloy; Ancre Heights; Ancre 1916, 18;
Arras 1917, 18; Scarpe 1917; Bullecourt;
Messines 1917; Pilckem; Menin Road; Polygon Wood;
Broodseinde; Passchendaele; Cambrai 1917, 18;
St. Quentin; Bapaume 1918; Rosières; Avre;
Villers Bretonneux; Lys; Hazebrouck; Bailleul; Kemmel;
Soissonnais-Ourcq; Amiens; Hindenburg Line; Epéhy;
St. Quentin Canal; Courtrai; Selle; Sambre;
France and Flanders 1914-18; Piave; **Vittorio Veneto;**
Italy 1917, 18; Suvla; Landing at Suvla; Scimitar Hill;
Gallipoli 1915; Rumani; Egypt 1915, 16; Gaza;
El Mughar; Jerusalem; Jericho; Tell Asur;
Palestine 1917-18; Khan Baghdadi; **Mesopotamia 1915-16; N.W. Frontier India 1916-17.**

Second World War:

Defence of Escaut; **Villers Bocage;** Mont Pincon;
Lower Maas; Roer; North-West Europe 1940, 44-45;
Syria 1941; Sidi Barrani; **Tobruk 1941;** Tobruk Sortie;
Deir el Munasib; **El Alamein;** Advance on Tripoli;
Medenine; Tunis; North Africa 1940-43; **Salerno;**
Monte Stella; Scafati Bridge; Volturno Crossing;
Monte Camino; Garigliano Crossing; Damiano; **Anzio;**
Gothic Line; **Gemmano Ridge;** Senio Pocket;
Senio Floodbank; Casa Fabbri Ridge; Menate; Filo;
Argenta Gap; Italy 1943-45; **North Arakan; Kohima;**
Yenangyaung 1945; Sittang 1945; Chindits 1944;
Burma 1943-45.

Pre-1914:

Gibraltar, 1704-5; **Dettingen** [1743]; **Martinique, 1794;**
Peninsula [1808-14]; **Talavera** [1809];
Guadeloupe, 1810; Albuhera [1811]; **Nive** [1813];
Nivelle [1813]; **Pyrenees** [1813]; **Vittoria** [1813];
Orthes [1814]; **Candahar, 1842; Ferozeshah** [1845];
Moodkee [1845]; **Aliwal** [1846]; **Sobraon** [1846];
Sevastopol [1854-55]; **Taku Forts** [1860];
New Zealand [1863-66]; **Afghanistan, 1878-1879;**
Suakin, 1885; South Africa, 1899-1902;
Relief of Ladysmith [1900].

First World War:

Mons; Le Cateau; Retreat from Mons; **Marne 1914;**
Aisne 1914; La Bassée 1914; Armentières 1914; Hill 60;
Ypres 1915, 17, 18; Gravenstafel; St. Julien;
Frezenberg; Bellewaarde; **Loos. Somme 1916, 18;**
Albert 1916, 18; Bazentin; Delville Wood; Pozières;
Guillemont; Flers-Courcelette; Morval; Thiepval;
Le Transloy; Ancre Heights; Ancre 1916; Arras 1917, 18;
Vimy 1917; Scarpe 1917; Messines 1917; Pilckem;
Langemarck 1917; Menin Road; Polygon Wood;
Broodseinde; Poelcapelle; Passchendaele;
Cambrai 1917, 18; St. Quentin; Bapaume 1918;
Rosières; Avre; Lys; Estaires; Hazebrouck; Amiens;
Hindenburg Line; Epéhy; Canal du Nord;
St. Quentin Canal; Courtrai; **Selle;** Sambre;
France and Flanders 1914-18; Italy 1917-18; Struma;
Doiran 1918; Macedonia 1915-18; Egypt 1915; Aden;
Mesopotamia 1917-18; Murman 1919.

Second World War:

Defence of Escaut; **Dunkirk 1940;**
North-West Europe 1940; Tebourba; Fort McGregor;
Oued Zarga; Djebel Ang; Jebel Djaffa Pass;
Medjez Plain; **Longstop Hill 1943;** Tunis; Montarnaud;
North Africa 1942-43; Adrano; Centuripe; **Sicily 1943;**
Trigno; **Sangro; Cassino;** Capture of Forli; Argenta Gap;
Italy 1943-45; Greece 1944-45; Kampar;
Malaya 1941-42.

Pre-1914:

Blenheim [1704]; **Ramillies** [1706]; **Oudenarde** [1708];
Malplaquet [1709]; **Dettingen** [1743];
Guadeloupe, 1759; Belleisle [1761];
Peninsula [1808-14]; **Douro** [1809]; **Talavera** [1809];
Nive [1813]; **Nivelle** [1813]; **Pyrenees** [1813];
Vittoria [1813]; **Orthes** [1814]; **Toulouse** [1814];
Punniar [1843]; **Sevastopol** [1854-55];
Taku Forts [1860]; **South Africa, 1879; Chitral** [1895];
Relief of Kimberley [1900]; **Paardeberg** [1900];
South Africa, 1900-02.

First World War:

Aisne 1914; **Armentières 1914; Ypres 1915, 17;**
Gravenstafel; St. Julien; Frezenberg; Bellewaarde;
Hooge 1915; **Loos; Somme 1916, 18;** Albert 1916, 18;
Bazentin; Delville Wood; Pozières; Flers-Courcelette;
Morval; Thiepval; Le Transloy; Ancre Heights;
Ancre 1916, 18; **Arras 1917;** Scarpe 1917; Pilckem;
Messines 1917; **Menin Road; Passchendaele;**
Cambrai 1917, 18; St. Quentin; Avre; **Amiens;**
Bapaume 1918; **Hindenburg Line;** Epéhy;
St. Quentin Canal; Selle; Sambre;
France and Flanders 1914-18; **Struma;** Doiran 1918;
Macedonia 1915-18; Gaza; **Jerusalem;** Tell'Asur;
Palestine 1917-18; Aden; Tigris 1916;
Kut al Amara 1917; **Baghdad;** Mesopotamia 1915-18.

Second World War:

Defence of Escaut; St. Omer-La Bassée;
Withdrawal to Seine; **North-West Europe 1940;**
Sidi Suleiman; **Alem Hamza;** Alam el Halfa; **El Alamein;**
El Agheila; Advance on Tripoli; Tebaga Gap; El Hamma;
Akarit; Djebel Azzag 1943; **Robaa Valley;** Djebel Bech;
Heidows; Medjez Plain; Longstop Hill 1943;
North Africa 1941-43; Centuripe; Monte Rivoglia;
Sicily 1943; Termoli; **Trigno;** Sangro; **Anzio;** Cassino I;
Liri Valley; Aquino; Rome; Trasimene Line; Coriano;
Monte Spaduro; Senio; **Argenta Gap;** Italy 1943-45;
Leros; Middle East 1943; Malta 1940-42; **Shweli;**
Myitson; Burma 1945.

Pre-1914:

Egypt (Sphinx) [1801]; Vimiera [1808];
Peninsula [1808-14]; **Corunna** [1809]; **Almaraz** [181.
Nive [1813]; **Pyrenees** [1813]; **Vittoria** [1813];
Orthes [1814]; **Punniar** [1843]; **Ferozeshah** [1845];
Moodkee [1845]; **Aliwal** [1846]; **Sobraon** [1846];
Alma [1854]; **Sevastopol** [1854-55];
Lucknow [1857-58]; **New Zealand** [1863-66]; South Africa, 1900-0
Egypt, 1882-84; **Nile, 1884-85; South Africa, 1900-0**

First World War:

Mons; Le Cateau; Retreat from Mons; Marne 1914;
Aisne 1914; La Bassée 1914; Messines 1914, 17;
Ypres 1914, 15, 17, 18; Hill 60; Gravenstafel; St. Juli
Frezenberg; Loos; **Somme 1916, 18;** Albert 1916, 18;
Bazentin; Delville Wood; Pozières; Guillemont;
Flers-Courcelette; Morval; Thiepval; Le Transloy;
Ancre Heights; Ancre 1916, 18; Arras 1917, 18;
Vimy 1917; Scarpe 1917; Oppy; Pilckem;
Langemarck 1917; Menin Road; Polygon Wood;
Broodseinde; Passchendaele; Cambrai 1917, 18;
St. Quentin; Rosières; Avre; Betonneux; Lys;
Hazebrouck; Kemmel; Amiens; Bapaume 1918;
Hindenburg Line; Epéhy; Canal du Nord;
St. Quentin Canal; Courtrai; Selle; Sambre;
France and Flanders 1914-18; **Italy 1917-18;** Suvla;
Landing at Suvla; Scimitar Hill; **Gallipoli 1915;** Ruma
Egypt 1915-16; **Gaza;** El Mughar; Jerusalem; Jericho
Tell Asur; Palestine 1917-18; **Defence of Kut al Ama**
Sharqat; Mesopotamia 1915-18.

Afghanistan 1919.

Second World War:

Defence of Escaut; Foret de Nieppe;
North-West Europe 1940; Alam el Halfa; **El Alamein**
Djebel Abiod; Djebel Azzag 1942; Oued Zarga;
Djebel Ang; **Medjez Plain;** Longstop Hill 1943;
Si Abdallah; North Africa 1942-43; **Centuripe;**
Monte Rivoglia; Sicily 1943; Termoli; San Salvo; **Sang**
Romagnoli; Impossible Bridge; Villa Grande; **Cass**
Castle Hill; Liri Valley; Piedimonte Hill; **Trasimene L**
Arezzo; Advance to Florence; Monte Scalari; Casa Fo
Rimini Line; Savio Bridgehead; Monte Planoerino;
Monte Spaduro; Senio; **Argenta Gap;** Italy 1943-45;
Greece 1944-45; Leros; **Malta 1940-42;** North Arakan
Rzabil; Mayu Tunnels; **Defence of Kohima;** Taungth
Sittang 1945; Burma 1943-45.

BATTLE HONOURS

THE ROYAL SUSSEX REGIMENT

Pre-1914:

..altar, 1704-5; **Louisburg** [1758]; **Quebec** [1759]; ..annah [1762]; **Martinique, 1762; St. Lucia, 1778;** ..la [1806]; **Egypt, 1882-84; Nile, 1884-85;** .. **Klea** [1885]; **South Africa, 1900-02.**

First World War:

..s; **Retreat from Mons, Marne 1914,18;** Aisne 1914; ..s **1914, 17, 18;** Gheluvelt; Nonne Bosschen; ..nchy 1914; Aubers. Loos; **Somme 1916, 18;** ..rt 1916, 18; Bazentin; Delville Wood; Pozières; ..-Courcelette; Morval; Thiepval; Le Transloy; ..e Heights; Ancre 1916, 18; Arras 1917, 18; .. 1917; Scarpe 1917; Arleux; Messines 1917; ..kem; Langemarck 1917; Menin Road; ..gon Wood; Broodseinde; Poelcapelle; ..schendaele; Cambrai 1917, 18; St. Quentin; ..aume 1918; Rosières; Avre; Lys; Kemmel; ..ce and Flanders 1914-18; Piave; Vittorio Veneto; ..erpenberg; Soissonnais-Ourcq; Amiens; ..ourt-Quéant; **Hindenburg Line;** Epéhy; ..uentin Canal; Beaurevoir; Courtrai; Selle; Sambre; ..ce and Flanders 1914-18; Piave; Vittorio Veneto; .. 1917-18; Suvla; Landing at Suvla; Scimitar Hill; ..poli 1915; Rumani; Egypt 1915-17; Gaza; ..ughar; Jerusalem; Jericho; Tell Asur; ..stine 1917-18; **N.W. Frontier India 1915, 1916-17;** ..man 1918-19.

..anistan 1919.

Second World War:

..nce of Escaut; Amiens 1940; St. Omer-La Bassée; ..t de Nieppe; **North-West Europe 1940;** ..ra-Marsa Taclai; Cubcub; Mescelit Pass; Keren; ..Engiahat; Massawa; **Abyssinia 1941; Omars;** ..ghazi; **Alam el Halfa; El Alamein; Akarit;** ..el Meida; Tunis; **North Africa 1940-43;** ..sino II; Monastery Hill; Gothic Line; Pian di Castello; ..e Reggiano; **Italy 1944-45;** North Arakan; Pinwe; ..eli; **Burma 1943-45.**

THE MIDDLESEX REGIMENT (Duke of Cambridge's Own)

Pre-1914:

Mysore [1789-91]; **Seringapatam** [1799]; **Peninsula** [1808-14]; **Albuhera** [1811]; **Badajos** [1812]; **Ciudad Rodrigo** [1812]; **Nive** [1813]; **Nivelle** [1813]; **Pyrenees** [1813]; **Vittoria** [1813]; **Alma** [1854]; **Inkerman** [1854]; **Sevastopol** [1854-55]; **New Zealand** [1860-61]; **South Africa, 1879; South Africa, 1900-02.**

First World War:

Mons; Le Cateau; Retreat from Mons; **Marne 1914;** Aisne 1914, 18; La Bassée 1914; Messines 1914, 17, 18; Armentières 1914; Neuve Chapelle; **Ypres 1915, 17, 18;** Gravenstafel; St. Julien; Frezenberg; Bellewaarde; Aubers; Hooge 1915; Loos; Somme 1916, 18; **Albert 1916, 18; Bazentin;** Delville Wood; Pozières; Ginchy; Flers-Courcelette; Morval; Thiepval; Le Transloy; Ancre Heights; Ancre 1916, 18; Bapaume 1918; Arras 1917, 18; Vimy 1917; Scarpe 1917, 18; Arleux; Pilckem; Langemarck 1917; Menin Road; Polygon Wood; Broodseinde; Poelcapelle; Passchendaele; **Cambrai 1917, 18;** St. Quentin; Rosières; Avre; Villers Bretonneux; Lys; Estaires; Hazebrouck; Bailleul; Kemmel; Scherpenberg; **Hindenburg Line;** Canal du Nord; St. Quentin Canal; Courtrai; Selle; Valenciennes; Sambre; France and Flanders 1914-18; Italy 1917-18; Struma; Doiran 1918; Macedonia 1915-18; **Suvla;** Landing at Suvla; Scimitar Hill; Gallipoli 1915; Rumani; Egypt 1915-17; Gaza; El Mughar; **Jerusalem;** Jericho; Jordan; Tell Asur; Palestine 1917-18; **Mesopotamia 1917-18;** Murman 1919; Dukhovskaya; Siberia 1918-19.

Second World War:

Dyle; Defence of Escaut; Ypres-Comines Canal; **Dunkirk 1940; Normandy Landing;** Cambes; Breville; Odon; **Caen;** Orne; Hill 112; Bourguebus Ridge; Troarn; **Mont Pincon;** Falaise; Seine 1944; Nederrijn; Le Havre; Lower Maas; Venraij; Meijel; Geilenkirchen; Venlo Pocket; Rhineland; Reichswald; Goch; **Rhine;** Lingen; Brinkum; Bremen; North-West Europe 1940, 40-45; **El Alamein;** Advance on Tripoli; Mareth; **Akarit;** Djebel Roumana; North Africa 1942-43; Francofonte; Sferro; Sferro Hills; **Sicily 1943; Anzio;** Carroceto; Gothic Line; Monte Grande; Italy 1944-45; **Hong Kong;** South-East Asia 1941.

THE ROYAL HAMPSHIRE REGIMENT

Pre-1914:

Blenheim [1704]; **Ramillies** [1706]; **Oudenarde** [1708]; **Malplaquet** [1709]; **Dettingen** [1743]; **Minden** [1759]; **Belleisle** [1761]; **Tournay** [1794]; **India** [1796-1826]; **Peninsula** [1808-14]; **Barrosa** [1811]; **Pekin, 1860; Taku Forts** [1860]; **Afghanistan, 1878-1880; Charasiah** [1879]; **Kabul** [1879]; **Burmah, 1885-1887; Paardeberg** [1900]; **South Africa, 1900-02.**

First World War:

Le Cateau; **Retreat from Mons;** Marne 1914, 18; Aisne 1914; Armentières 1914; **Ypres 1915, 17, 18;** St. Julien; Frezenberg; Bellewaarde; **Somme 1916, 18;** Albert 1916; Guillemont; Ginchy; Flers-Courcelette; Thiepval; Le Transloy; Ancre Heights; Ancre 1916; **Arras 1917, 18;** Vimy 1917; Scarpe 1917, 18; Messines 1917; Pilckem; Langemarck 1917; Menin Road; Polygon Wood; Broodseinde; Poelcapelle; Passchendaele; **Cambrai 1917, 18;** St. Quentin;

Bapaume 1918; Rosières; Lys; Estaires; Hazebrouck; Bailleul; Kemmel; Béthune; Tardenois; Drocourt-Quéant; Hindenburg Line; Havrincourt; Canal du Nord; Courtrai; Selle; Valenciennes; Sambre; France and Flanders 1914-18; Italy 1917-18; Kosturino; Struma; **Doiran 1917, 18;** Macedonia 1915-18; Helles; **Landing at Helles;** Krithia; **Suvla;** Sari Bair; Landing at Suvla; Scimitar Hill; Gallipoli 1915-16; Egypt 1915-17; **Gaza;** El Mughar; Nebi Samwil; Jerusalem; Jaffa; Tell Asur; Megiddo; Sharon; Palestine 1917-18; Aden; Shaiba; **Kut al Amara 1915, 17;** Tigris 1916; Baghdad; Sharqat; Mesopotamia 1915-18; Persia 1918-19; Archangel 1919; Siberia 1918-19.

Second World War:

Dunkirk 1940; Normandy Landing; Tilly sur Seulles; **Caen;** Hill 122; Mont Pincon; Jurques; St. Pierre la Vielle; Nederrijn; Roer; Rhineland; Goch; **Rhine;** North-West Europe 1940, 44-45; **Tebourba Gap;** Sidi Nsir; **Hunt's Gap;** Montagne Farm; Fondouk; Pichon; El Kourzia; Ber Rabai; North Africa 1940-43; Landing in Sicily; Regalbuto; Sicily 1943; Landing at Porto san Venere; **Salerno;** Salerno Hills; Battipaglia; Cava di Tirreni; Volturno Crossing; Garigliano Crossing; Damiano; Monte Ornito; Cerasola; **Cassino II;** Massa Vertecchi; Trasimene Line; Advance to Florence; **Gothic Line;** Monte Gridolfo; Montegaudio; Coriano; Montilgallo; Capture of Forli; Cosina Canal Crossing; Lamone Crossing; Pideura; Rimini Line; Montescudo; Frisoni; Italy 1943-45; Athens; Greece 1944-45; **Malta 1941-42.**

Post-1945:

THE MIDDLESEX REGIMENT (Duke of Cambridge's Own)

Naktong Bridgehead; Chongju; Chongchon II; Chaum-ni; Kapyong-chon; Kapyong; **Korea 1950-51.**

THE PRINCESS OF WALES'S ROYAL REGIMENT (Queen's and Royal Hampshires)

1674
Clare's Irish Regiment (1)

1688
Lloyd's Regiment (2)

5th

1747
5th Regiment of Foot

1751
5th (Northumberland)
Regiment of Foot

1836
5th Regiment of Foot
(Northumberland
Fusiliers)

1881
The Northumberland
Fusiliers

NOTES

(1) Raised in Holland by Lord Clare for Dutch service.

In 1675 ranked as the 1st English Regiment in Dutch service. Adopted St. George and the Dragon as regimental badge.

Recalled to English service during Monmouth's Rebellion in 1685.

(2) Later Tollemache's.

1674
Lillington's English
Regiment (3)

1688
Babington's Regiment (4)

6th

1747
6th Regiment of Foot

1782
6th (1st Warwickshire)
Regiment of Foot

1832
6th (Royal
1st Warwickshire)
Regiment of Foot

1881
The Royal Warwickshire
Regiment

NOTES

(3) Raised in Holland by Sir Walter Vane for Dutch service.

Recalled to English service during Monmouth's Rebellion in 1685.

(4) Taken on to the British Establishment in 1688 as Babington's Regiment.

1685
The Ordnance
Regiment (5)

1686
The Royal Regiment of
Fuziliers

7th

1747
7th Regiment of Foot
The Royal English
Fuziliers

1751
7th Regiment of Foot
(The Royal Fuziliers)

NOTES

(5) Raised by Lord Dartmouth from Tower of London guards during Monmouth's Rebellion. The name reflects the early role of fusiliers in guarding the artillery train on the march.

1688
Peyton's Regiment of
Foot (6)

1699
Peyton's Regiment of
Fuziliers

20th

1751
20th Regiment of Foot (7)

1782
20th (East Devonshire)
Regiment of Foot

NOTES

(6) Raised in Exeter [by] Sir Robert Peyton f[or] service under Willia[m] of Orange.

James Wolfe was commissioned into t[he] Regiment in 1742 a[nd] later commanded i[t.]

(7) Known at the tim[e] as Kingsley's Regiment.

1935
**THE ROYAL
NORTHUMBERLAND
FUSILIERS**

1963
**THE ROYAL
WARWICKSHIRE
FUSILIERS**

1881
THE ROYAL FUSILIERS
(City of London Regiment)

1881
**THE LANCASHIRE
FUSILIERS**

**1st
BATTALION** **2nd
BATTALION** **3rd
BATTALION** **4th
BATTALION**

1968
**THE ROYAL REGIMENT
OF FUSILIERS**

In **1969** the **4th Battalion** was disbanded and its personnel merged into the remaining three battalions.

In **1992** the **3rd Battalion** was disbanded and its personnel merged into the remaining two battalions.

REGIMENTAL HEADQUARTERS

HM Tower of London, Tower Hill, London
EC3N 4AB
Tel: Civ. 0203 166 6909 London Mil. 6909
Fax. 0203 166 6920
email: rhq@thefusiliers.org.uk
Website: www.thefusiliers.org

REGIMENTAL MARCHES

Quick March: The British Grenadiers

Slow Marches: Rule Britannia, De Normandie
St. George (Northumberland)
Macbean's Slow March (Warwickshire)
De Normandie (London)
The former Lancashire Fusiliers' slow march

ALLIANCES

Canadian Armed Forces:
The Royal Canadian Regiment
The Lorne Scots (Peel, Dufferin and Halton Regim[ent])
31 Combat Engineer Regiment (The Elgins)
The Royal Westminster Regiment
Les Fusiliers du St. Laurent

Australian Military Forces:
5th/6th Battalion The Royal Victoria Regiment

New Zealand Army:
The Hauraki Regiment

COLONEL-IN-CHIEF

Field Marshal HRH The Duke of Kent
KG, GCMG, GCVO, ADC

BATTLE HONOURS

THE ROYAL NORTHUMBERLAND FUSILIERS

Pre-1914:

Wilhelmstahl [1762]; **St. Lucia, 1778**; Vimiera [1804]; Rolica [1808]; **Peninsula** [1808-14]; **Corunna** [1809]; Busaco [1810]; **Ciudad Rodrigo** [1812]; Salamanca [1812]; **Nivelle** [1813]; **Vittoria** [1813]; Orthes [1814]; **Toulouse** [1814]; **Lucknow** [1857-58]; **Afghanistan, 1878-1880; Khartoum** [1898]; **Modder River** [1899]; **South Africa, 1899-1902.**

First World War:

Mons; Le Cateau; Retreat from Mons; **Marne 1914;** Aisne 1914,18; La Bassée 1914; Messines 1914, 17, 18; Armentières 1914; **Ypres 1914, 15, 17, 18;** Nonne Bosschen; Gravenstafel; **St. Julien;** Frezenberg; Bellewaarde; Loos; **Somme 1916, 18;** Albert 1916, 18; Bazentin; Delville Wood; Pozières; Morval; Thiepval; Le Transloy; Ancre Heights; Ancre 1916; Arras 1917, 18; **Scarpe 1917, 18;** Arleux; Pilckem; Langemarck 1917; Menin Road; Polygon Wood; Broodseinde; Passchendaele; Cambrai 1917, 18; St. Quentin; Bapaume 1918; Rosières; Lys; Estaires; Hazebrouck; Bailleul; Kemmel; Béthune; Scherpenberg; Drocourt-Quéant; Hindenburg Line; Epéhy; Selle; Valenciennes; Sambre; France and Flanders 1914-18; **Piave;** Vittorio Veneto; Italy 1917,18; **Struma;** Macedonia 1915-18; **Suvla;** Landing at Suvla; Scimitar Hill; Gallipoli 1915; Egypt 1916-17.

Second World War:

Defence of Escaut; Arras counter attack; St. Omer-La Bassée; **Dunkirk 1940;** Odon; **Caen;** Cagny; Falaise; Nederrijn; **Rhineland;** North-West Europe 1940, 44-45; **Sidi Barrani; Defence of Tobruk; Tobruk 1941;** Belhamed; Gauldron; Ruweisat Ridge; **El Alamein;** Advance on Tripoli; Medenine; North Africa 1940-43; **Salerno;** Volturno Crossing; Monte Camino; Garigliano Crossing; **Cassino II;** Italy 1943-45; Singapore Island.

Post-1945:

Seoul; **Imjin;** Kowang-San; **Korea 1950-51.**

THE ROYAL WARWICKSHIRE FUSILIERS

Pre-1914:

Namur, 1695; Martinique, 1794; Vimiera [1804]; **Peninsula** [1808-14]; **Rolica** [1808]; **Corunna** [1809]; **Niagara** [1813]; **Pyrenees** [1813]; **Vittoria** [1813]; **Orthes** [1814]; **South Africa, 1846-47; South Africa, 1851-53; Atbara** [1898]; **Khartoum** [1898]; **South Africa, 1899-1902.**

First World War:

Le Cateau; Retreat from Mons; **Marne 1914;** Aisne 1914, 18; Armentières 1914; Ypres 1914, 15, 17; Langemarck 1914, 17; Gheluvelt; Neuve Chapelle; St. Julien; Frezenberg; Bellewaarde; Aubers; Festubert 1915; Loos; **Somme 1916, 18;** Albert 1916, 18; Bazentin; Delville Wood; Pozières; Guillemont; Flers-Courcelette; Morval; Le Transloy; Ancre Heights; Ancre 1916; **Arras 1917, 18;** Vimy 1917; Scarpe 1917, 18; Arleux; Oppy; Bullecourt; Messines 1917, 18; Pilckem; Menin Road; Polygon Wood; Broodseinde; Poelcapelle; Passchendaele; Cambrai 1917, 18; St. Quentin; Bapaume 1918; Rosières; **Lys;** Estaires; Hazebrouck; Bailleul; Kemmel; Béthune; Drocourt-Quéant; **Hindenburg Line;** Epéhy; Canal du Nord; Beaurevoir; Selle; Valenciennes; Sambre; France and Flanders 1914-18; **Piave;** Vittorio Veneto; Italy 1917-18; Suvla; **Sari Bair;** Gallipoli 1915-16; Tigris 1916; Kut al Amara 1917; **Baghdad;** Mesopotamia 1916-18; Baku; Persia 1918.

Second World War:

Defence of Escaut; **Wormhoudt; Ypres-Comines Canal; Normandy Landing; Caen;** Bourguebus Ridge; **Mont Pincon;** Falaise; **Venrail;** Rhineland; Lingen; Brinkum; **Bremen; North-West Europe 1940, 44-45; Burma 1945.**

THE ROYAL FUSILIERS (CITY OF LONDON REGIMENT)

Pre-1914:

Namur, 1695; Peninsula [1808-14]; **Martinique** [1809]; **Talavera** [1809]; **Busaco** [1810]; **Albuhera** [1811]; **Badajos** [1812]; **Salamanca** [1812]; **Pyrenees** [1813]; **Vittoria** [1813]; **Orthes** [1814]; **Toulouse** [1814]; **Alma** [1854]; **Inkerman** [1854]; **Sevastapol** [1854-55]; **Afghanistan, 1879-1880; Kandahar, 1880; South Africa, 1899-1902; Relief of Ladysmith** [1900].

First World War:

Mons; Le Cateau; Retreat from Mons; **Marne 1914;** Aisne 1914; La Bassée 1914; Messines 1914, 17; Armentières 1914; **Ypres 1914, 15, 17, 18;** Nonne Bosschen; Gravenstafel; St. Julien; Frezenberg; Bellewaarde; Hooge 1915; Loos; **Somme 1916, 18;** Albert 1916, 18; Bazentin; Delville Wood; Pozières; Flers-Courcelette; Thiepval; Le Transloy; Ancre Heights; Ancre 1916, 18; **Arras 1917, 18;** Vimy 1917; Scarpe 1917; Arleux; Pilckem; Langemarck 1917; Menin Road; Polygon Wood; Broodseinde; Poelcapelle; Passchendaele; Cambrai 1917, 18; St. Quentin; Bapaume 1918; Rosières; Avre; Villers Bretonneux; Lys; Estaires; Hazebrouck; Béthune; Amiens; Drocourt-Quéant; **Hindenburg Line;** Havrincourt; Epéhy; Canal du Nord; St. Quentin Canal; Beaurevoir; Courtrai; Selle; Sambre; France and Flanders 1914-18; Italy 1917-18; **Struma;** Macedonia 1915-18; Helles; **Landing at Helles;** Krithia; Suvla; Scimitar Hill; Gallipoli 1915-16; Egypt 1916; Megiddo; Nablus; **Palestine 1918;** Troitsa; Archangel 1919; Kilimanjaro; Behobeho; Nyango; East Africa 1915-17.

Second World War:

Dunkirk 1940; North-West Europe 1940; Agordat; **Keren;** Syria 1941; Sidi Barrani; Djebel Tebaga; Peters Corner; **North Africa 1940, 43;** Sangro; **Mozzagrogna;** Caldari; **Salerno;** St. Lucia; Battipaglia; Teano; Monte Camino; **Gragliano Crossing;** Damiano; **Anzio; Cassino II;** Ripa Ridge; Gabbiano; Advance to Florence; Monte Scalari; **Gothic Line; Coriano;** Croce; Casa Fortis; Savio Bridgehead; Valli di Comacchio; Senio; Argenta Gap; Italy 1943-45; Athens; Greece 1944-45.

Post-1945:

Korea 1952-53.

THE LANCASHIRE FUSILIERS

Pre-1914:

Dettingen [1743]; **Minden** [1759]; **Egmont-op-Zee** [1799]; **Vimiera** [1804]; **Maida** [1806]; **Peninsula** [1808-14]; **Corunna** [1809]; **Pyrenees** [1813]; **Vittoria** [1813]; **Orthes** [1814]; **Toulouse** [1814]; **Alma** [1854]; **Inkerman** [1854]; **Sevastapol** [1854-55]; **Lucknow** [1857-58]; **Khartoum** [1898]; **South Africa, 1899-1902; Relief of Ladysmith** [1900].

First World War:

Le Cateau; **Retreat from Mons;** Marne 1914; **Aisne 1914, 18;** Armentières 1914; **Ypres 1915, 17, 18;** St. Julien; Bellewaarde; **Somme 1916, 18;** Albert 1916, 18; Bazentin; Delville Wood; Pozières; Ginchy; Flers-Courcelette; Moeval; Thiepval; Le Transloy; Ancre Heights; Ancre 1916, 18; **Arras 1917, 18;** Scarpe 1917, 18; Arleux; Messines 1917; Pilckem; Langemarck 1917; Menin Road; Polygon Wood; Broodseinde; Poelcapelle; **Passchendaele; Cambrai 1917, 18;** St. Quentin; Bapaume 1918; Rosières; Lys; Estaires; Hazebrouck; Bailleul; Kemmel; Béthune; Scherpenberg; Amiens; Drocourt-Quéant; **Hindenburg Line;** Epéhy; Canal du Nord; St. Quentin Canal; Courtrai; Selle; Sambre; France and Flanders 1914-18; Doiran 1917; **Macedonia 1915-18;** Helles; **Landing at Helles;** Krithia; Suvla; Landing at Suvla; Scimitar Hill; Gallipoli 1915; Rumani; Egypt 1915-17.

Second World War:

Defence of Escaut; St. Omer-La Bassée; **Caen;** North-West Europe 1940, 44; **Medjez el Bab;** Oued Zarga; North Africa 1942-43; Adrano; Sicily 1943; Termoli; Trigno; **Sangro; Cassino II;** Trasimene Line; Monte Ceco; Monte Spaduro; Senio; **Argenta Gap;** Italy 1943-45; **Malta 1941-42;** Rathedaung; Htizwe; **Kohima;** Naga Village; **Chindits 1944; Burma 1943-45.**

THE ROYAL REGIMENT OF FUSILIERS

Wadi al Batin; **Gulf 1991;** Al Basrah; **Iraq 2003.**

1685
Cornwall's Regiment
of Foot (1)

9th

1751
9th Regiment of Foot

1782
9th (East Norfolk)
Regiment of Foot

1881
The Norfolk Regiment

NOTES

(1) Raised in Gloucester
and south-west England
by Colonel Henry
Cornwall.

The Britannia badge was
granted to the Regiment
in 1707 by Queen Anne
in recognition of good
service in Spain

1685
The Duke of Norfolk's
Regiment of Foot (2)

1686
The Earl of Lichfield's
Regiment of Foot

12th

1751
12th Regiment of Foot

1782
12th (East Suffolk)
Regiment of Foot

NOTES

(2) Raised in East Anglia
by the Duke of Norfolk.

1685
Granville's Regiment
of Foot (3)

10th

1751
10th Regiment of Foot

1782
10th (North Lincolnshire)
Regiment of Foot

1881
The Lincolnshire
Regiment

NOTES

(3) Raised largely in
Plymouth by John
Granville, Earl of Bath.
Served as marines until
1742.

(4) Raised in Norwich by
Colonel Hon. James
Cholmondeley.

(5) Raised in the south-
west of England by Sir
Robert Anstruther mainly
from the 12th and 37th
Foot

1741
Cholmondeley's
Regiment of Foot (4)

1747
59th Regiment of Foot

48th

1751
48th Regiment of Foot

1782
48th (Northamptonshire)
Regiment of Foot

1755
60th Regiment of Foot (5)

58th

1757
58th Regiment of Foot

1782
58th (Rutlandshire)
Regiment of Foot

1935
THE ROYAL NORFOLK REGIMENT

1881
THE SUFFOLK REGIMENT

1946
THE ROYAL LINCOLNSHIRE REGIMENT

1881
THE NORTHAMPTONSHIRE REGIMENT

1959
1st Battalion
1st EAST ANGLIAN REGIMENT
(Royal Norfolk and Suffolk)
EAST ANGLIAN BRIGADE

1960
1st Battalion
2nd EAST ANGLIAN REGIMENT
(Duchess of Gloucester's Own Royal Lincolnshire and Northamptonshire)
EAST ANGLIAN BRIGADE

GIBRALTAR

The Castle and Key of Gibraltar which feature in the cap badge of the Royal Anglian Regiment and some of its antecedents commemorates the involvement of the Suffolk, Essex and Northamptonshire Regiments in the Great Siege of Gibraltar 1779-83.

This shared tradition is a strong unifying link within today's Regiment and strengthens its Alliance with the Royal Gibraltar Regiment, and its inclusion, for administrative purposes, in the Queen's Division.

1688
Douglas's Regiment of Foot (6)

16th

1751
16th Regiment of Foot

1782
16th (Buckinghamshire) Regiment of Foot

1809
16th (Bedfordshire) (7) Regiment of Foot

1881
The Bedfordshire Regiment

NOTES

(6) Raised in the southern counties by Colonel Archibald Douglas for service with King James II(VII). Douglas was replaced one month later by a supporter of William of Orange.

(7) By a swop of county designations with the 14th Foot.

(8) Raised in the southern counties by Colonel James Long.

1741
Long's Regiment of Foot (8)

1747
55th Regiment of Foot

44th

1751
44th Regiment of Foot

1782
44th (East Essex) Regiment of Foot

1756
58th Regiment of Foot (9)

56th

1757
56th Regiment of Foot (10)

1782
56th (West Essex) Regiment of Foot

NOTES

(9) Raised in the north by Lord Charles Manners.

(10) Long known as "The Pompadours" from the colour of their uniform facings — said to be the favourite colour of Madame de Pompadour. The title was retained by the 3rd Battalion Royal Anglian until its disbandment in 1992.

(11) Raised in London by Colonel Solomon Richards for service with King James II(VII). Later changed allegiance.

1688
Richard's Regiment of Foot (11)

17th

1751
17th Regiment of Foot

1782
17th (Leicestershire) Regiment of Foot

1881
The Leicestershire Regiment

1919
THE BEDFORDSHIRE AND HERTFORDSHIRE REGIMENT

1881
THE ESSEX REGIMENT

1946
THE ROYAL LEICESTERSHIRE REGIMENT

1958
1st Battalion
3rd EAST ANGLIAN REGIMENT
(16th / 44th Foot)
EAST ANGLIAN BRIGADE

1963
THE ROYAL LEICESTERSHIRE REGIMENT
JOINED EAST ANGLIAN BRIGADE

1st BATTALION   **2nd BATTALION**   **3rd BATTALION**   **4th BATTALION**

1964
THE ROYAL ANGLIAN REGIMENT
(9, 10, 12, 16, 17, 44, 48, 56, 58)

The **4th Battalion** was disbanded in **1965** and the **3rd Battalion** in **1992** their personnel and traditions being absorbed by the remaining two battalions.

REGIMENTAL HEADQUARTERS

The Keep, Gibraltar Barracks, Bury St. Edmunds,
Suffolk IP33 3RN

Tel: Civ. 01284 752394 Mil. Bury St. Edmunds 5124

Fax: 01284 752026

email: chief-clerk@anglian.army.mod.uk

Website: www.army.mod.uk/royalanglian

REGIMENTAL MARCHES

Quick March: Rule Britannia and Speed the Plough

Slow March: Slow March of the Northamptonshire Regiment

ALLIANCES

Canadian Armed Forces:
Sherbrooke Hussars
The Lincoln and Welland Regiment
The Essex and Kent Scottish
The Lake Superior Scottish Regiment

Australian Military Forces:
The Royal Tasmania Regiment

New Zealand Army:
3rd Battalion (Auckland (Countess of Ranfurly's Own) and Northland) Royal New Zealand Infantry Regiment

Pakistan Army:
5th Battalion The Frontier Force Regiment

Malaysian Armed Forces:
1st Battalion The Royal Malay Regiment

Barbados:
The Barbados Regiment

South African Defence Forces:
First City Regiment
Regiment de la Rey

Belize:
The Belize Defence Force

Colonial Forces:
The Bermuda Regiment
The Royal Gibraltar Regiment

Royal Navy:
HMS St Albans

COLONEL-IN-CHIEF

HRH Prince Richard, Duke of Gloucester KG, GCVO

BATTLE HONOURS

THE ROYAL NORFOLK REGIMENT

Pre-1914:

Belleisle [1761]; **Havannah** [1762]; **Martinique** [1794]; **Peninsula** [1808-14]; **Vimeira** [1808]; Rolica [1808]; **Corunna** [1809]; Busaco [1810]; **Salamanca** [1812]; Nive [1813]; San Sebastian [1813]; **Vittoria** [1813]; **Cabool, 1842; Candahar, 1842; Ferozeshah** [1845]; **Moodkee** [1845]; **Sevastapol** [1854-55]; **Sobraon** [1846]; **Afghanistan, 1879-1880; Kabul, 1879; Paardeberg** [1900]; **South Africa, 1900-02.**

First World War:

Mons; Le Cateau; Retreat from Mons; **Marne 1914;** Aisne 1914; La Bassée 1914; **Ypres 1914, 15, 17, 18;** Gravenstafel; St. Julien; Frezenberg; Bellewaarde; Loos; **Somme 1916, 18;** Albert 1916, 18; Delville Wood; Pozières; Guillemont; Flers-Courcelette; Morval; Thiepval; Le Transloy; Ancre Heights; Ancre 1916, 18; Arras 1917; Vimy 1917; Scarpe 1917; Arleux; Oppy; Pilckem; Langemarck 1917; Polygon Wood; Broodseinde; Poelcapelle; Passchendaele; Cambrai 1917, 18; St. Quentin; Bapaume 1918; Lys; Bailleul; Kemmel; Scherpenberg; Amiens; **Hindenburg Line;** Epéhy; Canal du Nord; St. Quentin Canal; Beaurevoir; Selle; Sambre; France and Flanders 1914-18; Italy 1917-18; Suvla; **Landing at Suvla;** Scimitar Hill; Gallipoli 1915; Egypt 1915-17; **Gaza;** El Mughar; Nebi Samwil; Jerusalem; Jaffa; Tell Asur; Megiddo; Sharon; Palestine 1917-18; **Shaiba; Kut al Amara 1915, 17;** Ctesiphon; Defence of Kut al Amara; Mesopotamia 1914-18.

Second World War:

Defence of Escaut; **St. Omer-La Bassée;** St. Valery-en-Caux; **Normandy Landing;** Caen; Le Perier Ridge; **Brieux Bridgehead; Venraij; Rhineland;** Hochwald; Lingen; Brinkum; **North-West Europe 1940, 44-45;** Johore; Muar; Batu Pahat; **Singapore Island;** Malaya 1942; **Kohima; Aradura;** Mandalay; **Burma 1944-45.**

Post-1945:

Korea 1951-52.

THE SUFFOLK REGIMENT

Pre-1914:

Dettingen [1743]; **Minden** [1759]; **Gibraltar, 1779-1783;** India [1796-1826]; **Seringapatam** [1799]; **South Africa, 1851-53; New Zealand** [1860-61]; **New Zealand** [1863-66]; **Afghanistan, 1878-1880; South Africa, 1899-1902.**

First World War:

Mons; **Le Cateau;** Retreat from Mons; Marne 1914; Aisne 1914; La Bassée 1914; Givenchy 1914; **Neuve Chapelle; Ypres 1915, 17, 18;** Gravenstafel; St. Julien; Frezenberg; Bellewaarde; Aubers; Hooge 1915; Loos; **Somme 1916, 18;** Albert 1916, 18; Bazentin; Delville Wood; Pozières; Flers-Courcelette; Morval; Thiepval; Le Transloy; Ancre Heights; Ancre 1916, 18; **Arras 1917, 18;** Scarpe 1917, 18; Arleux; Pilckem; Langemarck 1917; Menin Road; Polygon Wood; Poelcapelle; Passchendaele; **Cambrai 1917, 18;** St. Quentin; Bapaume 1918; Lys; Estaires; Messines 1918; Hazebrouck; Bailleul; Kemmel; Béthune; Scherpenberg; Amiens; **Hindenburg Line;** Epéhy; Canal du Nord; Courtrai; Selle; Valenciennes; Sambre; France and Flanders 1914-18; Struma; Doiran 1918; **Macedonia 1915-18;** Suvla; **Landing at Suvla;** Scimitar Hill; Gallipoli 1915; Egypt 1915-17; **Gaza;** El Mughar; Nebi Samwil; Jerusalem; Jaffa; Tell'Asur; Megiddo; Sharon; Palestine 1917-18.

Second World War:

Dunkirk 1940; Normandy Landing; Odon; Falaise; Venraij; Brinkum; North-West Europe 1940, 44-45; **Singapore Island;** Malaya 1942; **North Arakan; Imphal; Burma 1943-45.**

THE ROYAL LINCOLNSHIRE REGIMENT

Pre-1914:

Blenheim [1704]; **Ramillies** [1706]; **Oudenarde** [1708]; **Malplaquet** [1709]; **Peninsula** [1808-14]; **Sobraon** [1846]; **Punjaub** [1848-49]; **Goojerat** [1849]; **Mooltan** [1849]; **Lucknow** [1857-58]; **Atbara** [1898]; **Khartoum** [1898]; **Paardeberg** [1900]; **South Africa, 1900-02.**

First World War:

Mons; Le Cateau; Retreat from Mons; **Marne 1914;** Aisne 1914, 18; La Bassée 1914; **Messines 1914, 17, 18;** Armentières 1914; **Ypres 1914, 15, 17;** Nonne Bosschen; **Neuve Chapelle;** Gravenstafel; St. Julien; Frezenberg; Bellewaarde; Aubers; **Loos; Somme 1916, 18;** Albert 1916, 18; Bazentin; Delville Wood; Pozières; Flers-Courcelette; Morval; Thiepval; Ancre 1916, 18; Arras 1917, 18; Scarpe 1917, 18; Arleux; Pilckem; Langemarck 1917; Menin Road; Polygon Wood; Broodseinde; Poelcapelle; Passchendaele; Cambrai 1917, 18; St. Quentin; Bapaume 1918; **Lys;** Estaires; Bailleul; Kemmel; Amiens; Drocourt-Quéant; **Hindenburg Line;** Epéhy; Canal du Nord; St. Quentin Canal; Beaurevoir; Selle; Sambre; France and Flanders 1914-18; **Suvla;** Landing at Suvla; Scimitar Hill; Gallipoli 1915; Egypt 1916.

Second World War:

Vist; Norway 1940; **Dunkirk 19140; Normandy Landing;** Cambes; **Fontenay le Pesnil;** Defence of Rauray; Caen; Orne; Bourguebus Ridge; Troarn; Nederrijn; Le Havre; **Antwerp-Turnhout Canal;** Venraij; Venlo Pocket; **Rhineland;** Hochwald; Lingen; Bremen; Arnhem 1945; North-West Europe 1940, 44-45; Sedjenane I; Mine de Sedjenana; Argoub Sellah; **North Africa 1943; Salerno;** Vietri Pass; Capture of Naples; Cava di Terreni; Volturno Crossing; Garigliano Crossing; Monte Tuga; **Gothic Line;** Monte Gridolfo; Gemmano Ridge; Lamone Crossing; San Marino; Italy 1943-45; Donbaik; Point 201 (Arakan); North Arakan; Buthidaung; **Ngakyedauk Pass;** Ramree; **Burma 1943-45.**

THE NORTHAMPTONSHIRE REGIMENT

Pre-1914:

Louisburg [1758]; **Quebec, 1759; Havannah** [1762]; **Martinique** [1762]; **Gibraltar, 1779-1783; Martinique, 1794;** Maida [1806]; **Peninsula** [1808-14]; Douro [1809]; **Talavera** [1809]; **Albuhera** [1811]; **Badajos** [1812]; **Salamanca** [1812]; Nivelle [1813]; Pyrenees [1813]; **Vittoria** [1813]; Orthes [1814]; Toulouse [1814]; **New Zealand** [1846-47]; **Sevastapol** [1854-55]; South Africa, 1879; **Tirah** [1897-98]; Modder River [1899]; **South Africa, 1899-1902; Relief of Ladysmith** [1900].

First World War:

Mons; Retreat from Mons; **Marne 1914; Aisne 1914, 18; Ypres 1914, 17;** Langemarck 1914, 17; Gheluvelt; Nonne Bosschen; Givenchy 1914; **Neuve Chapelle;** Aubers; **Loos; Somme 1916, 18;** Albert 1916, 18; Bazentin; Delville Wood; Pozières; Flers-Courcelette; Morval; Thiepval; Le Transloy; Ancre Heights; Ancre 1916, 18; Bapaume 1917, 18; **Arras 1917, 18;** Vimy 1917; Scarpe 1917, 18; Arleux; Messines 1917; Pilckem; Passchendaele; Cambrai 1917, 18; St. Quentin; Rosières; Avre; Villers Bretonneux; Amiens; Drocourt-Quéant; Hindenburg Line; **Epéhy;** St. Quentin Canal; Selle; Sambre; France and Flanders 1914-18; Landing at Suvla; Scimitar Hill; Gallipoli 1915; Egypt 1915-17; **Gaza;** El Mughar; Nebi Samwil; Jerusalem; Jaffa; Tell Asur; Megiddo; Sharon; Palestine 1917-18.

Second World War:

Defence of Escaut; Defence of Arras; Ypres-Comines Canal; **North-West Europe 1940, 45;** Djedeida; Djebel Djaffa; Oued Zarga; Djebel Tanngoucha; Sidi Ahmed; **North Africa 1942-43;** Landing in Sicily; Adrano; Sicily 1943; Sangro; **Garigliano Crossing; Anzio; Cassino II;** Monte Gabbione; Trasimene Line; Monte la Pieve; Argenta Gap; **Italy 1943-45;** Madagascar; **Yu; Imphal;** Tamu Road; Bishenpur; Monywa 1945; **Myinmu Bridgehead;** Irrawaddy; **Burma 1943-45.**

THE
BEDFORDSHIRE
AND
HERTFORDSHIRE
REGIMENT

THE ESSEX
REGIMENT

THE ROYAL
LEICESTERSHIRE
REGIMENT

Pre-1914:

nur, 1695; Blenheim [1704]; **Ramillies** [1706]; Menarde [1708]; **Malplaquet** [1709]; Surinam [1804]; ral [1895]; **South Africa, 1900-02.**

First World War:

as; Le Cateau; Retreat from Mons; **Marne 1914;** ne 1914; La Bassée 1914; Ypres 1914, 15, 17; gemarck 1914, 17; Gheluvelt; Nonne Bosschen; ve Chapelle; Hill 60; St. Julien. Frezenberg; ewaarde; Aubers; Festubert 1915; **Loos;** me 1916, 18; Albert 1916, 18; Bazentin; ville Wood; Pozières; Guillemont; Flers-Courcelette; val; Thiepval; Le Transloy; Ancre Heights; re 1916, 18; **Arras 1917, 18;** Vimy 1917; rpe 1917; Arleux; Oppy; Messines 1917; Pilckem; gon Wood; Broodseinde; Poelcapelle; schendaele; **Cambrai 1917, 18;** St. Quentin; aume 1918; Rosières; Avre; Villers Bretonneux; Lys; ebrouck; Scherpenberg; Amiens; Drocourt-Quéant; denburg Line; Epéhy; Canal du Nord; Quentin Canal; Selle; **Sambre;** ice and Flanders 1914-18; Italy 1917-18; **Suvla;** ding at Suvla; Scimitar Hill; Gallipoli 1915; pt 1915-17; **Gaza;** El Mughar; Nebi Samwil; salem; Jaffa; Tell'Asur; Megiddo; Sharon; stine 1917-18.

Second World War:

kirk 1940; North-West Europe 1940; Tobruk 1941; ruk Sortie; Belhamed; Tunis; th Africa 1941, 43; Cassino II; Trasimene Line; 1944-45; Athens; Greece 1944-45; apore Island; Malaya 1942; **Chindits 1944;** na 1944.

Pre-1914:

Havannah [1762]; Moro [1762]; **Gibraltar, 1779-1783;** Peninsula [1808-14]; **Badajos** [1812]; Salamanca [1812]; **Bladensburg** [1814]; Waterloo [1815]; **Ava** [1824-26]; Alma [1854]; Inkerman [1854]; **Sevastopol** [1854-55]; Taku Forts [1860]; **Nile, 1884-85;** South Africa, 1899-1902; Relief of Kimberley [1900]; **Paardeberg** [1900].

First World War:

Le Cateau; Retreat from Mons; **Marne 1914;** Aisne 1914; Messines 1914; Armentières 1914; Ypres 1915, 17; St. Julien; Frezenberg; Bellewaarde; **Loos; Somme 1916, 18;** Albert 1916, 18; Bazentin; Delville Wood; Pozières; Flers-Courcelette; Morval; Thiepval; Le Transloy; Ancre Heights; Ancre 1916, 18; Bapaume 1917, 18; **Arras 1917, 18;** Scarpe 1917, 18; Arleux; Pilckem; Langemarck 1917; Menin Road; Broodseinde; Poelcapelle; Passchendaele; **Cambrai 1917, 18;** St. Quentin; Avre; Villers Bretonneux; Lys; Hazebrouck; Béthune; Amiens; Drocourt-Quéant; Hindenburg Line; Havrincourt; Epéhy; St. Quentin Canal; **Selle;** Sambre; France and Flanders 1914-18; Helles; Landing at Helles; Krithia; Suvla; Landing at Suvla; Scimitar Hill; **Gallipoli 1915-16;** Rumani; Egypt 1915-17; **Gaza;** Jaffa; Megiddo; Sharon; Palestine 1917-18.

Second World War:

St. Omer-La Bassée; Tilly sur Seulles; Le Havre; Antwerp-Turnhout Canal; Scheldt; **Zetten;** Arnhem 1945; **North-West Europe 1940, 44-45;** Abyssinia 1940; Falluja; Baghdad 1941; Iraq 1941; **Palmyra;** Syria 1941; **Tobruk 1941;** Belhamed; Mersa Matruh; **Defence of Alamein Line;** Deir el Shein; Ruweisat; Ruweisat Ridge; El Alamein; Matmata Hills; Akarit; **Enfidaville;** Djebel Garci; Tunis; Ragoubet Souissi; North Africa 1941-43; Trigno; **Sangro; Villa Grande; Cassino I;** Castle Hill; Hangman's Hill; Italy 1943-44; Athens; Greece 1944-45; Kohima; **Chindits 1944;** Burma 1943-45.

Pre-1914:

Namur, 1695; Louisburg [1758]; **Havannah** [1762]; **Martinique, 1762; Hindoostan** [1790-1823]; Afghanistan, 1839; **Ghuznee, 1839; Khelat** [1839]; **Sevastopol** [1854-55]; **Afghanistan, 1878-1879;** Ali Masjid [1878]; **Defence of Ladysmith** [1899-1900]; **South Africa, 1899-1902.**

First World War:

Aisne 1914,18; La Bassée 1914; Armentières 1914; Festubert 1914, 15; **Neuve Chapelle;** Aubers; Hooge 1915; **Somme 1916, 18;** Bazentin; Flers-Courcelette; Morval; Le Transloy; **Ypres 1917;** Polygon Wood; **Cambrai 1917, 18;** St. Quentin; **Lys;** Bailleul; Kemmel; Scherpenberg; Albert 1918; Bapaume 1918; Hindenberg Line; Epéhy; **St. Quentin Canal;** Beaurevoir; Selle; Sambre; **France and Flanders 1914-18;** Megiddo; Sharon; Damascus; **Palestine 1918;** Tigris 1916; Kut al Amara 1917; Baghdad; **Mesopotamia 1915-18.**

Second World War:

Norway 1940; Antwerp-Turnhout Canal; **Scheldt;** Zetten; **North-West Europe 1944-45;** Jebel Mazar; Syria 1941; **Sidi Barrani;** Tobruk 1941; Montagne Farm; **North Africa 1940-41, 43; Salerno;** Calabritto; **Gothic Line;** Monte Gridolfo; Monte Colombo; **Italy 1943-45; Crete;** Heraklion; Kampar; **Malaya 1941-42; Chindits 1944.**

Post-1945:

Maryang-San; **Korea 1951-52.**

As the Queen's Division was predominantly a southern division, so the King's Division is a staunchly northern division its present-day constituents having descended from seventeen great regiments forged in such disparate areas as, on one hand, the wild expanses of the Borders country, the Cumbria fells and Yorkshire Dales and, on the other, the great Port of Liverpool, the booming mill towns of Lancashire and the big industrial cities of South Yorkshire. The Division is proud of its northern character and sets great store on the gritty, plain speaking, no-nonsense nature of its soldiers.

Most of the regiments comprising today's Duke of Lancaster's Regiment were formed in the 17th and 18th centuries the oldest being "The King's Own" which was founded in 1680 and, as the 4th Foot, was the fourth most senior line infantry regiment in the British Army. Not far behind it was the 8th Foot, "The King's", which was traditionally the infantry regiment for Merseyside and Manchester.

Since the Wars of the Roses, there has always been a healthy rivalry between

The King's Division comprises two "large" regiments, one of two battalions and the other of three which have together descended from seventeen original regiments of the line.

the Red Rose of Lancashire and the White Rose of Yorkshire which has always been much in evidence in the splendid military and sporting records of the regiments of both regions. No doubt the performance of each battalion in the new King's Division will be sharpened with such inter-battalion competition within the overall context of striving to make the Division the best in the Army!

PRESENT ROLES & LOCATIONS OF THE REGULAR BATTALIONS THE KING'S DIVISION	
1 LANCS	Mechanised Infantry *(Catterick)*
2 LANCS	Light Role *(Cyprus)*
1 YORKS	Light Role *(20th Armoured Brigade, Münster)*
2 YORKS	Light Role *(11th Light Brigade, Preston)*
3 YORKS	Armoured Infantry *(12th Mechanised Brigade, Warminster)*

Today's Yorkshire Regiment represent the recent fusion of three great Yorkshire regiments with origins dating back 300 years. It might surprise many that "The Green Howards" — that most Yorkshire of Yorkshire regiments — was actually raised by the Luttrell family in Dunster from musketeers and pikemen in Somerset and Devon! It was also the first regiment to be raised for service with William of Orange.

Arthur Wellesley, the first Duke of Wellington, joined the 33rd Foot in 1793 and commanded the Regiment in the Netherlands and India. After his death, Queen Victoria granted the Regiment the unique honour of bearing his name — the only regiment in the Army to incorporate the name of a commoner in its title — The Duke of Wellington's Regiment, now the 3rd Battalion of The Yorkshire Regiment.

All the regiments of the North of England expanded enormously during both World Wars and it was largely from Lancashire and Yorkshire that the immortal "Pals" and "Chums" battalions of Kitchener's New Army emerged in 1916. The young men of whole towns would enlist together, fight together and all too often, die together in the ferocious battles of the First World War.

4th	55th
8th	59th
30th	63rd
34th	81st
40th	82nd
47th	96th

14th	
15th	33rd
19th	76th

1st BATTALION **2nd BATTALION**

THE DUKE OF LANCASTER'S REGIMENT
(KING'S, LANCASTER and BORDER)

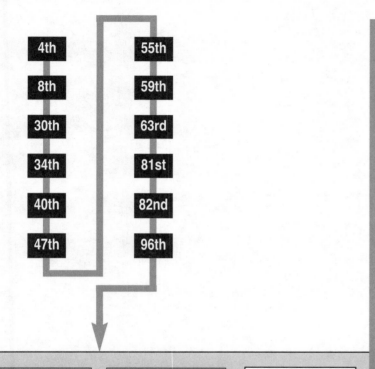

PAGE 94-97

1st BATTALION **2nd BATTALION** **3rd BATTALION**

THE YORKSHIRE REGIMENT

PAGE 98-99

THE KING'S DIVISION

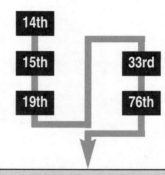

1680
The 2nd Tangier Regiment of Foot (Plymouth's) (1)

1684
The Duchess of York and Albany's (2) Regiment of Foot

1685
The Queen's Own Regiment of Foot

1702
The Queen's Own Regiment of Marines

1703
The Royal Regiment of Marines

1715
The King's Own Regiment of Foot (3)

4th

1751
4th (The King's Own) Regiment of Foot

1865
4th (The King's Own Royal) Regiment of Foot

1881
The King's Own (Royal Lancaster Regiment)

1702
Lucas's Regiment of Foot (5)

34th

1751
34th Regiment of Foot

1782
24th (Cumberland) Regiment of Foot

1755
57th Regiment of Foot (6)

55th

1757
55th Regiment of Foot

1782
55th (Westmoreland) Regiment of Foot

1685
The Princess Anne of Denmark's (7) Regiment of Foot

1702
The Queen's Regiment of Foot

1716
The King's (8) Regiment of Foot

8th

1751
8th (The King's) Regiment of Foot

1756
2nd Battalion 8th (The King's) Regiment of Foot

63rd

1758
63rd Regiment of Foot

1782
63rd (The West Suffolk) Regiment of Foot

96th

1824
96th Regiment of Fo[...]

1st BATTALION

2nd BATTALION

1st BATTALION

2nd BATTALION

1st BATTALION

2nd BATTALION

1881 (July)
THE KING'S OWN ROYAL REGIMENT
(Lancaster) (4)

1881
THE BORDER REGIMENT

1873
The King's (Liverpool) Regiment
1921
The King's Regiment (Liverpool)
1948
THE KING'S REGIMENT (9)

1881
The Manchester Regiment
1948
THE MANCHESTER REGIMENT (10)
(63rd / 96th)

1959
THE KING'S OWN ROYAL BORDER REGIMENT

1958
THE KING'S REGIMENT
(Manchester and Liverpool)
1968
THE KING'S REGIMENT

REGIMENTAL HEADQUARTERS
Fulwood Barracks, Preston, Lancs PR2 8AA
Tel: 01772 260426 / 260362 Fax: 01772 260583
email: rhqlancs@btconnect.com
Website: www.army.mod.uk/lancs/

County Office Carlisle
The Castle, Carlisle, Cumbria CA3 8UR
Tel and Fax: 01228 521275
email: admin-officer@kingsownborder.army.mod.uk

City Office Liverpool
New Zealand House, Water St., Liverpool L2 8TD
Tel: 0151 2366363 Fax: 0151 2360439
email: rhq@kings.army.mod.uk

City Office Manchester
TA Centre, Ardwick Green N., Manchester M12 6HD
Tel and Fax: 0161 2736191
email: rhqi@rhqkings.fsnet.co.uk

ALLIANCES
Canadian Armed Forces:
The King's Own Calgary Regiment
Australian Military Forces:
The Royal Queensland Regiment
Pakistan Army:
15th Battalion The Frontier Force Regiment

REGIMENTAL MARCHES
Quick March: Arrangement of "John Peel" and "Corn Rigs are Bonn[...]
Slow March: Trelawney

COLONEL-IN-CHIEF
HM The Queen

1702
Saunderson's
Regiment of Marines (11)

1715
Willis's
Regiment of Foot

30th

1751
30th Regiment
of Foot

1782
30th (1st
Cambridgeshire)
Regiment of Foot

1756
61st Regiment
of Foot (12)

59th

1757
59th Regiment
of Foot

1782
59th (2nd
Nottinghamshire)
Regiment of Foot

1717
Phillip's Regiment
of Foot (13)

40th

1751
40th Regiment
of Foot

1782
40th (2nd
Somersetshire)
Regiment of Foot

82nd

1793
82nd (The Prince of
Wales's Volunteers)
Regiment of Foot (14)

1741
Mordaunt's Regiment
of Foot (15)

47th

1751
47th Regiment
of Foot

1782
47th (Lancashire)
Regiment of Foot

1831
47th (Duke of
Lancaster's Own)
Regiment of Foot

81st

1793
81st (Royal
Lincolnshire Volunteers)
Regiment of Foot (16)

1794
81st Regiment
of Foot

1833
81st (Royal
Lincoln Volunteers)
Regiment of Foot

1881
**THE EAST LANCASHIRE
REGIMENT**

1881
The Prince of Wales's Volunteers
(South Lancashire Regiment)

1938
**THE SOUTH LANCASHIRE
REGIMENT**
(The Prince of Wales's Volunteers)

1881
THE LOYAL NORTH LANCASHIRE
REGIMENT

1921
THE LOYAL REGIMENT
(North Lancashire)

1958
THE LANCASHIRE REGIMENT
(Prince of Wales's Volunteers)
(30, 40, 59, 82)

1970
**THE QUEEN'S LANCASHIRE
REGIMENT**
(30, 40, 47, 59, 81 and 82)

**1st
BATTALION** | **2nd
BATTALION**

2006
**THE DUKE OF
LANCASTER'S REGIMENT**
(KING'S, LANCASHIRE &
BORDER)

NOTES

(1) Raised in London by the Earl of Plymouth for service in Tangier.

(2) Mary of Modena, wife of the future King James II(VII) and "Queen" the following year.

(3) King George I.

(4) The 1st Battalion of the King's Own Royal Regiment (Lancaster) was captured on Leros in 1943 and reformed from the 8th Battalion in 1944.

(5) Raised in East Anglia by Colonel Lord Lucas.

(6) Raised by Colonel George Perry in Stirling — the only regiment north of the central belt not to be designated "Highland".

(7) Princess Anne, 2nd daughter of King James II(VII) who became Queen Anne in 1702.

(8) King George I.

(9) In 1945 the 1st Battalion The King's Regiment (Liverpool) became the 15th (King's) Battalion The Parachute Regiment. It was disbanded in 1948 and the 2nd Battalion King's became the 1st Battalion.

(10) The 1st Battalion The Manchester Regiment was captured at Singapore in 1942 and reconstituted from the 6th TA Battalion.

(11) Raised by Colonel Thomas Saunderson in Lincolnshire and on Tyneside and designated 1st Marines. Later ranked as 32nd Foot.

(12) Raised by Colonel Montagu in Nottingham and Leicester.

(13) Raised from Independent Companies in Nova Scotia and Newfoundland by Col. Richard Phillips, Governor of Nova Scotia.

(14) Raised in Yorkshire and the North of England by Maj. Gen. Charles Leigh from The Prince of Wales's Volunteer Militia.

(15) Raised in Scotland by Colonel John Mordaunt.

(16) Raised by Major General Albermarle Bertie from Loyal Lincoln Volunteer Militia. The later title "Loyal" derives from his family motto — "Loyaute m'oblige" (Loyalty binds me).

BATTLE HONOURS

THE KING'S OWN ROYAL REGIMENT (Lancaster)

Pre-1914:

Namur [1695]; **Gibraltar, 1704-05; Guadaloupe, 1759;** **St. Lucia, 1778; Peninsula** [1808-14]; **Corunna** [1809]; **Badajos** [1812]; **Salamanca** [1812]; **Nive** [1813]; San Sebastian [1813]; **Vittoria** [1813]; **Bladensburg** [1814]; **Waterloo** [1815]; **Alma** [1854]; **Inkerman** [1854]; **Sevastopol** [1854-55]; **Abyssinia** [1867-68]; **South Africa, 1879;** **South Africa, 1899-1902; Relief of Ladysmith** [1900];

First World War:

Le Cateau; Retreat from Mons; **Marne 1914;** Aisne 1914; Armentières 1914; **Ypres 1915-17;** Gravenstafel; St. Julien; Frezenberg; Bellewaarde; Festubert 1915; Loos; **Somme 1916, 18;** Albert 1916, 18; Bazentin; Delville Wood; Pozières; Guillemont; Ginchy; Flers-Courcelette; Morval; Le Transloy; Ancre Heights; Ancre 1916; **Arras 1917, 18;** Scarpe 1917, 18; Arleux; **Messines 1917;** Pilckem; Menin Road; Polygon Wood; Broodseinde; Poelcapelle; Passchendaele; Cambrai 1917, 18; St. Quentin; **Lys;** Estaires; Hazebrouck; Béthune; Bapaume 1918; Drocourt-Quéant; Hindenburg Line; Canal du Nord; Selle; Valenciennes; Sambre; **France and Flanders 1914-18;** Struma; Doiran 1917, 18; **Macedonia 1915, 18;** Suvla; Sari Bair; **Gallipoli 1915;** Egypt 1916; Tigris 1916; Kut al Amara 1917; Baghdad; **Mesopotamia 1916, 18.**

Second World War:

St. Omer-La Bassée; **Dunkirk 1940;** **North-West Europe 1940; Defence of Habbaniya;** Falluja; Iraq 1941; **Merjayun;** Jebel Mazar; Syria 1941; Tobruk 1941; **Tobruk Sortie; North Africa 1940-42;** Montone; Citta di Castello; San Martino Sogliano; **Lamone Bridgehead;** Italy 1944-45; **Malta 1941-42; Chindits 1944;** Burma 1944.

THE BORDER REGIMENT

Pre-1914:

Havannah [1762]; **St. Lucia, 1778;** Peninsula [1808-14]; **Albuhera** [1811]; **Arroyo dos Molinos** [1811]; **Nive** [1813]; Nivelle [1813]; **Pyrenees** [1813]; **Vittoria** [1813]; Orthes [1814]; **Alma** [1854]; **Inkerman** [1854]; Sevastopol [1854-55]; Lucknow [1857-58]; **South Africa, 1899-1902; Relief of Ladysmith** [1900].

First World War:

Ypres 1914, 15, 17, 18; Langemarck 1914, 17; Gheluvelt; Neuve Chapelle; Frezenberg; Bellewaarde; Aubers; Festubert 1915; Loos; **Somme 1916, 18;** Albert 1916, 18; Bazentin; Delvill Wood; Pozières; Guillemont; Flers-Courcelette; Morval; Thiepval; Le Transloy; Ancre Heights; Ancre 1916; **Arras 1917, 18;** Scarpe 1917; Bullecourt; Messines 1917, 18; Pilckem; Polygon Wood; Broodseinde; Poelcapelle; Passchendaele; **Cambrai 1917, 18;** St. Quentin; Rosières; **Lys;** Estaires; Hazebrouck; Bailleul; Kemmel; Scherpenberg; Aisne 1918; Amiens; Bapaume 1918; Hindenburg Line; Epéhy; St. Quentin Canal; Beaurevoir; Courtrai; Selle; Sambre; **France and Flanders 1914-18;** Piave; **Vittorio Veneto;** Italy 1917-18; Doiran 1917-18; **Macedonia 1915-18;** Helles; Landing at Helles; Krithia; Suvla; Landing at Suvla; Scimitar Hill; **Gallipoli 1915-16;** Egypt 1916; N.W. Frontier India 1916-17.

Afghanistan 1919.

Second World War:

Defence of Escaut; **Dunkirk 1940;** Somme 1940; **Arnhem 1944; North-West Europe 1940, 44;** **Tobruk 1941; Landing in Sicily; Imphal;** Sakawng; Tamu Road; Shenam Pass; Kohima; Ukhrul; Mandalay; **Myinmu Bridgehead; Meiktila;** Rangoon Road; Pyawbwe; Sittang 1945; **Chindits 1943;** **Burma 1943-45.**

THE KING'S REGIMENT

Pre-1914:

Blenheim [1704]; **Ramillies** [1706]; **Oudenarde** [1708]; Malplaquet [1709]; **Dettingen** [1743]; **Niagara** [1813]; Delhi, 1857; Lucknow [1857-58]; Afghanistan, 1878-80; Peiwar Kotal [1878]; Burmah, 1885-87; Defence of Ladysmith [1899-1900]; South Africa, 1899-1902.

First World War:

Mons; **Retreat from Mons; Marne 1914; Aisne 1914;** **Ypres 1914, 15, 17;** Langemarck 1914, 17; Gheluvelt; Nonne Bosschen; Neuve Chapelle; Gravenstafel; St. Julien; Frezenberg; Bellewaarde; Aubers; **Festubert 1915; Loos; Somme 1916, 18;** Albert 1916, 18; Bazentin; Delville Wood; Guillemont; Ginchy; Flers-Courcelette; Morval; Le Transloy; Ancre 1916; Bapaume 1917, 18; **Arras 1917, 18;** **Scarpe 1917, 18;** Arleux; Pilckem; Menin Road; Polygon Wood; Poelcapelle; Passchendaele; **Cambrai 1917, 18;** St. Quentin; Rosières; Avre; Lys; Estaires; Messines 1918; Bailleul; Kemmel; Béthune; Scherpenberg; Drocourt-Quéant; Hindenburg Line; Epéhy; Canal du Nord; St. Quentin Canal; Selle; Sambre; France and Flanders 1914-18; Doiran 1917; Macedonia 1915-18; N.W. Frontier India 1915; Archangel 1918-19.

Afghanistan 1919.

Second World War:

Normandy Landing; North-West Europe 1944; **Cassino II; Trasimene Line; Tuori; Capture of Forli; Rimini Line;** Italy 1944-45; **Athens;** Greece 1944-45; **Chindits 1943; Chindits 1944;** Burma 1943-44.

Post-1945:

The Hook 1953; Korea 1952-53.

THE MANCHESTER REGIMENT (63rd / 96th)

Pre-1914:

Guadeloupe, 1759; Egmont-op-Zee [1799]; Peninsula [1808-14]; **Martinique, 1809; Guadeloupe, 1810; New Zealand** [1846-47]; **Alma** [1854]; **Inkerman** [1854]; **Sevastopol** [1854-55]; **Afghanistan, 1879-1880; Egypt, 1882;** Defence of Ladysmith [1899-1900]; South Africa, 1899-1902.

First World War:

Mons; Le Cateau; Retreat from Mons; Marne 1914; Aisne 1914; La Bassée 1915; Armentières 1914; **Givenchy 1914;** Neuve Chapelle; **Ypres 1915, 17, 1[8]** Gravenstafel; St. Julien; Frezenberg; Bellewaarde; Aubers; **Somme 1916, 18;** Albert 1916, 18; Bazenti[n] Delville Wood; Guillemont; Flers-Courcelette; Thiepva[l] Le Transloy; Ancre Heights; Ancre 1916, 18; Arras 1917, 18; Scarpe 1917; Bullecourt; Messines 1917; Pilckem; Langemarck 1917; Menin Road; Polygon Wood; Broodseinde; Poelcape[lle] Passchendaele; St. Quentin; Bapaume 1918; Rosière[s] Lys; Kemmel; Amiens; **Hindenburg Line;** Epéhy; Canal du Nord; St. Quentin Canal; Beaurevoir; Cambrai 1918; Courtrai; Selle; Sambre; France and Flanders 1914-18; **Piave;** Vittorio Veneto[.] Italy 1917-18; Doiran 1917; **Macedonia 1915-18;** Hel[les] Krithia; Suvla; Landing at Suvla; Scimitar Hill; **Gallipoli 1915;** Rumani; Egypt 1915-17; **Megiddo;** Sharon; Palestine 1918; Tigris 1916; Kut al Amara 19[17] **Baghdad;** Mesopotamia 1916-18.

Second World War:

Dyle; Withdrawal to Escaut; Defence of Escaut; **Defence of Arras;** St. Omer-La Bassée; Ypres-Comines Canal; **Caen;** Esquay; Falaise; Nede[r] **Scheldt;** Walcheren Causeway; Flushing; **Lower Ma[as]** Venlo Pocket; **Roer;** Ourthe; Rhineland; **Reichswal[d]** Goch; Weeze; Rhine; Ibbenburen; Dreirwalde; Aller; Bremen; North-West Europe 1940, 44-45; Gothic Lin[e] Monte Gridolfo; Coriano; San Clemente; Gemmano Ridge; Montilgallo; Capture of Forli; Lamone Crossing; Lamone Bridgehead; Rimini Line; Montescudo; Cesena; Italy 1944; **Malta 1940,** Singapore Island; Malaya 1941-42; North Arakan; **Kohima;** Pinwe; Shwebo; Myinmu Bridgehead; Irrawaddy; Burma 1944-45.

BATTLE HONOURS

THE EAST LANCASHIRE REGIMENT

THE SOUTH LANCASHIRE REGIMENT
(The Prince of Wales's Volunteers)

THE LOYAL REGIMENT
(North Lancashire)

Pre-1914:

...raltar, 1704-05; **Belleisle** [1761]; ...e of Good Hope [1806]; Peninsula [1808-14]; ...unna [1809]; **Java** [1811]; **Badajos** [1812]; ...amanca [1812]; **Nive** [1813]; **San Sebastian** [1813]; ...oria [1813]; **Waterloo** [1815]; **Bhurtpore** [1826]; ...a [1854]; **Inkerman** [1854]; **Sevastapol** [1854-55]; ...ton [1857]; Afghanistan. 1878-1880; ...ned Khel [1880]; **Chitral** [1895]; ...th Africa 1900-02.

First World War:

...Cateau; **Retreat from Mons; Marne 1914;** ...e 1914-18; Armentières 1914; **Neuve Chapelle;** ...es 1915, 17, 18; St. Julien; Frezenberg; Bellewaarde; ...ers; **Somme 1916, 18;** Albert 1916, 18; Bazentin; ...ières; Le Transloy; Ancre Heights; Ancre 1916, 18; ...oria 1813]; **Nivelle** [1813]; **as 1917, 18;** Vimy 1917; Scarpe 1917, 18; Arleux; ...y; Messines 1917; Pilckem; Langemarck 1917; ...nin Road; Polygon Wood; Broodseinde; Poelcapelle; ...schendaele; St. Quentin; Bapaume 1918; Rosières; ...rs Bretonneux; Lys; Etaires; Hazebrouck; Bailleul; ...mel; Hindenburg Line; Canal do Nord; ...nbrai 1918; Selle; Valenciennes; Sambre; ...nce and Flanders 1914-18; Kosturino; ...ran 1917, 18; Macedonia 1915-18; **Helles;** Krithia; ...la; Sari Bair; Gallipoli 1915; Rumani; Egypt 1915-17; ...is 1916; **Kut al Amara 1917;** Baghdad; ...sopotamia 1916-17.

Second World War:

...ence of Escaut; **Dunkirk 1940;** Caen; **Falaise;** ...lerrijn; **Lower Maas; Ourthe;** Rhineland; ...chswald; **Weeze;** Rhine; Ibbenburen; **Aller;** ...th-West Europe 1940, 44-45; **Madagascar;** ...th Arakan; **Pinwe; Burma 1944-45.**

Pre-1914:

Louisburg [1758]; **Havannah** [1762]; Martinique, 1762; St. Lucia, 1778; **Monte Video** [1807]; Peninsula [1808-14]; **Rolica** [1808]; **Vimiera** [1808]; **Corunna** [1809]; **Talavera** [1809]; **Badajos** [1812]; **Salamanca** [1812]; **Niagara** [1813]; **Nivelle** [1813]; **Pyrenees** [1813]; **Vittoria** [1813]; **Orthes** [1814]; **Toulouse** [1814]; **Waterloo** [1815]; **Cabool, 1842; Candahar, 1842; Ghuznee, 1842; Maharajpore** [1843]; **Sevastopol** [1854-55]; **Lucknow** [1857-58]; **New Zealand** [1860-61]; South Africa, 1899-1902; **Relief of Ladysmith** [1900].

First World War:

Mons; Le Cateau; Retreat from Mons; Marne 1914; **Aisne 1914, 18;** La Bassée 1914; **Messines 1914, 17, 18;** Armentières 1914; **Ypres 1914, 15, 17, 18;** Nonne Bosschen; St. Julien; Frezenberg; Bellewaarde; **Somme 1916, 18;** Albert 1916; Bazentin; Pozières; Guillemont; Ginchy; Flers-Courcelette; Morval; Le Transloy; Ancre Heights; Ancre 1916; Arras 1917, 18; Scarpe 1917, 18; Pilckem; Langemarck 1917; Menin Road; Polygon Wood; Passchendaele; Cambrai 1917, 18; St. Quentin; Bapaume 1918; Rosières; **Lys;** Estaires; Hazebrouck; Bailleul; Kemmel; Scherpenberg; Drocourt-Quéant; Hindenburg Line; Canal du Nord; Courtrai; Selle; Sambre; France and Flanders 1914-18; **Doiran 1917, 18;** Macedonia 1915-18; Suvla; **Sari Bair;** Gallipoli 1915; Egypt 1916; Tigris 1916; Kut al Amara 1917; **Baghdad;** Mesopotamia 1916-18; **Baluchistan 1918.**

Afghanistan 1919.

Second World War:

Dunkirk 1940; Normandy Landing; Odon; **Bourguebus Ridge;** Troarn; **Falaise;** Venraij; **Rhineland;** Hochwald; Bremen; **North-West Europe 1940, 44-45; Madagascar;** Middle East 1942; **North Arakan;** Mayu Tunnels; **Kohima;** Meiktila; **Nyaungu Bridgehead;** Letse; Irrawaddy; Burma 1943-45.

Pre-1914:

Louisburg [1758]; **Quebec, 1759; Maida** [1806]; Peninsula [1808-14]; **Corunna** [1809]; **Tarifa** [1811]; **Nive** [1813]; **San Sebastian** [1813]; **Vittoria** [1813]; **Ava** [1824-26]; **Alma** [1854]; **Inkerman** [1854]; **Sevastapol** [1854-55]; Afghanistan, 1878-1879; **Ali Masjid** [1878]; **Defence of Kimberley** [1899-1900]; South Africa, 1899-1902.

First World War:

Mons; Retreat from Mons; Marne 1914; Aisne 1914, 18; **Ypres 1914, 18;** Langemarck 1914, 17; Gheluvelt; Nonne Bosschen; **Neuve Chapelle;** Aubers; Festubert 1915; **Loos; Somme 1916, 18;** Albert 1916, 18; Bazentin; Delville Wood; Pozières; Flers-Courcelette; Morval; Thiepval; Le Transloy; Ancre Heights; Ancre 1916, 18; **Arras 1917, 18;** Scarpe 1917, 18; Arleux; Pilckem; Polygon Wood; Broodseinde; Poelcapelle; Passchendaele; **Cambrai 1917, 18;** St. Quentin; Bapaume 1918; **Lys;** Estaires; Bailleul; Kemmel; Béthune; Scherpenberg; Soissonnais-Ourcq; Drocourt-Quéant; **Hindenburg Line;** Epéhy; Canal do Nord; St. Quentin Canal; Courtrai; Selle; Sambre; France and Flanders 1914-18; Doiran 1917; Macedonia 1917; **Suvla;** Sari Bair; Gallipoli 1915; Egypt 1916; **Gaza;** Nebi Samwil; Jerusalem; Jaffa; Tell'Asur; Palestine 1917-18; Tigris 1916; Kut al Amara 1917; **Baghdad;** Mesopotamia 1916-18; **Kilimanjaro;** E. Africa 1914-16.

Second World War:

Dunkirk 1940; North-West Europe 1940; Banana Ridge; **Djebel Kesskiss;** Mediez Plain; **Gueriat el Atach Ridge;** Djebel bou Aoukaz 1943; Gab Gab Gap; **North Africa 1943; Anzio;** Rome; **Fiesole;** Gothic Line; Monte Gamberaldi; Monte Ceco; **Monte Grande; Italy 1944-45; Johore;** Batu Pahat; **Singapore Island;** Malaya 1941-42.

REGIMENTAL MUSEUMS OF THE KING'S DIVISION

THE YORKSHIRE REGIMENT

PRINCE OF WALES'S OWN REGIMENT OF YORKSHIRE MUSEUM
3 Tower Street, York YO1 9SB
Tel: 01904 461010 Fax: 01904 658824
email: regsec@pwoyorkshire.army.mod.uk
Website: www.yorkshireregiment.mod.uk

GREEN HOWARDS REGIMENTAL MUSEUM
Trinity Church Square, Richmond, Yorks DL10 4QN
Tel: 01748 822133 Fax: 01748 822133
email: greenhowardsmus@aol.com
Website: www.greenhowards.org.uk

DUKE OF WELLINGTON'S REGIMENT (WEST RIDING) MUSEUM
Boothtown Road, Halifax, Yorks HX3 6HG
Tel: 01422 354825 Fax: 01422 349020
email: rhq@dukesrhq.demon.co.uk
Website: www.dwr.org.uk/dwr.php?id=54

THE DUKE OF LANCASTER'S REGIMENT

KING'S OWN ROYAL REGIMENT MUSEUM
City Museum, Market Square, Lancaster LA1 1HT
Tel: 01524 555619 Fax: 01524 841692
email: kingsownmuseum@iname.com
Website: www.kingsownmuseum.plus.co.uk

BORDER REGIMENT and KING'S OWN ROYAL BORDER REGIMENT MUSEUM
Queen Mary's Tower, The Castle, Carlisle CA3 8UR
Tel: 01228 532774 Fax: 01228 545435
email: korbr@aol.com
Website: www.kingsownbordermuseum.btik.com

MANCHESTER REGIMENT MUSEUM
Town Hall, Market Place, Ashton-under-Lyne OL6 6DL
Tel: 01613 422254 Fax: 01613 432869
email: museum.manchester@tameside.gov.uk
Website: www.tameside.gov.uk/museumsgalleries/mom

KING'S REGIMENT COLLECTION
Museum of Liverpool Life, Pier Head, Liverpool L3 1PZ
Tel: 01514 784065 Fax: 01514 784090
email: matthew.buck@liverpoolmuseums.org.uk

QUEEN'S LANCASHIRE REGIMENT MUSEUM
Fulwood Barracks, Watling Street Road, Preston, Lancs PR2 8AA
Tel: 01772 260362 Fax: 01772 260583
email: qlrmuseum@btconnect.com

1685
Hales's
Regiment of Foot (1)

14th

1751
14th Regiment of Foot

1782
14th (Bedfordshire)
Regiment of Foot

1809
14th (Buckinghamshire)
Regiment of Foot (2)

1876
14th (Buckinghamshire
The Prince of Wales's
Own)(3) Regiment of Foot

1881
The Prince of Wales's
Own (West Yorkshire
Regiment)

NOTES

(1) Raised in Kent by Sir Edward Hales who remained loyal to King James II(VII) and was removed from command in 1688.

(2) By a swop of county designations with the 16th Foot.

(3) The future King Edward VII.

1685
Clifton's (4)
Regiment of Foot

15th

1751
15th Regiment of Foot

1782
15th (Yorkshire
East Riding)
Regiment of Foot

1881
The East Yorkshire
Regiment

NOTES

(4) Raised by Sir William Clifton mainly in Nottinghamshire

(5) Albert, Duke of York, the future King George VI.

(6) Raised by Francis Luttrell at Dunster Castle from Independent Companies of musketeers and pikemen in Somerset and Devon — the first regiment to be raised for service with William of Orange. On Luttrell's death the following year, the Regiment combined with Erle's Regiment to form the only 2-battalion regiment of the time.

1688
Luttrell's (6)
Regiment of Foot

19th

1751
19th Regiment of Foot

1782
19th (1st Yorkshire,
North Riding)
Regiment of Foot

1875
19th (1st Yorkshire,
North Riding, Princess
of Wales's Own) (7)
Regiment of Foot

1881
The Yorkshire Regiment

1885
The Princess of Wales's
Own (Yorkshire
Regiment)

NOTES

(7) Alexandra of Denmark, wife of the future King Edward VII.

(8) A title in unofficial use since 1744 when two regiments commanded by Colonels called Howard were billeted together in Flanders. To differentiate between the two, they were known by the colour of their uniform facings — "The Green Howards" and "The Buff Howards". The latter became "The Buffs".

(9) Raised by the Earl of Huntingdon in Yorkshire and the Midlands.

(10) Raised by Colonel Thomas Musgrave in Nottinghamshire and Leicestershire for service in India.

(11) Arthur Wellesley, later Duke of Wellington, joined the 33rd Foot in 1793 and subsequently commanded the Regiment in the Netherlands an India. It was also present, under his overall command, at Waterloo. On 18 June 1853, the fir anniversary of Waterloo following the Duke's dea the Regiment was granted the unique honour of bearing his name — the only regiment to incorporate the name of a commoner in its title.

1702
The Earl of Huntingdon's
Regiment of Foot (9)

33rd

1751
33rd Regiment of Foot

1782
33rd (1st Yorkshire
West Riding)
Regiment of Foot

1853
33rd (Duke of
Wellington's) (11)
Regiment of Foot

76th

1787
Musgrave's 76th
Regiment of Foot (1

1803
76th (Hindoostan)
Regiment of Foot

1812
76th Regiment of Fo

1920
**THE WEST YORKSHIRE
REGIMENT**
(The Prince of Wales's Own)

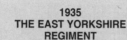

1935
**THE EAST YORKSHIRE
REGIMENT**
(The Duke of York's Own) (5)

1958
**THE PRINCE OF WALES'S
OWN REGIMENT OF
YORKSHIRE**

1921
THE GREEN HOWARDS (8)
(Alexandra, Princess of Wales's
Own Yorkshire Regiment)

1881
THE DUKE OF WELLINGTON'S
(West Riding Regiment)

1921
**THE DUKE OF
WELLINGTON'S REGIMENT**
(West Riding)

REGIMENTAL HEADQUARTERS

3 Tower Street, York YO1 9SB

Tel. Civ: 01904 461014 Fax Civ: 01904 461021

Tel. Mil: 94777 8114 Fax Mil: 94777 8121

email: rhqyorks@btconnect.com

Website: www.army.mod.uk/york

REGIMENTAL MARCHES

Quick March: Ça Ira
Slow March: The Duke of York

**1st
BATTALION**

**2nd
BATTALION**

**3rd
BATTALION**

**2006
THE YORKSHIRE
REGIMENT**
14th/15th, 19th & 33rd/76th Foot

ALLIANCES

Canadian Armed Forces:

The Rocky Mountain Rangers

The Queen's York Rangers
(1st American Regiment) RCAC

The Royal Montreal Regiment

1st Battalion The Royal New Brunswick
Regiment (Carleton and York)

Les Voltigeurs de Québec

Pakistan Army:
10th Battalion The Balloch Regiment

Falkland Islands:
The Falkland Islands Defence Force

COLONEL-IN-CHIEF
HRH The Duke of York KG, KCVO, ADC(P)

DEPUTY COLONEL-IN-CHIEF
Brigadier His Grace The Duke of Wellington
KG, LVO, OBE, MC, DL

BATTLE HONOURS

THE WEST YORKSHIRE REGIMENT (The Prince of Wales's Own)	THE EAST YORKSHIRE REGIMENT (The Duke of York's Own)	THE GREEN HOWARDS (Alexandra, Princess of Wales's Own Yorkshire Regiment)	THE DUKE OF WELLINGTON'S REGIMENT (West Riding)

THE WEST YORKSHIRE REGIMENT (The Prince of Wales's Own)

Pre-1914:

...mur, 1695; Tournay [1794]; Corunna [1809]; ...va [1811]; Waterloo [1815]; Bhurtpore [1826]; ...vastapol [1854-55]; New Zealand [1860-61]; ...w Zealand [1863-66]; Afghanistan, 1879-1880; ...uth Africa, 1899-1902; Relief of Ladysmith [1900].

First World War:

...ne 1914, 18; **Armentières 1914; Neuve Chapelle;** ...bers; Hooge 1915; Loos; **Somme 1916, 18;** ...ert 1916, 18; Bazentin; Pozières; Flers-Courcelette; ...rval; Thiepval; Le Transloy; Ancre Heights; ...cre 1916; Arras 1917, 18; Scarpe 1917, 18; ...llecourt; Hill 70; Messines 1917, 18; **Ypres 1917, 18;** ...ckem; Langemarck 1917; Menin Road; Polygon Wood; ...elcapelle; Passchendaele; **Cambrai 1917, 18;** ... Quentin; Rosières; **Villers Bretonneux; Lys;** ...zebrouck; Bailleul; Kemmel; Marne 1918; **Tardenois;** ...niens; Bapaume 1918; Drocourt-Quéant; ...ndenburg Line; Havrincourt; Epéhy; Canal du Nord; ...lle; Valenciennes; Sambre; ...ance and Flanders 1914-18; **Piave;** Vittorio Veneto; ...y 1917-18; **Suvla;** Landing at Suvla; Scimitar Hill; ...llipoli 1915; Egypt 1915-16.

Second World War:

...rth-West Europe 1940; Jebel Dafeis; Keren; ...Teclesan; Abysinnia 1940-41; Cauldron; ...fence of Alamein Line; North Africa 1940-42; ...gu 1942; Yenangyaung 1942; North Arakan; ...aungdaw; Defence of Sinzweya. Imphal; Bishenpur; ...nglatongbi; **Meiktila;** Capture of Meiktila; ...fence of Meiktila; Rangoon Road; Pyawbwe; ...ttang 1945; Burma 1942-45.

THE EAST YORKSHIRE REGIMENT (The Duke of York's Own)

Pre-1914:

Blenheim [1704]; **Ramillies** [1706]; **Oudenarde** [1708]; **Malplaquet** [1709]; **Louisburg** [1758]; Havannah [1762]; Quebec, **1759; Martinique** [1762]; Martinique [1794]; **St. Lucia** [1778]; **Martinique** [1809]; Guadeloupe, 1810; Afghanistan, 1879-1880; South Africa, 1900-02.

First World War:

Aisne 1914, 18; Armentières 1914; Ypres 1915, 17, 18; Gravenstafel; St. Julien; Frezenberg; Bellewaarde; Hooge 1915; **Loos; Somme 1916, 18;** Albert 1916, 18; Bazentin; Delville Wood; Pozières; Flers-Courcelette; Morval; Thiepval; Ancre Heights; Ancre 1916; **Arras 1917, 18;** Scarpe 1917, 18; Arleux; Oppy; Messines 1917, 18; Pilckem; Langemarck 1917; Menin Road; Polygon Wood; Broodseinde; Poelcapelle; Passchendaele; **Cambrai 1917, 18;** St. Quentin; Bapaume 1918; Rosières; Lys; Estaires; Hazebrouck; Kemmel; Scherpenberg; Amiens; Hindenburg Line; Epéhy; Canal du Nord; St. Quentin Canal; **Selle;** Sambre; France and Flanders 1914-18; Struma; **Doiran 1917;** Macedonia 1915-18; Suvla; Landing at Suvla; Scimitar Hill; **Gallipoli 1915;** Egypt 1915-16.

Second World War:

Withdrawal to Escaut; Defence of Escaut; Defence of Arras; French Frontier 1940; Ypres-Comines Canal; **Dunkirk 1940; Normandy Landing;** Tilly sur Seulles; **Odon;** Caen; Bourguebus Ridge; Troarn; Mont Pincon; St. Pierre la Vielle; Gheel; Nederrijn. Aam; Venraij; Rhineland; **Schaddenhof;** Brinkum; Bremen; **North-West Europe 1940, 44-45;** Gazala; Mersa Matruh; Defence of Alamein Line; **El Alamein; Mareth;** Wadi Zigzaou; Akarit; North Africa 1942-43; Primosole Bridge; **Sicily 1943;** Sittang 1945; **Burma 1945.**

THE GREEN HOWARDS (Alexandra, Princess of Wales's Own Yorkshire Regiment)

Pre-1914:

Malplaquet [1709]; **Belleisle** [1761]; **Alma** [1854]; **Inkerman** [1854]; **Sevastapol** [1854-55]; **Tirah** [1897-98]; **Relief of Kimberley** [1900]; **Paardeberg** [1900]; **South Africa, 1899-1902.**

First World War:

Ypres 1914, 15, 17; Langemarck 1914, 17; Gheluvelt; Neuve Chapelle; St. Julien; Frezenberg; Bellewaarde; Aubers; Festubert 1915; **Loos; Somme 1916, 18;** Albert 1916, 18; Bazentin; Pozières; Flers-Courcelette; Morval; Thiepval; Le Transloy; Ancre Heights; Ancre 1916; **Arras 1917, 18;** Scarpe 1917, 18; **Messines 1917, 18;** Pilckem; Menin Road; Polygon Wood; Broodseinde; Poelcapelle; Passchendaele; Cambrai 1917, 18; St. Quentin; Hindenburg Line; Canal du Nord; Beaurevoir; Selle; **Valenciennes; Sambre; France and Flanders 1914-18;** Piave; **Vittorio Veneto;** Italy 1917-18; **Suvla;** Landing at Suvla; Scimitar Hill; Gallipoli 1915; Egypt 1916; Archangel 1918.

Second World War:

Otta; **Norway 1940;** Defence of Arras; Dunkirk 1940; **Normandy Landing;** Tilly sur Seulles; St. Pierre la Vielle; Gheel; Nederrijn; **North-West Europe 1940, 44-45; Gazala;** Defence of Alamein Line; **El Alamein; Mareth; Akarit;** North Africa 1942-43; Landing in Sicily; Lentini; **Sicily 1943; Minturno; Anzio;** Italy 1943-44; Arakan Beaches; Burma 1945.

THE DUKE OF WELLINGTON'S REGIMENT (West Riding)

Pre-1914:

Dettingen [1743]; **Mysore** [1789-91]; **Seringapatam** [1799]; **Ally Ghur** [1803]; **Delhi 1803;** Leswarree [1803]; Deig [1804]; **Corunna** [1809]; Nive [1813]; **Peninsula** [1808-14]; **Waterloo** [1815]; **Alma** [1854]; **Inkerman** [1854]; **Sevastapol** [1854-55]; **Abyssinia** [1867-68]; **Relief of Kimberley** [1900]; **Paardeberg** [1900]; South Africa, 1900-02.

First World War:

Mons; Le Cateau; Retreat from Mons; **Marne 1914, 18;** Aisne 1914; La Bassée 1914; **Ypres 1914, 15, 17;** Nonne Bosschen; **Hill 60;** Gravenstafel; St. Julien; Aubers; **Somme 1916, 18;** Albert 1916; Bazentin; Delville Wood; Pozières; Flers-Courcelette; Morval; Thiepval; Le Transloy; Ancre Heights; **Arras 1917, 18;** Scarpe 1917, 18; Arleux; Bullecourt; Messines 1917, 18; Langemarck 1917; Menin Road; Polygon Wood; Broodseinde; Poelcapelle; Passchendaele; Cambrai 1917, 18; St. Quentin; Ancre 1918; Lys; Estaires; Hazebrouck; Bailleul; Kemmel; Béthune; Scherpenberg; Tardenois; Amiens; Bapaume 1918; Drocourt-Quéant; Hindenburg Line; Havrincourt; Epéhy; Canal du Nord; Selle; Valenciennes; Sambre; France and Flanders 1914-18; **Piave;** Vittorio Veneto; Italy 1917-18; Suvla; **Landing at Suvla;** Scimitar Hill; Gallipoli 1915; Egypt 1916.

Second World War:

Dunkirk 1940; St. Valéry-en-Caux; Tilly sur Seulles; **Odon; Fontenay le Pesnil; North-West Europe 1940, 44-45;** Banana Ridge; Medjez Plain; Gueriat el Atach Ridge; Tunis; **Djebel Bou Aoukaz 1943;** North Africa 1943; **Anzio;** Campoleone; Rome; **Monte Ceco;** Italy 1943-45; **Sittang 1942;** Paungde; Kohima; **Chindits 1944; Burma 1942-44.**

Post-1945:

The Hook 1953; Korea 1952-53; Iraq 2003.

The Prince of Wales's Division

The Prince of Wales's Division, as its name implies, has its heritage in Wales and the adjacent English counties of Cheshire, Staffordshire and Worcestershire, the important industrial region of the West Midlands and the counties of Derbyshire and Nottinghamshire.

The first element of the Division is also the most recently formed regiment of the Army — The Mercian Regiment, formed on 1st September 2007, the final infantry amalgamation in the "Future Army Structure". The Regiment takes its name from the ancient Kingdom of Mercia, its territory being the heartland of England bounded by the three great rivers — the Severn, the Mersey and the Trent.

The oldest of the constituent regiments of the Mercian is The Cheshire Regiment, formed in 1689 as The Duke of Norfolk's Regiment, numbered as 22nd of the Line in 1751 and first recording its connection with the county of Cheshire 31 years later in 1782. Not far behind, and formed in 1694 and 1701 respectively, the 29th and 36th, representing the counties of Worcestershire and Herefordshire, combined in the Cardwell Reforms to

As with the King's Division, the Prince of Wales's Division comprises two newly-formed "large" regiments, one of three regular battalions and the other of two, descended from thirteen original regiments of the line.

form The Worcestershire Regiment which, in turn, combined with The Sherwood Foresters, descended from the old 45th and 95th, to form the Worcestershire and Sherwood Foresters Regiment in 1970.

In 1881 The South Staffordshire Regiment, descended from the 38th and 80th, amalgamated with The North Staffordshire Regiment to form The Staffordshire Regiment which today forms the 3rd Battalion of The Mercians.

The second element of The Prince of Wales's Division, The Royal Welsh, formed in 2006, is descended from four famous Welsh regiments. The 1st Battalion of the new regiment comprises The Royal Welch Fusiliers, the old 23rd Foot, raised in the Welsh Marches by Lord Herbert in 1689. The 2nd Battalion absorbs the old 24th, 41st and 69th Regiments which were amalgamated into The Royal Regiment of Wales in 1969. The 24th, later The South Wales Borderers, achieved everlasting fame and their soldiers were awarded seven Victoria Crosses for their gallant defence of Rorke's Drift in the Anglo-Zulu War in 1879. During this action and the preceding Battle of Isandlwana the Regiment lost over 600 of its men.

The 41st Foot, an invalid regiment raised from Chelsea Out-Pensioners in 1719, and the 69th, originally the 2nd Battalion of the 24th, combined in 1881 into The Welsh (later Welch) Regiment.

As will be seen in the following pages these fine regiments from Wales and the heartland of England have as distinguished a record of service as any and will no doubt provide each other with solid mutual support as they carry forward their proud traditions in The Prince of Wales's Division.

PRESENT ROLES & ATTACHMENTS OF THE REGULAR BATTALIONS THE PRINCE OF WALES'S DIVISION	
1 MERCIAN	Light Role *(4th Brigade, Catterick)* .
2 MERCIAN	Light Role *(19th Brigade, Northern Ireland)*.
3 MERCIAN	Armoured Infantry *(12th Brigade, Tidworth)*. Moving to Fallingbostel in 2009.
1 R WELSH	Light Role *(Chester)*.
2 R WELSH	Armoured Infantry *(Tidworth)*.

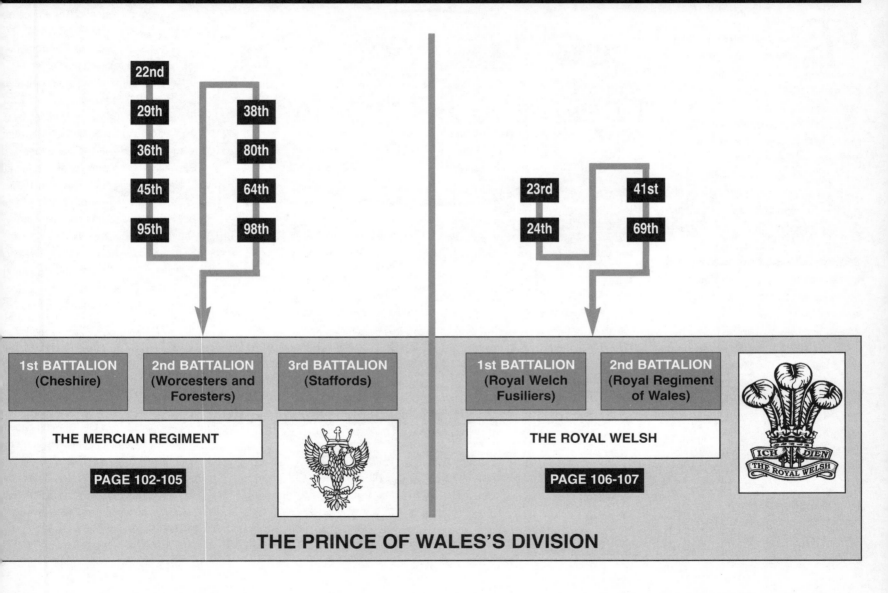

22nd	
29th	38th
36th	80th
45th	64th
95th	98th

| 23rd | 41st |
| 24th | 69th |

| 1st BATTALION (Cheshire) | 2nd BATTALION (Worcesters and Foresters) | 3rd BATTALION (Staffords) | 1st BATTALION (Royal Welch Fusiliers) | 2nd BATTALION (Royal Regiment of Wales) |

THE MERCIAN REGIMENT

PAGE 102-105

THE ROYAL WELSH

PAGE 106-107

THE PRINCE OF WALES'S DIVISION

1689
The Duke of Norfolk's
Regiment of Foot (1)

22nd

1751
22nd Regiment of Foot

1782
22nd (The Cheshire)
Regiment of Foot

NOTES:

(1) Raised by the Duke of
Norfolk in Chester for
service in Ireland.

1694
Farrington's
Regiment of Foot (2)

29th

1751
29th Regiment of Foot

1782
29th (Worcestershire)
Regiment of Foot

1701
Charlemont's
Regiment of Foot (3)

36th

1751
36th Regiment of Foot

1782
36th (Herefordshire)
Regiment of Foot

NOTES:

(2) Raised in London by
Colonel Thomas
Farrington of the
Coldstream Guards.

(3) Raised in Ireland by
Thomas Allnut and
Viscount Charlemont for
service as marines.

1741
Houghton's
Regiment of Foot (4)

45th

1751
45th Regiment of Foot (5)

1782
45th
(1st Nottinghamshire)
Regiment of Foot

1866
45th (Nottinghamshire
Regiment)
Sherwood Foresters

95th

1823
95th Regiment of Foot (6)

1825
95th (Derbyshire)
Regiment of Foot

NOTES:

(4) Raised by Colonel
Daniel Houghton in the
West Country and
originally ranked as 56th
of Foot.

(5) Initially employed as
marines and re-ranked
45th of Foot following
disbandment of the
regiments of marines in
1748.

(6) Raised in Winchester

1881
THE CHESHIRE
REGIMENT

1881
THE WORCESTERSHIRE
REGIMENT

1881
THE SHERWOOD FORESTERS
(Derbyshire Regiment)
1902
THE SHERWOOD
FORESTERS
(Nottinghamshire and Derbyshire
Regiment)

1970
THE WORCESTERSHIRE
AND SHERWOOD FORESTERS
REGIMENT
(29th / 45th Foot)

1st BATTALION
(Cheshire)

2nd BATTALION
(Worcesters
and Foresters)

3rd BATTALION
(Staffords)

2007
THE MERCIAN
REGIMENT

1705
Lillingston's
Regiment of Foot (7)

38th

1751
38th Regiment of Foot

1782
38th (1st Staffordshire)
Regiment of Foot

80th

1793
80th Regiment
of Foot (8)

80th (Staffordshire
Volunteers)
Regiment of Foot

NOTES:

(7) Raised by Colonel
Luke Lillingston at The
King's Head Hotel,
Lichfield.

(8) Raised at Chatham,
mainly from men of the
Staffordshire Militia, by
Lord Henry Paget, later
Marquess of Anglesey.

(9) Raised by Lieutenant
Colonel Mildmay Fane for
service in South Africa.

In 1837 the Regiment
was commanded by Colin
Campbell, later Field
Marshal Lord Clyde.

(10) The future King
Edward VII.

1756
2nd Battalion
11th Regiment of Foot

64th

1758
64th Regiment of Foot

1782
64th (2nd Staffordshire)
Regiment of Foot

98th

1824
98th Regiment
of Foot (9)

1876
98th (The Prince of
Wales's) (10) Foot

1881
THE SOUTH STAFFORDSHIRE REGIMENT

1881
THE NORTH STAFFORDSHIRE REGIMENT
(The Prince of Wales's)

1959
THE STAFFORDSHIRE REGIMENT
(The Prince of Wales's)

REGIMENTAL HEADQUARTERS

Heath Avenue, Lichfield, Staffs WS14 9TJ

ALLIANCES

Canadian Armed Forces:
2nd Battalion The Nova Scotia Highlanders
(Cape Breton)
The Grey and Simcoe Foresters
4ème Battalion Royal 22ème Régiment (Châteauguay)
Le Régiment de Maisonneuve

Australian Military Forces:
The Royal Victoria Regiment

Leeward Islands:
The Antigua & Barbuda Defence Force

Pakistan Army:
13th Battalion The Punjab Regiment
7th Battalion The Baluch Regiment

Jamaica Defence Force:
The Jamaica Regiment

Royal Navy:
HMS Albion
HMS Nottingham

REGIMENTAL MARCHES

Mercian Regiment Quick March
Mercian Regiment Slow March

COLONEL-IN-CHIEF

Lieutenant-General HRH The Prince of Wales
KG, KT, OM, GCB, AK, QSO, ADC

BATTLE HONOURS

THE CHESHIRE REGIMENT

THE WORCESTERSHIRE REGIMENT

THE SHERWOOD FORESTERS (Nottinghamshire and Derbyshire Regiment)

Pre-1914:

Louisburg [1758]; **Havannah** [1762]; **Martinique, 1762; Hyderabad** [1843]; **Meeanee** [1843]; **Scinde** [1843]; **South Africa, 1900-02.**

First World War:

Mons; Le Cateau; Retreat from Mons; Marne 1914, 18; Aisne 1914, 18; La Bassée 1914; Armentières 1914; **Ypres 1914, 15, 17, 18;** Nonne Bosschen; Gravenstafel; St. Julien; Frezenburg; Bellewaarde; Loos; **Somme 1916, 18;** Albert 1916, 18; Bazentin; Delville Wood; Pozières; Guillemont; Flers-Courcelette; Morval; Thiepval; Le Transloy; Ancre Heights; Ancre 1918; **Arras 1917, 18;** Vimy 1917; Scarpe 1917, 18; Oppy; **Messines 1917, 18;** Pilckem; Langemarck 1917; Menin Road; Polygon Wood; Broodseinde; Poelcapelle; Passchendaele; Cambrai 1917, 18; St. Quentin; **Bapaume 1918;** Rosières; Lys; Estaires; Hazebrouck; Bailleul; Kemmel; Scherpenberg; Soissonnais-Ourcq; Hindenburg Line; Canal du Nord; Courtrai; Selle; Valenciennes; Sambre; France and Flanders 1914-18; Italy 1917-18; Struma; **Doiran 1917, 18;** Macedonia 1915-18; **Suvla;** Sari Bair; Landing at Suvla; Scimitar Hill; Gallipoli 1915; Egypt 1915-17; **Gaza;** El Mughar; Jerusalem; Jericho; Tell'Asur; Palestine 1917-18; Tigris 1916; **Kut al Amara 1917;** Baghdad; Mesopotamia 1916-18.

Second World War:

Dyle; Withdrawal to Escaut; **St. Omer-La Bassée;** Wormhoudt; Cassel; Dunkirk 1940; **Normandy Landing;** Mont Pincon; St. Pierre la Vielle; Gheel; Nederrijn; Aam; Aller; North-West Europe 1940, 44-45; Sidi Barrani; **Capture of Tobruk;** Gazala; Mersa Matruh; Defence of Alamein Line; Deir el Shein; **El Alamein; Mareth;** Wadi Zeuss East; Wadi Zigzaou; Akarit; Wadi Akarit East; Enfidaville; North Africa 1940-43; Landing in Sicily; Primosole Bridge; Simeto Bridgehead; **Sicily 1943;** Sangro; **Salerno;** Santa Lucia; Battipaglia; Volturno Crossing; Monte Maro; Teano; Monte Camino; Garigliano Crossing; Minturno; Damiano; Anzio; **Rome; Gothic Line;** Coriano; Gemmano Ridge; Savignano; Senio Floodbank; Rimini Line; Ceriano Ridge; Valli di Comacchio; Italy 1943-45; **Malta 1941-42.**

Pre-1914:

Ramillies [1706]; **Belleisle** [1761]; **Mysore** [1789-91]; **Hindoostan** [1790-1823]; **Peninsula** [1808-14]; **Vimiera** [1808]; **Rolica** [1808]; **Corunna** [1809]; **Talavera** [1809]; **Albuhera** [1811]; **Salamanca** [1812]; **Nive** [1813]; **Nivelle** [1813]; **Pyrenees** [1813]; **Orthes** [1814]; **Toulouse** [1814]; **Ferozeshah** [1845]; **Sobraon** [1846]; **Punjaub** [1848-49]; **Chillianwallah** [1849]; **Goojerat** [1849]; **South Africa, 1900-02.**

First World War:

Mons; Le Cateau; Retreat from Mons; Marne 1914; Aisne 1914, 18; La Bassée 1914; Armentières 1914; **Ypres 1914, 15, 17, 18;** Langemarck 1914, 17; **Gheluvelt;** Nonne Bosschen; **Neuve Chapelle;** Aubers; Festubert 1915; Loos; **Somme 1916, 18;** Albert 1916; Bazentin; Delville Wood; Pozières; Le Transloy; Ancre Heights; Ancre 1916; Arras 1917; Scarpe 1917; Arleux; Messines 1917, 18; Pilckem; Menin Road; Polygon Wood; Broodseinde; Poelcapelle; **Cambrai 1917, 18;** St. Quentin; Bapaume 1918; Rosières; Villers Bretonneux; **Lys;** Estaires; Hazebrouck; Bailleul; Kemmel; Scherpenberg; Hindenburg Line; Canal du Nord; St. Quentin Canal; Beaurevoir; Courtrai; Selle; Valenciennes; Sambre; France and Flanders 1914-18; Piave; Vittorio Veneto; **Italy 1917-18;** Doiran 1917, 18; Macedonia 1915-18; Helles; Landing at Helles; Krithia; Suvla; Sari Bair; Scimitar Hill; **Gallipoli 1915-16;** Egypt 1916; Tigris 1916; Kut al Amara 1917; **Baghdad;** Mesopotamia 1916-18; Baku; Persia 1918.

Second World War:

Defence of Escaut; St. Omer-La Bassée; Wormhoudt; Odon; Borguebus Ridge; Maltot; **Mont Pincon;** Jurques; La Varinière; Noireau Crossing; **Seine 1944;** Nederrijn; **Geilenkirchen;** Rhineland; **Goch;** Rhine; **North-West Europe 1940, 44-45;** Gogni; Barentu; **Keren;** Amba Alagi; Abyssinia 1940-41; **Gazala;** Via Balbia; North Africa 1941-42; **Kohima;** Naga Village; Mao Songsang; Shwebo; **Mandalay;** Irrawaddy; Mt. Popa; **Burma 1944-45.**

Pre-1914:

Louisburg [1758]; **Peninsula** [1808-14]; **Rolica** [1808]; **Vimiera** [1808]; **Talavera** [1809]; **Busaco** [1810]; **Fuentes D'Onor** [1811]; **Badajos** [1812]; **Ciudad Rodrigo** [1812]; **Salamanca** [1812]; **Nivelle** [1813]; **Pyrenees** [1813]; **Vittoria** [1813]; **Orthes** [1814]; **Toulouse** [1814]; **Ava** [1824-26]; **South Africa, 1846-47; Alma** [1854]; **Inkerman** [1854]; **Sevastopol** [1854-55]; **Central India** [1857-58]; **Abyssinia** [1867-68]; **Egypt, 1882; Tirah** [1897-98]; **South Africa, 1899-1902.**

First World War:

Aisne 1914, 18; Armentières 1914; **Neuve Chapelle;** Aubers; Hooge 1915; Loos; **Somme 1916, 18;** Albert 1916, 18; Bazentin; Delville Wood; Pozières; Ginchy; Flers-Courcelette; Morval; Thiepval; Le Transloy; Ancre Heights; Ancre 1916; Arras 1917, 18; Vimy 1917; Scarpe 1917, 18; Messines 1917; **Ypres 1917, 18;** Pilckem; Langemarck 1917; Menin Road; Polygon Wood; Broodseinde; Poelcapelle; Passchendaele; **Cambrai 1917, 18;** St. Quentin; Bapaume 1918; Rosières; Villers Bretonneux; Lys; Bailleul; Kemmel; Scherpenberg; Amiens; Drocourt-Quéant; Hindenburg Line; Epéhy; Canal du Nord; **St. Quentin Canal;** Beaurevoir; Courtrai; Selle; Sambre; **France and Flanders 1914-18;** Piave; **Italy 1917-18;** Suvla; Landing at Suvla; Scimitar Hill; **Gallipoli 1915;** Egypt 1916.

Second World War:

Norway 1940; St. Omer-La Bassée; Ypres-Comines Canal; Dunkirk 1940; North-West Europe 1940; **Gazala; El Alamein;** Djebel Guerba; Tamera; Medjez Plain; **Tunis;** North Africa 1942-43; **Salerno;** Volturno Crossing; Monte Camino; **Anzio; Campoleone;** Advance to Tiber; **Gothic Line; Coriano;** Cosina Canal Crossing; Monte Ceco; Italy 1943-45; **Singapore Island; Malaya 1942.**

BATTLE HONOURS

THE SOUTH STAFFORDSHIRE REGIMENT

THE NORTH STAFFORDSHIRE REGIMENT (The Prince of Wales's)

THE STAFFORDSHIRE REGIMENT (The Prince of Wales's)

Pre-1914:

adeloupe, 1759; **Martinique, 1762;**
nte Video [1807]; **Peninsula** [1808-14];
'ica [1808]; **Vimiera** [1808]; **Corunna** [1809];
saco [1810]; **Badajos** [1812]; **Salamanca** [1812];
re [1813]; **San Sebastian** [1813]; **Vittoria** [1813];
a [1824-26]; **Ferozeshah** [1845]; **Moodkee** [1845];
braon [1846]; **Pegu** [1852-53]; **Alma** [1854];
erman [1854]; **Sevastopol** [1854-55];
ntral India [1857-58]; **Lucknow** [1857-58];
uth Africa, 1878-79; **Egypt, 1882; Nile, 1884-85;**
bekan [1885]; **South Africa, 1900-02.**

First World War:

ns; Retreat from Mons; **Marne 1914;**
sne 1914, 18; **Ypres 1914, 17;** Langemarck 1914, 17;
eluvelt; Nonne Bosschen; Neuve Chapelle; Aubers;
stubert 1915; **Loos; Somme 1916, 18;**
ert 1916, 18; Bazentin; Delville Wood; Pozières;
rs-Courcelette; Morval; Thiepval; Ancre 1916;
paume 1917, 18; Arras 1917, 18; Scarpe 1917, 18;
eux; Bullecourt; Hill 70; Messines 1917, 18;
nin Road; Polygon Wood; Broodseinde; Poelcapelle;
sschendaele; **Cambrai 1917, 18;** St. Quentin; Lys;
illeul; Kemmel; Scherpenberg; Drocourt-Quéant;
adenburg Line; Havrincourt; Canal du Nord;
Quentin Canal; Beaurevoir; Selle; Sambre;
ance and Flanders 1914-18; Piave; **Vittorio Veneto;**
y 1917-18; **Suvla;** Landing at Suvla; Scimitar Hill;
llipoli 1915; Egypt 1916.

Second World War:

en; Noyers; Falaise; **Arnhem 1944;**
rth-West Europe 1940, 44; Sidi Barrani;
rth Africa 1940; Landing in Sicily; **Sicily 1943;**
y 1943; **Chindits 1944; Burma 1944.**

Pre-1914:

Guadeloupe, 1759; Martinique, 1794; St. Lucia, 1803;
Surinam [1804]; **Punjaub** [1848-49]; **Bushire** [1856];
Persia [1856-57]; **Reshire** [1856]; **Kosh-Ab** [1857];
Lucknow [1857-58]; **Hafir** [1896];
South Africa, 1900-02.

First World War;

Aisne 1914, 18; **Armentières 1914;** Loos;
Somme 1916, 18; Albert 1916, 18; Bazentin;
Delville Wood; Pozières; Guillemont; Ancre Heights;
Ancre 1916; **Arras 1917;** Scarpe 1917; Arleux;
Messines 1917,18; Ypres 1917, 18; Pilckem;
Langemarck 1917; Menin Road; Polygon Wood;
Broodseinde; Poelcapelle; Passchendaele;
Cambrai 1917, 18; St. Quentin; Bapaume 1918;
Rosières; Avre; Lys; Bailleul; Kemmel; Hindenburg Line;
Havrincourt; Canal du Nord; **St. Quentin Canal;**
Beaurevoir; Courtrai; **Selle;** Valenciennes; Sambre;
France and Flanders 1914-18; Suvla; **Sari Bair;**
Gallipoli 1915-16; Egypt 1916; Tigris 1916;
Kut al Amara 1917; Baghdad; Mesopotamia 1916-18;
Baku; Persia 1918; **N.W. Frontier India 1915.**

Afghanistan 1919.

Second World War:

Dyle; Defence of Escaut; **Ypres-Comines Canal; Caen;**
Orne; Noyers. Mont Pincon; **Brieux Bridgehead;**
North-West Europe 1940, 44; Djebel Kesskiss;
Medjez Plain; Gueriat el Atach Ridge; Gab Gab Gap;
North Africa 1943; Anzio; Carroceto; **Rome;**
Advance to Tiber; Gothic Line; **Marradi;** Italy 1944-45;
Burma 1943.

Post-1945:

Gulf 1991; Wadi al Batin.

REGIMENTAL MUSEUMS

CHESHIRE MILITARY MUSEUM
The Castle, Chester CH1 2DN
Tel: 01244 327617 Fax: 01244 401700
email: museum@chester.ac.uk
Website: www.chester.ac.uk/militarymuseum

WORCESTERSHIRE REGIMENT COLLECTION
City Museum and Art Gallery, Foregate Street,
Worcester WR1 1DT
Tel: 01905 354359 Fax: 01905 353871
email: rhq@wfr.army.mod.uk
Website: www.wfrmuseum.org.uk

STAFFORDSHIRE REGIMENT MUSEUM
Whittington Barracks, Lichfield, Staffs WS14 9PY
Tel: 01543 434394/5 Fax: 01543 434391
email: curator@staffordshireregimentmuseum.com
Website: www.army.mod.uk/staffords

THE SHERWOOD FORESTERS (Nottinghamshire and Derbyshire) REGIMENT COLLECTION
The Castle, Nottingham NG1 6EL
Tel: 01159 465415 Fax: 01559 469853
email: rhqwfr-nottm@lineone.net
Website: www.wfrmuseum.org.uk

1689
Lord Herbert's
Regiment of Foot (1)

1712
The Royal Regiment of
Welch Fuzileers

1714
The Prince of Wales's (2)
Own Royal Regiment of
Welch Fusiliers

1727
The Royal Welch
Fusiliers

23rd

1751
23rd Regiment of Foot
(Royal Welch Fusiliers)

1881
The Royal Welsh
Fusiliers

NOTES:

(1) Raised in the Welsh
Marches by Colonel Lord
Herbert of Chirbury from
thirteen independent
companies of foot.

(2) The future King
George II.

1689
Dering's
Regiment of Foot (3)

24th

1751
24th Regiment of Foot

1782
24th (2nd Warwickshire)
Regiment of Foot

NOTES:

(3) Raised in Kent by
Colonel Sir Edward
Dering for service in
Ireland.

(4) Raised by Colonel
Edmund Fielding from
army pensioners.

1719
Fielding's Regiment of
Invalids (4)

41st

1751
41st Royal Invalids
Regiment of Foot

1787
41st Regiment of Foot

1831
41st (The Welsh)
Regiment of Foot

1756
2nd Battalion
24th Regiment of Foot

69th

1758
69th Regiment of Foot

1782
69th (South Lincolnshire)
Regiment of Foot

1881
THE SOUTH WALES
BORDERERS

1881
THE WELSH REGIMENT

1920
THE WELCH REGIMENT

1920
THE ROYAL WELCH
FUSILIERS

1969
THE ROYAL REGIMENT OF
WALES
(24th / 41st Foot)

1st BATTALION
(The Royal Welch
Fusiliers)

2nd BATTALION
(The Royal
Regiment of Wales)

2007
THE ROYAL WELSH

REGIMENTAL HEADQUARTERS
Maindy Barracks, Whitchurch Road, Cardiff CF14 3

REGIMENTAL MARCHES
Quick March: Men of Harlech
Slow March: Men of Glamorgan: Forth to the Battl

ALLIANCES

Canadian Armed Forces:
Le Royal 22e Régiment
The Ontario Regiment (RCAC)

Australian Military Forces:
The Royal New South Wales Regiment

Pakistan Army:
3rd Battalion The Frontier Force Regiment
4th Battalion The Baluch Regiment

Malaysian Armed Forces:
4th Battalion The Royal Malay Regiment

South African Defence Forces:
Pretoria Regiment
121 South African Infantry Battalion

COLONEL-IN-CHIEF:
HM The Queen

REGIMENTAL MUSEUMS

THE ROYAL WELCH FUSILIERS
REGIMENTAL MUSEUM
Caernarfon Castle, Caernarfon, Gwynedd LL55 2A'
Tel: 01286 673362
Website: www.rwfmuseum.org.uk

THE REGIMENTAL MUSEUM OF
THE ROYAL WELSH
The Barracks, Brecon, Powys LD3 7EB
Tel: 01874 613310
Website: www.rrw.org.uk

FIRING LINE: THE CARDIFF CASTLE MUSEUM
OF THE WELSH SOLDIER
Cardiff Castle, Cardiff CF10 2RB
Tel: 02920 788370
Website: www.cardiffcastlemuseum.org.uk

The Cardiff Castle Museum includes the collections of the
The Queen's Dragoon Guards and The Royal Welsh (Sout
Wales Borderers and Welch Regiment). Opens mid-2010.

BATTLE HONOURS

THE ROYAL WELCH FUSILIERS

THE SOUTH WALES BORDERERS

THE WELCH REGIMENT

Pre-1914:

Device: SPHINX (1801).

amur, 1695; Blenheim [1704]; **Ramillies** [1706]; udenarde [1708]; **Malplaquet** [1709]; ettingen [1743]; **Minden** [1759]; **Peninsula** [1808-14]; orunna [1809]; **Martinique, 1809; Albuhera** [1811]; adajos [1812]; **Salamanca** [1812]; **Nivelle** [1813]; yrenees [1813]; **Vittoria** [1813]; **Orthes** [1814]; oulouse [1814]; **Waterloo** [1815]; **Alma** [1854]; kerman [1854]; **Sevastapol** [1854-55]; ucknow [1857-58]; **Ashantee, 1873-74;** urmah, **1885-87; South Africa, 1899-1902;** elief of Ladysmith [1900]; **Pekin, 1900.**

First World War:

ons; Le Cateau; Retreat from Mons; **Marne 1914;** sne 1914,18; La Bassée 1914; Messines 1914, 17, 18; rmentières 1914; **Ypres 1914, 17, 18;** angemarck 1914, 17; Gheluvelt; Givenchy 1914; euve Chapelle; Aubers; Festubert 1915; Loos; omme 1916, 18; Albert 1916, 18; Bazentin; elville Wood; Pozières; Guillemont; Flers-Courcelette; orval; Le Transloy; Ancre Heights; Ancre 1916, 18; ras 1917; Scarpe 1917; Arleux; Bullecourt; Pilckem; nin Road; Polygon Wood; Broodseinde; Poelcapelle; asschendaele; Cambrai 1917, 18; St. Quentin; apaume 1918; Lys; Bailleul; Kemmel; Scherpenberg; **indenburg Line;** Havrincourt; Epéhy; t. Quentin Canal; Beaurevoir; Selle; Valenciennes; ambre; France and Flanders 1914-18; Piave; **ittorio Veneto;** Italy 1917-18; **Doiran 1917, 18;** acedonia 1915-18; Suvla; Sari Bair; Landing at Suvla; cimitar Hill; **Gallipoli 1915-16;** Rumani; **gypt 1915-17; Gaza;** El Mughar; Jerusalem; Jericho; ell'Asur; Megiddo; Nablus; Palestine 1917-18; gris 1916; Kut al Amara 1917; **Baghdad;** esopotamia 1916-18.

Second World War:

yle; Defence of Escaut; **St. Omer-La Bassée; Caen;** squay; Falaise; Nederrijn; **Lower Maas;** Venlo Pocket; urthe; Rhineland; **Reichswald;** Goch; **Weeze; Rhine;** benburen; Aller; North-West Europe 1940, 44-45; **ladagascar;** Middle East 1942; **Donbaik;** orth Arakan; **Kohima;** Mandalay; Ava; urma 1943-45.

Pre-1914:

Devices: SPHINX (1801); SILVER WREATH (1879).

Blenheim [1704]; **Ramillies** [1706]; **Oudenarde** [1708]; **Malplaquet** [1709]; **Cape of Good Hope, 1806; Peninsula** [1808-14]; **Talavera** [1809]; **Busaco** [1810]; **Fuentes D'Onor** [1811]; **Salamanca** [1812]; **Nivelle** [1813]; **Pyrenees** [1813]; **Vittoria** [1813]; **Orthes** [1814]; **Punjaub** [1848-49]; **Chillianwallah** [1849]; **Goojerat** [1849]; **South Africa, 1877-79; Burmah, 1885-87; South Africa, 1900-02.**

First World War:

Mons; Retreat from Mons; **Marne 1914;** Aisne 1914, 18; **Ypres 1914, 17, 18;** Langemarck 1914, 17; **Gheluvelt;** Nonne Bosschen; Givenchy 1914; Aubers; Loos; **Somme 1916, 18;** Albert 1916, 18; Bazentin; Pozières; Flers-Courcelette; Morval; Ancre Heights; Ancre 1916; Arras 1917, 18; Scarpe 1917; Messines 1917, 18; Pilckem; Menin Road; Polygon Wood; Broodseinde; Poelcapelle; Passchendaele; **Cambrai 1917, 18;** St. Quentin; Bapaume 1918; Lys; Estaires; Hazebrouck; Bailleul; Kemmel; Béthune; Scherpenberg; Drocourt-Quéant; Hindenburg Line; Havrincourt; Epéhy; St. Quentin Canal; Beaurevoir; Courtrai; Selle; Valenciennes; Sambre; France and Flanders 1914-18; **Doiran 1917, 18; Macedonia 1915-18;** Helles; **Landing at Helles;** Krithia; Suvla; Sari Bair; Scimitar Hill; Gallipoli 1915-16; Egypt 1916; Tigris 1916; Kut al Amara 1917; **Baghdad;** Mesopotamia 1916-18; **Tsingtao.**

Second World War:

Norway 1940; Normandy Landing; Sully; Odon; **Caen;** Falaise; Risle Crossing; **Le Havre;** Antwerp-Turnhout Canal; Scheldt; Zetten; Arnhem 1945; **North-West Europe 1944-45;** Gazala; **North Africa 1942;** North Arakan; **Mayu Tunnels; Pinwe;** Schweli; Myitson; **Burma 1944-45.**

Pre-1914:

Device: NAVAL CROWN (1792, 1797).

Belleisle [1761]; **Martinique, 1762; India** [1796-1826]; **St. Vincent, 1797; Bourbon** [1810]; **Java** [1811]; Detroit [1812]; Queenstown [1812]; Miami [1813]; Niagara [1814]; **Waterloo** [1815]; Ava [1824-26]; **Cabool, 1842; Candahar, 1842; Ghuznee, 1842; Alma** [1854]; **Inkerman** [1854]; **Sevastapol** [1854-55]; **South Africa, 1899-1902; Relief of Kimberley** [1900]; **Paardeberg** [1900].

First World War:

Mons; Retreat from Mons; Marne 1914; **Aisne 1914, 18; Ypres 1914, 15, 17;** Langemarck 1914, 17; **Gheluvelt;** Nonne Bosschen; Givenchy 1914; Gravenstafel; St. Julian; Frezenberg; Bellewaarde; Aubers; Loos; **Somme 1916, 18;** Albert 1916, 18; Bazentin; Pozières; Flers-Courcelette; Morval; Ancre Heights; Ancre 1916, 18; Messines 1917, 18; **Pilckem;** Menin Road; Polygon Road; Broodseinde. Poelcapelle; Passchendaele; **Cambrai 1917, 18;** St. Quentin; Bapaume 1918; Lys; Estaires; Hazebrouck; Bailleul; Kemmel; Béthune; Scherpenberg; Arras 1918; Drocourt-Quéant; Hindenburg Line; Epéhy; St. Quentin Canal; Beaurevoir; Selle; Valenciennes; Sambre; France and Flanders 1914-18; Struma; Doiran 1917, 18; **Macedonia 1915-18;** Suvla; Sari Bair; Landing at Suvla; Scimitar Hill; **Gallipoli 1915;** Egypt 1915-17; Gaza; El Mughar; Jerusalem; Tell'Asur; Megiddo; Nablus; **Palestine 1917-18;** Aden; Tigris 1916; Kut al Amara 1917; Baghdad; **Mesopotamia 1916-18.**

Second World War:

Falaise; Lower Maas; Reichswald; North-West Europe 1944-45; Benghazi; North Africa 1940-42; Sicily 1943; Coriano; **Croce;** Rimini Line; Ceriano Ridge; Argenta Gap; **Italy 1943-45;** Crete; **Canea;** Withdrawal to Sphakia; Middle East 1941; **Kyaukmyaung Bridgehead;** Maymyo; Rangoon Road; **Sittang 1945; Burma 1944-45.**

Post-1945:

Korea 1951-52.

ADDITIONAL BATTLE HONOURS OF THE ROYAL REGIMENT OF WALES (24th / 41st FOOT) AND THE ROYAL WELSH

In addition to the Battle Honours of its antecedent regiments shown on the left, The Royal Regiment of Wales (24th / 41st Foot), and then The Royal Welsh, also inherited the *additional* Battle Honours earned by The Monmouthshire Regiment, a TA regiment of The South Wales Borderers now disbanded:

Second World War:

Borguebus Ridge; Mont Pincon; Souleuvre; Le Perier Ridge; Antwerp; Hochwald.

"DEVICES"

A "Device" is a Battle Honour awarded to a regiment which appears on the Colour as a badge or an emblem rather than the usual scroll with the name of the action.

The original Royal Irish Regiment was raised in Ireland by the Earl of Granard in 1684. After 238 years of loyal and distinguished service to the Crown, it was disbanded in 1922 following Irish independence and bears no relation, other than in name, with the present-day Royal Irish Regiment.

Its successor to the proud title started life in 1689 as Tiffin's Regiment and in the Cardwell Reforms of 1881 five distinguished Irish regiments of the line and one Madras regiment from the East India Company combined to form the three legendary Irish regiments whose pedigrees are shown on the following pages — The Royal Inniskilling Fusiliers, The Royal Irish Rifles and The Royal Irish Fusiliers. These three amalgamated in 1968 to form The Royal Irish Rangers which 24 years later amalgamated with The Ulster Defence Regiment to create today's Royal Irish.

The Ulster Defence Regiment was formed in 1970 as a result of a wave of civil unrest in Northern Ireland which threatened to overwhelm the Royal Ulster Constabulary. With an initial establishment of 6,000 men in seven battalions, it was the largest

The Royal Irish Regiment

Until quite recently the Royal Irish Regiment was the largest regiment in the British Army with nine regular battalions and, at its peak, some 10,000 personnel. Today, with a more pacific political climate in Northern Ireland, the Regiment has been reduced to a single battalion.

regiment in the British Army and at its peak its strength rose to 10,000 men in eleven battalions. Its duties were confined purely to service within the province.

The majority of the 197 Ulster Defence Regiment soldiers who lost their lives during the life of the Regiment were killed while off duty and a further 60 were murdered after they had left the Army.

In 1992 the UDR battalions became Northern Ireland Resident (formerly Home Service) Battalions of the Royal Irish and, after further amalgamations, the remaining three battalions were disbanded on 1st August 2007 when the Army ended its support of the civil power in Northern Ireland in response to the promised renouncement of violence by the Provisional IRA.

PRESENT ROLE & ATTACHMENT OF THE REGULAR BATTALION OF THE ROYAL IRISH REGIMENT	
1 R IRISH	Light Role *(16th Air Assault Brigade)* Moving to Tern Hill in 2008.

REGIMENTAL HEADQUARTERS
Palace Barracks, Hollywood, Co. Antrim BT43 7BH
Tel: Civ. 02890 420629 Mil. Ballymena 32380
Fax. 02890 420627
email: rhqrirish-mailbox@mod.uk
Website: www.army.mod.uk/royalirish

REGIMENTAL MARCHES
Quick March: Regimental March of The Royal Irish Regiment "Killaloe"
Slow March: "Eileen Alannah"

ALLIANCES
Canadian Armed Forces:
  The Princess Louise Fusiliers
  2nd Battalion The Irish Regiment of Canada (Sudbury)
  The Irish Fusiliers of Canada (Vancouver Regiment) (Ceased)
Australian Military Forces:
  Adelaide University Regiment
New Zealand Army:
  2nd Battalion (Canterbury, Nelson, Marlborough and West Coast) Royal New Zealand Infantry Regiment
Pakistan Army:
  1st Battalion The Punjab Regiment
  9th Battalion (Wilde's) The Frontier Force Regiment
South African Defence Force:
  South African Irish Regiment
Gibraltar:
  The Royal Gibraltar Regiment
Royal Navy:
  HMS Bulwark

COLONEL-IN-CHIEF
HRH The Duke of York KCVO ADC

On 6th October 2006 HM The Queen awarded the Conspicuous Gallantry Cross to The Royal Irish Regiment in recognition of the 36 years of continuous operational service in Northern Ireland by the Ulster Defence Regiment and the home service battalions of the Royal Irish Regiment. It is the first and only instance of the award being made to a formation rather than an individual.

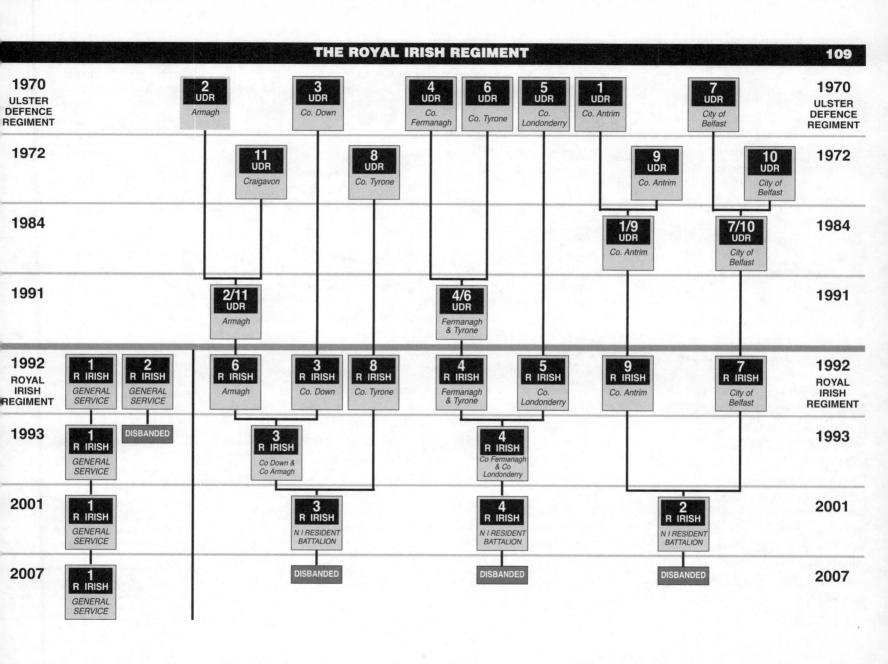

1684
The Earl of Granard's
Regiment of Foot (1)

1695
The Royal Regiment
of Ireland

18th

1751
18th (The Royal Irish)
Regiment of Foot

1689
Tiffin's Regiment
of Foot (3)

27th

1751
27th (Inniskilling)
Regiment of Foot

1854
3rd (Madras European
Infantry) Regiment (4)

1858
3rd (Madras) Regiment

108th

1861
108th (Madras Infantry)
Regiment

1793
Fitch's Grenadiers (5)

83rd

1794
83rd Regiment of Foot

1859
83rd (County of Dublin)
Regiment of Foot

1793
Cuyler's Shropshire
Volunteers (6)

86th

1794
86th Regiment of Foot

1809
86th (The Leinster)
Regiment of Foot

1812
86th (Royal County
Down) Regiment

87th

1793
87th (The Prince of
Wales's Irish) (7)
Regiment of Foot (8)

1811
87th (The Prince of
Wales's Own Irish)
Regiment of Foot

1827
87th (Royal Irish
Fusiliers) Regiment

89th

1793
89th Regiment of Foot (9)

1866
89th (Princess Victoria's)
Regiment of Foot (10)

1881
THE ROYAL IRISH REGIMENT

1922
DISBANDED (2)

1881
**THE ROYAL INNISKILLING
FUSILIERS**

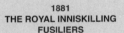

1881
THE ROYAL IRISH RIFLES

1921
THE ROYAL ULSTER RIFLES

1881
THE ROYAL IRISH FUSILIERS
(Princess Victoria's)

1970
**THE ULSTER DEFENCE
REGIMENT**

1968
THE ROYAL IRISH RANGERS
(27th (Inniskilling), 83rd and 87th)

1992
**THE ROYAL IRISH
REGIMENT**
(27th (Inniskilling), 83rd, 87th and
The Ulster Defence Regiment)

REGIMENTAL MUSEUMS

ROYAL INISKILLING FUSILIERS MUSEUM
The Castle, Enniskillen, Co Fermanagh BT74 7HL
Tel: 02866 323142 Fax: 02866 320359
email: museum@inniskilling.com
Website: www.inniskilling.com

ROYAL ULSTER RIFLES MUSEUM
5 Waring Street, Belfast BT1 2EW
Tel: 02890 232086 Fax: 02890 232086
email: rurmuseum@yahoo.co.uk

ROYAL IRISH FUSILIERS REGIMENTAL MUSEUM
Sovereign's House, The Mall, Armagh, BT16 9DL
Tel: 02837 522911 Fax: 02827 522911
email: Rylirfusiliermus@aol.com
Website: rirfus-museum.freeserve.co.uk

ROYAL IRISH REGIMENT MUSEUM
St Patrick's Barracks, Ballymena, Co Antrim BT43 7BH
Tel: 02825 661386 Fax: 02825 661378
email: hqrirish@royalirishregiment.co.uk
Website: www.royalirishregiment.co.uk

NOTES

(1) Raised in Ireland from independent companies of musketeers and pikemen.

(2) Disbanded during the Irish Civil War. Raised nine battalions during World War I.

(3) Raised in Ireland by Gustavus Hamilton for the defence of Enniskillen.

(4) Hon. East India Co. Service. Taken on to Crown strength after the Mutiny.

(5) Raised by Colonel William Fitch with recruits mainly from Dublin.

(6) Raised in Shrewsbury by General Sir Cornelius Cuyler.

(7) The future King George IV.

(8) Raised in Ireland by Colonel Sir John Doyle.

(9) Raised in Ireland by Colonel William Crosbie.

(10) Presented with new Colours by Queen Victoria in 1866 when the title "Princess Victoria's" was granted to commemorate the previous presentation in 1822 when she was still "Princess Victoria".

BATTLE HONOURS

THE ROYAL IRISH REGIMENT
∽∾∿
DISBANDED 1922

Pre-1914:

Namur, 1695; Blenheim [1704]; Ramillies [1706]; Oudenarde [1708]; Malplaquet [1709]; China [1840-42]; Pegu [1852-53]; Sevastapol [1854-55]; New Zealand [1863-66]; Afghanistan, 1879-80; Tel-el-Kebir [1882]; Nile, 1884-85; South Africa, 1900-02.

First World War:

Mons; Le Cateau; Retreat from Mons; Marne 1914; Aisne 1914; La Bassée 1914; Ypres 1915, 17, 18; Gravenstafel; St. Julien; Frezenberg; Bellewaarde; Somme 1916, 18; Albert 1916, 18; Bazentin; Delville Wood; Guillemont; Ginchy; Messines 1917; Pilckem; Langemarck 1917; St. Quentin; Rosières; Arras 1918; Drocourt-Quéant; Hindenburg Line; Canal du Nord; St. Quentin Canal; Beaurevoir; Cambrai 1918; Courtrai; France and Flanders 1914-18; Struma; Macedonia 1915-17; Suvla; Landing at Suvla; Gallipoli 1915; Gaza; Jerusalem; Tell Asur; Megiddo; Nablus; Palestine 1917-18.

REGIMENT DISBANDED 1922

THE ROYAL INNISKILLING FUSILIERS

Pre-1914:

Havannah [1762]; Martinique, 1762; St. Lucia, 1778; St. Lucia, 1796; Maida [1806]; Peninsula [1808-14]; Badajos [1812]; Salamanca [1812]; Nivelle [1813]; Pyrenees [1813]; Orthes [1814]; Waterloo [1815]; South Africa, 1835; South Africa, 1846-47; Central India [1857-58]; South Africa, 1899-1902]; Relief of Ladysmith [1900].

First World War:

Le Cateau; Retreat from Mons; Marne 1914, 18; Aisne 1914; Messines 1914, 17; Armentières 1914; Aubers; Festubert 1915; Somme 1916, 18; Albert 1916; Bazentin; Guillemont; Ginchy; Ancre 1916; Arras 1917; Scarpe 1917; Ypres 1917, 18; Pilckem; Langemarck 1917; Polygon Wood; Broodseinde; Poelcapelle; Cambrai 1917, 18; St. Quentin; Rosières; Hindenburg Line; Beaurevoir; Courtrai; Selle; Sambre; France and Flanders 1914-18; Kosturino; Struma; Macedonia 1915-18; Helles; Landing at Helles; Krithia; Suvla; Landing at Suvla; Scimitar Hill; Gallipoli 1915-16; Egypt 1916; Gaza; Jerusalem; Tell'Asur; Palestine 1917-18.

Second World War:

Defence of Arras; Ypres-Comines Canal; North-West Europe 1940; Two Tree Hill; Bou Arada; Oued Zarga; Djebel Bel Mahdi; Djebel Tanngoucha; North Africa 1942-43; Landng in Sicily; Solarino; Simeto Bridgehead; Adrano; Centuripe; Simeto Crossing; Pursuit to Messina; Sicily 1943; Termoli; Trigno; San Salvo; Sangro; Garigliano Crossing; Minturno; Anzio; Cassino II; Massa Tambourini; Liri Valley; Rome; Advance to Tiber; Trasimene Line; Monte Spaduro; Argenta Gap; Italy 1943-45; Middle East 1942; Yenangyaung 1942; Donbaik; Burma 1942-43.

THE ROYAL IRISH RIFLES
(THE ROYAL ULSTER RIFLES)

Pre-1914:

India [1796-1826]; Cape of Good Hope, 1806; Peninsula [1808-14]; Talavera [1809]; Bourbon [1810]; Busaco [1810]; Fuentes d'Onor [1811]; Badajos [1812]; Ciudad Rodrigo [1812]; Salamanca [1812]; Nivelle [1813]; Vittoria [1813]; Orthes [1814]; Toulouse [1814]; Central India [1857-58]; South Africa, 1899-1902.

First World War:

Mons; Le Cateau; Retreat from Mons; Marne 1914; Aisne 1914; La Bassée 1914; Messines 1914, 17, 18; Armentières 1914; Ypres 1914, 15, 17, 18; Nonne Bosschen; Neuve Chapelle; Frezenberg; Aubers; Somme 1916, 18; Albert 1916; Bazentin; Pozières; Guillemont; Ginchy; Ancre Heights; Pilckem; Langemarck 1917; Cambrai 1917; St. Quentin; Rosières; Lys; Bailleul; Kemmel; Courtrai; France and Flanders 1914-18; Kosturino; Struma; Macedonia 1915-17; Suvla; Sari Bair; Gallipoli 1915; Gaza; Jerusalem; Tell'Asur; Palestine 1917-18.

Second World War:

Dyle; Dunkirk 1940; Normandy Landing; Cambes; Caen; Troarn; Venlo Pocket; Rhine; Bremen; North-West Europe 1940, 44-45.

Post-1945:

Seoul; Imjin; Korea 1950-51.

THE ROYAL IRISH FUSILIERS
(Princess Victoria's)

Pre-1914:

Monte Video [1807]; Peninsula [1808-14]; Talavera [1809]; Barrosa [1811]; Java [1811]; Tarifa [1811]; Niagara [1813]; Nivelle [1813]; Vittoria [1813]; Orthes [1814]; Toulouse [1814]; Ava [1824-26]; Sevastapol [1854-55]; Egypt, 1882-84; Tel-el-Kebir [1882]; South Africa, 1899-1902; Relief of Ladysmith [1900].

First World War:

Le Cateau; Retreat from Mons; Marne 1914; Aisne 1914; Armentières 1914; Ypres 1915, 17, 18; Gravenstafel; St. Julien; Frezenberg; Bellewaarde; Somme 1916, 18; Albert 1916; Guillemont; Ginchy; Le Transloy; Arras 1917; Scarpe 1917; Messines 1917, 18; Langemarck 1917; Cambrai 1917; St. Quentin; Rosières; Lys; Bailleul; Kemmel; Courtrai; France and Flanders 1914-18; Kosturino; Struma; Macedonia 1915-17; Suvla; Landing at Suvla; Scimitar Hill; Gallipoli 1915; Gaza; Jerusalem; Tell'Asur; Megiddo; Nablus; Palestine 1917-18.

Second World War:

Withdrawal to Escaut; St. Omer-La Bassée; Bou Arada; Stuka Farm; Oued Zarga; Djebel Bel Mahdi; Djebel Ang; Djebel Tanngoucha; Adrano; Centuripe; Salso Crossing; Simeto Crossing; Malleto; Termoli; Trigno; Sangro; Fossacesia; Cassino II; Liri Valley; Trasimene Line; Monte Spaduro; Monte Grande; Argenta Gap; San Nicolo Canal; Leros; Malta 1940.

───────────

THE ROYAL IRISH REGIMENT
(27th (Inniskilling), 83rd, 87th and The Ulster Defence Regiment)

Post-1945:

Iraq 2003.

The concept of Light Infantry – fast moving, lightly-equipped troops with special training in marksmanship and self-reliance — was first considered within the British Army during the late 18th-century campaigns in North America where a stealthy and fleet-footed enemy often confounded traditional infantry tactics.

Over the next 50 years, experimental Light Companies were formed within several regiments of the British and East India Company Armies and these were sometimes mustered together as a single battalion to undertake specific tasks where stealth and mobility were of paramount importance.

In 1799 the Duke of York, impressed by the successes of the French *Tiraillers* — skirmishers detached from the main body of the army — ordered the formation of an Experimental Rifle Corps at Shorncliffe in Kent under the command of Colonel Coote Manningham. This comprised a detachment of three officers

The Bugle-Horn replaced the Drum for passing battlefield orders and has become the symbol of Light Infantry formations.

The Light Infantry element of the British Army is now contained in one large regiment of five regular battalions — The Rifles — which has evolved from twenty-two original infantry regiments of the line.

and 34 men from each of 15 different line regiments *(see page 122)* which, three years later, became the 95th Foot.

In 1803 the experiment was extended with the formation of a Corps of Light Infantry at Shorncliffe commanded by

Major-General John Moore who devised and established the first large-scale training programme for Light Troops. His riflemen were equipped with the Baker rifle, shorter, lighter and with better sights than the "Brown Bess" used by the rest

PRESENT ROLES & ATTACHMENTS OF THE REGULAR BATTALIONS THE RIFLES	
1 RIFLES	Commando. *(3rd Commando Brigade).* Chepstow.
2 RIFLES	Light Role. *(19th Light Brigade).* Ballykinler, Northern Ireland.
3 RIFLES	Light Role. *(52nd Infantry Brigade).* Edinburgh.
4 RIFLES	Mechanised Infantry role. *(1st Mechanised Brigade).* Bulford.
5 RIFLES	Armoured Infantry role. *(20th Armoured Brigade).* Paderborn, Germany.

of the infantry. They were trained to operate in small groups, to move with stealth using the ground for cover and to make tactical decisions on their own initiative — indeed, very much the forerunner of the requirements of a modern-day infantryman.

Specific regiments then began to adopt the title and role of Light Infantry and these regiments eventually formed the nucleus of the famous Light Division which served with such distinction under Sir John Moore in the Peninsula.

Riflemen of the Light Infantry did not carry Colours into battle, which would impede rapid movement, and orders were passed by bugle-horn rather than by cumbersome drums; their drill was simplified and their marching pace increased from the standard 120 to 140 paces per minute.

These are among the many traditions which have been carried forward into today's Light Regiment — **The Rifles** — which incorporates no less than 22 former regiments most of which have a Light Infantry background. As they bear no Colours on which to emblazon their Battle Honours, a representative selection is borne on the belt badge of the new Regiment.

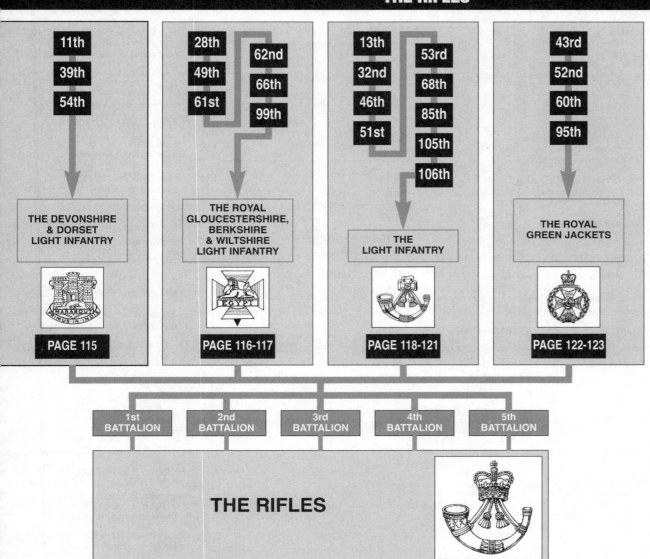

11th
39th
54th

THE DEVONSHIRE
& DORSET
LIGHT INFANTRY

PAGE 115

28th
49th
61st

62nd
66th
99th

THE ROYAL
GLOUCESTERSHIRE,
BERKSHIRE
& WILTSHIRE
LIGHT INFANTRY

PAGE 116-117

13th
32nd
46th
51st

53rd
68th
85th
105th
106th

THE
LIGHT INFANTRY

PAGE 118-121

43rd
52nd
60th
95th

THE ROYAL
GREEN JACKETS

PAGE 122-123

1st
BATTALION

2nd
BATTALION

3rd
BATTALION

4th
BATTALION

5th
BATTALION

THE RIFLES

REGIMENTAL HEADQUARTERS

Peninsula Barracks, Romsey Road, Winchester, Hampshire SO 23 8TS

Tel: 01962 828527

email: rhq@the-rifles.co.uk

Website: www.army.mod.uk/infantry/
regiments/3469.aspx

COLONEL-IN-CHIEF THE RIFLES

Field Marshal HRH The Prince Philip,
Duke of Edinburgh, KG KT GBE OM AC QSO

ROYAL COLONELS of the Regular Battalions

1st Battalion:
Field Marshal HRH The Duke of Kent,
KG GCMG GCVO ADC

2nd Battalion:
HRH The Earl of Wessex, KCVO

3rd Battalion:
HRH The Princess Alexandra,
The Hon. Lady Ogilvy, KG GCVO

4th Battalion:
HRH The Duchess of Cornwall

5th Battalion:
HRH The Countess of Wessex

REGIMENTAL MARCHES

Quick March:	"The Rifles"
Double March:	"Keel Row"
	"Road to the Isles"
Slow March:	"Old Salamanca"

ALLIANCES

Canadian Armed Forces:
The Royal Canadian Regiment
Princess Patricia's Canadian Light Infantry
The Queen's Own Rifles of Canada
The Brockville Rifles
The Royal Winnipeg Rifles
The Royal Regina Rifles
Les Fusiliers de Sherbrooke
The Lincoln and Welland Regiment
The Algonquin Regiment
The British Columbia Regiment
(Duke of Connaught's Own) RCAC
The Royal Hamilton Light Infantry
Le Régiment de Maisonneuve
The North Saskatchewan Regiment

Australian Military Forces:
Monash University Regiment
Melbourne University Regiment
11th/28th Battalion, The Royal Western Australia
Regiment
The Royal New South Wales Regiment

New Zealand Army:
The Royal New Zealand Infantry Regiment
The Canterbury and Nelson-Marlborough and
West Coast Regiment
The Hauraki Regiment

Pakistan Army:
11th, 13th Battalions, The Baloch Regiment
1st Battalion, The Sind Regiment
2nd and 13th Battalions, The Frontier Force Regiment

Kenya Army:
1st and 3rd Battalions, The Kenya Rifles

Mauritius:
The Mauritius Special Mobile Force

South African Defence Forces:
The Capetown Rifles
The Rand Light Infantry
The Durban Light Infantry
The Kaffrarian Rifles

Malaysian Armed Forces:
6th Battalion, The Royal Malay Regiment

Ghana:
1st Battalion, The Ghana Regiment

Royal Navy:
HMS Astute
HMS Cornwall
HMS Exeter
HMS Gloucester
HMS Somerset

BONDS OF FRIENDSHIP

South Africa
5th Battalion, South African Infantry

France
2ème Régiment Étranger d'Infanterie

**THE KEEP MILITARY MUSEUM
(The Devonshire and Dorset Regiment)**
Bridport Road, Dorchester, Dorset DT1 1RN
Tel: 01305 264066 Fax: 01305 250373
email: curator@keepmilitarymuseum.org
Website: www.keepmilitarymuseum.org

**SOMERSET MILITARY MUSEUM
(Somerset Light Infantry)**
Somerset County Museum, The Castle,
Taunton TA1 4AA
Tel: 01823 320201 Fax: 01823 320229
email: info@sommilmuseum.org.uk
Website: www. sommilmuseum.org.uk

DURHAM LIGHT INFANTRY MUSEUM
DLI Museum and Art Gallery,
Aykley Heads, Durham DH1 5TU
Tel: 01913 842214 Fax: 01903 861770
email: dli@durham.gov.uk
Website: www.durham.gov.uk/dli

**DUKE OF CORNWALL'S LIGHT INFANTRY
REGIMENTAL MUSEUM**
The Keep, Bodmin, Cornwall PL31 1EG
Tel: 01208 72810 Fax: 01208 72810
email: dclimus@talk21.com
Website: www.lightinfantry.org.uk/regiments/dcli/
duke_museum.htm

ROYAL GREEN JACKETS MUSEUM
Peninsula Barracks, Romsey Road, Winchester,
Hampshire SO23 8TS
Tel: 01962 828549 Fax: 01962 828500
email: museum@royalgreenjackets.co.uk
Website: www.royalgreenjackets.co.uk

**KING'S OWN YORKSHIRE LIGHT INFANTRY
MUSEUM**
Doncaster Museum and Art Gallery, Chequer Road,
Doncaster, South Yorks DN1 2AE
Tel: 01302 734293 Fax: 01302 735409
email: museum@doncaster.gov.uk
Website: www.doncaster.gov.uk/museums

**OXFORDSHIRE AND BUCKINGHAMSHIRE LIGHT
INFANTRY MUSEUM**
Slade Park TA Barracks, Headington, Oxford OX3 7J
Tel: 01865 780128

**SHROPSHIRE REGIMENTAL MUSEUM
(The King's Shropshire Light Infantry)**
The Castle, Shrewsbury, Shropshire SY1 2AT
Tel: 01743 262292 Fax: 01743 270023
email: shropsrm@zoom.co.uk
Website: www.lightinfantry.org.uk/regiments/ksli/
shrop_museum.htm

1685
The Duke of Beaufort's
Musketeers (1)

11th

1751
11th Regiment of Foot

1782
11th (North Devonshire)
Regiment of Foot

NOTES

(1) Raised by Henry, Duke of Beaufort in Devonshire, Dorset and Somerset.

(2) Raised in Ireland by Colonel Richard Coote.

(3) In 1754 the 39th Foot was the first British regiment to arrive for service in India thus earning the motto *"Primus in Indus"*.

1702
Coote's
Regiment of Foot (2)

39th

1751
39th Regiment of Foot (3)

1782
39th (East Middlesex)
Regiment of Foot

1807
39th (Dorsetshire)
Regiment of Foot

1755
56th Regiment of Foot

54th

1757
Renumbered
54th Regiment of Foot

1782
54th (West Norfolk)
Regiment of Foot

1881
THE DEVONSHIRE REGIMENT

1881
The Dorsetshire Regiment

1951
THE DORSET REGIMENT

1958
THE DEVONSHIRE AND DORSET REGIMENT

2005
THE DEVONSHIRE AND DORSET LIGHT INFANTRY

On 20th July 2005, as part of the infantry restructure, The Devonshire and Dorset Regiment was re-roled as Light Infantry with the title *The Devonshire and Dorset Light Infantry.* From this date, the regiment adopted the differences in dress and ceremonial exclusive to Light Infantry units.

2007
THE RIFLES

BATTLE HONOURS

THE DEVONSHIRE REGIMENT

Pre-1914:

Dettingen [1743]; **Peninsula** [1808-14]; **Salamanca** [1812]; **Nive** [1813]; **Pyrenees** [1813]; **Orthes** [1814]; **Toulouse** [1814]; **Afghanistan, 1879-1880; South Africa, 1899-1902; Defence of Ladysmith** [1899-1900]; **Relief of Ladysmith** [1900].

First World War:

Aisne 1914-18; **La Bassée 1914;** Armentières 1914; Neuve Chapelle; Hill 60; **Ypres 1915, 17;** Gravenstafel; St. Julien; Frezenberg; Aubers; **Loos; Somme 1916, 18;** Albert 1916; Bazentin; Delville Wood; Guillemont; Flers-Courcelette; Morval; Arras 1917; Vimy 1917; Scarpe 1917; Bullecourt; Pilckem; Langemarck 1917; Polygon Wood; Broodseinde; Poelcapelle; Passchendaele; Rosières; Villers Bretonneux; Lys; Hazebrouck; **Bois des Buttes;** Marne 1918; Tardenois; Bapaume 1918; **Hindenburg Line;** Havrincourt; Epéhy; Canal du Nord; St. Quentin Canal; Beaurevoir; Cambrai 1918; Selle; Sambre; France and Flanders 1914-18; Piave; **Vittorio Veneto;** Italy 1917-18; **Doiran 1917, 18;** Macedonia 1915-18; Egypt 1916-17; Gaza; Nebi Samwil; Jerusalem; Tell'Asur; **Palestine 1917-18;** Tigris 1916; Kut al Amara 1917; **Mesopotamia 1916-18.**

Second World War:

Normandy Landing; Port en Bessin; Tilly sur Seulles; **Caen;** St Pierre la Vielle; Nederrijn; Roer; **Rhine;** Ibbenburen; **North-West Europe 1944-45; Landing in Sicily; Regalbuto;** Sicily 1943; Landing at Porto San Venere; Italy 1943; **Malta 1940-42; Imphal;** Shenam Pass; Tamu Road; Ukhrul; **Myinmu Bridgehead;** Kyaukse 1945; **Burma 1943-45.**

THE DORSET REGIMENT

Pre-1914:

Plassey [1757]; **Gibraltar, 1779-1783; Martinique, 1794; Marabout** [1802]; **Peninsula** [1808-14]; **Albuhera** [1811]; **Nive** [1813]; **Nivelle** [1813]; **Vittoria** [1813]; **Orthes** [1814]; **Ava** [1824-26]; **Maharajpore** [1843]; **Sevastopol** [1854-55]; **Tirah** [1897-98]; **South Africa, 1899-1902; Relief of Ladysmith** [1900].

First World War:

Mons; Le Cateau; Retreat from Mons; **Marne 1914;** Aisne 1914; La Bassée 1914; Armentières 1914; **Ypres 1915, 17;** Gravenstafel; St. Julien; Bellewaarde; **Somme 1916, 19;** Albert 1916, 18; Flers-Courcelette; Thiepval; Ancre 1916, 18; Arras 1917; Scarpe 1917; Messines 1917; Langemarck 1917; Polygon Wood; Broodseinde; Poelcapelle; Passchendaele; St. Quentin; Amiens; Bapaume 1918; **Hindenburg Line;** Epéhy; Canal du Nord; St. Quentin Canal; Beaurevoir; Cambrai 1918; Selle; **Sambre;** France and Flanders 1914-18; **Suvla;** Landing at Suvla; Scimitar Hill; Gallipoli 1915; Egypt 1916; **Gaza;** El Mughar; Nebi Samwil; Jerusalem; Tell'Asur; Megiddo; Sharon; Palestine 1917-18; Basra; **Shaiba;** Kut al Amara 1915, 17; **Ctesiphon;** Defence of Kut al Amara; Baghdad; Mesopotamia 1914-18.

Second World War:

St. Omer-La Bassée; Normandy Landing; Villers Bocage; Tilly sur Seulles; **Caen;** Mont Pincon; St. Pierre la Vielle; **Arnhem 1944; Aam;** Geilenkirchen; Goch; Rhine; Twente Canal; North-West Europe 1940, 44-45; **Landing in Sicily;** Agira; Regalbuto; Sicily 1943; Landing at Porto San Venere; Italy 1943; **Malta 1940-42; Kohima; Mandalay;** Mt. Popa; Burma 1944-45.

1694
Gibson's
Regiment of Foot (1)

28th

1751
28th Regiment of Foot

1782
28th (North
Gloucestershire)
Regiment of Foot

1756
2nd Battalion
3rd Regiment of Foot

61st

1758
61st Regiment of Foot

1782
61st (South
Gloucestershire)
Regiment of Foot

NOTES

(1) Raised by Sir John Gibson in Portsmouth.

(2) Raised from six independent companies by Colonel Edward Trelawney, Governor of Jamaica. Also known as "The Jamaica Volunteers".

(3) Princess Charlotte, daughter of the future King George IV.

1744
Trelawney's
Regiment of Foot (2)

1747
63rd Regiment of Foot

49th

1751
49th Regiment of Foot

1782
49th (Hertfordshire)
Regiment of Foot

1816
49th (The Princess
Charlotte of Wales's) (3)
Hertfordshire Regiment
of Foot

1755
2nd Battalion
19th Regiment of Foot

66th

1758
66th Regiment of Foot

1782
66th (Berkshire)
Regiment of Foot

1756
2nd Battalion
4th King's Own
Regiment (4)

62nd

1758
62nd Regiment of Foot

1782
62nd (Wiltshire)
Regiment of Foot

99th

1824
99th Regiment of Foot (5)

1832
99th (Lanarkshire)
Regiment of Foot

1874
99th (The Duke of
Edinburgh's) (6)
Regiment of Foot

NOTES

(4) Raised by Colonel Alexander Duroure in Exeter.

(5) Raised in Lanarkshire by Major-General Gage John Hall.

(6) Prince Alfred, Duke of Edinburgh, second son of Queen Victoria.

1881
**THE GLOUCESTERSHIRE
REGIMENT**

1881
PRINCESS CHARLOTTE OF
WALES'S
(Berkshire Regiment)

1885
PRINCESS CHARLOTTE OF
WALES'S
(Royal Berkshire Regiment)

1921
**THE ROYAL BERKSHIRE
REGIMENT**
(Princess Charlotte of Wales's)

1881
THE WILTSHIRE REGIMENT
(Duke of Edinburgh's)

1994
THE ROYAL
GLOUCESTERSHIRE,
BERKSHIRE AND
WILTSHIRE REGIMENT

2005
**THE ROYAL
GLOUCESTERSHIRE,
BERKSHIRE AND
WILTSHIRE LIGHT
INFANTRY**

On 20th July 2005, as part of the infantry restructure, The Royal Gloucestershire, Berkshire and Wiltshire Regiment was re-roled as Light Infantry with the title *The Royal Gloucestershire, Berkshire and Wiltshire Light Infantry.* From this date, the Regiment adopted the differences in dress and ceremonial exclusive to Light Infantry units.

1959
**THE DUKE OF EDINBURGH'S
ROYAL REGIMENT**
(Berkshire and Wiltshire)

2007
THE RIFLES

BATTLE HONOURS

THE [G]LOUCESTERSHIRE REGIMENT

THE ROYAL BERKSHIRE REGIMENT (Princess Charlotte of Wales's)

THE WILTSHIRE REGIMENT (Duke of Edinburgh's)

Pre-1914:

[Ra]millies [1706]; **Louisburg** [1758]; [Gu]adeloupe, **1759**; **Quebec, 1759**; **Havannah** [1762]; [Ma]rtinique, **1762**; **St. Lucia, 1778**; **Maida** [1806]; [Pe]ninsula [1808-14]; **Corunna** [1809]; **Talavera** [1809]; [Bu]saco [1810]; **Albuhera** [1811]; **Barrosa** [1811]; [Sa]lamanca [1812]; **Pyrenees** [1813]; **Nive** [1813]; [Ni]velle [1813]; **Vittoria** [1813]; **Orthes** [1814]; [Tou]louse [1814]; **Waterloo** [1815]; **Punjaub** [1848-49]; [Mooltan/Chillianwallah] [1849]; **Goojerat** [1849]; **Alma** [1854]; [In]kerman [1854]; **Sevastapol** [1854-55]; **Delhi, 1857**; [De]fence of Ladysmith [1899-1900]; [So]uth Africa, 1899-1902; **Relief of Kimberley** [1900]; [Paa]rdeberg, 1900.

First World War:

[Mo]ns; Retreat from Mons; Marne 1914, 18; [Ai]sne 1914, 18; **Ypres 1914, 15, 17;** [Lan]gemarck 1914, 17; Gheluvelt; Nonne Bosschen; [Gi]venchy 1914; Gravenstafel; St. Julien; Frezenberg; [Bel]lewaarde; Aubers; **Loos; Somme 1916, 18;** [Al]bert 1916, 18; Bazentin; Delville Wood; Pozières; [Gu]illemont; Flers-Courcelette; Moeval; Ancre Heights; [An]cre 1916; Arras 1917, 18; Vimy 1917; Scarpe 1917; [M]essines 1917, 18; Pilckem; Menin Road; Broodseinde; [Pol]ygon Wood; Poelcapelle; Passchendaele; [Ca]mbrai 1917, 18; St. Quentin; Bapaume 1918; [Ro]sières; Avre; **Lys;** Estaires; Hazebrouck; Bailleul; [Ke]mmel; Béthune; Drocourt-Quéant; Hindenburg Line; [Ep]éhy; Canal du Nord; St. Quentin Canal; Beaurevoir; [Sel]le; Valenciennes; Sambre; France and Flanders [19]14-18; Piave; **Vittorio Veneto;** Italy 1917-18; Struma; [Do]iran 1917; Macedonia 1915-18; Suvla; **Sari Bair;** [Kr]ithia/Krimitar Hill; Gallipoli 1915-16; Egypt 1916; Tigris 1916; [Ku]t al Amara 1917; **Baghdad;** Mesopotamia 1916-18; [Pe]rsia 1918.

Second World War:

[De]fence of Escaut; St. Omer-La Bassée; Wormhoudt; [Cas]sel; Villers Bocage; **Mont Pincon; Falaise;** [I]sle Crosing; Le Havre; Zetten; [No]rth-West Europe 1940, 44-45; **Taukyan; Paungde;** [Kon]ywa 1942; North Arakan; Mayu Tunnels; **Pinwe;** [S]hweli; **Myitson; Burma 1942, 44-45.**

Post-1945:

[Hi]ll 327; **Imjin; Korea 1950-51.**

Pre-1914:

St. Lucia, 1778; Egmont-op-Zee [1799]; **Copenhagen** [1801]; **Peninsula** [1808-14]; Douro [1809]; **Talavera** [1809]; **Albuhera** [1811]; **Queenstown** [1812]; **Nive** [1813]; **Nivelle** [1813]; **Pyrenees** [1813]; **Vittoria** [1813]; **Orthes** [1814]; **Alma** [1854]; **Inkerman** [1854]; **Sevastapol** [1854-55]; **Afghanistan, 1879-80; Kandahar, 1880; Egypt, 1882-84; Suakin, 1885; Tofrek** [1885]; **South Africa, 1899-1902;**

First World War:

Mons; Retreat from Mons; Marne 1914; Aisne 1914, 18; **Ypres 1914, 18;** Langemarck 1914, 17; Gheluvelt; Nonne Bosschen; **Neuve Chapelle;** Aubers; Festubert 1915; **Loos; Somme 1916, 18;** Albert 1916, 18; Bazentin; Delville Wood; Pozières; Flers-Courcelette; Morval; Thiepval; Le Transloy; Ancre Heights; Ancre 1916, 18; **Arras 1917, 18;** Scarpe 1917, 18; Arleux; Pilckem; Polygon Wood; Broodseinde; Poelcapelle; Passchendaele; Cambrai 1917, 18; St. Quentin; Bapaume 1918; Rosières; Avre; Villers Bretonneux; Lys; Hazebrouck; Béthune; Amiens; Hindenburg Line; Havrincourt; Epéhy; Canal du Nord; St. Quentin Canal; **Selle;** Valenciennes; Sambre; France and Flanders 1914-18; Piave; **Vittorio Veneto;** Italy 1917-18; **Doiran 1917, 18;** Macedonia 1915-18.

Second World War:

Dyle; St. Omer-La Bassée; **Dunkirk 1940; Normandy Landing; Rhine;** North-West Europe 1940, 44-45; Pursuit to Messina; **Sicily 1943;** Monte Camino; Calabritto; Garigliano Crossing; **Damiano; Anzio;** Carroceto; Italy 1943-45; Donbaik; **Kohima;** Mao Songsang; Shwebo; Kyaukmyaung Bridgehead; **Mandalay;** Fort Dufferin; Rangoon Road; Toungoo; **Burma 1942-45.**

Pre-1914:

Louisburg [1758]; **Peninsula** [1808-14]; **Nive** [1813]; **Ferozeshah** [1845]; **New Zealand** [1846-47]; **Sobraon** [1846]; **Sevastapol** [1854-55]; **Pekin, 1860; South Africa, 1879; South Africa, 1900-02.**

First World War:

Mons; Le Cateau; Retreat from Mons; Marne 1914; Aisne 1914, 18; La Bassée 1914; **Messines 1914, 17, 18;** Armentières 1914; **Ypres 1914, 17;** Langemarck 1914; Nonne Bosschen; Neuve Chapelle; Aubers; Festubert 1915; Loos; **Somme 1916, 18;** Albert 1916, 18; Bazentin; Pozières; Le Transloy; Ancre Heights; Ancre 1916; **Arras 1917;** Scarpe 1917; Pilckem; Menin Road; Polygon Wood; Broodseinde; Poelcapelle; Passchendaele; St. Quentin; Lys; Bailleul; Kemmel; Scherpenberg; **Bapaume 1918;** Hindenburg Line; Epéhy; Canal du Nord; St. Quentin Canal; Beaurevoir; Cambrai 1918; Selle; Sambre; France and Flanders 1914-18; Doiran 1917; **Macedonia 1915-18;** Suvla; Sari Bair; **Gallipoli 1915-16;** Gaza; Nebi Samwil; Jerusalem; Megiddo; Sharon; **Palestine 1917-18;** Tigris 1916; Kut al Amara 1917; **Baghdad;** Mesopotamia 1916-18.

Second World War:

Defence of Arras; Ypres-Comines Canal; Odon; Caen; **Hill 112; Bourguebus Ridge; Maltot; Mont Pincon;** La Varinière; **Seine 1944;** Nederrijn; Roer; Rhineland; **Cleve;** Goch; Xanten; Rhine; Bremen; North-West Europe 1940, 44-45; Solarino; Simeto Bridgehead; Sicily 1943; **Garigliano Crossing;** Minturno; **Anzio; Rome;** Advance to Tiber; Italy 1943-44; Middle East 1942; **North Arakan;** Point 551; Mayu Tunnels; Ngakyedauk Pass; Burma 1943-44.

1685
Huntingdon's (1)
Regiment of Foot

1706
Pearce's Dragoons

13th

1751
13th Regiment of Foot

1782
13th (1st Somersetshire)
Regiment of Foot (2)

1822
13th (1st Somersetshire)
Light Infantry

1842
13th (1st Somersetshire)
Light Infantry
(Prince Albert's) (3)

1881 (May)
The Somersetshire
Regiment (Prince Albert's
Light Infantry)

1881 (July)
Prince Albert's Light
Infantry (Somersetshire
Regiment)

1911
Prince Albert's (Somerset
Light Infantry)

NOTES:

(1) Raised by Colonel the
Earl of Huntingdon mainly
in Buckinghamshire.

(2) In 1776 the Regiment
was stationed at Wells
which was the start of its
association with
Somerset.

(3) Albert, Prince Consort
to Queen Victoria.

1702
Fox's 3rd Regiment
of Marines (4)

1715
Borr's Regiment of Foot

32nd

1751
32nd Regiment of Foot

1782
32nd (Cornwall)
Regiment of Foot

1858
32nd (Cornwall)
Light Infantry

1741
Price's Regiment
of Foot (5)

1747
57th Regiment of Foot

46th

1751
46th Regiment of Foot

1782
46th (South Devonshire)
Regiment of Foot

NOTES:

(4) Raised by Colonel
Edward Fox as Marines
and converted to Infantry
of the Line in 1714.

(5) Raised by Colonel
James Price in the North
of England.

(6) The future King
Edward VII.

(7) Raised by Colonel
Robert Napier in
Yorkshire with a nucleus
of two companies each
from the 15th and 37th
Regiments of Foot.

(8) King George IV.

(9) Raised by Colonel
Archibald Brown-Dyce for
service with the Hon.
East India Company.
Came under Crown
control in 1858.

1755
53rd Regiment of Foot (7)

51st

1757
51st Regiment of Foot

1782
51st (2nd Yorkshire
West Riding)
Regiment of Foot

1809
51st (2nd Yorkshire
West Riding Light
Infantry) Regiment

1821
51st (2nd Yorkshire
West Riding The King's
Own (8) Light Infantry)
Regiment

1839
2nd Madras
(European Light Infantry
Regiment (9)

1858
2nd Madras
(Light Infantry) Regimen

105th

1861
105th Regiment of Foot
(Madras Light Infantry)

1921
**THE SOMERSET LIGHT
INFANTRY**
(Prince Albert's)

1881
**THE DUKE OF
CORNWALL'S (6)
LIGHT INFANTRY**

1959
**THE SOMERSET AND
CORNWALL LIGHT INFANTRY**

1881 (May)
THE SOUTH YORKSHIRE REGIMENT
(King's Own Light Infantry)

1881 (July)
**THE KING'S OWN
YORKSHIRE LIGHT
INFANTRY**

| 1st BATTALION | 2nd BATTALION | 3rd BATTALION | 4th BATTALION |

1968
THE LIGHT INFANTRY

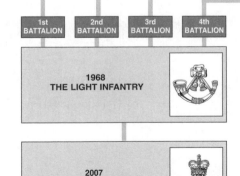

2007
THE RIFLES

1755
55th Regiment of
Foot (10)

53rd

1757
53rd Regiment of Foot

1782
53rd (Shropshire)
Regiment of Foot

85th

1793
Nugent's 85th Regiment
of Foot (11)

1794
85th (Bucks Volunteers)
Regiment of Foot

1815
85th (Duke of York's
Own) (12) (Light Infantry)
Regiment of Foot

1827
85th King's (13) Regiment
of Light Infantry
(Bucks Volunteers)

NOTES:

(10) Raised by Col.
William Whitmore in
Shropshire.

(11) Raised by Col. Sir
George Nugent in
Buckinghamshire.

(12) Frederick, Duke of
York, 2nd son of King
George III.

(13) An honour gained for
protecting King George IV
from a hostile crowd
during his attempt to
divorce Queen Caroline.

(14) The Regiment has its
origins in the South
Durham Militia dating
back to the 13th century.

1756
2nd Battalion
23rd Regiment of
Foot (14)

68th

1758
68th Regiment of Foot

1782
68th (Durham) Regiment
of Foot

1808
68th (Durham) Regiment
of Foot (Light Infantry)

1839
2nd Bombay (European)
Light Infantry (15)

1859
2nd Bombay Light
Infantry

106th

1862
106th Regiment of Foot
(Bombay Light Infantry)

NOTES:

(15) Raised for service
with the Hon. East India
Company. Came under
Crown control in 1858.

1881 (May)
THE SHROPSHIRE REGIMENT
(King's Light Infantry)
1881 (July)
**THE KING'S
SHROPSHIRE LIGHT
INFANTRY**

1881
**THE DURHAM LIGHT
INFANTRY**

BATTLE HONOURS

THE SOMERSET LIGHT INFANTRY (Prince Albert's)

Pre-1914:

Gibraltar, 1704-1705; Dettingen [1743];
Martinique, 1809; Ava, 1824-26; **Afghanistan, 1839**;
Ghuznee, 1839; **Jellalabad, 1842**; Cabool, 1842;
Sevastapol [1854-55]; **South Africa, 1878-79**;
Burmah, 1885-87; **South Africa, 1899-1902**;
Relief of Ladysmith [1900].

First World War:

Le Cateau; Retreat from Mons; **Marne 1914** 13, 18;
Aisne 1914; Armentières 1914; **Ypres 1915, 17, 18**;
St. Julien; Frezenberg; Bellewaarde; Hooge 1915; Loos;
Mount Sorrel; **Somme 1916, 18; Albert 1916, 18**;
Delville Wood; Guillemont; Flers-Courcelette; Morval;
Le Transloy; Ancre 1916, 18; **Arras 1917, 18**;
Vimy 1917; Scarpe 1917, 18; Arleux; Langemarck 1917;
Menin Road; Polygon Wood; Broodseinde; Poelcapelle;
Passchendaele; **Cambrai 1917, 18**; St. Quentin;
Bapaume 1918; Rosières; Avre; Lys; Hazebrouck;
Béthune; Soissonais-Ourcq; Drocourt-Quéant;
Hindenburg Line; Havrincourt; Epéhy; Canal du Nord;
Courtrai; Selle; Valenciennes; Sambre;
France and Flanders 1914-18; Gaza; El Mughar;
Nebi Samwil; Jerusalem; Megiddo; Sharon;
Palestine 1917-18; Tigris 1916; Sharqat;
Mesopotamia 1916-18; N.W. Frontier India 1915.

Afghanistan 1919.

Second World War:

Odon; Caen; **Hill 112; Mont Pincon;** Noireau Crossing;
Seine 1944; Nederrijn; Geilenkirchen; Roer; **Rhineland;**
Cleve; Goch; Hochwald; Xanten; **Rhine;** Bremen;
North-West Europe 1944-45; Cassino II;
Trasimene Line; Arezzo; Advance to Florence;
Capture of Forli; **Cosina Canal Crossing; Italy 1944-45;**
Athens; Greece 1944-45; **North Arakan;** Buthidaung;
Ngakyedauk Pass; Burma 1943-44.

THE DUKE OF CORNWALL'S LIGHT INFANTRY

Pre-1914:

Gibraltar, 1704-1705; Dettingen [1743];
St. Lucia, 1778; Dominica [1805]; **Peninsula** [1808-14];
Rolica [1808]; Vimiera [1808]; **Corunna** [1809];
Salamanca [1812]; Nive [1813]; **Nivelle** [1813];
Pyrenees [1813]; **Orthes** [1814]; **Waterloo** [1815];
Punjaub [1848-49]; Goojerat [1849]; Mooltan [1849];
Sevastapol [1854-55]; **Lucknow** [1857-58];
Egypt, 1882-84; Tel-el-Kebir [1882]; Nile, 1884-85;
South Africa, 1899-1902; Paardeberg [1900].

First World War:

Mons; **Le Cateau;** Retreat from Mons; **Marne 1914;**
Aisne 1914; La Bassée 1914; Armentières 1914;
Ypres 1915, 17; Gravenstafel; St. Julien; Frezenberg;
Bellewaarde; Hooge 1915; Mount Sorrel;
Somme 1916, 18; Delville Wood; Guillemont;
Flers-Courcelette; Morval; Le Transloy; Ancre 1916;
Bapaume 1917, 18; **Arras 1917, 18;** Vimy 1917;
Scarpe 1917; Arleux; Langemarck 1917; Menin Road;
Polygon Wood; Broodseinde; Poelcapelle;
Passchendaele; Cambrai 1917, 18; St. Quentin;
Rosières; Lys; Estaires; Hazebrouck; Albert 1918;
Hindenburg Line; Havrincourt; Canal du Nord; Selle;
Sambre; France and Flanders 1914-18; Italy 1917-18;
Struma; Doiran 1917-18; Macedonia 1915-18; **Gaza;**
Nebi Samwil; Jerusalem; Tell'Asur; Megiddo; Sharon;
Palestine 1917-18; Aden.

Second World War:

Defece of Escaut; Cheux; **Hill 112; Mont Pincon;**
Noreau Crossing; **Nederrijn;** Opheusden;
Geilenkirchen; Rhineland; Goch; Rhine;
North-West Europe 1940, 44-45; Gazala;
Medjez Plain; Si Abdallah; North Africa 1942-43;
Cassino II; Trasimene Line; Advance to Florence;
Incontro; Rimini Line; Italy 1944-45.

THE KING'S OWN YORKSHIRE LIGHT INFANTRY

Pre-1914:

Minden [1759]; **Corunna** [1809]; **Peninsula** [1808-14];
Fuentes D'Onor [1811]; **Salamanca** [1812];
Nivelle [1813]; **Pyrenees** [1813]; **Vittoria** [1813];
Orthes [1814]; **Waterloo** [1815]; **Pegu** [1852-53];
Afghanistan,1878-1880; Ali Masjid [1878];
Burmah, 1885-87; Modder River [1899];
South Africa, 1899-1902.

First World War:

Mons; **Le Cateau;** Retreat from Mons; **Marne 1914, 18;**
Aisne 1914, 18; La Bassée 1914;
Messines 1914, 17, 18; Ypres 1914, 15, 17, 18; Hill 60;
Gravenstafel; St. Julien; Frewzenberg; Bellewaarde;
Hooge 1915; Loos; **Somme 1916, 18;** Albert 1916, 18;
Bazentin; Delville Wood; Pozières; Guillemont;
Flers-Courcelette; Morval; Le Transloy; Ancre 1916;
Arras 1917, 18; Scarpe 1917; Langemarck 1917;
Menin Road; Polygon Wood; Broodseinde; Poelcapelle;
Passchendaele; **Cambrai 1917, 18;** St. Quentin;
Bapaume 1918; Lys; Hazebrouck; Bailleul; Kemmel;
Scherpenberg; Tardenois; Amiens; Hindenburg Line;
Havrincourt; Epéhy; Canal du Nord; St. Quentin Canal;
Beaurevoir; Selle; Valenciennes; **Sambre;**
France and Flanders 1914-18; Piave; Vittorio Veneto;
Italy 1917-18; Struma; **Macedonia 1915-17;**
Egypt 1915-16.

Second World War:

Kvam; **Norway 1940; Fontenay le Pesnil;** Le Havre;
Antwerp-Turnhout Canal; Lower Maas;
North-West Europe 1944-45; Mine de Sedjenane;
Argoub Sellah; North Africa 1943; **Sicily 1943;**
Salerno; Salerno Hills; Cava di Tirreni;
Volturno Crossing; Garigliano Crossing; **Minturno;**
Monte Tuga; **Anzio; Gemmano Ridge;** Carpineta;
Lamone Bridgehead; Italy 1943-45; Sittang 1942;
Burma 1942.

BATTLE HONOURS

THE KING'S SHROPSHIRE LIGHT INFANTRY

THE DURHAM LIGHT INFANTRY

THE LIGHT INFANTRY

Post-1945:

Iraq 2003; Al Basrah.

Pre-1914:

Nieuport [1793]; Tournay [1794]; **St. Lucia, 1796;** Peninsula [1808-14]; Talavera [1809]; Fuentes D'onor [1811]; **Salamanca** [1812]; Busaco [1813]; **Nivelle** [1813]; **Pyrenees** [1813]; Vittoria [1813]; **Bladensburg** [1814]; Toulouse [1814]; Aliwal [1846]; Sobraon [1846]; Punjaub [1848-49]; Goojerat [1849]; **Lucknow** [1857-58]; **Afghanistan, 1879-80;** Egypt, 1882-84; Suakin, 1885; **South Africa, 1899-1902; Paardeberg** [1900].

First World War:

Aisne 1914,18; **Armentières 1914; Ypres 1915, 17;** Gravenstafel; St. Julien; **Frezenberg;** Bellewaarde; Hooge 1915; Mount Sorrel; **Somme 1916, 18;** Albert 1916, 18; Bazentin; Delville Wood; Guillemont; Flers-Courcelette; Morval; Le Transloy; Ancre 1916; **Arras 1917, 18;** Scarpe 1917; Arleux; Hill 70; Langemarck 1917; Menin Road; Polygon Wood; Passchendaele; **Cambrai 1917, 18;** St. Quentin; Bapaume 1918; Lys; Estaires; Messines 1918; Hazebrouck; Bailleul; Kemmel; Béthune; **Bligny;** Hindenburg Line; **Epéhy;** Canal du Nord; Selle; Valenciennes; Sambre; France and Flanders 1914-18; **Doiran 1917, 18;** Macedonia 1915-18; **Jerusalem;** Jericho; Tell'Asur; Palestine 1917-18.

Second World War:

Defence of Escaut; **Dunkirk 1940; Normandy Landing;** Odon; Caen; Bourguebus Ridge; Troarn; Mont Pincon; Couleuvre; Le Perier Ridge; Falaise; **Antwerp;** Nederrijn; Venraij; Rhineland; **Hochwald;** Ibbenburen; Lingen; Aller; **Bremen; North-West Europe 1940, 44-45;** Gueriat el Atach Ridge; **Tunis;** Djebel Bou Aoukaz 1943, II; North Africa 1943; **Anzio;** Campoleone; Carroceto; Gothic Line; Monte Ceco; Monte Grande; **Italy 1943-45.**

Post-1945:

Hill 227, I; **Kowang-San; Korea 1951-52.**

Pre-1914:

Peninsula [1808-14]; **Fuentes D'Onor** [1811]; **Salamanca** [1812]; **Nivelle** [1813]; **Pyrenees** [1813]; **Vittoria** [1813]; **Orthes** [1814]; Alma [1854]; Inkerman [1854]; **Sevastapol** [1854-55]; Bushire [1856]; **Persia** [1856-57]; Reshire [1856]; Koosh-Ab [1857]; **New Zealand** [1863-66]; **South Africa, 1899-1902; Relief of Ladysmith** [1900].

First World War:

Aisne 1914, 18; Armentières 1914; **Ypres 1915, 17, 18;** Gravenstafel; St. Julien; Frezenberg; Bellewaarde; **Hooge 1915; Loos; Somme 1916, 18;** Albert 1916, 18; Bazentin; Delville Wood; Pozières; Guillemont; Flers-Courcelette; Morval; Le Transloy; Ancre Heights; **Arras 1917, 18;** Scarpe 1917; Arleux; Hill 70; **Messines 1917;** Pilckem; Langemarck 1917; Menin Road; Polygon Wood; Broodseinde; Passchendaele; Cambrai 1917, 18; St. Quentin; Rosières; **Lys;** Estaires; Hazebrouck; Bailleul; Kemmel; Scherpenberg; Marne 1918; Tardenois; Bapaume 1918; **Hindenburg Line;** Havrincourt; Epéhy; Canal du Nord; St. Quentin Canal; Beaurevoir; Courtrai; Selle; **Sambre;** France and Flanders 1914-18; Piave; Vittorio Veneto; Italy 1917-18; Macedonia 1916-18; Egypt 1915-16; N.W. Frontier India 1915, 1916-17; Archangel 1918-19.

Afghanistan 1919.

Second World War:

Dyle; Arras counter attack; St. Omer-La Bassée; **Dunkirk 1940;** Villers Bocage; **Tilly sur Seulles; Defence of Rauray;** St. Pierre la Vielle; **Gheel;** Roer; Ibbenburen; North-West Europe 1940, 44-45; Syria1941; Halfaya 1941; **Tobruk 1941;** Relief of Tobruk; Gazala; Gabr el Fachri; Zt el Mrasses; Mers Matruh; Point 174; **El Alamein; Mareth;** Sedjenane I; El Kourzia; North Africa 1940-43; Landing in Sicily; Solarino; **Primosole Bridge;** Sicily 1943; **Salerno;** Volturno Crossing; Teano; Monte Camino; Monte Tuga; Gothic Line; Gemmano Ridge; Cosina Canal Crossing; Pergola Ridge; Cesena; Sillaro Crossing; Italy 1943-45; Athens; Greece 1944-45; Cos; Middle East 1943; Malta 1942; Donbaik; **Kohima;** Mandalay; Burma 1943-45.

Post-1945:

Korea 1952-53.

1741
Fowkes's 54th Regiment of Foot (1)

43rd

1748
43rd Regiment of Foot

1782
43rd (Monmouthshire) Regiment of Foot

1803
43rd (Monmouthshire) Light Infantry (2)

NOTES

(1) Raised in Bedfordshire by Colonel Thomas Fowkes for service in Flanders.

(2) 1804 1st Battalion joined Sir John Moore's Light Brigade at Shorncliffe.

(3) Raised by Colonel Hedworth Lambton in the south of England.

1755
54th Regiment of Foot (3)

52nd

1757
52nd Regiment of Foot

1804
52nd (Oxfordshire) Regiment of Foot

NOTES

(4) Raised by Colonel Lord Loudon from settlers in Pennsylvania, Maryland and Virginia for service in North America.

(5) Frederick, Duke of York, second son of King George III.

(6) King George IV.

1755
The German Legion (4)
62nd Loyal American Provincials

60th

1759
60th Royal Americans

1816
60th Royal American Light Infantry

1818
60th Royal Americans

1824
60th (The Duke of York's (5)) Rifle Corps

1830
60th The King's (6) Royal Rifle Corps

NOTES

(7) An experimental corps of Riflemen raised by Colonel Coote Manningham. A detachment of 3 officers and 34 men were taken from the 1st, 21st, 23rd, 25th, 27th, 29th, 49th, 55th, 67th, 69th, 71st, 72nd, 79th, 85th and 92nd Regiments of Foot.

1800
Manningham's Sharpshooters (7)

95th

1802
95th Regiment of Foot

1812
95th Regiment of Foot (Riflemen)

1816
The Rifle Brigade (8)

1862
The Prince Consort's (9) Own Rifle Brigade

NOTES

(8) Taken out of the numbered regiments of the line and called "The Rifle Brigade" (4 battalions).

(9) Prince Albert, husband of Queen Victoria. (The honour was granted in the year of Prince Albert's death.)

1st BATTALION

2nd BATTALION

1881
THE OXFORDSHIRE LIGHT INFANTRY

1908
THE OXFORDSHIRE AND BUCKINGHAMSHIRE LIGHT INFANTRY

1958
1st GREEN JACKETS
(43rd and 52nd)

1881
THE KING'S ROYAL RIFLE CORPS

1958
2nd GREEN JACKETS
(The King's Royal Rifle Corps)

1922
THE RIFLE BRIGADE
(Prince Consort's Own)

1958
3rd GREEN JACKETS
(The Rifle Brigade)

1st BATTALION

2nd BATTALION

3rd BATTALION

1966
THE ROYAL GREEN JACKETS

2007
THE RIFLES

BATTLE HONOURS

HE OXFORDSHIRE AND UCKINGHAMSHIRE LIGHT INFANTRY

THE KING'S ROYAL RIFLE CORPS

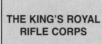

THE RIFLE BRIGADE (Prince Consort's Own)

Pre-1914:

uebec [1759]; Havannah [1762]; Martinique, 1762; ysore [1789-91]; Hindoostan [1790-1823]; artinique, 1794; **Peninsula [1808-14]**; Vimiera [1808]; **orunna [1809]**; Busaco [1810]; Fuentes d'Onor [1811]; **adajos [1812]**; Ciudad Rodrigo [1812]; **alamanca [1812]**; Nive [1813]; Nivelle [1813]; yrenees [1813]; **Vittoria [1813]**; Orthes [1814]; oulouse [1814]; **Waterloo [1815]**; outh Africa, 1851-53; **Delhi, 1857**; ew Zealand [1863-66]; Relief of Kimberley [1900]; aardeberg [1900]; South Africa, 1900-02.

First World War:

ons; Retreat from Mons; Marne 1914; **Ypres 1914, 17; angemarck 1914, 17**; Gheluvelt; **Nonne Bosschen;** ubers; Festubert 1915; Hooge 1915; Loos; ount Sorrel; **Somme 1916, 18**; Albert 1916, 18; azentin; Delville Wood; Pozières; Guillemont; ers-Courcelette; Morval; Le Transloy; Ancre Heights; ncre 1916; Bapaume 1917, 18; Arras 1917; Vimy 1917; carpe 1917; Arleux; Menin Road; Polygon Wood; oodseinde; Poelcapelle; Passchendaele; ambrai 1917, 18; St. Quentin; Rosières; Avre; Lys; azebrouck; Béthune; Hindenburg Line; Havrincourt; anal du Nord; Selle; Valenciennes; rance and Flanders 1914-18; **Piave;** Vittorio Veneto; aly 1917-18; **Doiran 1917-18;** Macedonia 1915-18; **ut al Amara** 1915; **Ctesiphon;** efence of Kut al Amara; Khan Baghdadi; esopotamia 1914-18; Archangel 1919.

Second World War:

efence of Escaut; **Cassel; Ypres-Comines Canal; ormandy Landing; Pegasus Bridge;** Caen; Esquay; wer Maas; Ourthe; Rhineland; **Reichswald; Rhine;** benburen; North-West Europe 1940, 44-45; **Salerno;** St. Lucia; fidaville; North Africa 1943; **Salerno;** St. Lucia; alerno Hills; Teano; Monte Camino; arigliano Crossing; Damiano; **Anzio;** Coriano; emmano Ridge; Italy 1943-45; Arakan Beaches; amandu; Burma 1943-45.

Pre-1914:

Louisburg [1758]; **Quebec [1759]**; Havannah [1762]; Martinique, 1762; North America, 1763-64; **Peninsula [1808-14]**; Rolica [1808]; Vimiera [1808]; Martinique, 1809; Talavera [1809]; Busaco [1810]; Albuhera [1811]; Fuentes d'Onor [1811]; **Badajos [1812]**; Ciudad Rodrigo [1812]; **Salamanca [1812]**; Nive [1813]; Nivelle [1813]; Pyrenees [1813]; **Vittoria [1813]**; Orthes [1814]; Toulouse [1814]; Punjaub [1848-49]; Goojerat [1849]; Mooltan [1849]; South Africa, 1851-53; **Delhi, 1857**; Pekin, 1860; Taku Forts [1860]; **Afghanistan, 1878-80**; South Africa, 1879; Ahmed Khel [1880]; Kandahar, 1880; Egypt, 1882-84; Tel-el-Kebir [1882]; Chitral [1895]; **Defence of Ladysmith [1899-1900];** South Africa, 1899-1902; Relief of Ladysmith [1900].

First World War:

Mons; Retreat from Mons; **Marne 1914;** Aisne 1914; **Ypres 1914, 15, 17, 18;** Langemarck 1914, 17; Gheluvelt; Nonne Bosschen; Givenchy 1914; Gravenstafel; St. Julien; Frezenberg; Bellewaarde; Aubers; Festubert 1915; Hooge 1915; Loos; **Somme 1916, 18;** Albert 1916, 18; Bazentin; Pozières; Delville Wood; Guillemont; Flers-Courcelette; Morval; Le Transloy; Ancre Heights; Ancre 1916, 18; Arleux; **Arras 1917, 18;** Scarpe 1917; **Messines 1917, 18;** Pilckem; Menin Road; Polygon Wood; Broodseinde; Poelcapelle; Passchendaele; Cambrai 1917, 18; St. Quentin; Rosières; Avre; Lys; Bailleul; Kemmel; Béthune; Bapaume 1918; Drocourt-Quéant; Hindenburg Line; Havrincourt; **Epéhy; Canal du Nord;** St. Quentin Canal; Beaurevoir; Courtrai; **Selle; Sambre;** France and Flanders 1914-18; Italy 1917-18; Macedonia 1916-18.

Second World War:

Calais 1940; Mont Pincon; Falaise; Roer; **Rhineland;** Cleve; Goch; Hochwald; Rhine; Dreirwalde; Aller; **North-West Europe 1940, 44-45;** Sidi Barrani; **Egyptian Frontier 1940;** Derna Aerodrome; Gazala; Tobruk 1941; **Sidi Rezegh 1941;** Bir Hacheim; Knightsbridge; Defence of Alamein Line; Ruweisat; Fuka Airfield; **Alam el Halfa; El Alamein;** Capture of Halfaya Pass; Nofilia; Tebaga Gap; Argoub el Megas; Tunis; **North Africa 1940-43;** Sangro; Arezzo; Coriano; Lamone Crossing; Argenta Gap; **Italy 1943-45;** Veve; **Greece 1941, 44-45;** Crete; Middle East 1941.

Pre-1914:

Copenhagen [1801]; Monte Video [1807]; **Peninsula [1808-14];** Rolica [1808]; Vimiera [1808]; **Corunna [1809];** Busaco [1810]; Barrosa [1811]; Fuentes d'Onor [1811]; **Badajos [1812];** Ciudad Rodrigo [1812]; **Salamanca [1812];** Nive [1813]; Nivelle [1813]; Pyrenees [1813]; **Vittoria [1813];** Orthes [1814]; Toulouse [1814]; **Waterloo [1815];** South Africa,1846-47; South Africa, 1851-63; Alma [1854]; **Inkerman [1854];** Sevastapol [1854-55]; Lucknow [1857]; Ashantee [1873-74]; **Afghanistan, 1878-79;** Ali Masjid [1878]; Burmah, 1885-87; Khartoum [1898]; **Defence of Ladysmith [1899-1900];** Relief of Ladysmith [1900]; South Africa, 1899-1902

First World War:

Le Cateau; Retreat from Mons; **Marne 1914;** Aisne 1914, 18; Armentières 1914; **Neuve Chapelle; Ypres 1915, 17;** Gravenstafel; St. Julien; Frezenberg; Aubers; Bellewaarde; Hooge 1915; **Somme 1916, 18;** Albert 1916, 18; Bazentin; Delville Wood; Guillemont; Flers-Courcelette; Morval; Le Transloy; Ancre Heights; Ancre 1916, 18; **Arras 1917, 18;** Vimy 1917; Scarpe 1917, 18; Arleux; **Messines 1917;** Pilckem; Langemarck 1917; Menin Road; Polygon Wood; Broodseinde; Poelcapelle; Passchendaele; Cambrai 1917, 18; St. Quentin; Avre; Rosières; Villers Bretonneux; Lys; Hazebrouck; Béthune; Drocourt-Quéant; **Hindenburg Line;** Havrincourt; Canal du Nord; Selle; Valenciennes; Sambre; France and Flanders 1914-18; **Macedonia 1915-18.**

Second World War:

Calais 1940; Villers Bocage; Odon; Bourguebus Ridge; Mont Pincon; Le Perier Ridge; Falaise; Antwerp; Hechtel; Nederrijn; Lower Maas; Roer; Leese; Aller; **North-West Europe 1940, 44-45;** Egyptian Frontier 1940; **Beda Fomm;** Mersa el Brega; Agedabia; Derna Aerodrome; Tobruk 1941; **Sidi Rezegh 1941;** Chor es Sufan; Saunnu; Gazala; Knightsbridge; Defence of Alamein Line; Ruweisat; **Alam el Halfa; El Alamein;** Tebaga Gap; Medjez el Bab; Kasserine; Thala; Fondouk; Fondouk Pass; El Kourzia; Djebel Kournine; Tunis; Hammam Lif; **North Africa 1940-43;** Cardito; Cassino II; Liri Valley; Melfa Crossing; Monte Rotondo; **Capture of Perugia;** Monte Malbe; Arezzo; Advance to Florence; Gothic Line; Orsara; Tossignano; Argenta Gap; Fossa Cembalina; **Italy 1943-45.**

The discovery of hydrogen gas by Henry Cavendish in 1760 allowed, for the first time, the lifting of a weight from the ground attached to a gas-filled balloon. The first manned balloon ascent in Britain was in 1784 and the French were experimenting with balloons for military purposes as early as 1794. Balloons were used during the American Civil War, between 1860 and 1864, at which time a group of officers of the Royal Engineers were making persistent applications for ballooning to be adopted by the British Army. It was not, however, until 1879 that the first British military balloon was produced; in the following year balloon training was instituted at Aldershot and a Balloon Detachment attended the Aldershot manoeuvres of 1880.

Balloon Sections were deployed in South Africa and China and in 1900 a Balloon Section was formed in the Indian Army. As the development of military balloons and airships continued into the 20th century, the first experiments in powered flight were taking place in Farnborough, Hampshire, which was to become the national home of experimental aviation.

Army Aviation & Airborne Forces

The Parachute Regiment, the Special Air Service Regiment and the present-day Army Air Corps all trace their origins back to the pioneers of military ballooning in the 1880s.

In 1908, Samuel Cody, an American who had received a grant from the War Office for the purpose, made the first official powered flight in Britain. Two years later in 1910, two Royal Artillery officers, Captain Bertram Dickson and Lieutenant Lancelot Gibbs, obtained permission to attempt reconnaissance flights as a private venture. This was the first use of aircraft in the British Army. Dickson, sadly, died of his injuries received in the first ever mid-air collision later in the year.

In 1911 the Air Battalion Royal Engineers was established at Larkhill and the following year the responsibility for Army Aviation was handed over to the newly-formed Royal Flying Corps.

During the First World War the role of military aircraft was extended from the traditional observation, reconnaissance and artillery spotting to include bombing and air combat. The RFC entered the War with 48 aircraft and by 1918 had a front line strength of 1,782.

In 1918 The Royal Air Force was formed from the Royal Flying Corps and Royal Naval Air Service but the need to keep gunner officers in the air for the observation and direction of artillery fire

was recognised and Army Cooperation Squadrons were established with RA pilots seconded to the RAF. In 1940 the first experimental Air Observation Post Unit was formed (see next page) which came under the control of the Army Air Corps which was disbanded at the end of the War in 1945.

In 1957 the Corps was reconstituted with the initial primary roles of observation, reconnaissance and artillery fire control which soon expanded into forward air control, radio relay and battlefield liaison. During the 1960s helicopters joined the traditional fixed-wing aircraft in the Corps thereby greatly increasing the scope of its potential activities in a support role.

The greatest change, however, was during the 1970s when the Corps was equipped with the first Scout helicopters armed with SS11 anti-tank guided missiles introducing a combat role for the first time. The regimental structure of the Corps, now a teeth-arm as well as a support formation, was developed through the 1980s and 90s to its present form as shown on the following pages.

Today, with two regiments equipped with the powerful Apache attack helicopter, the Army Air Corps constitute a vital part of Britain's front line force.

1880
Military balloon training initiated at Aldershot.

1882
School of Ballooning established at Chatham as part of the School of Military Engineering.

1890
(5 May) Formation of first Balloon Section — the first Air Unit of the Regular Forces.

1907
First powered Army Airship became operational.

1908
(5 Oct) Samuel Cody makes first official powered flight in Britain at Laffan's Plain, Farnborough.

1910
First use of an aeroplane with the British Army flown by Captain Bertram Dickson RHA.

1911
AIR BATTALION ROYAL ENGINEERS
formed at Larkhill

No. 1 Company
AIRSHIPS, BALLOONS & KITES

No. 2 Company
AIRCRAFT

1912
ROYAL FLYING CORPS
founded (May) with one squadron of airships and three squadrons of aircraft

DISBANDED 1918

1918
ROYAL AIR FORCE
founded (Jan.) from the Royal Flying Corps and the Royal Naval Air Service

---

1940
CENTRAL LANDING ESTABLISHMENT

| No: 1 PARACHUTE TRAINING SCHOOL | No: 1 GLIDER TRAINING SCHOOL |

1942
THE ARMY AIR CORPS

1945
DISBANDED

1957
RECONSTITUTED INTO ITS PRESENT FORM

PAGE 128-129

1942
THE GLIDER PILOT REGIMENT

1957
DISBANDED

PAGE 127

1942
THE PARACHUTE REGIMENT

1949
TRANSFERRED TO INFANTRY OF THE LINE

PAGE 126

1944
THE SPECIAL AIR SERVICE REGIMENT

1946
DISBANDED

1947
RECONSTITUTED AS A SEPARATE UNIT

PAGE 127

AIR OBSERVATION POST SQUADRONS

The first experimental Air Observation Post unit — 'D' Flight — was formed in February 1940 and conducted its operational trials in France during the general withdrawal of the British Expeditionary Force. In August 1941, at Old Sarum, it became 651 Air OP Squadron the first of twelve squadrons which were deployed in every major theatre during the Second World War.

These squadrons were commanded by a Royal Artillery major with Royal Artillery pilots, drivers, signallers and ground defence personnel but the adjutant was a Royal Air Force officer and the aircraft were maintained by RAF technicians and riggers.

Although primarily intended for the direction and control of artillery fire, the Air OP Squadrons also undertook the important secondary roles of reconnaissance, photography and battlefield liaison.

From disbandment of The Army Air Corps in 1945, Army aviators were employed until 1956 on flying duties in Air Observation Post Flights with RA aircrew and with Light Liaison Flights manned by pilots of the Glider Pilot Regiment. The modern Army Air Corps was formed on 1st September 1957 which coincided with the disbandment of the Glider Pilot Regiment.

In 1958 the Royal Electrical and Mechanical Engineers took over the maintenance of Army aircraft from the Royal Air Force.

1942
THE
PARACHUTE
REGIMENT

REGIMENTAL HEADQUARTERS

Flagstaff House, 4 Napier Road, Colchester,
Essex CO2 7SW

Tel: 01206 782102 Fax: 01206 782199

email: rhq@parachuteregiment.com

website: www.army.mod.uk/para/

REGIMENTAL MARCHES

Quick March: "Ride of the Valkyries"
Slow March: "Pomp and Circumstance No 4"

ALLIANCES

Australian Military Forces:
8th/9th Battalion (Disbanded) The Royal
                     Australian Regiment
Canadian Armed Forces:
The Canadian Airborne Regiment (Disbanded)

COLONEL-IN-CHIEF

HRH The Prince of Wales,
        KG KT OM GCB AK QSO ADC

NOTES:

The Parachute Regiment was formed from No. 2
Commando, an elite special service force set up on the
instructions of Winston Churchill in response to the
success of German airborne units in the invasion of
Norway and the Low Countries.

The first British airborne assault was in Italy in 1941 the
success of which, and the need for a great number of
paratroops, led to the formation of The Parachute
Regiment the following year.

Initially under command of the Army Air Corps, The
Parachute Regiment was transferred to infantry of the
line in 1949.

BATTLE HONOURS

Second World War:

Bruneval; Normandy Landing; Pegasus Bridge;
Merville Battery; **Breville;** Dives Crossing;
La Touques Crossing; **Arnhem 1944;** Ourthe; **Rhine;**
Southern France; North-West Europe 1942, 44-45;
Soudia; **Oudna;** Djebel Azzag 1943; El Hadjeba;
Tamera; Djebel Dhara; Kef el Debna;
North Africa 1942-43; **Primosole Bridge;** Sicily 1943;
Taranto; Orsogna; Italy 1943-44; **Athens;**
Greece 1944-45.

Post-1945:

Goose Green; Mount Longdon; Wireless Ridge;
Falkland Islands 1982; Al Basrah, Iraq 2003.

PRESENT ROLES & ATTACHMENTS OF THE REGULAR BATTALIONS OF THE PARACHUTE REGIMENT

1 PARA   Ranger Unit *(Special Forces Support Group, RAF St. Athan).*

*The Special Forces Support Group (SFSG) is a joint-service special forces unit providing infantry and
specialised support to SAS and SBS operations. The Group's main constituent is 1 PARA but it also
contains elements of the Royal Marines and RAF Regiment. Soldiers must serve a minimum of 2 years
in the 2nd or 3rd battalion before they are eligible for service in 1 PARA.*

2 PARA   Air Assault/Light Role. *(16th Air Assault Brigade, Colchester).*

3 PARA   Air Assault/Light Role. *(16th Air Assault Brigade, Colchester).*

*The 2nd and 3rd battalions are the permanent airborne infantry element of 16th Air Assault Brigade
the composition of which is shown alongside.*

16th AIR ASSAULT BRIGADE

The Brigade was formed in 1999 from the existing 24 Airmobile and 5 Airborne Brigades to provide
the Army with a lightly-equipped, fast moving, rapidly deployable, multi-function force with massive
striking power and supported by the very latest in military technology.

Operating under the Joint Helicopter Command (controlling the helicopter forces of all three services)
the Brigade comprises almost 10,000 personnel including the elite, parachute-trained elements of its
supporting corps. Its composition is at present as follows:

RECONNAISSANCE

Reconnaissance Squadron, The Household Cavalry Regiment (Recce Sqn HCR)

The Pathfinder Platoon — responsible for the covert location and marking of drop zones, tactical
landing zones and helicopter landing sites prior to an air assault operation.

INFANTRY

2nd Battalion Parachute Regiment (2 PARA)

3rd Battalion Parachute Regiment (3 PARA) (including the Guards Parachute Platoon)

1st Battalion The Royal Irish Regiment (1 R IRISH)

ATTACK HELICOPTERS

3rd Regiment Army Air Corps (3 AAC)

4th Regiment Army Air Corps (4 AAC)

9th Regiment Army Air Corps (9 AAC)

ARTILLERY

7th Parachute Regiment Royal Horse Artilley (7 RHA)

21st Air Defence Battery, 47th Regiment Royal Artillery (47 Regt RA)

ENGINEERING

23rd (Air Assault) Engineer Regiment, Royal Engineers (23 Eng Regt)

7th (Air Assault) Battalion, Royal Electrical & Mechanical Engineers (7 Bn REME)

HEADQUARTERS & SIGNALS

216 16 Air Assault Brigade HQ & Signal Squadron Royal Corps of Signals (216 Signal Sqn)

SUPPORT

13 (Air Assault) Support Regiment, Royal Logistic Corps (13 Regt RLC)

16 Close Support Medical Regiment, Royal Army Medical Corps

156 Provost Company, Royal Military Police, Adjutant General's Corps (156 Pro Coy)

89 Airborne Close Support Military Intelligence Section, Intelligence Corps

1942
GLIDER PILOT REGIMENT

1957 DISBANDED

NOTES:

In October 1940, 66 men with previous flying experience were selected from No. 2 Commando for preliminary training as "Glider Coxswains". These were to form the nucleus of the Glider Pilot Regiment when in February 1942 the Army Air Corps was founded as the parent formation for the new airborne regiments —the Glider Pilot Regiment, the Parachute Regiment and the Special Air Service.

The very high casualty rate associated with glider landings coupled with the advent of the jet aircraft made the assault glider redundant and its role today is performed by support helicopters of the Army Air Corps and Royal Air Force.

1944
SPECIAL AIR SERVICE REGIMENT

1946 DISBANDED

1947 RECONSTITUTED

1952 Formally became
22nd SPECIAL AIR SERVICE REGIMENT

NOTES:

Formed as 'L' Detachment, SAS Brigade, by Lieutenant David Stirling, Scots Guards, in the Middle East in 1941, the predecessor of today's SAS Regiment had an initial establishment of 68 officers and men and was tasked with conducting raids and sabotage deep behind enemy lines in the Western Desert.

Together with the Special Boat Service (SBS) of the Royal Marines, the SAS forms the major part of Britain's Special Forces responsible for a wide range of special duties including behind-the-lines intelligence gathering and sabotage and counter-terrorist operations.

REGIMENTAL HEADQUARTERS

In view of the covert nature of much of its work, The Special Air Service retains a very low profile and no contact details for the Regiment are published.

REGIMENTAL MARCHES;

Quick March: "Marche des Parachutistes Belges"

Slow March: "Lilli Marlene"

ALLIANCES

Australian Military Forces:
Special Air Service Regiment

Canadian Armed Forces:
Joint Task Force 2

New Zealand Army:
1st New Zealand Special Air Service Group

MUSEUMS OF ARMY AVIATION & AIRBORNE FORCES

THE MUSEUM OF ARMY FLYING
Army Air Corps and Glider Pilot Regiment
Middle Wallop, Stockbridge, Hampshire SO20 8DY
Tel: 01264 784421 Fax: 01264 781694
email: enquiries@flying-museum.org.uk
Website: www.flying-museum.org.uk

AIRBORNE ASSAULT
Museum of The Parachute Regiment
Imperial War Museum, Duxford,
Cambridgeshire CB22 4QR
Tel: 01223 839909
email: curatorairbornemuseum@btconnect.com
Website: www.airborneassault.org.uk

BATTLE HONOURS

Second World War:

rmandy Landing; Pegasus Bridge; rville Battery; Rhine; Southern France; th-West Europe 1944-45; Landing in Sicily; ly 1943.

In 2007 HM The Queen gave Royal Assent for the Battle Honours of the Glider Pilot Regiment, to be taken over by the Army Air Corps.

BATTLE HONOURS

Second World War:

North-West Europe 1944-45; Tobruk 1941; Benghazi Raid; North Africa 1940-43; Landing in Sicily; Sicily 1943; Termoli; Valli di Comacchio; Italy 1943-45; Greece 1944-45; Adriatic; Middle East 1943-44.

Post-1945:

Falkland Islands 1982; Gulf 1991; Western Iraq.

1942
ARMY AIR CORPS

1945
DISBANDED

1957
RECONSTITUTED

CORPS HEADQUARTERS

HQ Army Air Corps, Middle Wallop,
Stockbridge, Hants SO20 8DY
Tel: 01264 784294/784405
Fax: 01264 784481
email:aacassociation@btconnect.com
website: www.rmy.mod.uk/aviation/air.aspx

REGIMENTAL MARCHES;

Quick March:	"Recce Flight"
Slow March:	"The Thievish Magpie"

ALLIANCES

Australian Military Forces:
Australian Army Aviation Corps

Royal Navy
HMS Chatham

COLONEL-IN-CHIEF

HRH The Prince of Wales
    KG, KT, OM, GCB, AK, QSO, PC, ADC

REGIMENTAL MUSEUM
SEE PAGE 127

NOTES:

The Army Air Corps of World War 2 was founded in 1942 and was the parent formation for the new Airborne Forces which included the Glider Pilot Regiment, the Parachute Regiment and, later, the Special Air Service.

The wartime Army Air Corps was disbanded in 1945 and its units placed under command of the Infantry. The Parachute Regiment joined the regiments of line infantry and the Special Air Service became an independent unit in Special Forces.

In 1957 the Glider Pilot Regiment was disbanded and its personnel formed the nucleus of a reconstituted Army Air Corps which was developed over the next 50 years into its present, multi-role status.

ROLES OF THE ARMY AIR CORPS

Offensive action.

ISTAR — Intelligence, Surveillance, Target Acquisition, Reconnaissance.

Control and Direction of Firepower.

Command Support & Control.

Movement of Personnel & Material.

AIRCRAFT OF THE ARMY AIR CORPS

Apache AH Mk 1	*Lynx Mk 7*	*Lynx Mk 9*
Gazelle AH 1	*BN Islander*	*Defender*
Bell 212	*Squirrel*	

ACTIVE REGULAR ARMY AIR CORPS REGIMENTS AND OTHER UNITS

HEADQUARTERS AAC	SCHOOL OF ARMY AVIATION	1 REGIMENT AAC	3 REGIMENT AAC	4 REGIMENT AAC	9 REGIMENT AAC	5 REGIMENT AAC	OTHER AAC UNITS
Middle Wallop, Hants.	Middle Wallop, Hants.	Gütersloh, Germany	Wattisham, Suffolk	Wattisham, Suffolk	Dishforth, Yorkshire	Aldergrove, N. Ireland	657 SQN AAC Odiham
			16 AIR ASSAULT BRIGADE	16 AIR ASSAULT BRIGADE	16 AIR ASSAULT BRIGADE		660 SQN AAC (Defence Helicopter Flying School)
HQLF / JHC HQ	JHC HQ / ARTD	1 (UK) DIVISION	JHC HQ	JHC HQ	JHC HQ	JHC HQ	674 SQN AAC (Defence Elementary Flying School)
HQ AAC	HQ SAAvn	RHQ	RHQ	RHQ	RHQ	RHQ	7 FLIGHT AAC Brunei
	2 (TRG) REGT AAC						
RHQ AAC	668 (TRG) SQN AAC	652 SQN AAC	653 SQN AAC	654 SQN AAC	659 SQN AAC	651 SQN AAC	8 FLIGHT AAC Hereford Garrison
	676 SQN						
667 SQN AAC	HQ SQN	661 SQN AAC	662 SQN AAC	664 SQN AAC	669 SQN AAC	665 SQN AAC	25 FLIGHT AAC Belize
	7 (TRG) REGT AAC						
	670 SQN AAC	HQ SQN	663 SQN AAC	656 SQN AAC	672 SQN AAC		
	671 SQN AAC						
	673 SQN AAC		HQ SQN	HQ SQN	HQ SQN		
	The Blue Eagles Helicopter Display Team						
	The Army Historic Aircraft Flight						

The School of Army Aviation provides the focus for aviation and ground training.

Providing Aviation Support to 1 (UK) Division with light utility helicopters (Lynx).

Aviation Attack equipped with Apache AH 1 helicopters.

Aviation Attack equipped with Apache AH 1 helicopters.

Providing Aviation Support with Light Utility Helicopters (Lynx).

Providing Aviation Reconnaissance with Light Aircraft and Gazelle Helicopters.

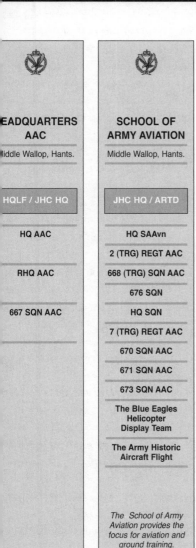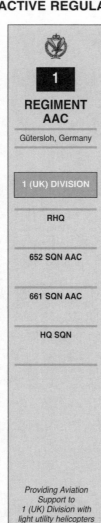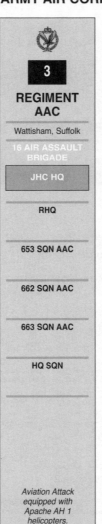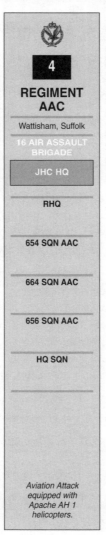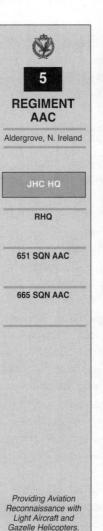

In 1816, as a result of border disputes between Britain and Nepal, an army of British and East India Company troops invaded Nepal with the intention of forcing the fierce Gurkha nation to ratify the Treaty of Sagauli which would settle their differences.

After some ferocious fighting, with many casualties on both sides, the greatly outnumbered Gurkhas realised that they could not hope to win and the Treaty was duly ratified.

However, in the course of the fighting, the British and Indian troops had been deeply impressed by the bravery of the Gurkhas and a high level of mutual respect and regard had been established. The potential of recruiting Gurkhas into the British Indian Army was recognised and this was to be the start of one of the most enduring and worthwhile international alliances which Britain has ever had the privilege ro enjoy. Gurkha regiments were raised and soon proved their worth as loyal and highly efficient infantrymen.

In the Indian Mutiny of 1857, every Gurkha unit remained true to its vow of allegiance and 12,000 Government

The Brigade of Gurkhas

For nearly 200 years Gurkhas have fought alongside British troops with gallantry and distinction proving themselves as Britain's staunchest allies and most loyal and respected friends. Today, the Brigade of Gurkhas forms an integral and important part of the British Army.

troops from Nepal marched into India, under the personal command of the Nepalese Prime Minister, to assist their British friends. During the Siege of Delhi the Sirmoor Gurkhas, with the 60th Foot, held the British position, under continuous fire from the mutineers, for over three months suffering 327

PRESENT ROLES & ATTACHMENTS OF THE ROYAL GURKHA RIFLES	
1 RGR	Light Role (Jungle) *(Brunei)*.
2 RGR	Light Role *(52nd Infantry Brigade, Shorncliffe)*.
D (Tamandu) Company	Reinforcement Company.
Demonstration Companies	Royal Military Academy Sandhurst. Infantry Training Centre, Wales.

The two battalions rotate on a three-year cycle. The home-based battalion, together with 1 R IRISH and 5 SCOTS, will rotate as part of 16 Air Assault Brigade spending five years with this formation from 2010 before returning for two years to 52nd Infantry Brigade.

casualties out of a total strength of 490 and losing eight of their nine British officers. As a result of their loyal and courageous service during the Mutiny, the bond of affection between British and Gurkha soldiers was consolidated and strengthened and Gurkhas were granted privileges which had never before been enjoyed by native troops.

In many imperial campaigns in Burma, Afghanistan, the North-East and the North-West Frontiers of India, Malta, Cyprus, Malaya, China and Tibet, and subsequently through the two World Wars, the Gurkha regiments served Britain with distinction. Their involvement can be seen from their Battle Honours shown on the following pages and from the numerous awards for personal gallantry, which include 23 Victoria Crosses, won by personnel of the Gurkha regiments.

In 1947, with the Independence and Partition of India, the Gurkha regiments were divided between the armies of Britain and India as shown on the following page. Since then these loyal and courageous soldiers have continued to serve Britain with distinction, notably Malaya and the Falkland Islands, and remain an intregral and important part of the British Army today.

1st REGIMENT OF GURKHA RIFLES	2nd REGIMENT OF GURKHA RIFLES	3rd REGIMENT OF GURKHA RIFLES	4th REGIMENT OF GURKHA RIFLES	5th REGIMENT OF GURKHA RIFLES	6th REGIMENT OF GURKHA RIFLES	7th REGIMENT OF GURKHA RIFLES	8th REGIMENT OF GURKHA RIFLES	9th REGIMENT OF GURKHA RIFLES	10th REGIMENT OF GURKHA RIFLES	11th REGIMENT OF GURKHA RIFLES
1947	1947	1947	1947	1947	1947	1947	1947	1947	1947	1947
INDIAN ARMY	BRITISH ARMY	INDIAN ARMY	INDIAN ARMY	INDIAN ARMY	BRITISH ARMY	BRITISH ARMY	INDIAN ARMY	INDIAN ARMY	BRITISH ARMY	INDIAN ARMY
PAGE 134		PAGE 134	PAGE 134	PAGE 134			PAGE 135	PAGE 135		PAGE 135

2nd King Edward VII's Own Gurkha Rifles (The Sirmoor Rifles)
PAGE 132

6th Queen Elizabeth's Own Gurkha Rifles
PAGE 132

7th Duke of Edinburgh's Own Gurkha Rifles
PAGE 133

10th Princess Mary's Own Gurkha Rifles
PAGE 133

1st BATTALION   2nd BATTALION   3rd BATTALION

THE ROYAL GURKHA RIFLES

PAGE 132-133

3rd BATTALION DISBANDED November 1996

1951
Formed in Hong Kong from elements of the Royal Engineers (1)

1955
17th Gurkha Divisional Engineers

The Gurkha Engineers

1977 THE QUEEN'S GURKHA ENGINEERS

1948
X Brigade Signal Squadron (2)

1949
Gurkha Royal Signals

1955
Gurkha Signals

1977 QUEEN'S GURKHA SIGNALS

1958
Gurkha Army Service Corps (3)

1959
Gurkha Transport Company

1965
Gurkha Transport Regiment

1992
The Queen's Own Gurkha Transport Regiment

2001 THE QUEEN'S OWN GURKHA LOGISTIC REGIMENT

NOTES

(1) 67th and 68th Field Squadrons RE formed at Kluang, Malaya in 1948 and 1950 respectively. Moved to Hong Kong in 1950. RHQ 50th Field Engineer Regiment RE formed in Hong Kong 1951.

(2) Formed in Malaya to provide a training cadre for Gurkha signals units within 17th Gurkha Infantry Division.

(3) Formed in Malaya as 28th and 30th Gurkha Army Service Corps companies.

Though the three Gurkha "corps", Engineers, Signals and Logistics, were formed to support the Gurkha Infantry Division during the Malayan Emergency (1948-60), Gurkha soldiers had been employed in these fields for many years previously. Gurkhas had served as Sappers and Miners in the three presidency armies of the Hon. East India Company, Bengal, Bombay and Madras, during the 19th century and had been employed as signalmen in the British Indian Army since 1857.

The Brigade of Gurkhas

Headquarters:
Airfield Camp, Netheravon, Salisbury, Wiltshire SP4 9SF
Tel: Civ. 01908 628088
Fax: 01980 62 8564
website: www.army.mod.ok/brigade_of_gurkhas/

2nd

REGIMENT OF GURKHA RIFLES

1815
The Sirmoor Battalion (1)

1823
8th Sirmoor (Gorkha)

1850
Sirmoor (Rifle) Battalion

1858
Sirmoor Rifle Regiment (2)

1861
17th Bengal Native Infantry

2nd Goorkha (The Sirmoor Rifle) Regiment

1876
2nd (Prince of Wales's Own (3)) Goorkha Regiment (The Sirmoor Rifles)

1891
2nd (Prince of Wales's Own) Gurkha (Rifle) Regiment (The Sirmoor Rifles)

1903
2nd Prince of Wales's Own Gurkha Rifles (The Sirmoor Rifles)

1906
2nd King Edward's Own Gurkha Rifles (The Sirmoor Rifles)

1936
2nd King Edward VII's Own Gurkha Rifles (The Sirmoor Rifles)

1948
2nd King Edward VII's Own Gurkha Rifles (The Sirmoor Rifles) Brigade of Gurkhas

1994
1st Battalion
THE ROYAL GURKHA RIFLES

NOTES

(1) Raised at Nahan in Sirmoor by Lieutenant F. Young from Gurkha soldiers who enlisted in the British service during the Nepal War.

(2) Granted the right to wear red facings after exemplary service during the Siege of Delhi. Special association formed with The King's Royal Rifle Corps.

(3) The future King Edward VII.

In 1897 a special association was formed with The Gordon Highlanders after storming the Heights of Dargai together.

2nd KING EDWARD VII's OWN GURKHA RIFLES (The Sirmoor Rifles)

BATTLE HONOURS

Pre-1914:

Bhurtpore [1826]; **Aliwal** [1846]; **Sobraon** [1846]; **Delhi 1857**; India 1857-58; **Kabul** [1879]; **Kandahar** [1880]; **Afghanistan 1878-80**; **Tirah** [1897-98]; **Punjaub Frontier** [1897-98].

First World War:

La Bassée 1914; Festubert 1914-15; Givenchy 1914; Neuve Chapelle; Aubers; Loos; France and Flanders 1914-15; Egypt 1915; **Tigris 1916; Kut al Amara 1917; Baghdad;** Mesopotamia 1916-18; **Persia 1918;** Baluchistan 1918.

Afghanistan 1919; Waziristan 1921; **North-West Frontier India 1937-40.**

Second World War:

El Alamein; Mareth; **Akarit;** Djebel el Meida; Enfidaville; **Tunis;** North Africa 1942-43; **Cassino I;** Monastery Hill; Pian di Maggio; **Gothic Line;** Coriano; Poggio San Giovanni; Monte Reggiano; Italy 1944-45; Greece 1944-45; North Malaya; **Jitra;** Central Malaya; Kampar; **Slim River;** Johore; Singapore Island; Malaya 1941-42; Chindits 1943; **North Arakan;** Point 1433; Arakan Beaches; Myebon; **Tamandu; Irawaddy;** Magwe; Sittang 1945; Burma 1943-45.

GURKHA REGIMENTS IN BRITISH SERVICE

Over the years, since the first recruitment of Gurkhas into British Service, there have been constant changes to the designations of individual regiments which would be cumbersome, and unnecessary, to reproduce here. These tables therefore only include the most major and significant changes in titles. There were also discrepancies between different official documents and, as with all Indian proper names during the 18th and 19th centuries, wide inconsistencies in their spelling notably with the name 'Gurkha' itself which appears as 'Gorka', 'Gorkha', 'Goorka' and 'Goorkha'. Since 1891 the official spelling for those in British Service has been 'Gurkha' and those in Indian Army service since 1945 have reverted to the older form of 'Gorkha'. It is interesting to note that many soldiers with extensive Indian service before World War 2 often pronounced the word 'Goorka'.

Readers seeking more detailed information on these matters are referred to the definitive work produced by, and obtainable from, the Gurkha Museum:
"The Lineages and Composition of Gurkha Regiments in British Service".
It should also be noted that the Gurkha Regiments which transferred to the Indian Army on Independence, were never a part of the British Army; their origins and Battle Honours are recorded here as a tribute to their long and gallant service to the Crown and the unique relationship between Britain and her Gurkha soldiers.

6th

REGIMENT OF GURKHA RIFLES

1817
The Cuttack Legion (1)

1823
10th Rungpoor Light Infantry

1826
8th Rungpoor Light Infantry

1828
8th Assam Light Infantry

1844
1st Assam Light Infantry

1861
46th (1st Assam) Bengal Native Infantry

1864
42nd (Assam) Bengal Native (Light) Infantry

1885
42nd (Assam) Bengal (Light) Infantry

1886
42nd Regiment Goorkha (Light) Infantry

1889
42nd (Goorkha) Regiment of Bengal (Light) Infantry

1891
42nd Gurkha (Rifle) Regiment of Bengal Infantry

1901
42nd Gurkha Rifles

1903
6th Gurkha Rifles

1959
6th Queen Elizabeth's Own Gurkha Rifles

1994
1st Battalion
THE ROYAL GURKHA RIFLES

NOTES

(1) Raised at Chaubiaganj in Orissa by Captain S. Fraser.

6th QUEEN ELIZABETH's OWN GURKHA RIFLES

BATTLE HONOURS

Pre-1914:

Assam [1824-25]; Ava [1824-26]; **Burma, 1885-87;** North-East Frontier India, 1889-93.

First World War:

Helles; Krithia; Suvla; Sari Bair; Gallipoli 1915; Suez Canal; Egypt 1915-16; **Khan Baghdadi; Mesopotamia 1916-18;** Waziristan 1917; **Persia 1918;** North-West Frontier India 1915; Afghanistan 1919.

Waziristan 1921; **North-East Frontier India 1936-37; North-West Frontier India 1937-40.**

Second World War:

Coriano; Santarcangelo; **Monte Chicco;** Lamone Crossing; Senio Floodbank; **Medicina;** Gaiana Crossing; **Italy 1944-45; Chindits 1944;** Schwebo; **Kyaukmyaung Bridgehead; Mandalay; Fort Dufferin;** Maymyo; **Rangoon Road;** Toungoo; **Sittang 1945; Burma 1942-45.**

ROYAL GURKHA RIFLES

REGIMENTAL HEADQUARTERS
Sir John Moore Barracks, Shorncliffe, Kent CT20 3HJ

REGIMENTAL MARCHES

Quick March:	"Bravest of the Brave"
Double March:	"The Keel Row"
Slow March (Band):	"God Bless The Prince of Wales"
Slow March (Pipes & Drums):	"The Garb of Old Gaul"

ALLIANCES

Canadian Armed Forces:
The Queen's Own Rifles of Canada

COLONEL-IN-CHIEF
Lieutenant-General HRH The Prince of Wales
KG, KT, OM, GCB, AK, QSO, ADC

7th

REGIMENT OF GURKHA RIFLES

1902
8th Gurkha Rifles (1)

1903
2nd Battalion 10th
Gurkha Rifles

1907
7th Gurkha Rifles
(two battalions) (2)

1959
7th Duke of
Edinburgh's (3) Own
Gurkha Rifles

1994
2nd Battalion
**THE ROYAL GURKHA
RIFLES**

NOTES

(1) Raised at Thayetmyo
in Burma by Major E.
Vansittart from personnel
of 1st Gurkha Rifles to
replace the disbanded 8th
Madras Native Infantry.

(2) In 1907 a new 2nd
Battalion was raised from
10th Gurkha Rifles.

In 1910 the Regiment
absorbed the 78th
Moplah Rifles.

(3) HRH Prince Philip,
Duke of Edinburgh,
husband of Queen
Elizabeth II.

7th DUKE OF EDINBURGH's OWN GURKHA RIFLES

BATTLE HONOURS

First World War:

Suez Canal; **Egypt 1915; Megiddo; Sharon;
Palestine 1918;** Shaiba; **Kut al Amara 1915, 17;
Ctesiphon; Defence of Kut al Amara; Baghdad;
Sharquat; Mesopotamia 1915-18.**

Afghanistan 1919.

Second World War:

Tobruk 1942; North Africa 1942; **Cassino I;** Campriano;
Poggio del Grillo; Tavoleto;
Montebello-Scorticata Ridge; Italy 1944;
Sittang 1942, 45; Pegu 1942; **Kyaukse 1942;**
Shwegyin; **Imphal; Bishenpur; Meiktila;**
Capture of Meiktila; Defence of Meiktila;
Rangoon Road; Pyawbwe; Burma 1942-45.

Post-1945:

Falkland Islands.

10th

REGIMENT OF GURKHA RIFLES

1766
14th Coast Sepoys (1)

1784
10th Madras Native
Infantry

1885
10th Madras Infantry

1890
1st (Burma) Regiment
of Madras Infantry (2)

1891
10th Regiment
(1st Burma Battalion)
Madras Infantry

1892
10th (1st Burma Rifles)
Madras Infantry

1895
10th (1st Burma Gurkha
Rifles) Madras Infantry

1901
10th Gurkha Rifles

1950
10th Princess Mary's (3)
Own Gurkha Rifles

1994
3rd Battalion
**THE ROYAL GURKHA
RIFLES**

1996
DISBANDED

NOTES

(1) Madras Army of Hon.
East India Company.

(2) An amalgamation of
the 10th Madras Infantry
and the Kubo Valley
Police Battalion which
had been raised by Lieut.
Colonel C. R. MacGregor
in 1887.

(3) Princess Mary,
Princess Royal,
the only daughter of
King George V.

10th PRINCESS MARY's OWN GURKHA RIFLES

BATTLE HONOURS

First World War:

**Helles; Krithia; Suvla; Sari Bair; Gallipoli 1915;
Suez Canal; Egypt 1915; Sharquat;
Mesopotamia 1916-18.**

Afghanistan 1919.

Second World War:

Iraq 1941; Deir ez Zor; Syria 1941; **Coriano;
Santarcengelo;** Senio Floodbank; **Bologna;**
Sillaro Crossing; Gaiana Crossing; Italy 1944-45;
Monywa 1942; **Imphal; Tuitum;** Tamu Road;
Shenam Pass; Litan; Bishenpur; **Tengnoupal;
Mandalay; Myinmu Bridgehead;** Kyaukse 1945;
Meiktila; Capture of Meiktila; Defence of Meiktila;
Irrawaddy; **Rangoon Road;** Pegu 1945; Sittang 1945;
Burma 1942-45.

*Gurkha soldiers are recruited in their native Nepal where the Army maintains
a base to administer welfare and recruitment. Pride in the profession of arms
and competition to join the Brigade is fierce. During 2008 out of 28,000
applicants only 230 were selected and enlisted.*

1st REGIMENT OF GURKHA RIFLES

1815
1st & 2nd Nasiri Battalions (1)

1843
4th (Nasiri) Rifle Battalion

1850
66th Gurkha Regiment (2)

1858
66th Gurkha Light Infantry

1861
1st Gurkha Regiment (Light Infantry)

1891
1st Gurkha Rifle Regiment

1903
1st Gurkha Rifles (The Malaun Regiment)

1906
1st Prince of Wales's Own Gurkha Rifles (The Malaun Regiment)

1910
1st King George's Own Gurkha Rifles (The Malaun Regiment)

1937
1st King George V's Own Gurkha Rifles (The Malaun Regiment)

1950
Transferred to Indian Army as
1st GORKHA RIFLES (The Malaun Regiment)

(1) Raised from soldiers of Amar Singh Thapa's army after the fall of Malaun.

(2) Reconstitution of 66th Bengal Native Infantry following its mutiny and disbandment.

BATTLE HONOURS

Pre-1914:

Bhurtpore [1826]; **Aliwal** [1846]; **Sobraon** [1846]; North-West Frontier India [1849-57]; India [1857-58]; Perak 1875; Khyber Pass 1880; **Afghanistan 1878-80**; Sikkim [1888]; Mohmund [1897]; **Tirah** [1897-98]; **Punjab Frontier** [1897-98].

First World War:

Givenchy 1914; Neuve Chapelle; Ypres 1915; St Julien; Festubert 1915; Loos; France and Flanders 1914-15; Megiddo; Sharon; Palestine 1918; Tigris 1916; Kut al Amara 1917; Baghdad; Mesopotamia 1916-18; North-West Frontier India 1915-17.

Afghanistan 1919; Waziristan 1921; North-West Frontier India 1930; North-West Frontier India 1936-37; North-West Frontier India 1937-40.

Second World War:

Jitra; Kampar; Malaya 1942-42; Shenam Pass; Ukhrul; Myinmu Bridgehead; Kyaukse 1945; Burma 1942-45.

3rd REGIMENT OF GURKHA RIFLES

1815
The Kumaon Battalion (1)

1816
The Kumaon Provincial Battalion

1823
9th (or Kumaon) Local Battalion

1826
7th (or Kumaon) Local Battalion

1860
The Kumaon Battalion

1861
18th Bengal Native Infantry

3rd Gurkha (The Kumaon) Regiment

1864
3rd (The Kumaon) Goorkha Regiment

1887
3rd Gurkha Regiment

1891
3rd Gurkha (Rifle) Regiment

1908
3rd Queen Alexandra's (2) Own Gurkha Rifles

1950
Transferred to Indian Army as
3rd GORKHA RIFLES

(1) Raised from Gurkha soldiers after the fall of Malaun and Kumaon.

(2) Queen Alexandra, wife of King Edward VII.

BATTLE HONOURS

Pre-1914:

Delhi 1857; India [1857-58]; Bhutan [1864-66]; **Ahmed Khel** [1880]; **Afghanistan 1878-80**; Burma 1885-87; North-East Frontier India [1889-91]; **Chitral** [1895]; Waziristan 1895; **Tirah** [1897-98]; Dargai [1897]; **Punjab Frontier** [1897-98].

First World War:

La Bassée 1914; Armentières 1914; Festubert 1914, 15; Givenchy 1914; Neuve Chapelle 1915; Aubers; France and Flanders 1914-15; Egypt 1915-16; Gaza; El Mughar; Nebi Samwil; Jerusalem; Tell'Asur; Megiddo; Sharon; Palestine 1917-18; Sharquat; Mesopotamia 1917-18.

Afghanistan 1919; Waziristan 1921; North-West Frontier India 1930, 1936-37, 1937-40.

Second World War:

Deir el Shein; North Africa 1940-43; Monte Della Gorgace; Il Costello; Monte Farneto; Monte Cavallo; Italy 1943-45; Sittang 1942; Kyaukse 1942; Imphal; Tuitum; Sakwng; Shenam Pass; Bishenpur; Tengnoupal; Meiktila; Rangoon Road; Pyawbwe; Pegu 1945; Burma 1942-45.

4th REGIMENT OF GURKHA RIFLES

1857
The Extra Goorkha Regiment (1)

1861
19th Bengal Native Infantry

4th Goorkha Regiment

1891
4th Gurkha (Rifle) Regiment

1901
4th Gurkha Rifles

1924
4th Prince of Wales's (2) Own Gurkha Rifles

1947
Transferred to Indian Army as
4th GORKHA RIFLES

(1) Raised from part of the 1st Nasiri Battalion.

(2) The future King Edward VII.

BATTLE HONOURS

Pre-1914:

Umbeyla [1863]; North-West Frontier India [1868]; **Ali Masjid** [1878]; **Kabul 1879**; **Kandahar 1880**; **Afghanistan 1878-80**; North-East Frontier India [1889-93]; Waziristan 1895; **Chitral** [1895]; **Tirah** [1897-98]; **Punjab Frontier** [1897-98]; China 1900.

First World War:

Givenchy 1914; Neuve Chapelle; Ypres 1915; St. Julien; Aubers; Festubert 1915; France and Flanders 1914-15; Gallipoli 1915; Egypt 1916; Tigris 1916; Kut al Amara 1917; Baghdad 1917; Mesopotamia 1916-18.

Afghanistan 1919; Waziristan 1921; North-West Frontier India 1930, 1936-37, 1937-40.

Second World War:

Iraq; Syria; The Cauldron; North Africa 1940-43; Trestina; Monte Cedrone; Italy 1943-45; Pegu 1942; Chindits 1944; Mandalau; Burma 1942-45.

5th REGIMENT OF GURKHA RIFLES

1857
25th Punjab Infantry (1) or Hazara Gurkha Battalion

1861
7th Regiment of Infantry (Hazara Goorkha Battalion) (2)

1886
5th Goorkha Regiment (the Hazara Goorkha Battalion)

1887
5th Goorkha Regiment

1891
5th Gurkha (Rifle) Regiment

1901
5th Gurkha Rifles

1903
5th Gurkha Rifles (Frontier Force)

1921
5th Royal Gurkha Rifles (Frontier Force)

1947
Transferred to Indian Army as
5th GORKHA RIFLES (FRONTIER FORCE)

(1) Raised at Abbottabad by Captain H. M. Boisdragon.

(2) Punjab Irregular Force

BATTLE HONOURS

Pre-1914:

North-West Frontier India 1857-61, 1868; Umbeyla; **Peiwar Kotal** [1878]; **Charasiah** [1879]; **Kabul 1879**; **Kandahar 1880**; **Afghanistan 1878-80**; Hazara 1888, 1891; Samana 1891; **Punjab Frontier 1897-98**.

First World War:

Helles; Krithia; Suvla; Sari Bair; Gallipoli 1915; Suez Canal; Egypt 1915-16; Khan Baghdadi; Mesopotamia 1916-18; North-West Frontier India.

Afghanistan 1919; Waziristan 1921; North-West Frontier India 1930, 1936-39.

Second World War:

The Sangro; Cassino II; St Angelo in Teodice; Rocca D'Arce; Ripa Ridge; Femmina Morta; Monte San Bartolo; Italy 1943-45; Sittang 1942; Kyaukse 1942; Yenangyaung 1942; The Stockades; Buthidaung; Imphal; Sakawng; Shenam Pass; Bishenpur; The Irrawaddy; Sittang 1945; Burma 1942-45.

1824	1864	1835	1885
16th or Sylhet Local Battalion (1)	44th (Sylhet) Bengal Native (Light) Infantry	The Assam Sebundy Corps (2)	43rd (Assam) Bengal (Light) Infantry
1827	**1885**	**1844**	**1886**
11th or Sylhet Light Infantry	44th (Sylhet) Bengal (Light) Infantry	2nd Assam Light Infantry	43rd Regiment Goorkha Light Infantry
1861	**1886**	**1861**	**1891**
48th (Sylhet) Light Infantry	44th Goorkha (Light) Infantry	47th (2nd Assam) Light Infantry	43rd Gurkha (Rifle) Regiment Bengal Infantry
44th (Sylhet) Light Infantry	**1901**	43rd (Assam) Light Infantry	**1901**
	44th Gurkha Rifles		43rd Gurkha Rifles
	1903	**1864**	**1903**
	8th Gurkha Rifles	43rd (2nd Assam) Bengal Native Infantry	7th Gurkha Rifles

) Raised in Sylhet by
aptain P. Dudgeon.

(2) Raised at Gauhati by Captain W. Simonds from two companies of Assam Light Infantry.

1st BATTALION   **2nd BATTALION**

8th

1907
8th REGIMENT OF GURKHA RIFLES

1949
Transferred to Indian Army as
8th GORKHA RIFLES

9th

REGIMENT OF GURKHA RIFLES

1817 The Fatehgarh Levy (1)	**1893** 9th (Gurkha Rifle) Regiment of Bengal Infantry
1819 The Mainpuri Levy	**1901** 9th Gurkha Rifles
1823 32nd Bengal Native Infantry	**1949** Transferred to Indian Army as **9th GORKHA RIFLES**
1824 63rd Bengal Native Infantry	
1861 9th Bengal Native Infantry (2)	
1885 9th Bengal Infantry	

(1) Raised at Fatehgarh by Major C. S. Fagan.

(2) 63rd BNI disarmed at Berhampore during the Mutiny and later reconstituted as 9th BNI.

11th

REGIMENT OF GURKHA RIFLES

1918
Raised at Kut al Amara in Mesopotamia (1)

1921
REGIMENT DISBANDED

1948
Reraised in the Indian Army after partition as
11th GORKHA RIFLES

(1) Four battalions of the Regiment were raised — two in Mesopotamia and two in India.

The 1st Battalion, raised at Kut al Amara, drew its personnel from 1/5, 2/5, 1/6 and 2/6GR.

The 2nd Battalion, raised at Baghdad, drew from 1/1, 1/3, 2/4 and 1/7GR.

BATTLE HONOURS

Pre-1914:

Ava [1824-26]; India 1856-58; Bhutan [1864];
Burma 1885-87; North-East Frontier India [1890-93];
Thibet 1904.

First World War:

La Bassée 1914; Festubert 1914, 15; Givenchy 1914;
Neuve Chapelle; Aubers;
France and Flanders 1914-15; Egypt 1915-16;
Megiddo; Sharon; Palestine 1918; Tigris 1916;
Kut al Amara 1917; Baghdad; Mesopotamia 1916-17.

Afghanistan 1919; Malabar 1921; Waziristan 1921;
North-West Frontier India 1937-40.

Second World War:

Iraq 1941; North Africa 1940-43; Gothic Line;
Coriano; Santarcangelo; Gaiana Crossing;
Italy 1944-45; Point 551; Imphal; Tamu Road;
Bishenpur; Kanglatongbi; Mandalay;
Myinmu Bridgehead; Singhu; Shandatgyi;
Sittang 1945; Burma 1942-45.

BATTLE HONOURS

Pre-1914:

Ava [1824-26]; Arracan [1825]; **Bhurtpore [1826];**
Moodkee [1845]; Ferozeshah [1845]; **Sobraon [1846];**
Afghanistan 1879-80; Khyber Pass [1880];
North-East Frontier India 1889-90; Mohmund [1897];
Tirah {1897-98]; **Punjab Frontier 1897-98.**

First World War:

La Bassée 1914; Armentières 1914;
Festubert 1914, 15; Givenchy 1914; Neuve Chapelle;
Aubers; Loos 1915; France and Flanders 1914-15;
Tigris 1916; Kut al Amara 1917; Baghdad;
Mesopotamia 1916-18.

Afghanistan 1919; Malabar; Waziristan 1921;
North-West Frontier India 1937-40.

Second World War:

Djebel el Meida; Djebel Garci; Ragoubet Souissi;
North Africa 1940-43; Cassino I; Hangman's Hill;
San Marino; Italy 1943-45; Greece 1944-45;
Malaya 1941-42; Chindits 1944; Burma 1942-45.

BATTLE HONOUR

Aghanistan 1919.

The Royal Logistic Corps

The Royal Logistic Corps is the largest formation in the British Army with the most diverse responsibilities and the widest range of specialist trades. Its origins go back more than four centuries since when the paths of its main constituents have run a meandering course until they were rationalised with the formation of the Corps in 1993.

The effectiveness of any battle force is entirely dependent upon the efficiency of its transport and supply organisation. Napoleon maintained that an army marches on its stomach and the Duke of Wellington recommended that, in the event of his death, Sir William Beresford should succeed him in the Peninsula because he, alone, "knew how to feed an army".

The roots of transport and supply in the British Army are embedded in such ancient offices as the "Master of the Baggage Train" and "Master of the Ordnance" who were responsible for logistics in King Henry V's army at Agincourt. It was not until 1544, however, that the first formal logistics organisation was established by King Henry VIII. This was the Office of Ordnance which became the Board of Ordnance in 1597 and, for nearly three centuries, was the body which controlled artillery, military engineering, transport and supply. It was a civilian organisation, answerable to the Treasury, and it was not until 1855 that the Board was abolished and these functions came under military control.

Until 1870 transport and supply had developed separately but in 1870 all logistic officers were streamed into a Control Department with other ranks forming the first Army Service Corps. However, this arrangement only lasted for five years when transport and supply were again separated with officers and other ranks still in separate formations.

In 1889 officers and other ranks on the transport side united in a newly-formed Army Service Corps which in 1965 became the Royal Corps of Transport. Seven years later the supply side developed separately but in 1870 all followed suit with formation of the Army Ordnance Corps which together with the ASC became Royal in 1918.

In 1993 transport and supply came together finally with the formation of the multi-roled Royal Logistic Corps. They were joined by the Royal Pioneer Corps, with its long experience of labour management and control, and by the Postal & Courier Service of the Royal Engineers which handled the Army's mail from its central post office in Northolt and through British Army Post Offices (BFPOs) throughout the world where British servicemen were deployed. The final element of the RLC was the Army Catering Corps, a young formation but one which, in its short history, had already established a high reputation in professional catering circles.

With over 15,000 personnel, comprising some 16% of the Army's total strength, the Royal Logistic Corps is its largest formation and has the most diverse range of responsibilities.

The acquisition, storage, maintenance, transport and supply of almost everything the Army needs to live, move and fight – food, water, weapons, ammunition, vehicles, spares, fuel, clothing and equipment — is the reponsibility of the Corps.

Rations and ammunition are distributed to front-line troops by RLC soldiers in specialist armoured vehicles; RLC chefs prepare the Army's meals; RLC Postal & Courier personnel deliver the mail; RLC railway tradesmen drive the Army's trains; RLC maritime officers and soldier crew the Army's ships and man the military ports; RLC Air Despatch specialists handle the air-dropped supplies both in military operations and during international civil emergencies;

ROYAL CORPS OF TRANSPORT

PAGE 138

ROYAL ARMY ORDNANCE CORPS

PAGE 138

ROYAL PIONEER CORPS

PAGE 138

ARMY CATERING CORPS

PAGE 138

POSTAL & COURIER SERVICE

ROYAL ENGINEERS

PAGE 57, 138

1993 THE ROYAL LOGISTIC CORPS

LC personnel support the vast, state-of-e-art warehouses and depots which use everything the Army uses from ain battle tanks to belt buckles; LC drivers transport the tanks to their ea of operation on huge transporters nd deliver ammunition to the Royal rtillery batteries on Dismountable Rack ff-load and Pick-up System vehicles OROPS). Not least in the duties of the

Corps is its original ordnance role as the Army's ammunition experts. RLC personnel man the ammunition depots at Kineton and the Defence Explosive Munitions Search School at Temple Herdewyke, and Ammunition Technicians of the Corps undertake the hazardous duties of Explosive Ordnance Disposal when terrorist devices are located.

Pioneers of the RLC provide Labour Support and Artisan Skills as well as having responsibility for Mortuary Affairs and War Graves Services.

Although, in common with the other technical corps, the RLC no longer receives Battle Honours, it does carry forward five awards earned in the days when the Transport Corps of the Army was sometimes employed as light cavalry. These are shown on the right.

With its huge establishment and enormous range of trades and responsibilities, the RLC certainly justifies its popular sobriquet of the "Really Large Corps"!

CORPS MUSEUM

ROYAL LOGISTIC CORPS MUSEUM
Princess Royal Barracks, Deepcut, Camberley, Surrey GU16 6RW
Tel: 01252 833371 Fax: 01252 833484
email: information@rlcmuseum.com
Website: www.army-rlc.uk

REGIMENTAL HEADQUARTERS
Dettingen House, The Princess Royal Barracks, Deepcut, Camberley, Surrey GU16 6RW
Tel (Civ): 01252 833364 Fax: 01252 833375
Website: www.army-rlc.co.uk

REGIMENTAL MARCH
Quick March: *On Parade*

ALLIANCES

Australian Military Forces:
The Royal Australian Corps of Transport
The Royal Australian Army Ordnance Corps
The Royal Australian Catering Corps

New Zealand Army:
The Royal New Zealand Army Logistic Regiment

Indian Army:
Army Service Corps of India
Army Ordnance Corps of India

Pakistan Army:
Army Service Corps of Pakistan
Army Ordnance Corps of Pakistan

Sri Lanka Army:
The Sri Lanka Army Service Corps
The Sri Lanka Army Ordnance Corps

Malaysian Armed Forces:
The Malaysian Service Corps
The Malaysian Army Ordnance Corps

South African Defence Forces:
Personnel Service Corps of the South African Defence Force

Canadian Forces:
The Canadian Forces Logistic Branch

AFFILIATED REGIMENT
The Queen's Own Gurkha Logistic Regiment

COLONEL-IN-CHIEF
HRH The Princess Royal KG, KT, GCVO, QSO

DEPUTY COLONELS-IN-CHIEF
HRH The Duke of Gloucester KG, GCVO
HRH The Duchess of Kent GCVO

HEAD OF CORPS
The Master General of Logistics

BATTLE HONOURS
Peninsula; Waterloo; Lucknow; Taku Forts; Pekin.

LINEAGE OF THE ROYAL LOGISTIC CORPS

| | = | *OFFICERS* |
| | = | *OTHER RANKS* |

1794
Royal Waggoners (1)

1796
Royal Waggon Train

1799
Royal Waggon Corps

1802
Royal Waggon Train

1833
DISBANDED

1855
Land Transport Corps

1856
Military Train

1859
Commissariat Staff Corps

BOARD OF ORDNANCE

In 1544 King Henry VIII created the Office of Ordnance, which in 1597 became the Board of Ordnance, with its Headquarters in the Tower of London. This was a civilian organisation, answerable to Parliament and, by the time of its abolishment in 1855, was the effective controlling body for Artillery, Engineering, Munitions, Stores, Medical and Transport. In 1855 these functions came under the military orders of the Commander-in-Chief and the Board of Ordnance was absorbed into the War Office as The Department of the Master-General of the Ordnance.

1853
Purveyors Department (Officers)

1858
Commissariat Department (Officers)

1857
Military Store Department (Officers)

1858
Corps of Armourer-Sergeants

1865
Military Store Staff Corps

1870
Control Department (2) (3) (Officers)

1870
Army Service Corps (2) (Other Ranks)

1875
Commissariat & Transport Department (Officers)

1877
Commissariat & Transport Branch

1880
Commissariat & Transport Staff

1881
Commissariat & Transport Corps

1875
Ordnance Store Department (Officers)

1896
Army Ordnance Department

1877
Ordnance Store Branch

1881
Ordnance Store Corps

1882
Corps of Ordnance Artificers

1889
Army Service Corps

1918
Royal Army Service Corps

1965
ROYAL CORPS OF TRANSPORT

1896
Army Ordnance Corps

1918
ROYAL ARMY ORDNANCE CORPS

NOTES

(1) Raised from the prisons of the land and known popularly as "The Newgate Blues".

(2) In 1870 Transport and Supply personnel were united — officers in the Control Department and other ranks in the Army Service Corps. In 1875 the two functions were separated again and would remain separate until formation of the Royal Logistic Corps in 1993.

(3) Officers of the Barrack Department were also absorbed into the Control Department.

(4) A non-combatant corps raised for service in France and containing over 100,000 Chinese.

(5) A fully-combatant corps which by the end of World War II had a strength of over 400,000 excluding civilian and prisoners-of-war.

(6) In 1950 the Corps was taken on to the Regular Establishment ceasing to be an auxiliary organisation.

(7) Prior to the formation of a catering corps within the Royal Army Service Corps, there was no central control with battalions providing their own regimental cooks some of whom had received training at one of two Army catering schools at Aldershot and at Poona in India.

1762
Royal Pioneers

1763
DISBANDED

1855
Army Works Corps

1856
DISBANDED

1915
Labour Corps (4)

1919
DISBANDED

1939
Auxiliary Military Pioneer Corps (5)

1940
Pioneer Corps

1946
ROYAL PIONEER CORPS (6)

1902
Mechanical Transport Section of Royal Engineers transferred to Army Service Corps

1914
Responsibility for Inland Water Transport transferred from Army Service Corps to Royal Engineers

1965
Transportation & Movement Control transferred from Royal Engineers to Royal Corps of Transport

1993
POSTAL & COURIER SERVICE RE
became constituent of newly-formed Royal Logistic Corps

1941
Catering Corps of Royal Army Service Corps (7)

1965
ARMY CATERING CORPS

ACTIVE REGULAR ROYAL LOGISTIC CORPS REGIMENTS

1

LOGISTIC SUPPORT REGIMENT RLC

2

LOGISTIC SUPPORT REGIMENT RLC

3

LOGISTIC SUPPORT REGIMENT RLC

4

LOGISTIC SUPPORT REGIMENT RLC

6

REGIMENT RLC

7

REGIMENT RLC

8

REGIMENT RLC

9

REGIMENT RLC

10

UEEN'S OWN GURKHA LOGISTIC REGIMENT

11

EOD REGIMENT RLC

(EXPLOSIVE ORDNANCE DISPOSAL)

12

LOGISTIC SUPPORT REGIMENT RLC

13

AIR ASSAULT SUPPORT REGIMENT RLC

17

PORT and MARITIME REGIMENT RLC

23

PIONEER REGIMENT RLC

24

REGIMENT RLC

(POSTAL, COURIER & MOVEMENT)

25

TRAINING REGIMENT RLC

27

REGIMENT RLC

29

REGIMENT RLC

(POSTAL, COURIER & MOVEMENT)

ROYAL LOGISTIC CORPS ESTABLISHMENTS

Defence School of Mechanical Transport, Leconfield

Defence Storage and Distribution Agency at Ashchurch, Bicester and Donnington

Defence Munitions Depot, Kineton

Defence Explosives, Munitions and Search School North, Temple Herdewyke

Defence Petroleum Centre, West Moors

Defence Vehicle Depot, Ashchurch

Defence Food Services School, Worthy Down

British Forces Post Office, Northolt

Defence College of Logistics and Personnel Administration, (HQ at Deepcut)

*I*n the early days of the post-reformation standing army, each regiment employed a qualified Medical Officer in the rank of Surgeon, assisted by an Assistant Surgeon, a warrant officer. They were suppported by such orderlies as could be spared from the ranks of the regiment — often soldiers with disabilities or who were themselves convalescing from injuries. This medical team operated from a hospital provided by the regiment which would be tented when the regiment was on operations.

 Both Marlborough and Wellington, with the concern which every good commander has for the health and welfare of his men, had established field hospitals and attempted the formation of some sort of central medical service within their armies.

 However, during the 40 years of peace which followed the end of the Napoleonic Wars, the lessons learned in the Peninsula were forgotten and Britain entered the Crimean War in 1854 with no organised medical service and as poorly equipped as she had been 100 years before.

The Army's sick and wounded have been tended by Regimental Surgeons since the first standing army but it was not until the late 19th century that formal bodies were established for the administration and development of army medicine and nursing.

MEDICAL

 In a campaign blighted by disease and a heavy volume of battlefield casualties, Regimental Surgeons could not cope. The lack of medical care provided to the troops and the appalling conditions in which the sick and wounded were confined caused a national scandal. Clearly, as with most other aspects of Army administrative and supporting services, fundamental reform was urgently required.

 In 1855 an attempt to provide a pool of trained orderlies was made with the formation of the Medical Staff Corps for which were sought *"...men able to read and write, of regular habits and good temper and of a kindly disposition".* In 1857 the name was changed to Army Hospital Corps then back again in 1884.

 Meanwhile, medical officers had remained in the separate, officer-only Army Medical Department which, in turn, changed its name to Army Medical Staff

in 1873 to coincide with a raft of radical improvements in the structure of Army Medical Services. Regimental hospitals were abolished and replaced by fewer, much larger military hospitals with better facilities and more specialised staff and equipment.

 Then in 1898 medical officers and orderlies amalgamated into the newly-formed Royal Army Medical Corps which has supported the Army ever since. The Corps has provided a superb medical service both at home and on the field of battle with astonishing bravery and commitment which has been recognised with the award of 28 Victoria Crosses plus two Bars to its personnel. There have only been three awards of Bars to the Victoria Cross (ie a second award of the VC) and two of the three, Noel Chevasse and Arthur Martin-Leake, were medical officers.

NURSING

 There were women nursing in the Army during the Civil War and regulations for nurses in army hospitals in the late 18th century, but it was not until the arrival of Florence Nightingale in the Crimea with 38 volunteer nurses that the first serious attempt to address the basic problems ygiene and organisation in military ospitals was made. Their achievements the Crimea are well known and ontributed to the reputation for edication and legendary high standards hich army nursing was to acquire over e next 150 years.

After the Crimea, in 1860, formal aining of Army Nurses began at the oyal Victoria Hospital, Netley, and six ears later nurses were appointed to all ilitary General Hospitals. Although ursing sisters were sent to South Africa r the Zulu War of 1879/80, it was not ntil 1881 that the Army Nursing Service as officially instituted.

From there on nursing sisters began to ppear in British Military Hospitals verseas and by 1883, every BMH with ore than 100 beds had its complement f nurses. In the 2nd Boer War of 1899 ,400 Army nurses, including 80 from anada, Australia and New Zealand, erved in South Africa.

In 1902 the Army Nursing Service eceived Royal Patronage with the ersonal interest of Queen Alexandra ho became its President until her death 1925 and gave her name to the new ueen Alexandra's Imperial Military

Nursing Service. Its members gave outstanding service through two World Wars on every front, in every campaign, many suffering the privations of prison camps in the Far East and many giving their lives while tending the sick and wounded. Testament abounds to the courage, dedication and professionalism of the QAs.

After World War II the importance of the service was at last recognised with its incorporation into the Army as a separate corps called Queen Alexandra's Royal Army Nursing Corps. Today, their numbers have shrunk and the great BMHs have gone but the dedication and spirit of the QAs remains wherever the British Army serves.

DENTAL

Strong incisors in the ranks of the infantry were always important as soldiers were required to bite off the end of their cartridges before loading their rifles. In the 18th and 19th centuries, such dental treatment as was available in the Army was from the Regimental Surgeon and was usually confined to the extraction of rotten teeth which had reached the stage where the patient

considered that their removal, without any form of anaesthetic, was probably less painful than leaving them in place!

As a result of heavy demand for dental treatment during the 2nd Boer War, a Dental Service Branch was created within the RAMC in 1901 but the massive mobilisation of World War I, with millions rather than thousands of potential patients, emphasised the need for regular, high-quality preventative dental care and education. In 1921 the Army Dental Corps was formed which in 1946 acquired its "Royal" title as a result of excellent service during World War II.

Today, Army Dentists, Hygienists, Dental Nurses and Technicians provide a first-class service to soldiers and their families worldwide.

VETERINARY

The fourth element of the Army Medical Services, the Royal Army Veterinary Corps, has a history dating back to 1796 when an Army Veterinary Service was formed *'to improve the practice of Farriery in the Corps of Cavalry'*. In the days of mounted cavalry and horse-drawn artillery and transport, the number of service horses and mules was almost

as great as the number of soldiers and the responsibilities of the Corps were immense. As late as 1939, when the 1st Cavalry Division was deployed in Palestine with 20,000 animals, the RAVC played a major role in animal husbandry. With mechanisation, the size of the Corps and the demands for its services naturally declined but today, with a strength of around 200, the Corps is still responsible for the welfare of the Army's horses and dogs and provides an important professional advisory service to the civil authorities during certain international emergencies in which the Army is involved.

The Corps is also responsible for the Army's explosives and drugs sniffer dogs; in July 2008 Lance Corporal Kenneth Rowe of the RAVC, attached to 2 PARA, was killed in action with his search dog "Sasha" in Afghanistan.

MUSEUM

ARMY MEDICAL SERVICES MUSEUM

Royal Army Medical Corps
Royal Army Veterinary Corps
Royal Army Dental Corps
Queen Alexandra's Royal Army Nursing Corps

Keogh Barracks, Ash Vale, Aldershot,
Hants. GY12 5RQ
Tel: 01252 868612 Fax: 01252 340332
email: museum@keogh72.freeserve.co.uk
Website: www.ams-museum.org.uk

Royal Army Medical Corps

Army Medical Department (Medical Officers)	1855 Medical Staff Corps (Orderlies)
1873 Army Medical Staff (Medical Officers) (1)	1857 Army Hospital Corps
	1884 Medical Staff Corps

1884 ARMY MEDICAL STAFF CORPS

1898 ROYAL ARMY MEDICAL CORPS (2)

CORPS HEADQUARTERS

Slim Road, Camberley, Surrey GU15 4NP

Tel: 01276 412752 Fax: 01276 412793

email: rhq_ams@hotmail.com

Website: www.army.mod.uk/medical/
royal_army_medical_corps/

REGIMENTAL MARCHES

Quick March: Here's a Health unto His Majesty

Slow March: Her Bright Smile Haunts Me Still

ALLIANCES

Canadian Armed Forces:
Medical Branch

Australian Military Forces:
The Royal Australian Army Medical Corps

New Zealand Army:
Royal New Zealand Army Medical Corps

Pakistan Army:
Army Medical Corps

Sri Lanka Army:
The Sri Lankan Army Medical Corps

Zambia Army:
Zambia Army Medical Service

South African Defence Forces:
South African Medical Service

COLONEL-IN-CHIEF

HRH The Duke of Gloucester KG, GCVO

NOTES

(1) In 1873 mobile regimental hospitals were abolished and were replaced by fewer, but much larger, military hospitals with better facilities and more specialised medical staff.

(2) The newly-formed Corps first took its place in the field in the Khartoum Expedition of 1898 as part of the Nile Expeditionary Force.

Though it is an armed corps, under the terms of the Geneva Convention members of the RAMC may only use their weapons for defence. In recognition of this tradition, when on parade RAMC officers do not draw their swords; they hold the scabbard in the left hand while saluting with the right. NCOs and other ranks do not fix bayonets.

Queen Alexandra's Royal Army Nursing Corps

1881 Army Nursing Service	1897 Princess Christian's (5) Army Nursing Reserve

1902 Queen Alexandra's (3) Imperial Military Nursing Service (4)

1949 QUEEN ALEXANDRA'S ROYAL ARMY NURSING CORPS

CORPS HEADQUARTERS

RHQ Queen Alexandra's Royal Army Nursing Corp
Headquarters Army Medical Services
Slim Road, Camberley, Surrey GU15 4NP

Tel: 01276 412754 Fax: 01276 412793

email: regtsecqaranc@hotmail.com

Website: www.army.mod.uk/qaranc

REGIMENTAL MARCH

Quick March: Grey and Scarlet

ALLIANCES

Australian Military Forces:
The Royal Australian Army Nursing Corps

New Zealand Army:
The Royal New Zealand Nursing Corps

COLONEL-IN-CHIEF

HRH The Countess of Wessex

(3) Queen Alexandra. wife of King Edward VII. On her death in 1925 she was succeeded as President of the Service by Queen Mary, wife of King George V. The present Colonel-in-Chief is HRH The Countess of Wessex.

(4) QA nursing sisters have always been accorded officer status. Before World War II they were designated Principal Matron, Matron, Senior Sister and Sister but during the War were given normal military rank though they did not hold commissions. From 1949, QARANC has been a Corps within the Army with its officers holding full, commissioned rank.

(5) The 3rd daughter of Queen Victoria.

With their tin hats and gas masks, the QAs followed the troops during every major campaign of World War II during which over 10,000 were engaged and 1,369 received orders and decorations for exceptional service. Today, the strength of the Corps is around 850 comprising female and male personnel in both commissioned and non-commissioned rank.

Royal Army Dental Corps

1901
Dental Service Branch
Royal Army Medical
Corps

1921
ARMY DENTAL CORPS

1946
**ROYAL ARMY DENTAL
CORPS**

CORPS HEADQUARTERS

RHQ Royal Army Dental Corps,
Headquarters Army Medical Services
Slim Road, Camberley, Surrey GU15 4NP

Tel: 01276 412753 Fax: 01276 412793

email: rhq_radc@hotmail.com

Website: www.army.mod.uk/medical/dental/

REGIMENTAL MARCHES

Quick March: Green Facings

ALLIANCE

Australian Military Forces:
The Royal Australian Army Dental Corps

New Zealand Army:
The Royal New Zealand Dental Corps

COLONEL-IN-CHIEF

HRH The Duchess of Gloucester GCVO

Royal Army Veterinary Corps

1796
Army Veterinary Service
(Veterinary Surgeons) (1)

1859
Veterinary Medical
Department
(Officers)

1903
Army Veterinary Corps
(Other Ranks)

1903
ARMY VETERINARY CORPS

1918
**ROYAL ARMY VETERINARY
CORPS**

(1) John Shipp was the first Veterinary Officer to be
commissioned into the Army. He was appointed to the
11th Light Dragoons on 25th June 1796 celebrated since
as the Corps's Foundation Day — John Shipp Day.

CORPS HEADQUARTERS

RHQ Royal Army Veterinary Corps,
Headquarters Army Medical Services
Slim Road, Camberley, Surrey GU15 4NP

Tel: Camberley Mil. 94261 Ext. 2749

Website: www.army.mod.uk/medical/
royal_army_veterinary_corps/

REGIMENTAL MARCHES

Quick March: Arrangement of
"Drink Puppy Drink" and
"A Hunting We Will Go"
(Regimental March of the RAVC)

Slow March: "Golden Spurs"

ALLIANCE

Pakistan Army:
Pakistan Remounts, Veterinary and Farm Corps

COLONEL-IN-CHIEF

HRH The Princess Royal KG, KT, GCVO, QSO

The necessity of keeping weapons and equipment in first class order has always been recognised as an essential requirement for a battle-winning military force. Until the technical advances of the early 20th century, when weapons and equipment were relatively unsophisticated, this was the responsibility of the individual soldier supported by the skills of his unit armourer, farrier, carpenter and wheelwright.

With the advent of machine guns, internal-combustion engines, wireless sets and military aircraft, the responsibility for servicing and repairing these new equipments devolved upon the technical corps existing at the time in which the appropriate skills were to be found. The Army Ordnance Corps, specialists in weapons and ammunition, maintained the new weapons; the Army Service Corps, the transport and logistics experts, serviced and repaired the newly-introduced motor vehicles; after its formation in 1920, Royal Signals were responsible for the emerging communications systems and the Royal Engineers continued with a wide range of engineering commitments.

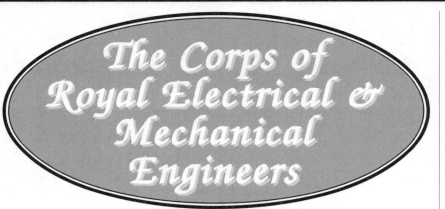

The Corps of Royal Electrical & Mechanical Engineers

Forged in the furnace of war, the Royal Electrical & Mechanical Engineers were formed in 1942 to rationalise technical support for the Army's vehicles and equipment. Taking over the principal electrical and mechanical responsibilities of the existing technical corps, REME soon developed into an essential constituent of every front line formation.

By the early part of the Second World War, electrical and mechanical equipment had become so universally essential to every formation that the War

REME REGULAR UNIT LOCATIONS AND ATTACHMENTS

There are presently 7 regular REME battalions, 2 integrated (regular/TA), and 2 TA battalions.

1	Close Support Battalion REME	Catterick	4 Mechanised Brigade
2	Close Support Battalion REME	Fallingbostel	7 Armoured Brigade
3	Close Support Battalion REME	Paderborn	20 Armoured Brigade
4	Close Support Battalion REME	Bordon	12 Mechanised Brigade
6	Close Support Battalion REME	Tidworth	1 Mechanised Brigade
19	Combat Service Support Light Battalion REME	Northern Ireland	19 Light Brigade
7	Air Assault Battalion REME	Wattisham	16 Air Assault Brigade
101	Force Support Battalion REME (integrated)		102 Logistic Brigade
104	Force Support Battalion REME (integrated)		101 Logistic Brigade

REME personnel are also serving in Canada, Belize, the United States, the Falklands, Gibraltar, Bosnia, Cyprus, Sierra Leone, Tanzania, Kenya, Iraq, Oman, Kuwait, Afghanistan, Nepal, Brunei and Australia.

Cabinet directed an enquiry, chaired by Sir William Beveridge, into the employment of technical manpower in the Army. The findings of this report led to the formation of the Corps of Royal Electrical & Mechanical Engineers (REME) in 1942. Drawing its personnel mainly from the existing technical corps, it was ready for its first operational role at the decisive Battle of El Alamein soon after which REME units were to be deployed in every theatre of the War.

Raised and configured in actual war conditions, the new Corps very quickly found its feet and was providing invaluable engineering support throughout the Army. By the end of the War it had a total strength of 158,000 officers and men plus 100,000 civilians under its command. After the War, as part of the occupying forces, it was a REME unit which recognised the potential of the Volkswagen "Beetle" and against all advice from the motor industry, insisted on the bomb-destroyed factory being put back into production.

Today, with a strength of around 9,500 officers and men, REME units are to be found wherever the Army is deployed ensuring expert and rapid support for its vehicles and equipment.

REME IN ACTION

REME battalions vary in size and structure according to their role and the requirements of the formation they support. Typically, a battalion might have an all-ranks strength of around 900 and comprise three companies — 2 x Armoured Companies and a Field Company.

LIGHT AID DETACHMENTS (LADs)

Every armoured and mechanised infantry regiment has its own REME Light Aid Detachment which is deployed with its parent regiment. LADs vary in size according to the equipment of the units they support and can range between 25 and 90 craftsmen and technicians commanded by a REME captain. The role of the LAD is to undertake instant repairs at the point of failure with spares and tools carried by the parent regiment. If the work is beyond the capability of the LAD, a supporting CS company will be called forward or, in the case of major failure, the equipment backloaded to a REME base workshop.

ROYAL ARMY ORDNANCE CORPS

CORPS OF ROYAL ENGINEERS

ROYAL ARMY SERVICE CORPS

ROYAL CORPS OF SIGNALS

ROYAL AIR FORCE

1942
CORPS OF ROYAL ELECTRICAL & MECHANICAL ENGINEERS
formed with technical personnel drawn from the above four corps from which it took over the principal electrical and mechanical engineering functions

1958
Took over from Royal Air Force responsibility for maintaining Army aircraft

CORPS HEADQUARTERS

Regimental Headquarters REME,
(Box H075) HQ DEME(A), Hazebrouck Barracks,
Isaac Newton Road, Arborfield,
Reading, Berkshire RG2 9NJ

Tel: Civ. 0118 976 3220 Arborfield Mil. 2220

Fax: 0118 976 3672

email: DEME-corpssecRO1@mod.uk

Website: www.army.mod.uk/reme/

REGIMENTAL MARCHES

Quick Marches: Lillibulero
                     Auprès de ma Blonde

Slow March: Duchess of Kent

ALLIANCES

Canadian Armed Forces:
Electrical & Mechanical Engineers Branch of the Canadian Armed Forces

South African Defence Forces:
Technical Services Corps

Australian Military Forces:
The Corps of Royal Australian Electrical & Mechanical Engineers

Indian Army:
Corps of Electronics & Mechanical Engineers

Pakistan Army:
Corps of Electrical & Mechanical Engineers

Sri Lanka Army:
The Sri Lanka Electrical & Mechanical Engineers

Malaysian Armed Forces:
The Royal Malaysian Electrical & Mechanical Engineers

COLONEL-IN-CHIEF

Field Marshal HRH The Prince Philip
Duke of Edinburgh KG, KT, OM, GBE, AC, QSO

CORPS MUSEUM

REME MUSEUM OF TECHNOLOGY
Isaac Newton Road, Arborfield, Reading RG2 9NJ
Tel: 0118 976 3375 Fax: 0118 976 2017
email: enquiries@rememuseum.org.uk
Website: www.rememuseum.org.uk

*T*he Adjutant General's Corps is a recent formation which consolidates several important offices within the Army — some with ancient antecedents and others of more recent origin.

STAFF AND PERSONNEL SUPPORT BRANCH (SPS)

Soldiers have always needed to be paid and the roots of the SPS Branch lie in the civilian paymasters who, prior to 1797, were appointed to individual regiments by civilian agencies.

In 1797 pay came under military control and full-time Army Paymasters were commissioned in the rank of Captain. This system lasted until 1870 when all officers providing support services to the field army — supply, transport, pay, etc. — were streamed into the newly-formed Control Department which only lasted for seven years and from which the individual, specialist corps began to evolve. The Army Pay Department of 1877 eventually became the Royal Army Pay Corps which in 1992 combined with the staff clerks of the Royal Army Ordnance Corps, all-arms clerks from every regiment and corps of the Army

The Adjutant General's Corps

With its origins in the civilian paymasters of Marlborough's armies, today's Adjutant General's Corps is the personnel organisation of the Army responsible for administration, records, accountancy, policing, guarding, educational support, resettlement and legal support.

and those members of the Women's Royal Army Corps who had not been rebadged into individual regiments, to form the SPS Branch — the major building block of the Adjutant General's Corps. Its responsibilities are far more diverse than pay alone incorporating the whole range of administrative, personnel records, management and accountancy functions within the Army.

PROVOST BRANCH (PRO)

The position of Provost-Marshal has existed in the Army since medieval times but it was only in Wellington's army in the Peninsular War that a formal military police force was first raised. This eventually became the Corps of Royal Military Police, "The Redcaps", which today carries forward its proud traditions as a constituent of the AGC. In 1992 the Military Provost Staff Corps who manned the Army's Detention Centres and Corrective Establishments, and were the Army's experts in all custodial matters, including the management of prisoners-of-war, combined with the RMP to form the Provost Branch of the AGC. In 1997 the Military Provost Guard Service (MPGS) was formed.

EDUCATIONAL AND TRAINING SERVICES BRANCH (ETS)

Education within the Army is a comparatively recent innovation which stems from the formation of the Corps of Army Schoolmasters in 1846. This became the Royal Army Educational Corps which undertook the whole range of general and vocational education within the Army as well as training support for other formations and the important function of resettlement — preparing personnel for their return to civilian employment. In 1992 the RAEC became the ETS Branch of the AGC.

ARMY LEGAL SERVICES BRANCH (ALS

The origins of the Army Legal Service lie in the office of the Judge Advocate General though a formal legal department was not created until 1923. In 1992 the Army Legal Corps became the ALS Branch of the AGC. Its tradition duties remain the same including the prosecution of offenders at Courts-Martial, the provision of expert advice or all aspects of military and civil law and the drafting and maintenance of Army legal documents. Additionally nowadays the Branch provides advice on all legal matters to Army personnel and their families at all levels.

ROYAL ARMY PAY CORPS

PAGE 148

ROYAL ARMY ORDNANCE CORPS

STAFF CLERKS

PAGE 138

WOMEN'S ROYAL ARMY CORPS

PERSONNEL NOT REBADGED INTO OTHER CORPS OR REGIMENTS

PAGE 148

CORPS OF ROYAL MILITARY POLICE

PAGE 149

MILITARY PROVOST STAFF CORPS

PAGE 149

ROYAL ARMY EDUCATIONAL CORPS

PAGE 149

ARMY LEGAL CORPS

PAGE 149

STAFF AND PERSONNEL SUPPORT BRANCH (SPS)

PROVOST BRANCH (PRO)

EDUCATIONAL AND TRAINING SERVICES BRANCH (ETS)

ARMY LEGAL SERVICES BRANCH (ALS)

1992
ADJUTANT GENERAL'S CORPS

ADJUTANT GENERAL'S CORPS

REGIMENTAL HEADQUARTERS

Worthy Down, Winchester, Hants. SO21 2RG

Tel: Civ. 01962 887820 Mil. Ext. 2820

Website: www.rhqagc.com

COLONEL-IN-CHIEF

HM The Queen

DEPUTY COLONELS-IN-CHIEF

HRH The Duchess of Gloucester GCVO
HRH The Duchess of Kent GCVO

REGIMENTAL MARCHES

Quick March: Pride of Lions

Slow March: Greensleeves

CORPS MUSEUM

ADJUTANT GENERAL'S CORPS MUSEUM COLLECTION
The Guardroom, Peninsula Barracks, Romsey Road, Winchester, Hants. SO23 8TS
Tel: 01962 877826 Fax: 01962 887690
email: agcmuseum@milnet.uk.net

1797
Commissioned Paymasters introduced into Army (1)

1870
Control Department Pay Sub-Department

1877
Army Pay Department (officers)

1905
Army Accounts Department

1909
Army Pay Department (2)

1893
Army Pay Corps (other ranks)

1920
ROYAL ARMY PAY CORPS

1992
Became part of AGC (SPS)

NOTES

(1) In the 17th and 18th centuries professional accountancy agents provided civilian Paymasters to individual regiments. In 1797 pay came under the Army's control with Paymasters commissioned in the rank of Captain.

(2) In 1912 the recommendations of the Clayton Commission were introduced whereby regimental officers paid their own soldiers with the Paymasters keeping central accounts in Fixed Centre Pay Offices (FCPOs) in the United Kingdom.

This system was in force during World War I at the start of which there were 170 Paymasters and 400 clerks. By the end of the War there were an additional 844 Acting Paymasters plus 11,000 military and 15,000 civilian clerks employed in the FCPOs.

(3) A voluntary organisation of gentlewomen who, during World War I, drove ambulances in the front line, ran canteens, mobile baths and cinemas for the troops often in conditions of extreme danger.

(4) Granted official status though its members remained unpaid volunteers.

(5) During World War II many FANYs served in covert communications activities and as agents with the Special Operations Executive (SOE). Among those who were dropped behind enemy lines were such famous names as Odette Hallowes, Violette Szabo and Noor Inayat Khan. Twelve FANYs died in concentration camps.

(6) Though still not an official corps in the Army, the FANYs are still active and perform invaluable voluntary service in support of the military and civil authorities during national emergencies.

(7) Queen Mary, wife of King George V.

(8) Another corps of volunteers raised to drive ambulances and run canteens for the troops.

1907
First Aid Nursing Yeomanry (3)

1927
First Aid Nursing Yeomanry (Ambulance Car Corps) (4)

1933
Women's Transport Service (FANY)

1939
Most personnel transferred to ATS forming nucleus of Motor Driver Companies (5)

1999
FIRST AID NURSING YEOMANRY (The Princess Royal's Volunteer Corps) (6)

1917
Women's Auxiliary Corps

1917
Absorbed Women's Legion (except Transport Section)

1918
Queen Mary's Auxiliary Army Corps (7)

1919
DISBANDED

1915
Women's Legion (8)

1917
Transferred all personnel except Transport Section to WAC

1919
DISBANDED

1938
AUXILIARY TERRITORIAL SERVICE (ATS)

1939
Absorbed most FANY personnel

1949
WOMEN'S ROYAL ARMY CORPS

1992
Most personnel were rebadged into the regiments or corps in which they were serving. The remainder became part of AGC (SPS)

STAFF AND PERSONNEL SUPPORT BRANCH (SPS)

BRANCH HEADQUARTERS

DSPS (A), Gould House, Worthy Down, Winchester, Hants. SO21 2RG

Tel: Civ. 0962 887333 Mil. 94271 2333

Website: www.army.mod.uk/agc/
staff_personnel_support_branch

ANTECEDENT CORPS MARCH

Quick March: Imperial Echoes

ALLIANCES

South African Defence Force:
Finance Service Corps

ARMY LEGAL SERVICES BRANCH (ALS)

BRANCH HEADQUARTERS

Directorate of Army Legal Services, Trenchard Lines, Upavon, Pewsey, Wilts. SN6 6BE

Tel: Civ. 01980 615703 Mil. Ext. 8703

Website: www.army.mod.uk/agc/
army_legal_services

ANTECEDENT CORPS MARCH

Quick March: Scales of Justice

ALLIANCES

Canadian Armed Forces:
Canadian Forces Legal Branch
Australian Military Forces:
The Australian Army Legal Corps

PROVOST

(1) Sir Henry Guyleford.

(2) Reformed after Waterloo, by orders of the Duke of Wellington, to combat drunken looting in France.

(3) Raised in Ireland, mainly from men of the Irish Constabulary, for service in the Crimean War.

(4) Twenty-one NCOs and troopers were seconded from four cavalry regiments for patrol duties in the garrison town of Aldershot. The early Military Policemen wore a red scarf around their right shoulder to distinguish them from ordinary troopers. It is thought that this was the origin of the red brassard worn to this day on the upper right arm and the red-topped service cap which gives the Corps their name "The Redcaps".

(5) Raised initially for service in Egypt.

(6) Formed to implement the recommendations of the Monkswell Commission on penal reform in military prisons. Today, the old "Glasshouse" has been replaced by the Military Corrective Training Centre, manned by members of the former Military Provost Staff, where the emphasis is on correction and rehabilitation.

EDUCATION

Although the Army had provided education for artillery and engineer officers since 1806 at the Royal Military Academy Woolwich, it was another 40 years before any formal education body was in place for the rest of the Army. In 1857 the Council for Military Education was formed to control all army schools and libraries and opportunities for general education and vocational training have developed since this date. Today the ETS Branch is concerned, not only with in-service education, but with the important duty of preparing soldiers for civilian life through vocational training during their final months of service at the Army's Resettlement Centres.

(7) Changes in the structure of the Army and the increased threat of terrorist activities led to the formation of the Military Provost Guard Service in 1997.

It comprises a body of armed, trained and experienced soldiers responsible for the security of military sites.

It is part of the AGC and is under the command of the Provost-Marshal (Army).

LEGAL SERVICES

A large increase after World War I in the need for legal advice, principally on Courts-Martial procedure, led to the formation of a Military Department in the Office of the Judge Advocate General (JAG). Previously this had been provided by Deputy JAGs appointed to major headquarters.

After World War II a Directorate of Army Legal Services was formed and the Department was much involved in the trials of Nazi war criminals. Though its principal role remains that of supervising and providing advice on the administration of Military Law, the AGC (ALS) today extends its services to all levels of the Army where guidance on legal matters of any type is required.

The cap badges of the RMP, the MPSC, the RAEC and the ALC have been retained by their respective branches within the Adjutant General's Corps.

1511
First recorded Provost Marshal (1)

1810
Staff Corps of Cavalry

1814
DISBANDED

1815
Staff Corps of Cavalry (2)

1817
DISBANDED

1854
Mounted Staff Corps (3)

1855
Mounted Military Police (4)

1877
Corps of Military Mounted Police

1882
Corps of Military Foot Police (5)

1926
Corps of Military Police

1946
CORPS OF ROYAL MILITARY POLICE

1992
Became part of AGC (PRO)

1901
Military Prison Staff Corps (6)

1906
MILITARY PROVOST STAFF CORPS

1992
MPSC became part of AGC (PRO)

1997
MILITARY PROVOST GUARD SERVICE (7)
formed as part of AGC (PRO)

1846
Corps of Army Schoolmasters

1920
Army Educational Corps

1946
ROYAL ARMY EDUCATIONAL CORPS

1992
Became part of AGC (ETS)

1923
Military Department Office of the Judge Advocate General

1948
Directorate of Army Legal Services formed

1978
ARMY LEGAL CORPS

1992
Became part of AGC (ALS)

PROVOST BRANCH (PRO)

BRANCH HEADQUARTERS

Trenchard Lines, Upavon, Pewsey, Wilts. SN9 6BE
Tel: Civ. 01980 615656 Mil. Ext. 5656
Website: www.army.mod.uk/agc/provost_branch

ANTECEDENT CORPS MARCHES

Quick Marches: The Watchtower (RMP)
The New Colonial (MPS)
Steadfast and True (MPGS)

ALLIANCES

Canadian Armed Forces:
Canadian Forces Security Branch

Australian Military Forces:
The Royal Australian Corps of Military Police

New Zealand Army:
Royal New Zealand Military Police

Pakistan Army:
Corps of Military Police (Pakistan)

Sri Lanka Army:
The Sri Lanka Corps of Military Police

Malaysian Armed Forces:
Malaysian Military Police

EDUCATIONAL AND TRAINING SERVICES BRANCH (ETS)

BRANCH HEADQUARTERS

Trenchard Lines, Upavon, Pewsey, Wilts. SN9 6BE
Tel: Civ. 01980 615703 Mil. Ext. 8703
Website: www.army.mod.uk/agc/dets_a

ANTECEDENT CORPS MARCH

Quick Marches: Guadeamus Igitur
The Good Comrade

ALLIANCES

Australian Military Forces:
The Royal Australian Army Educational Corps

New Zealand Army:
The Royal New Zealand Army Education Corps

The first structured intelligence units within the British Army were introduced during the Civil War when both sides employed "Scoutmasters" described as "The Chief Reconnoitres of the Army". Later, in the Napoleonic Wars, the Duke of Wellington instituted Codebreakers and "Exploring Officers" who, in full uniform, so they would not be taken for spies, moved in amongst and behind the enemy's lines to draw maps, sketch defensive positions and gather the intelligence so necessary for informed command. One of the most famous of these was Colonel Colquhoun Grant who became Wellington's Commander of Intelligence at Waterloo.

As with so many of the important support services for the Army, the years of peace and stability which followed the defeat of Bonaparte saw intelligence matters ignored and undeveloped. The Crimean War highlighted the serious lack of sound intelligence, the urgent need for effective maps and a formal intelligence staff structure but it was not until the Boer War of 1900 that a Directorate of Military Intelligence (South Africa) was created — the first official intelligence formation. This was headed by Colonel

From earliest times, British commanders in the field have recognised the importance of good intelligence and have employed persons to gather information on locations and movement of enemy forces. The great Duke of Marlborough himself once said: "No war can be conducted successfully without early and good intelligence".

David Henderson who defined the first principles of intelligence and during World War I was appointed as Commandant of the Military Wing, Royal Flying Corps, where he oversaw the development of the new techniques of aerial photography.

During the uneasy years which preceded World War I, when espionage was rife and international suspicions ran high, the two famous security sections of the War Office were formed — MI5 for counter-intelligence and MI6 concerned with the gathering of overseas intelligence, the former under the command of Captain Vernon Kell and the latter of Commander Mansfield Cumming, the original 'C'.

On the outbreak of war in 1914, telegrams were sent to some 50 previously-identified individuals, mainly serving army and Metropolitan Police officers, inviting them to join a newly-formed Intelligence Corps. One of the early commanders of this unit was Captain Archibald Wavell, later Field-

Marshal Lord Wavell. Often mounted on motorcycles, intelligence officers performed sterling service on the Western Front, in the spirit of Wellington's Exploring Officers, obtaining much invaluable intelligence. The Corps had no formal badges, though members wore a distinguishing "green insignia", and was eventually disbanded in 1929.

The military collapse resulting in the evacuation from Dunkirk saw the formation of the present "badged" Corps in July 1940. During World War II the Corps grew to a strength of 14,000 officers and men who handled every aspect of security and operational intelligence including codebreaking, SOE operations, air photography, censorship, interrogation, security control of our ports and the ultimate arrest of war criminals.

The post-war demands of the Cold War and the spread of international terrorism resulted in the formation in 1957 of an all-Regular Intelligence Corps. Over the last 60 years, some 40 worldwide military situations, ranging from Korea to Northern Ireland, Malaya to Yugoslavia, Aden to Cyprus and Afghanistan, coupled with ever-advancing technology, have placed heavy demands upon this small but expanding Corps.

1900
Directorate of
Military Intelligence (South Africa) (1)

1909
MI5 Counter Intelligence Section formed

1912
MI6 Special Intelligence Section formed (2)

1914
Intelligence Corps (3)

1929
DISBANDED

1940
Intelligence Corps reformed (4)

1957
Taken on to Regular
Establishment

**INTELLIGENCE
CORPS**

NOTES

(1) Field Intelligence Officers were appointed to combat units and Staff Intelligence Officers to formation HQs to analyse and evaluate the intelligence gathered in the field.

(2) For overseas intelligence gathering.

(3) Under the command of Major T.G.J. Torrie, 17th Light Cavalry, Indian Army, the infant Corps comprised an HQ and Mounted, Dismounted, Motorcycle and Security Duties Sections.

(4) A body of experienced intelligence personnel had been mustered in 1939 though the official formation of the Corps was not until the following year.

CORPS HEADQUARTERS

Chicksands, Shefford, Bedfordshire SG17 5PR

Tel: 01462 752340/01 Fax: 01462 752374

email: dinticacorpssec-el@disc.mod.uk

Website: www.army.mod.uk/intelligencecorps/

REGIMENTAL MARCHES
Quick March: The Rose and the Laurel
Slow March: Trumpet Tune (and Ayre)

ALLIANCES
Canadian Armed Forces:
   The Intelligence Branch Canadian Armed Forces

Australian Military Forces:
   The Australian Intelligence Corps

BONDS OF FRIENDSHIP
   Malaysian Intelligence Corps
   United States Army Military Intelligence Corps
   HMS Talent

COLONEL-IN-CHIEF
   Field Marshal HRH The Prince Philip,
   Duke of Edinburgh KG, KT, OM, GBE, AC, QSO

CORPS MUSEUM

THE MILITARY INTELLIGENCE MUSEUM
Headquarters Directorate Intelligence Corps,
Building 200, Chicksands, Shefford, Beds. SG17 5PR
Tel: 01462 752342 Fax: 01462 752374
email: dint@armymail.co.uk

1796
Army Chaplains' Department (Anglican)
1836
Roman Catholic Officiating Chaplains recognised (1)
1881
Wesleyan Officiating Chaplains recognised (2)
1892
First Jewish Chaplain admitted

NOTES

(1) Although recognised in 1836, the first RC Chaplains were not commissioned into the Department until 1859.

(2) Recognised but did not receive fully-commissioned status until 1914.

(3) They are not commissioned or uniformed but are managed by the RAChD.

1919
ROYAL ARMY CHAPLAINS' DEPARTMENT
2002
First Regular Female Chaplain appointed.
2004
Civilian Chaplains to the Military (3) appointed by MOD for the Buddhist, Hindu, Muslim and Sikh faiths.

DEPARTMENT HEADQUARTERS

MOD Chaplains (Army), Trenchard Lines, Upavon, Pewsey, Wiltshire SN9 6BE
Tel: 01980 615804
email: armychaplains@armymail.mod.uk
Website: www.army.mod.uk/chaplains/

NOTE: MOD Chaplains (Army) will relocate to Andover as part of the move of HQUKLF (possibly Spring 2010)

REGIMENTAL MARCH
　　Trumpet Voluntary

ALLIANCES

Canadian Armed Forces:
　　Chaplains' Branch

Australian Military Forces:
　　The Royal Australian Army Chaplains' Department

New Zealand Army:
　　Royal New Zealand Chaplains' Department

PATRON
　　HM The Queen

Royal Army Chaplains' Department

The Royal Army Chaplains' Department is the only remaining example of an old officer-only "Department" as opposed to a "Corps". Army Chaplains have accompanied British soldiers to war and provided spiritual leadership, moral guidance and pastoral support in every campaign over the past two centuries.

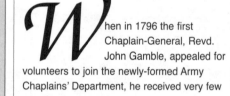

When in 1796 the first Chaplain-General, Revd. John Gamble, appealed for volunteers to join the newly-formed Army Chaplains' Department, he received very few applicants and on the outbreak of the Crimean War in 1854, there was only one deployable Chaplain, Revd. Henry Press Wright, for some 26,000 troops! The reports of William Russell in *"The Times"* eventually prompted the Society for the Propagation of the Gospel to provide funds for further Chaplains and by the end of the War 60 had deployed of which 12 had lost their lives.

Chaplains of the Department have brought comfort to British soldiers in circumstances of extreme discomfort and danger and there have been many examples of astonishing acts of bravery and selflessness by Army Padres in the worst and most dangerous possible situations. In 1879 during the Second Afghan War, Revd. James Adams, an Irishman serving as Chaplain to the Kabul Field Force, rushed to extricate troopers of the 9th Lancers trapped beneath their dead horses in a flooded nullah under heavy enemy fire. He received the first Victoria Cross to be awarded to a Chaplain.

Three more were to follow during World War I, among many other awards for gallantry: Revd. Theodore Hardy, VC, DSO, MC; Revd. Edward Mellish, VC, MC and Revd. William Addison. During the First World War 179 Army Padres were killed and many iconic characters emerged whose names would become part of the folk history of that awful conflict — "Woodbine Willie", Revd. Geoffrey Kennedy, who won an MC at Messines Ridge; and "Tubby Clayton", Revd. Philip Clayton, who founded TocH from Talbot House (TocH in signals terminology) the rest house for soldiers which he established behind the lines at Poperinge in Belgium.

In 1919 the exemplary service performed by Army Padres was recognised by the addition "Royal" to the Department's title.

During World War II Army Chaplains further enhanced their reputation for fortitude and devotion with countless memorable instances of dedicated service. British prisoners-of-war suffering the appalling conditions of the notorious Burma-Siam Railway Camps testified to the comfort and encouragement they received from Padres such as "Happy Harry" Thorpe and Revd. H. L. O. Davies. Another legendary figure was Revd. Fraser Macluskey, "The Parachute Padre" who, as Chaplain to 1 SAS, jumped behind enemy lines where he ministered to his flock during three months of dangerous covert operations. Later in his career he became Moderator of the General Assembly of the Church of Scotland. During World War II 134 British and Commonwealth Padres lost their lives.

Since 1945 Chaplains have continued to serve wherever the Army has been deployed: Korea, Suez, Aden, Northern Ireland, the Falklands, the Balkans, Iraq and Afghanistan. Wherever the British Army may serve in the future, in war or peace, the Padres will be there to provide spiritual leadership, moral guidance and pastoral support to soldiers and their families, irrespective of denomination, faith or lack of it.

DEPARTMENT MUSEUM

MUSEUM OF ARMY CHAPLAINCY
Forces Chaplaincy Centre, Amport House, Andover, Hants. SP11 8BG
Tel: 01264 773144 Fax: 01264 771042
email: rachdcurator@tiscali.co.uk
Website: www.army.mod.uk/chaplains/museum/

Small Arms School Corps

When, in the mid-19th century, the French Minié Rifle began to offer a more accurate alternative to the long-established "Brown Bess", it was clear that a change in infantry tactics, and a new standard of marksmanship would be necessary.

| 1853 |
| The School of Musketry (1) |
| **1919** |
| Small Arms School |

NOTES

(1) Founded with a grant of £1,000 to form an "Establishment for the Instruction of the Army in Rifle and Target Practice".

In 1926 the Small Arms School absorbed the Machine Gun School which had been formed at the start of World War I. The Vickers machine gun was then incorporated into its cap badge.

| 1929 |
| **SMALL ARMS SCHOOL CORPS** |

CORPS HEADQUARTERS

Land Warfare Centre, Warminster, Wilts. BA12 0DJ.
Tel: Civ. 01985 222612 Warminster Mil. 2612
Fax: 01985 222211
email: ci@sasc.info
Website: www.army.mod.uk/sasc/

REGIMENTAL MARCH

March of the Bowmen

COLONEL-IN-CHIEF

HRH The Duke of York KCVO, ADC

The smooth-bored, muzzle-loading "Brown Bess" musket was the standard issue to the British infantry from the early-18th to the mid-19th centuries. Its range was short and it relied for its effectiveness on being fired in massed volleys by carefully-drilled, tightly-disciplined ranks of soldiers.

When in 1851 the rifled Minié began to replace it, the greatly improved range and accuracy of the new weapon demanded new standards of marksmanship. Lord Hardinge, Master General of Ordnance at the time, therefore ordered the establishment of a School of Musketry at Hythe in Kent to develop training practices in the Army.

Acquiring Corps status in 1929, the Small Arms School Corps continues with the training of instructors in all aspects of small arms discipline and weapon handling, and the testing and appraisal of new weapons.

CORPS MUSEUM

INFANTRY AND SMALL ARMS SCHOOL CORPS WEAPONS COLLECTION
HQ SASC, Land Warfare Centre, Imber Road, Warminster, Wilts. BA12 0DJ
Tel: 01985 222487 Fax: 01985 222211
email: regsecsasc@aol.com

Army Physical Training Corps

One of several fundamental weaknesses in the British Army exposed during the Crimean War was the seriously unfit physical condition of many Britsh soldiers. This was addressed in 1860 with the formation of the Army Gymnastic Staff.

| 1860 |
| Army Gymnastic Staff |
| **1918** |
| Army Physical Training Staff |

NOTES

The first army gymnasium was opened in Wellington Lines, Aldershot, in 1866.

| 1940 |
| **ARMY PHYSICAL TRAINING CORPS** |

CORPS HEADQUARTERS

HQ APTC, Fox Lines, Queen's Avenue, Aldershot, Hants. GU11 2LB
Tel: 01252 347168
email: aspt-regsec@aspt.mod.uk
Website: www.army.mod.uk/aptc

REGIMENTAL MARCH

Be Fit — (Words from *"Land and Sea Tales"* by Rudyard Kipling) Regimental March of the Army Physical Training Corps.

In 1860, Major Frederick Hammersley took 12 sergeants from different regiments to Oxford University to undergo the first 6-month Army Physical Training Instruction Course under Mr. Archibald McLaren. They became known as the "Twelve Apostles" and were the start of a formal physical training organisation in the Army. Known originally as the Army Gymnastic Staff, it became the Army Physical Training Staff in 1918 and in 1940 was granted Corps status.

Soldiers wishing a career in the APTC must first attend a 9-week course to qualify as Regimental PTIs then, after a further period of experience with their own unit, may apply for selection for the APTC. If selected, they must then undertake a 30-week intensive course before qualifying as APTCIs,

Today, the Corps is responsible for the supervision of all fitness training and sporting activities in the Army. Its members have included many international class athletes and sportsmen including Warrant Officer 2 Kris Akabussi. Dame Kelly Holmes also was a sergeant PTI in the Army.

CORPS MUSEUM

ARMY PHYSICAL TRAINING CORPS MUSEUM
Army School of Physical Training, Fox Lines, Queen's Avenue, Aldershot, Hants. GU11 2LB
Tel: 01252 347168
email: aspt-regsec@aspt.mod.uk
Website: www.army.mod.uk/aptc

Music has always played an important role in the British Army. From earliest times orders have been promulgated on the battlefield by drums, bugles and trumpets and drumbeat has acted as the metronome for marching and other military drills. Since its beginnings, military music has stirred the souls of fighting men and enhanced their pride in themselves and their regiments.

Until recently almost every battalion had its own Band which moved with it wherever in the world it might be posted. The number of Bands was therefore proportional to the number of active battalions and at one point during World War I there were nearly 200 Regimental Bands in commission. Bands were considered so important to morale that, in the 19th century, they were often financed by the officers of the regiment where no public funding was available.

The longest-established Band is that of the Grenadier Guards which has claim to origins in 1685; the Bands of the Royal Artillery and the Coldstream and Scots Guards all date from the 18th century.

The Corps of Army Music was formed in 1994 at which time there were 58

Corps of Army Music

**1994
CORPS OF ARMY
MUSIC**

CORPS HEADQUARTERS
Kneller Hall, Twickenham, Middlesex TW2 7DU
Tel: 020 8744 8652 Fax: 020 8744 8668
Website: www.army.mod.uk/music

REGIMENTAL MARCH
Quick March:　　The Minstrel Boy

ALLIANCE
Australian Military Forces:
The Australian Army Band Corps

Regimental and Corps Bands in commission which, under the requirements of the "Options for Change" Defence Cuts, had to be reduced to 32. The formation of the Corps provided a central authority for Army musicians which would take over responsibility for their recruitment, training and career planning and for the manning and deployment of all Army Bands.

With a strength of around 1,100, the Corps is the largest employer of musicians in Britain and is one of the largest musical organisations in the world. The professionalism and versatility of Army musicians is well known in the civilian musical world and this standard of excellence is maintained at Kneller

Hall, the Headquarters and Training Establishment of the Corps at Twickenham, with basic and advanced training courses conducted up to and beyond nationally-recognised levels by some of the most distinguished musical tutors in the country.

The rousing marches played by the immaculately turned-out soldiers of the Corps are not the only type of music in their repertoires: today's Army musicians are proficient in more than one instrument and can turn their hands to a wide variety of disciplines. Every Band has the ability to field classical and jazz ensembles as well as rock, pop and folk groups which are always much in demand within both the Army and the

civilian communities in which the Bands are stationed.

In 2006/07, as part of the changes called for in the "Future Army Structure", the Regimental and Corps Bands were further reduced from 32 to the 24 which today form the Corps of Army Music and which are shown, together with their origins, on the following pages.

In addition to their Regimental Bands, the Scottish and Irish Regiments, and elements of other regiments and corps with Celtic traditions, maintain their individual Pipes & Drums; these are shown on page 157. In 1999 all Pipe & Drum schools within the Army merged to form "The Army School of Bagpipe Music & Highland Drumming" which is located at Redford Barracks, Edinburgh and is affiliated to the Corps of Army Music.

Though greatly reduced in numbers from past years, today's Army musicians continue to bolster morale and self-pride within the units they support and to maintain the standards of musical excellence for which they have always been renowned.

CORPS MUSEUM

ROYAL MILITARY SCHOOL OF MUSIC MUSEUM
Kneller Hall, Twickenham, Middlesex TW2 7DU
Tel: 020 8898 5533 Ext: 8652 Fax: 020 8744 8652
email: corpssec@hq.dcamus.mod.uk
(Entry by appointment only)

HOUSEHOLD CAVALRY		ROYAL ARTILLERY	ROYAL ENGINEERS	ROYAL SIGNALS	FOOT GUARDS				
Established 1805	Established 1762	Established 1763	Established 1856	Established 1921	Established 1685	Established 1785	Established 1716	Established 1900	Established 1915
THE BAND OF THE LIFE GUARDS	THE BAND OF THE BLUES AND ROYALS	THE BAND OF THE ROYAL REGIMENT OF ARTILLERY	THE BAND OF THE CORPS OF ROYAL ENGINEERS	THE BAND OF THE ROYAL CORPS OF SIGNALS	THE BAND OF THE GRENADIER GUARDS	THE BAND OF THE COLDSTREAM GUARDS	THE BAND OF THE SCOTS GUARDS	THE BAND OF THE IRISH GUARDS	THE BAND OF THE WELSH GUARDS

| The Band of 1st The Queen's Dragoon Guards | The Band of The Royal Scots Dragoon Guards | The Band of The Royal Dragoon Guards | The Cambrai Band of the Royal Tank Regiment | The Alamein Band of the Royal Tank Regiment | The Rhine Band of the Royal Tank Regiment | The Band of The Queen's Royal Hussars | The Band of The King's Royal Hussars | The Band of The Light Dragoons | The Band of The 9th/12th Royal Lancers | The Band of The Queen's Royal Lancers |

1994
The Band of The Dragoon Guards

1947
The Cambrai Band Royal Tank Regiment

The Hussars and Light Dragoons Band

The Royal Lancers Band

2006
THE HEAVY CAVALRY AND CAMBRAI BAND

ROYAL ARMOURED CORPS

2006
THE LIGHT CAVALRY BAND

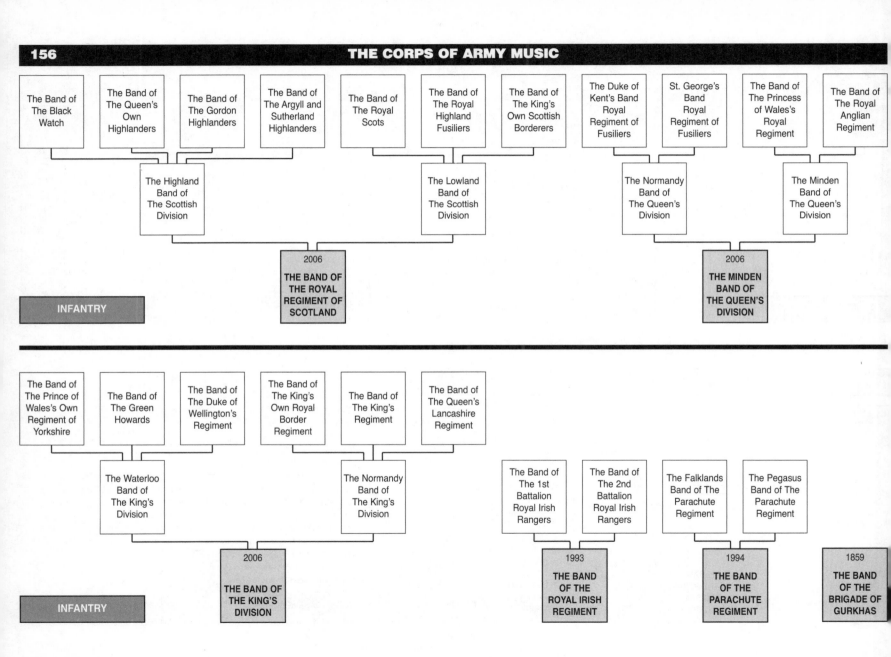

The Band of The Devonshire and Dorset Regiment

The Band of The Cheshire Regiment

The Band of The Royal Welch Fusiliers

The Band of The Royal Regiment of Wales

The Band of The Royal Gloucestershire Berkshire and Wiltshire Regiment

The Band of The Worcestershire and Sherwood Foresters Regiment

The Band of The Staffordshire Regiment

The Corunna Band of The Light Infantry

The Salamanca Band of The Light Infantry

The Normandy Band of The Royal Green Jackets

The Peninsula Band of The Royal Green Jackets

The Lucknow Band of The Prince of Wales's Division

The Clive Band of The Prince of Wales's Division

The Band of The Light Division

INFANTRY

2006

THE BAND OF THE PRINCE OF WALES'S DIVISION

2007

THE BAND AND BUGLES OF THE RIFLES

AAC

RLC

REME

AGC

PIPES & DRUMS

In addition to the Bands comprising the Corps of Army Music, the following Regular Army units maintain their individual Pipe & Drum Bands:

Established 1993

The Band of The Royal Corps of Transport

The Band of The Royal Army Ordnance Corps

Established 1947

The Band of the Women's Royal Army Corps

Royal Scots Dragoon Guards
1st Royal Tank Regiment
1st Battalion Scots Guards
1st Battalion Irish Guards
Royal Scots Borderers, 1st Battalion Royal Regiment of Scotland
Royal Highland Fusiliers, 2nd Battalion Royal Regiment of Scotland
Black Watch, 3rd Battalion Royal Regiment of Scotland
Highlanders, 4th Battalion Royal Regiment of Scotland
Argyll and Sutherland Highlanders, 5th Battalion Royal Regiment of Scotland
1st Battalion Royal Irish Regiment
1st Battalion Royal Gurkha Rifles
2nd Battalion Royal Gurkha Rifles
19th Regiment Royal Artillery
40th Regiment Royal Artillery
Royal Corps of Signals

1994

THE BAND OF THE ROYAL LOGISTIC CORPS

THE BAND OF THE CORPS OF ROYAL ELECTRICAL AND MECHANICAL ENGINEERS

1992

THE BAND OF THE ADJUTANT GENERAL'S CORPS

THE BAND OF THE ARMY AIR CORPS

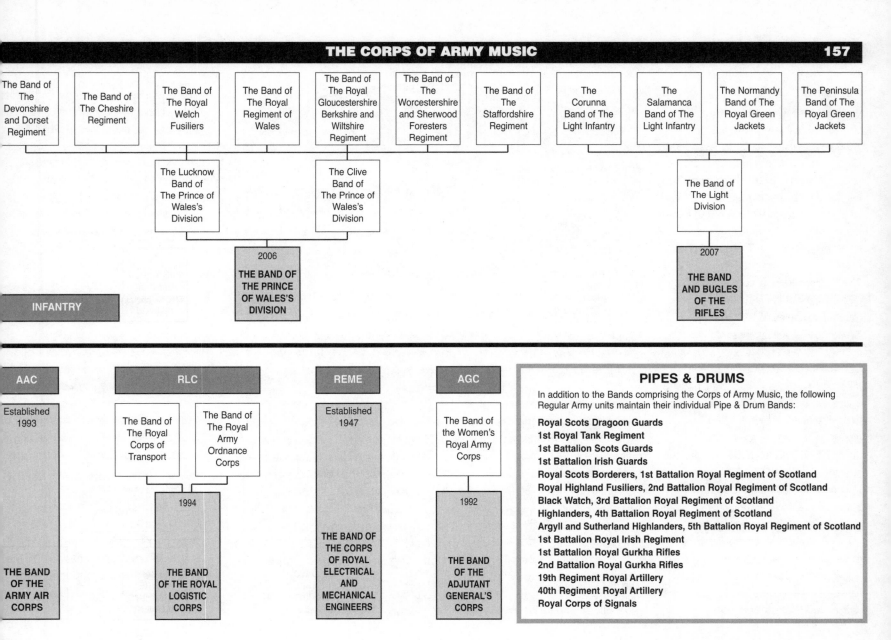

The Disbanded Regiments

There were two regiments in the British Army which in the defence cuts of the late 1960s chose, actively, to disband rather than lose their identity by amalgamation. The names of both regiments lived on for a time in their TA battalions but, with the further cuts in the 1990s, they were finally expunged from The Army List.

The Cameronians (Scottish Rifles)

The origins of the regiment lie in the religious struggles of 17th century Scotland. In the south-west of the country, the secret church services of the Covenanters — a group dedicated to maintenance of the reformed church and opposition to Roman catholicism — had to be guarded from government disruption by armed pickets who eventually formed the nucleus of the new regiment raised in 1689. The name of the Regiment derives from Richard Cameron a famous presbyterian preacher who was a leader of the Covenant movement.

The Regiment served the Crown with distinction until 1968 when it chose disbandment rather than amalgamation. Its recruiting area was taken over by The King's Own Scottish Borderers.

The majority of regiments which have ceased to exist as separate entities have been absorbed into new, amalgamated regiments which preserve the honours of their former constituents and carry forward their traditions. The six regiments in this section, however, have gone for ever but the contribution they made to the progress of the free world should not be forgotten and is recorded here.

The York and Lancaster Regiment

The name of this regiment is confusing deriving, as it does, from its original recruiting areas in the two Duchies of York and Lancaster in South Yorkshire. It was thus a wholly-Yorkshire regiment which recruited in Sheffield, Barnsley and Rotherham.

The Regiment established a fine reputation during its two centuries of service. On 1st July 1916, the first day of the Battle of the Somme, the Regiment fielded 8 battalions including several of the famous "Pals" battalions where young men from the same town, area or even employment, had enlisted together and were to train, fight and, all too often, to die together. During World War 1 the Regiment suffered 48,650 casualties out of 57,000 serving.

Choosing disbandment in 1968, the name of the Regiment lived on in its TA battalions until 1999 when it was finally expunged from the strength.

The Southern Irish Infantry Regiments

In 1922, following the establishment of the Irish Free State, the five Southern Irish infantry regiments were disbanded and their Colours laid up in Windsor Castle. Of these, the Royal Irish Regiment was the only one with a long-established tradition as an Irish formation and this Regiment, in name at least, is now back on the British Army establishment. The origins and Battle Honours of the old Regiment are therefore shown with those of the new Royal Irish Regiment on pages 110/111.

The other four, fine and ancient regiments as they were, had their origins mainly in the pre-Mutiny regiments of the East India Company and were only given Irish identities in the Cardwell Reforms of 1881 when their Irishness was augmented by the merging of the long-established militia units, previously only deployed within Ireland. It must however be remembered that there was a massive number of Irishmen in other British regiments; around one third of Wellington's soldiers were Irish and, despite independence, many thousands of Southern Irish chose to enlist in the British Army before and during the Second World War.

1689
The Earl of Angus's Regiment (1)

26th

1751
26th Foot
(The Cameronians)

1786
26th Cameronian Regiment

90th

1794
The 90th Perthshire Volunteers (2)

1815
90th Perthshire Light Infantry

1881 (May)
The Scotch Rifles
(Cameronians)

1881 (July)
THE CAMERONIANS
(Scottish Rifles)

⚔

DISBANDED 1968

BATTLE HONOURS

Pre-1914:

Blenheim [1704]; **Ramillies** [1706]; **Oudenarde** [1708]; **Malplaquet** [1709]; **Egypt** [1801]; **Mandora** [1801]; **Corunna** [1809]; **Martinique, 1809; Guadaloupe, 1810; China** [1840-42]; **South Africa, 1846-47; Lucknow** [1857-58]; **Abyssinia** [1867-68]; **South Africa, 1877-79, 1899-1902; Relief of Ladysmith** [1900].

First World War:

Mons; Le Cateau; Retreat from Mons; **Marne 1914, 18;** Aisne 1914; La Bassée 1914; Messines 1914; Armentières 1914; **Neuve Chapelle;** Aubers; **Loos; Somme 1916, 18;** Albert 1916; Bazentin. Pozières; Flers-Courcelette; Le Transloy; Ancre Heights; Arras 1917, 18; Scarpe 1917, 18; Arleux; **Ypres 1917, 18;** Pilckem; Langemarck 1917; Menin Road; Polygon Wood; Passchendaele; St. Quentin; Rosières; Avre; **Lys;** Hazebrouck; Bailleul; Kemmel; Scherpenberg; Soissonnais-Ourcq; Drocourt-Quéant; **Hindenburg Line;** Epéhy; Canal du Nord; St. Quentin Canal; Cambrai 1918; Courtrai; Selle; Sambre; France and Flanders 1914-18; Doiran 1917, 18; **Macedonia 1915-18; Gallipoli 1915;** Rumani; Egypt 1916-17; Gaza; El Mughar; Nebi Samwil; Jaffa; **Palestine 1917-18.**

Second World War:

Ypres-Comines Canal; **Odon;** Cheux; Caen; Mont Pincon; Estry; Nederrijn; Best; **Scheldt;** South Beveland; Walcheron Causeway; Asten; Roer; **Rhineland;** Reichswald; Moyland; Dreirwalde; Bremen; Artenburg; **North-West Europe 1940, 44-45;** Landing in Sicily; Simeto Bridgehead; **Sicily 1943;** Garigliano Crossing; **Anzio;** Advance to Tiber; **Italy 1943-44;** Pegu 1942; Paungde; Yenangyaung 1942; **Chindits 1944; Burma 1942, 44.**

NOTES

(1) Raised in Glasgow by the 19 year-old Earl of Angus to oppose Viscount Dundee's Jacobite rising.

(2) Raised by Colonel Thomas Graham of Balgowan, later General Lord Lynedoch, on his lands in Perthshire and originally known as "Balgowan's Grey Breeks".

REGIMENTAL MUSEUM

THE CAMERONIANS (SCOTTISH RIFLES) MUSEUM COLLECTION
Low Parks Museum, 129 Muir Street, Hamilton, South Lanarkshire ML3 6BJ
Tel: 01698 328232 Fax: 01698 328412
email: lowparksmuseum@southlanarkshire.gov.uk
Website: www.southlanarkshire.gov.uk

1756
2nd Battalion
12th Foot

65th

1758
65th Foot

1782
65th (2nd Yorkshire, North Riding) Foot (1)

84th

1793
84th Foot

1809
84th (York & Lancaster) Foot

1881
THE YORK AND LANCASTER REGIMENT

⚔

DISBANDED 1968

BATTLE HONOURS

Pre-1914:

Guadaloupe, 1759; Martinique, 1794; Peninsula [1808-14]; **Arabia** [1809]; **Lucknow** [1857-58]; **Egypt, 1882-84; Tel-el-Kebir** [1882]; **South Africa, 1899-1902.**

First World War:

Aisne 1914; Armentières 1914; **Ypres 1915, 17, 18;** Gravenstafel; St. Julien; Frezenberg; Bellewaarde; Hooge 1915; Loos; **Somme 1916, 18;** Albert 1916; Pozières; Flers-Courcelette; Morval; Thiepval; Le Transloy; Ancre Heights; Ancre 1916; Arras 1917,18; Scarpe 1917, 18; Arleux; Oppy; **Messines 1917, 18;** Langemarck 1917; Menin Road; Polygon Wood; Broodseinde; Poelcapelle; **Passchendaele; Cambrai 1917, 18;** St. Quentin; Bapaume 1918; **Lys;** Hazebrouck; Bailleul; Kemmel; Scherpenberg; Marne 1918; Tardenois; Drocourt-Quéant; Hindenburg Line; Havrincourt; Epéhy; Canal du Nord; **Selle;** Valenciennes; Sambre; France and Flanders 1914-18; **Piave;** Vittorio Veneto; Italy 1917-18; Struma; Doiran 1917; **Macedonia 1915-18;** Suvla; Landing at Suvla; Scimitar Hill; **Gallipoli 1915;** Egypt 1916.

Second World War:

Norway 1940; Odon; **Fontenay le Pesnil;** Caen; La Vie Crossing; La Touques Crossing; Forêt de Bretonne; Le Havre; **Antwerp-Turnhout Canal;** Scheldt; Lower Maas; Arnhem 1945; North-West Europe 1940, 44-45; **Tobruk 1941;** Tobruk Sortie 1941; **Mine de Sedjenane;** Djebel Kournine; North Africa 1941, 43; Landing in Sicily; Simeto Bridgehead; Pursuit to Messina; **Sicily 1943; Salerno;** Vietri Pass; Capture of Naples; Cava di Terreni; Volturno Crossing; Monte Camino; Calabritto; Colle Cedro; Garigliano Crossing; **Minturno;** Monte Tuga; Anzio; Advance to Tiber; Gothic Line; Coriano; San Clemente; Gemmano Ridge; Carpineta; Lamone Crossing; Defence of Lamone Bridgehead; Rimini Line; San Marino; Italy 1943-45; **Crete;** Heraklion; Middle East 1941; **North Arakan;** Maungdaw; Rangoon Road; Toungoo; Arakan Beaches; **Chindits 1944;** Burma 1943-45.

NOTES

(1) The regiment served in New Zealand from 1846 to 1865 and is still commemorated there by a uniformed re-enactment group. Its nickname, "The Hickety Pips", comes from the Maori pronunciation of 65th.

REGIMENTAL MUSEUM

YORK AND LANCASTER REGIMENT MUSEUM
Central Library and Arts Centre, Walker Place, Rotherham, South Yorks. S65 1JH
Tel: 01709 336624 Fax: 01709 336628
email: karl.noble@rotherham.gov.uk
Website: www.rotherham.gov.uk

88th

1760
88th (Royal Highland
Volunteers) Foot

1763
DISBANDED

1779
88th Foot

1783
DISBANDED

1793
88th (Connaught
Rangers) Foot (1)

94th

1760
94th (Royal Welsh
Volunteers) Foot

1763
DISBANDED

1779
94th Foot

1783
DISBANDED

1794
94th (Irish) Foot

1795
DISBANDED

1803
94th (Scots Brigade)
Foot (2)

1818
DISBANDED

1823
94th Foot (3)

1881

THE CONNAUGHT RANGERS

88th and 94th

✕

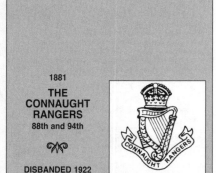

DISBANDED 1922

BATTLE HONOURS

Pre-1914:

Seringapatam [1799]; **Egypt** [1801];
Peninsula [1808-14]; **Talavera** [1809]; **Busaco** [1810];
Fuentes d'Onor [1811]; **Badajos** [1812];
Ciudad Rodrigo [1812]; **Salamanca** [1812];
Nivelle [1813]; **Pyrenees** [1813]; **Vittoria** [1813];
Orthes [1814]; **Toulouse** [1814]; **Alma** [1854];
Inkerman [1854]; **Sevastapol** [1854-55];
Central India [1857-58]; **South Africa, 1877-79,
South Africa, 1899-1902; Relief of Ladysmith, 1900.**

First World War:

Mons; Retreat from Mons; Marne 1914; **Aisne 1914**;
Messines 1914, 17; Armentières 1914;
Ypres 1914, 15, 17; Langemarck 1914, 17; Gheluvelt;
Nonne Bisschen; Festubert 1914; Givenchy 1914;
Neuve Chapelle; St. Julien; Aubers; Somme 1916, 18;
Guillemont; Ginchy; St. Quentin; Bapaume 1918;
Rosières; Hindenburg Line; **Cambrai 1918**; Selle;
France and Flanders 1914-18; **Kosturino**; Struma;
Macedonia 1915-17; Suvla; Sari Bair; **Scimitar Hill**;
Gallipoli 1915; Gaza; Jerusalem; Tell'Asur; **Megiddo**;
Sharon; Palestine 1917-18; Tigris 1916;
Kut al Amara 1917; Baghdad; Mesopotamia 1916-18.

NOTES

(1) Raised in Connaught by Colonel Hon. Thomas
de Burgh, later Earl of Clanricarde.

(2) Prior to 1803 the regiment was part of the Scots
Brigade in Dutch service.

(3) Raised in Glasgow by Sir Thomas Bradford.

100th

1761
100th (Highland)
Regiment

1763
DISBANDED

1780
100th (Royal
Lincolnshire) Foot (1)

1785
DISBANDED

1805
100th (Prince Regent's (2)
County of Dublin) Foot

1818
DISBANDED (3)

1858
100th (Prince of
Wales's (4)
Royal Canadian) Foot (5)

109th

1761
109th Foot (6)

1763
DISBANDED

1794
100th (Aberdeenshire)
Foot (7)

1795
DISBANDED (8)

1854
3rd (Bombay European)
Regiment HEIC (9)

1861
109th (Bombay Infantry)
Regiment

1881 (May)
The Prince of Wales's (4)
Royal Canadian
Regiment

1881 (July)

THE PRINCE OF WALES'S LEINSTER REGIMENT (ROYAL CANADIANS)

100th and 109th

✕

DISBANDED 1922

BATTLE HONOURS

Pre-1914:

Niagara [1813]; **Central India** [1857-58];
South Africa, 1900-02.

First World War:

Aisne 1914; Armentières 1914; **Ypres 1915, 17, 18**;
Gravenstafel; St. Julien; Frezenberg; **Somme 1916, 18**;
Delville Wood; **Guillemont**; Ginchy; Arras 1917;
Vimy 1917; Messines 1917; Pilckem;
Langemarck 1917; **St. Quentin**; Bapaume 1918;
Rosières; Courtrai; France and Flanders 1914-18;
Kosturino; Struma; **Macedonia 1915-17**; Suvla;
Sari Bair; **Gallipoli 1915**; Gaza; **Jerusalem**; Tell'Asur;
Megiddo; Nablus; Palestine 1917-18.

NOTES

(1) Raised in Ireland by Colonel
T. F. M. Humberstone.

(2) The future King George IV.

(3) Disbanded in Canada where most of the
members settled.

(4) The future King Edward VII.

(5) Raised in Canada from patriotic volunteers,
many from the old 100th Foot. The regiment was
given to Britain by Canada as a gift.

(6) Raised in London by Major John Nairne.

(7) Raised in Aberdeenshire by Colonel Alexander
Hay of Rannes.

(8) Regiment disbanded but its personnel were
drafted into the 53rd Foot.

(9) In 1858 the regiment was brought up to
strength by absorption of the remnants of the
British German Legion, raised for the Crimea. This
was one of the first regiments to wear khaki.

1652
The Guard of Honour
Bengal

1765
The Bengal (European)
Regiment HEIC (1)

1840
1st Bengal (European)
Regiment HEIC

1841
1st (Bengal European)
Light Infantry HEIC

1846
1st (Bengal European)
Fusiliers HEIC

1858
1st Bengal Fusiliers

101st

1862
101st (Royal Bengal
Fusiliers) Foot

1839
2nd Bengal (European)
Regiment HEIC

1850
2nd (Bengal European)
Fusiliers HEIC

1859
2nd Bengal Fusiliers

104th

1861
104th (Bengal Fusiliers)
Foot

BATTLE HONOURS

Pre-1914:

Plassey [1757]; **Condore** [1758]; **Badara** [1759]; **Masulipatam** [1759]; **Buxar** [1764]; **Rohillund, 1774, 1794**; **Guzerat** [1776-82]; **Carnatic** [1778-91]; **Sholinghur** [1781]; **Deig** [1804]; **Bhurtpore** [1826]; **Afghanistan** [1839]; **Ghuznee, 1839**; **Ferozeshah** [1845]; **Sobraon** [1846]; **Punjaub** [1848-49]; **Chillianwallah** [1849]; **Goojerat** [1849]; **Pegu** [1852-53]; **Delhi, 1857**; **Lucknow** [1857-58]; **Burmah, 1885-87**; **South Africa, 1899-1902**.

First World War:

Retreat from Mons; Marne 1914; Aisne 1914; **Ypres 1914, 17**; Langemarck 1914, 17; Gheluvelt; Nonne Bosschen; Givenchy 1914; **Aubers**; Loos; Somme 1916, 18; Albert 1916; Bazentin; Pozières; **Guillemont**; Ginchy; Flers-Courcelette; Morval; Messines 1917; Passchendaele; **St. Quentin**; Bapaume 1918; Rosières; Avre; Arras 1918; Scarpe 1918; **Drocourt-Quéant**; Hindenburg Line; Canal du Nord; St. Quentin Canal; Beaurevoir; Cambrai 1918; **Selle**; Sambre; France and Flanders 1914-18; Italy 1917-18; Kosturino; Struma; Macedonia 1915-17; Helles; **Landing at Helles**; Krithia; Suvla; **Landing at Suvla**; Scimitar Hill; Gallipoli 1915-16; Egypt 1916; Gaza; **Jerusalem**; Tell'Asur; Palestine 1917-18.

NOTES

(1) Comprising 3 battalions. The strength of the regiment fluctuated between 1 and 6 battalions during the course of its service with the HEIC.

(2) The new regiment also absorbed 3 long-established militia regiments from South Cork, Kerry and Limerick.

In World War I the regiment raised 11 battalions.

1881
THE ROYAL MUNSTER FUSILIERS (2)

DISBANDED 1922

1644
The Madras Europeans (1)

1746
The Madras (European)
Regiment HEIC

1839
1st Madras (European)
Regiment HEIC

1843
1st Madras (European)
Fusiliers HEIC

1859
1st Madras Fusiliers

102nd

1862
102nd (Royal Madras
Fusiliers) Foot

1661
The Bombay Regiment (2)

1668
The Bombay (European)
Regiment HEIC

1839
1st Bombay (European)
Regiment HEIC

1844
1st Bombay (European)
Fusiliers HEIC

1859
1st Bombay Fusiliers

103rd

1862
103rd (Royal Bombay
Fusiliers) Foot (3)

BATTLE HONOURS

Pre-1914:

Arcot [1751]; **Plassey** [1757]; **Condore** [1758]; **Wandewash** [1760]; **Pondicherry** [1761, 1778, 1793]; **Buxar** [1764]; **Amboor** [1767]; **Carnatic** [1774-91]; **Guzerat** [1776-82]; **Sholinghur** [1781]; **Mysore** [1789-91]; **Nundy Droog** [1791]; **Amboyna** [1796, 1810]; **Banda** [1796, 1810]; **Seringapatam** [1799]; **Ternate** [1801, 1810]; **Kirkee** [1817]; **Maheidpore** [1817]; **Beni Boo Alli** [1821]; **Ava** [1824-26]; **Aden** [1839]; **Punjaub** [1848-49]; **Goojerat** [1849]; **Mooltan** [1849]; **Pegu** [1852-53]; **Lucknow** [1857-58]; **South Africa, 1899-1902**; **Relief of Ladysmith** [1900].

First World War:

Le Cateau; **Retreat from Mons**; **Marne 1914**; Aisne 1914; Armentières 1914; **Ypres 1915, 17, 18**; St. Julien; Frezenberg; Bellewaarde; **Somme 1916, 18**; Albert 1916; Guillemont; Ginchy; Le Transloy; Ancre 1916; Arras 1917; Scarpe 1917; Arleaux; Messines 1917; Langemarck 1917; Polygon Wood; **Cambrai 1917, 18**; St. Quentin; Bapaume 1918; Rosières; Avre; **Hindenburg Line**; St. Quentin Canal; Beaurevoir; Courtrai; **Selle**; Sambre; France and Flanders 1914-18; Kosturino; Struma; **Macedonia 1915-17**; Helles; Landing at Helles; Krithia; Suvla; Sari Bair; Landing at Suvla; Scimitar Hill; **Gallipoli 1915-16**; Egypt 1916; Gaza; Jerusalem; Tell'Asur; **Palestine 1917-18**.

NOTES

(1) The oldest Indian regiment. Formed from 7 independent companies raised by the HEIC to protect their factories on the Coromandel Coast and on the islands of what is today Indonesia.

(2) Raised to take possession of Bombay as part of the dowry of Catherine of Braganza, Queen Consort of King Charles II.

(3) In 1871 the regiment came to England for the first time after 210 years service in India.

(4) The new regiment also absorbed long-established militia regiments from Kildare, Carlow and Dublin. In World War I it raised 11 battalions.

1881
THE ROYAL DUBLIN FUSILIERS (4)

DISBANDED 1922

	Protection of Queen Catherine of Braganza's Dowry
1662-80	Tangier 1662-80

	War of the League of Augsburg
1695	Namur 1695

	War of the Spanish Succession
1704-05	Gibraltar 1704-05
1704	Blenheim
1706	Ramillies
1708	Oudenarde
1709	Malplaquet

	War of the Austrian Succession
1743	Dettingen

	Seven Years War (Conquest of India)
1751	Arcot
1757	Plassey
1758	Condore
1759	Masulipatam
	Badara
1760	Wandewash
1761	Pondicherry

	Seven Years War (Conquest of Canada)
1758	Louisburg
1759	Guadeloupe 1759
	Quebec 1759

	Seven Years War (Europe)
1759	Minden
1760	Emsdorf
	Warburg
1762	Wilhelmsthal

	Seven Years War (Atlantic & West Indies)
1761	Belleisle
1762	Martinique 1762
	The Moro
	Havannah

	Campaign in Hindoostan against Surajah Doolah of Oude
1764	Buxar

	Pontiac's Indian Campaign
1763-64	North America 1763-64

The movements, and therefore history, of any regiment can be followed by studying its Battle Honours. The following pages show a chronological list of Battle Honours awarded to regular regiments of the British Army from 1662 to 2008. Awards which were exclusively for Commonwealth or Territorial Forces are not included.

	Hyder Ali's Campaign
1767	Amboor
1771	Tanjore

	1st Rohilla War
1774	Rohilcund 1774

	War with France & Spain
1778	St. Lucia 1778
1782	The Saints (Naval Crown)
1779-83	Defence of Gibraltar 1779-83

	Campaign in Guzerat
1778-82	Guzerat

	1st, 2nd, 3rd & 4th Mysore Wars
1781	Sholinghur
1783-84	Mangalore
1791	Nundy Droog
1747-92	Carnatic
	Mysore
1799	Seringapatam 1799

	Campaign in Pondicherry
1793	Pondicherry

	2nd Rohilla War
1794	Rohilcund 1794

	French Revolution (Europe)
1793	Lincelles
	Nieuport
1794	Villers-en-Cauchies
	Beaumont
	Willems
	Tournay
1799	Egmont-op-Zee

	French Revolution (West Indies)
1794	Martinique 1794
1796	St. Lucia 1796

	French Revolution (Sea Battles)
1794	Glorious First of June (Naval Crown)
1797	St. Vincent 1797
1801	Copenhagen (Naval Crown)

	Napoleonic War (Egypt)
1801	Mandora
	Marabout
	Egypt (Sphinx)

	Napoleonic War (West Indies & South America)
1803	St. Lucia 1803
1804	Surinam
1805	Dominica
1807	Monte Video
1809	Martinique 1809
1810	Guadaloupe 1810

	1st & 2nd Mahratta Wars
1803	Ally Ghur
	Delhi 1803
	Assaye
	Leswaree
1804	Deig

	Napoleonic War (Italy)
1806	Maida

	South Africa
1806	Cape of Good Hope 1806

	Napoleonic War (Peninsula)
1808	Rolica
	Vimiera
	Sahagun
1809	Corunna
	Douro
	Talavera
1810	Busaco
1811	Barrosa

1811 (cont.)	Fuentes d'Onor
	Albuhera
	Arroyo dos Molinos
1812	Tarifa
	Ciudad Rodrigo
	Badajoz
	Almaraz
	Salamanca
1813	Vittoria
	San Sebastian
	Pyrenees
	Nivelle
	Nive
1814	Orthez
	Toulouse
1808-14	Peninsula

	Napoleonic War (Far East)
1810	Amboyne
	Bourbon
	Banda
	Ternate
1811	Java

	American War of 1812
1812	Detroit
	Queenstown
1813	Miami
1814	Niagara
	Bladensburg

	Napoleonic War (Flanders)
1815	Waterloo

	3rd Mahratta War (Campaign against the Pindaris)
1817	Kirkee
	Nagpore
	Maheidpore

	Campaigns in India
1796-1819	India 1796-1819
1780-1823	Hindoostan

	Arabia & Persian Gulf Campaign against Arab Pirates
1819	Arabia
1821	Beni Boo Alli

	1st Burma War
1824-26	Ava

Jat War	
1825-26	Bhurtpore
6th Kaffir War	
1834-35	South Africa 1835
Aden	
1839	Aden
1st Afghan War	
1839	Ghuznee 1839
	Khelat
	Afghanistan 1839
1841-42	Jellalabad
1842	Candahar 1842
1841-42	Ghuznee 1842
1842	Cabul 1842
1st China War	
1840-42	China Coast
Conquest of Scinde	
1843	Meeanee
	Hyderabad
Gwalior Campaign	
1843	Maharajpore
	Punniar
1st Maori War	
1845-47	New Zealand
1st Sikh War	
(Sutlej Campaign)	
1845	Moodkee
	Ferozeshah
1846	Aliwal
	Sobraon
7th Kaffir War	
1846-47	South Africa 1846-7
2nd Sikh War	
(Punjab Campaign)	
1848-49	Mooltan
1849	Chillianwallah
	Goojerat
1848-49	Punjaub
8th Kaffir War	
1850-53	South Africa 1851-52-53

2nd Burma War	
1852-53	Pegu
Crimean War	
1854	Alma
	Balaclava
	Inkerman
1854-55	Sevastapol
Persian War	
1856	Reshire
	Bushire
1857	Kush-Ab
1856-57	Persia
Indian Mutiny	
1857	Delhi 1857
1857-58	Central India
	Lucknow
2nd China War	
1857-58	Canton
1860	Taku Forts
	Pekin 1860
2nd Maori War	
1860-61	New Zealand 1860-61
1863-66	New Zealand 1863-66
Abyssinian War	
1867-68	Abyssinia
Ashanti War (West Africa)	
1873-74	Ashantee 1873-4
Zulu War (South Africa)	
1877-79	South Africa 1877-8-9
2nd Afghan War	
1878	Ali Masjid
	Peiwar Kotal
1879	Charasiah
	Kabul 1879
1880	Ahmed Khel
	Kandahar 1880
1878-80	Afghanistan 1878-80
Egypt 1882	
1882	Tel-el-Kebir
	Egypt 1882

Suakin Expedition	
1884	Egypt 1884
1st Sudan War	
1885	Abu Klea
	Kirbokan
1884-85	Nile 1884-85
1885	Suakin 1885
	Tofrek
3rd Burma War	
1885-87	Burma 1885-87
India, N.W. Frontier 1895-98	
1895	Chitral
1879-98	Tirah
2nd Sudan War	
1896	Hafir
1898	Atbara
	Khartoum (Omdurman)
2nd Boer War	
(South African War)	
1899-1900	Defence of Kimberley
	Defence of Ladysmith
1899	Modder River
1900	Relief of Kimberley
	Paardeberg
	Relief of Ladysmith
1899-1902	South Africa 1899-1902
3rd China War (Boxer Rebellion)	
1900	Pekin 1900
	China 1900
First World War (France & Flanders)	
1914	Mons
	Le Cateau
	Retreat from Mons
	Marne 1914
	Aisne 1914
	La Bassée 1914
	Messines 1914
	Armentières 1914
	Ypres 1914
	Langemarck 1914
	Gheluvelt
	Nonne Boschen
	Festubert 1914
	Givenchy 1914

1915	Neuve Chapelle
	Hill 60
	Ypres 1915
	Gravenstafel
	St. Julien
	Frezenberg
	Bellewarde
	Aubers
	Festubert 1915
	Hooge 1915
	Loos
1916	Mount Sorrel
	Somme 1916
	Albert 1916
	Bazentin
	Delville Wood
	Pozières
	Guillemont
	Ginchy
	Flers Courcelette
	Morval
	Thiepval
	Le Transloy
	Ancre Heights
	Ancre 1916
1917	Bapaume 1917
	Arras 1917
	Vimy 1917
	Scarpe 1917
	Arleux
	Oppy
	Bullecourt
	Hill 70
	Messines 1917
	Ypres 1917
	Pilckem
	Langemarck 1917
	Menin Road
	Polygon Wood
	Broodseinde
	Poelcappelle
	Passchendaele
	Cambrai 1917
1918	Somme 1918
	St. Quentin
	Bapaume 1918
	Rosières
	Arras 1918
	Avre
	Ancre 1918
	Villers-Bretonneaux

1918 (cont.)	Lys
	Estaires
	Messines 1918
	Hazebrouck
	Bailleul
	Kemmel
	Béthune
	Scherpenberg
	Aisne 1918
	Bligny
	Bois des Buttes
	Hamel
	Marne 1918
	Soissonais-Ourcq
	Tardenois
	Amiens
	Albert 1918
	Scarpe 1918
	Drocourt-Quéant
	Hindenberg Line
	Havrincourt
	Epéhy
	Canal du Nord
	St. Quentin Canal
	Beaurevoir
	Cambrai 1918
	Ypres 1918
	Courtrai
	Selle
	Valenciennes
	Sambre
	Pursuit to Mons
1914-1918	France & Flanders 1914-1918

First World War (Italy)

1918	Piave
	Vittorio Veneto
1917-18	Italy 1917-18

First World War (Macedonia)

1915	Kosturino
1916	Struma
1917	Doiran 1917
1918	Doiran 1918
1915-18	Macedonia 1915-18

First World War (Dardanelles)

1915	Helles
	Landing at Helles
	Krithia
	Defence of Anzac

1915 (cont.)	Suvla
	Sari Bair
	Landing at Suvla
	Scimitar Hill
1915-16	Gallipoli 1915-16

First World War (Egypt)

1915-16	Suez Canal
1916	Rumani
1915-17	Egypt 1915-17

First World War (Palestine)

1917	Gaza
	El Mughar
	Nebi Samwil
	Jerusalem
	Jaffa
1918	Jericho
	Jordan
	Tell'Asur
	Megiddo
	Sharon
	Nablus
	Damascus
1917-18	Palestine 1917-18

First World War (Aden)

1915-18	Aden

First World War (Mesopotamia)

1914-15	Basra
1915	Shaiba
	Kut al Amara 1915
	Ctesiphon
1915-16	Defence of Kut al Amara
1916	Tigris 1916
1916-17	Kut al Amara 1917
1917	Baghdad
1918	Khan Baghdadi
	Sharquat
1914-18	Mesopotamia 1914-18
1920-21	Iraq 1920

First World War (Persia)

1918	Baku
1916-19	Persia 1916-19

First World War (India)

1914-18	North-West Frontier 1914-18
1917	Waziristan 1917
1918	Baluchistan 1918

First World War (Russia)

1918-19	Murman 1918-19
	Archangel 1918-19
1918	Dukhovskaya
1919	Troitsa
1918-19	Siberia 1918-19

First World War (China)

1914	Tsingtao

First World War (East Africa)

1916	Kilimanjaro
1917	Beho Beho
	Nyangao
1914-18	East Africa 1914-18

3rd Afghan War

1919	Afghanistan 1919

India, N.W. Frontier 1930-40

1930	North-West Frontier 1930
1936-37	North-West Frontier 1936-37
1937-40	North-West Frontier 1937-40

2nd World War (Norway)

1940	Vist
	Kvam
	Otta
	Stien
	Pothus
	Norway 1940
1941	Vaagso

2nd World War (North-West Europe 1940-42)

1940	The Dyle
	Withdrawal to the Escaut
	Defence of the Escaut
	Amiens 1940
	Defence of Arras
	Arras Counterattack
	Boulogne 1940
	Calais 1940
	French Frontier 1940
	St.Omer-la Bassée
	Wormhoudt
	Cassel
	Forêt de Nieppe
	Ypres-Comines Canal
	Dunkirk 1940
	The Somme 1940

1940 (cont.)	Withdrawal to the Seine
	Withdrawal to Cherbourg
	St. Valery-en-Caux
	Saar
1942	Bruneval
	St. Nazaire
	Dieppe
1940-42	North-West Europe 1940-42

2nd World War (North-West Europe 1944-45)

1944	Normandy Landings
	Pegasus Bridge
	Merville Battery
	Port en Bessin
	Sully
	Cambes
	Putot en Bassin
	Breville
	Villers Bocage
	Tilly sur Seulles
	The Odon
	Fontenay le Pesnil
	Cheux
	Tourmauville Bridge
	Defence of Rauray
	Caen
	The Orne (Buron)
	Hill 112
	Esquay
	Noyers
	Cagny
	Borguebus Ridge
	Troarn
	Faubourg de Vaucelles
	Maltot
	Mont Pincon
	Quarry Hill
	Jurques
	La Varinière
	The Souleuvre
	Le Perier Ridge
	Brieux Bridgehead
	St. Pierre la Vielle
	Estry
	Noireau Crossing
	Falaise
	Falaise Road
	Southern France
	Dives Crossing
	La Vie Crossing

1944 (cont.)	1945 (cont.)	1941	1942 (cont.)

1944 (cont.) Lisieux
La Touques Crossing
Risle Crossing
The Seine 1944
Forêt de Bretonne
Amiens 1944
Brussels
Antwerp
Hechtel
Gheel
Heppen
Neerpelt
Aart
Le Havre
Antwerp-Turnhout Canal
The Nederrijn
Arnhem 1944
Nijmegen
Veghel
Best
The Scheldt
South Beveland
Walcheren Causeway
Flushing
Westkapelle
The Lower Maas
Aam
Opheusden
Venraij
Asten/Meijel
Geilenkirchen
Venlo Pocket
1945 The Roer
Zetten
The Ourthe
The Rhineland
The Reichswald
Waal Flats
Cleve
Goch
Moyland/Moyland Wood
Weeze
The Hochwald
Schaddenhof
Xanten
The Rhine
Ibbenburen
Lingen
Benthelm
Twente Canal
Dreirwalde

1945 (cont.) Leese
The Aller
Arnhem 1945
Brinkum
Uelzen
Bremen
Artlenberg
1944-45 North-West Europe 1944-45

2nd World War (Abyssinia)
1941 Jebel Dafeis
Jebel Shiba
Gogni
Agordat
Barentu
Karora-Marsa Tacial
Cubcub
Mescelit Pass
Keren
Mount Englahat
Ad Teclesan
Massawa
Amba Alagi
1940-41 Abyssinia 1940-41

2nd World War (British Somaliland)
1940 Barkasan
British Somaliland 1940

2nd World War (Iraq 1941)
1941 Defence of Habbaniya
Falluga
Baghdad 1941
Iraq 1941

2nd World War (Syria 1941)
1941 The Litani
Merjayun
Palmyra
Deir ez Zor
Jebel Mazar
Syria 1941

2nd World War (North Africa) 8th Army Operations
1940 Egyptian Frontier 1940
Withdrawal to Matruh
Bir Enba
Sidi Barrani
Buq Buq

1941 Bardia 1941
Capture of Tobruk
Beda Fomm
Mersa el Brega
Agedabla
Derna Aerodrome
Halfaya 1941
Sidi Suleiman
Defence of Tobruk
Tobruk 1941
Gubi I
Gabr Saleh
Sidi Rezegh 1941
Tobruk Sortie 1941
Omars
Taleb el Essom
Belhamed
Gubi II
Relief of Tobruk 1941
Alem Hamza
Chor es Sufan
1942 Saunnu
Msus
Benghazi
Carmusa
Gazala
Retma
Bir el Igela
Bir el Aslagh
Bir Hacheim
The Cauldron
Knightsbridge
Gabr el Fachri
Via Balbia
Zt el Mrasses
Sidi Rezegh 1942
Tobruk 1942
Mersa Matruh
Point 174
Fuka
Defence of Alamein Line
Deir el Shein
Ruweisat
Fuka Airfield
Ruweisat Ridge
Alam el Halfa
Benghazi Raid
Deir el Munassib
El Alamein
Capture of Halfaya Pass 1942
El Agheila

1942 (cont.) Nofilia
1943 Advance on Tripoli
Medenine
Zemiet el Lebene
Tadjera Khir
Mareth
Wadi Zeuss East
Wadi Zigzaou
Tebaga Gap
Point 201 (Roman Wall)
El Hamma
Matmata Hills
Akarit
Djebel el Meida
Wadi Akarit East
Enfidaville
Djebel Garci
Djebel Tabaga

2nd World War (North Africa) 1st Army Operations
1942 Djebel Abiod
Soudia
Medjez el Bab
Tebourba
Djedeida
Djebel Azzag 1942
Oudna
Tebourba Gap
Longstop Hill 1942
1943 Djebel Azzag 1943
Two Tree Hill
Bou Arada
Robaa Valley
Djebel Alliliga
Kasserine
Sbiba
Thala
El Hadjeba
Djebel Djaffa
Sidi Nsir
Fort McGregor
Stuka Farm
Steamroller Farm
Hunt's Gap
Montagne Farm
Kef Oulba Pass
Djebel Guerba
Sedjenane I
Tamera
Djebel Dahra

1943 (cont.) Djebel Choucha
Kef el Debna
Mine de Sedjenane
Fondouk
Pichon
Djebel el Rhorab
Fondouk Pass
Kalrouan
Bordj
Oued Zarga
Djebel bel Mahdi
Djebel bech Chekaoul
Djebel Ang
Djebel Tanngoucha
Heldous
Banana Ridge
Djebel Kesskiss
Djebel Djaffa Pass
El Kourzia
Ber Rabal
Argoub Sellah
Medjez Plain
Grich el Oued
Gueriat el Atach Ridge
Longstop Hill 1943
Peter's Corner
Si Mediene
Djebel bou Aoukaz 1943, I
Si Abdallah
Gab Gab Gap
Sid Ahmed
Djebel Kournine
Argoub el Megas

2nd World War (North Africa)
1st / 8th Army Operations
1943   Tunis
Djebel bou Aoukaz 1943, II
Montarnaud
Ragoubet Souissi
Hammam Lif
Creteville Pass
Gromballa
Bou Ficha
1940-43   North Africa 1940-43

2nd World War (Sicily)
1943   Landing in Sicily
Solarino
Vizzini
Augusta

1943 (cont.) Francofonte
Lentini
Primosole Bridge
Sferro
Simeto Bridgehead
Gerbini
Agira
Adrano
Regalbuto
Sferro Hills
Centuripe
Salso Crossing
Simeto Crossing
Monte Rivoglia
Malleto
Pursuit to Messina
Sicily 1943

2nd World War (Italy)
1943   Landing at Porto San Venere
Taranto
Salerno
St. Lucia
Vietri Pass
Salerno Hills
Battipaglia
Capture of Naples
Cava di Terreni
Cappezano
Monte Stella
Scafati Bridge
Cardito
Termoli
The Trigno
Volturno Crossing
Monte Maro
Rocchetta e Croce
Teano
San Salvo
Monte Camino
Calabritto
The Sangro
Mozzagrogna
Fossacesia
Romagnoli
Orsogna
Moro Bridge (Impossible Bridge)
Caldari
Villa Grande
1944   Colle Cedro
Garigliano Crossing

1944 (cont.) Minturno
Damiano
Monte Tuga
Monte Ornito
Cerasola
Cassino I
Monastery Hill
Castle Hill
Hangman's Hill
Anzio
Aprilia
Campoleone
Carroceto
Cassino II
Massa Vertechi
Massa Tambourini
Casa Sinagogga
Liri Valley
Aquino
Piedimonte Hill
Melfa Crossing
Monte Piccolo
Rocca d'Arce
Rome
Advance to the Tiber
Monte Rotondo
Monte Gabbione
Citta Della Pieve
Capture of Perugia
Ripa Ridge
Monte Malbe
Trasimene Line
Sanfatucchio
Gabbiano
Ancona
Arezzo
Tuori
Montone
Citta di Castello
Pian di Maggio
Advance to Florence
Monte San Michelle
Monte Domini
Monte Scalari
Il Castello
Incontro
Campriano
Citerna
Poggio del Grillo
Fiesole
Montorsoli

1944 (cont.) Gothic Line
Monte Gridolfo
Tavoleto
Montegaudio
Coriano
San Clemente
Poggio San Giovanni
Pian di Castello
Croce
Gemmano Ridge
Rimini Line
Monte Colombo
Casa Fabbri Ridge
Montescudo
Frisoni
San Marino
Ceriano Ridge
Montebello-Scorticata Ridge
Santarcangelo
Monte Reggiano
Savignano
Marradi
Monte Gamberaldi
Catarelto Ridge
San Martino-Sogliano
Monte Farneto
Montilgallo
Carpineta
Monte Chicco
Monte Cavallo
Casena
Savio Bridgehead
Battaglia
Monte Casalino
Monte Ceco
Monte la Pieve
Monte Pianoereno
Monte Spaduro
Orsara
Capture of Forli
Casa Fortis
Cosina Canal Crossing
Monte San Bartolo
Monte Grande
Lamone Crossing
Pideura
Defence of Lamone Bridgehead
Pergola Ridge
Capture of Ravenna
Tossignano
1945   Conventello-Comacchio

1945 (cont.)	Senio Pocket	1942 (cont.)	Johore
	Senio Floodbank		The Muar
	Valli di Commacchio		Batu Pahat
	The Senio		Singapore Island
	Santerno Crossing	1941-42	Malaya 1942-42
	Menate		

2nd World War (Hong Kong & South-East Asia 1941-42)

1941	Hong Kong
1941-42	South-East Asia 1941-42

Col 1 continued:

	Filo
	Argenta Gap
	Fossa Cembalina
	San Nicolo Canal
	Bologna
	Sillaro Crossing
	Medecina
	Gaina Crossing
	Idice Bridgehead
	Traghetto
1943-45	Italy 1943-45

2nd World War (Greece)

1941	Veve
	Proasteion
	Corinth Canal
	Greece 1941
1944-45	Athens
	Greece 1944-45

2nd World War (Crete)

1941	Crete
	Canea
	Heraklion
	Retimo
	Withdrawal to Sphakia

2nd World War (Madagascar)

1942	Madagascar

2nd World War (Adriatic, Aegean & Mediterranean Islands)

1940-42	Malta 1940-42
1943	Cos
	Leros
1944	Adriatic
1941-44	Middle East 1941-44

2nd World War (Malaya 1941-42)

1941	North Malaya
	Grik Road
1941-42	Central Malaya
1941	Ipoh
1941-42	Kampar
1942	Slim River

2nd World War (Burma)

1942	Sittang 1942
	Pegu 1942
	Taukyan
	Paungde
	Yenangyaung 1942
	Kyaukse 1942
	Monywa 1942
	Shwegyin
1942-43	Rathedaung
1943	Donbaik
	Htizwe
	Point 201 (Arakan)
	The Stockades
	Chindits 1943
1944	The Yu
	North Arakan
	Buthidaung
	Razabil
	Point 551
	Alethangyaw
	Mayu Tunnels
	Maungdaw
	Ngakeydauk Pass
	Defence of Sinzweya
	Chindits 1944
	Imphal
	Tuitum
	Sakawng
	Tamu Road
	Shenam Pass
	Nungshigum
	Litan
	Bishenpur
	Kanglatongbi
	Kohima
	Defence of Kohima
	Relief of Kohima
	Naga Village
	Aradura

1944 (cont.)	Mao Songsang		
	Ukhrul		
	Tengnoupal		
	Kennedy Peak		
	Pinwe		
1945	Shwebo		
	Monywa 1945		
	The Shweli		
	Kyaukmyaung Bridgehead		
	Sagaing		
	Arakan Beaches		
	Myebon		
	Ramree		
	Kangaw		
	Tamandu		
	Mandalay		
	Myitson		
	Ava		
	Myinmu Bridgehead		
	Fort Dufferin		
	Maymyo		
	Kyaukse 1945		
	Meiktila		
	Nyaungu Bridgehead		
	Capture of Meiktila		
	Defence of Meiktila		
	Taungtha		
	Letse		
	Singce		
	The Irrawaddy		
	Mount Popa		
	Yenangyaung 1945		
	Shandatgyi		
	Kama		
	Rangoon Road		
	Pyawbwe		
	Toungoo		
	Pegu 1945		
	Sittang 1945		
1942-1945	Burma 1942-45		

Korean War

1950	Naktong Bridgehead
	Chongju
	Pakchon
	Chong Chon II
1951	Seoul
	Chuam-Ni
	Hill 327
	Kapyong-Chon
	The Imjin

1951 (cont.)	Kapyong
	Kowang-San
	Maryang-San
	Hill 227, I
	The Hook 1952
1953	The Hook 1953
1950-1953	Korea 1950-53

Falkland Islands 1982

1982	Goose Green
	Mount Longdon
	Tumbledown Mountain
	Wireless Ridge
	Falkland Islands 1982

Gulf War

1991	Gulf 1991
	Wadi al Batin
	Western Iraq

Iraq

2003	Iraq 2003
	Al Basrah